The greater Washington Park neighborhood stretches from the south of Cherry Creek to South Colorado Boulevard on the right, South Broadway, the heavy line near the left, and Interstate 25, here denoted as the tracks of the Colorado & Southern Railway on this map dating from the 1930s.

The History of South Denver

The Haunts of Washington Park

Volume two of a three-volume work

By Phil Goodstein

Denver
New Social Publications
2009

To Jim Peiker:
A South Denver native, gracious host,
community activist, and a fount of wisdom.

The front cover photo is an aerial view of the northern
half of Washington Park, c. 1930, courtesy DPL.
The back cover drawing is by Walt Young.

The History of South Denver
Volume One: *The Spirits of South Broadway*
Volume Two: *The Haunts of Washington Park*
Volume Three: *The Ghosts of University Park, Platt Park, and Beyond*

New Social Publications
Box 18026; Denver, Colorado 80218
(303)333-1095

Printed in Denver, Colorado
All Rights Reserved
First Edition: October 2009

Library of Congress Control Number 2009924964
ISBN 0–9742264–4–0

Contents

Abbreviations vi

Introduction 1

1. The Gem of South Denver 7

2. Washington Park West 53

3. Myrtle Hill 76

4. South High School 120

5. South of the Country Club 138

6. Northwest of Washington Park 162

7. Bonnie Brae and Beyond 184

8. Cory-Merrill...225

9. Papers and Politicians 256

Index 287

Abbreviations

CCN: *Cherry Creek News*
CD: *City of Denver*
CH: *Colorado Heritage*
CHS: Colorado Historical Society
CJ: *Cervi's Journal*
CL: *Colorado Lawyer*
CM: *Colorado Magazine*
DBJ: *Denver Business Journal*
DCR: *Denver Catholic Register*
DLPC: Denver Landmark Preservation Commission
DMF: *Denver Municipal Facts*
DOC: Denver Organizing Committee for the 1976 Winter Olympics
DP: *Denver Post*
DPL: Denver Public Library
DPS: Denver Public Schools
DR: *Denver Republican*
DT: *Denver Times*
DU: University of Denver
DUWC: Denver Union Water Company
DWD: Denver Water Department
DX: *Denver Express*
GCCC: *Glendale Cherry Creek Chronicle*
HD: Historic Denver
ITT: International Telephone & Telegraph
KKK: Ku Klux Klan
kluxer: a member of the Ku Klux Klan
LCH: *Life on Capitol Hill*
LWV: League of Women Voters
NRHP: National Register of Historic Places
RMJ: *Rocky Mountain Journal*

RMN: *Rocky Mountain News*
SCIA: South Central Improvement Association
SCJ: *Straight Creek Journal*
SCOPE: Steele–Crofton Organization of Parents and Educators
SDCA: South Denver Civic Association
SDE: *South Denver Eye*. It also refers to the *Denver Eye*, and *South Denver Eye and Bulletin*.
SDS: Students for a Democratic Society
SDM: *South Denver Monitor*
Seventeenth Street: Denver's commanding business boulevard. Used to emphasize the power of the city's leading banks and corporate interests.
UPCC: University Park Community Council
UPN: *University Park News*. It also refers to *University Park and Cherry Creek News*.
Valley Highway: Interstate 25
VOC: Volunteers for Outdoors Colorado
WPGC: Washington Park Garden Club
WPP: *Washington Park Profile*
WW: *Westword*
WWPNA: West Washington Park Neighborhood Association
YAL: Young American League
YMCA: Young Men's Christian Association
YWCA: Young Women's Christian Association

Introduction

*J*ust as the intrepid sailor was about to launch his canoe at dusk on a peaceful summer evening onto the northern lake in Washington Park, Smith Lake, huge waves suddenly started wildly convulsing the water. Or so he thought. Nobody else saw the storm, at least at that time. Nonetheless, the park's lore is that at sunset on the summer solstice, for a brief moment the previously placid lake sometimes appears to churn wildly. Psychically gifted observers then see a struggling, drowning man desperately clinging to a canoe, about 40 feet from the northern shore. No sooner does he vanish into the water than the lake calms down, resuming its role as a central attraction in Denver's foremost greenery. Even so, mysterious splashes and cries are occasionally heard coming from Smith Lake.

The tale might stem from the fate of Chester Sirkle, 20. An expert swimmer, he went out on the lake in a canoe with Julius Rosenbloom around 8:00 PM on Sunday, June 21, 1914, right about when the guards ordered everybody out of the lake with the impending dusk. As Sirkle and Rosenbloom glided near the end of the women's pier on the lake, about 40 feet from the shore, Rosenbloom ducked to avoid hitting the diving board while Sirkle apparently smacked his head against it. Hearing his companion plunge into the water, Rosenbloom unsuccessfully dove in the hope of rescuing his friend. Alerted by Rosenbloom's cries for help, bathhouse custodian Hugo R. Siebers of 644 South Williams Street, hauled Sirkle from the lake. By the time rescuers had Sirkle on shore, the boater had been underwater between ten and thirty minutes—newspaper accounts of the event vastly differed.

Neither Siebers nor anyone else present knew how to work the first-aid device to pump out swimmers. A call to city hall led to the dispatch of the police ambulance. The patrolmen responding were also unable to operate the equipment to save those who had swallowed too much water. In the face of this, Sirkle died. Since then, irresponsible boaters have sometimes been scared to the shore when they witness some sort of ghostly image flailing about in the lake, possibly the shade of Sirkle warning them of the deadly result of his misadventure.

1

Such is the legend of the Flying Dutchman (a sailor condemned to sail end-lessly in stormy conditions) on Smith Lake. As Washington Park emerged as Denver's most popular open space in the 1980s, stories about the greenery and the surrounding neighborhood have soared. An influx of affluent settlers has drasti-cally transformed the surrounding neighborhood from what had been a staunch middle-class area into something of the city's ultimate yuppie village. How this has happened, the area's heritage, people, places, institutions, and folklore are the scope of this volume.

In the 19th century, South Denver was an isolated part of the metropolis. It generally referred to the land east of the South Platte River to the south of West Sixth Avenue and Cherry Creek. Farms popped up in the section in the 1860s and 1870s. Before long, elite villas lined Broadway south of Cherry Creek. For a while, the Broadway Terrace/Baker neighborhood—the land south of West Sixth Avenue to the west of Broadway—rivaled Capitol Hill as the city's foremost resi-dential enclave. The area never recovered from the Panic of 1893. Henceforth, the South Side was primarily home to wage workers, clerks, storekeepers, sales-men, and numerous other everyday people who formed the heart of the Queen City of Mountain and Plain, a community which exploded from 4,700 residents in 1870 to more than 100,000 in 1890.

Land speculators and puritans were active at a very early date in South Denver. In 1886, seeing that the Mile High City ended at Alameda Avenue while rowdy bars plagued the unincorporated area to the south, settlers created the Town of South Denver, an independent jurisdiction stretching from the Denver city limits to Yale Avenue between the South Platte River and South Colorado Boulevard. Residents adopted strict morals legislation, outlawing liquor and behavior which they found offensive. Despite settlers' high hopes, the community verged on bank-ruptcy in the wake of the Panic of 1893, leading to its annexation by Denver on February 7, 1894.

Though city hall promised South Denver would be a full and equal part of the community, many residents felt ignored by the administration. South Siders in-creasingly emphasized their own institutions and identity. Citizens were immensely proud of their schools and churches as evidence that they lived in a sedate, pros-perous, civilized area. Pointing to massive public works projects north of Cherry Creek, especially on Capitol Hill, they demanded their fair share of improvement programs when Denver presented itself as the city beautiful in the early 20th cen-tury—a community filled with open spaces, fountains, and monumental statuary.

Before long, there were numerous different worlds of South Denver. The Uni-versity of Denver was something of an isolated community, especially among resi-dents of University Park. Those living east of Washington Park, an area once known as Myrtle Hill, saw themselves as better than those dwelling off to the west. South Broadway near Mississippi Avenue was the heart of an industrial district with Gates Rubber, Shwayder Brothers (Samsonite), and a Ford assembly plant. Off to the west, factories intermingled with residences toward the river. Numer-ous simple cottages and shacks dotted the land near Overland Park at West Jewell Avenue and South Santa Fe Drive. Separate yet were those dwelling near the old

Photo by Phil Goodstein

A Flying Dutchman allegedly haunts placid Smith Lake in Washington Park.

Town of South Denver city hall at South Grant Street and Florida Avenue in Platt Park. Orphans occupying the State Home for Dependent and Neglected Children near South Clarkson Street and Iliff Avenue formed an additional dimension of the South Side. The secluded manors north of Alameda Avenue on the southern boundary of the Denver Country Club were another world of South Denver.

Neighborhood youths have mingled at South High School, the area's defining public institution. A wide variety of improvement associations have come and gone. Newspapers have sought to serve the community. Houses have ranged from tiny units of 600 to 800 square feet to huge manors in such gated villages as the Polo Club to the south of Alameda Avenue and east of South University Boulevard.

Distinctive business strips have emerged. The Miracle Mile was the name of the shops along Broadway from about Sixth Avenue to Exposition Avenue in the 1920s, 1930s, 1940s, and 1950s. Closer to Washington Park, shopping areas emerged along South University Boulevard between Exposition and Ohio avenues and on South Gaylord Street between Tennessee and Mississippi avenues. Stretches of South Pearl Street have likewise been commercial areas. All the while, urban legends have popped up, giving residents a sense of community and place.

I first looked at Denver south of Cherry Creek in my 1991 *South Denver Saga*. When I started revising it in 2007, the text quickly grew. Rather than overwhelming readers with a 900–page volume, I carved my *Haunted History of South Denver* into three parts. Volume one, which came out in 2008, *The Spirits of South Broadway*, looks at the rise of the South Side, the Town of South Denver, and the Broadway corridor from Cherry Creek to Englewood. It includes the story of

Overland Park, the landmark Baker neighborhood, the evolution of the Miracle Mile, and the rise and decline of the industrial district. Along the way, I featured a few ghost stories to highlight the area's traditions.

It is impossible to say exactly where the South Broadway corridor ends and the West Washington Park section begins. Consequently, I paid a good deal of attention to the area near the old Byers Junior High School at South Pearl Street and Bayaud Avenue in *The Spirits of South Broadway*. I likewise mentioned hippie happenings along South Pennsylvania and South Pearl streets. But these places are also very much part of the story of Washington Park and its surrounding neighborhoods. Some repetition between the volumes has been unavoidable. The index cross references subjects in volumes one and three.

The primary focus is on the people who have made the Washington Park region their home. The volume looks at the evolution of the greenery and the stories and traditions associated with it. From there, it examines the adjacent residential districts, especially to the east, north, and west of the park. This includes attention to such sections as Belcaro, Bonnie Brae, and Cory-Merrill. Generally, South Colorado Boulevard is the eastern boundary of historic South Denver. In focusing on how that road was the center of such attractions as Celebrity Lanes, the Cooper Theatre, and Writers' Manor in the 1960s and 1970s, I occasionally glance at areas farther to the east. Cherry Creek and the Denver Country Club form the northern border of the Washington Park district.

The South High story, of course, is of foremost importance while I highlight some of the churches in the area. It is not possible to mention every congregation, school, and institution in a manageable history. *The Ghosts of University Park, Platt Park, and Beyond*, the concluding volume, will take up the story, focusing on the neighborhoods south of the Washington Park district. The Valley Highway (Interstate 25) is a most visible dividing line between the two areas.

In keeping with historic Denver usages, streets not specifically designated as south are north of Ellsworth Avenue, the dividing line of the roads. Similarly, avenues are automatically east unless prefaced as being west. Rather than cluttering the text with footnotes, I have added essays on sources after each chapter. Volume three will include a bibliography.

Official city neighborhood names and boundaries are not trustworthy. They stem from a 1972 Denver Planning Office effort designed to get Model City monies from Washington for "endangered" and "blighted" sections. In the process, the planners systematically denigrated parts of South Denver. Typical of their sloppiness is how they labeled Platt Park at South Logan Street and Florida Avenue, named for James H. Platt, "Platte" Park. Rather than relying on planning definitions, I have focused on real estate records, customary usages, and natural divisions and unities between areas.

Haunted houses have come and gone. Seemingly, every generation of neighborhood children has developed its own stories about apparitions. Until the 1970s, the city as a whole paid very little attention to its ghostly lore. As locals and newcomers started to discover Denver's marvelous Victorian heritage during that decade, tales of spirits became ever more popular. For the most part, ghosts pri-

Bizarre creatures protect South High School, the institution which has brought together generations of South Denver youths.

marily seemed to haunt the surviving 19th-century mansions on Capitol Hill. The 20th-century bungalows of Washington Park did not appear to have the right flavor for spirits.

Increasingly, however, spooks have become omnipresent. Virtually any old house of any character has strange creaking sounds, uneven heating patterns, and occasional flickering lights. For the most part, however, South Denver does not have the same colorful ghost lore as Capitol Hill. Nor is it possible to document the specters. Consequently, I have relied on oral tradition, hearsay, and lively accounts. The ghost dimension of this volume is not nearly as rich as I would have wished. It is merely a complement to the core focusing on the residents of Washington Park neighborhoods and the world they have created.

$\mathcal{N}$umerous friends and South Denver residents have encouraged me in my research and writing. Librarians are at the top of the list of those deserving thanks. Steve Fisher opened the archives at the University of Denver to me. He allowed me to look at a draft of his forthcoming *University Park and South Denver* (Charleston, SC: Arcadia Publishing, 2009). His wife, Katie, urged me to visit Taylor Library of the Iliff School of Theology which has a rich repository on area churches.

The librarians at the Colorado Historical Society readily pulled requested materials and gave me hints about collections I should investigate. The same is true with those working at the Western History Department of the Denver Public Library (DPL). Those staffing the desk of the Government Documents collection of

DPL were also of utmost assistance. The crew at the Auraria Archives similarly welcomed me. I further received valued assistance in occasional visits to the Colorado State Archives and Colorado Supreme Court library.

Bill Good, who grew up near Washington Park in the 1930s, shared his many stories of the area as a boy. He also has plugged my books and occasionally provided me with taxi service in exploring the area. Members of the Walla family of Roach Photography, along with John Davenport, assisted in photography. They shared their invaluable collections with me. Lee Raen, another product of South Denver, helped design the cover. Doug Gerash especially assisted in research and stories about movie theaters and the evolution of South Colorado Boulevard.

Shortly after *South Denver Saga* appeared, South Denver native Alvan Morrison wrote me an extremely detailed letter commenting on the book. The epistle and his further commentary have been most enlightening and useful. Jim Peiker, also a South Denver native, likewise shared his rich lore of stories about the neighborhood. He arranged for me to meet with members of his 1953 class of South High School on February 17, 2008. I cite this as the South Denver history seminar. Patsy Vail and Bob Sheets joined Peiker at another session on the history of the neighborhood on December 7, 2008. The late Mary Dell Simmons and Carl Ott told me of their many memories of South Denver and Washington Park after the appearance of *South Denver Saga*. Charlotte Winzenburg opened her home to me, sharing her collection of documents on the West Washington Park neighborhood.

Bill Wiederspan of the South High Alumni and Friends Incorporated welcomed me to its Historic Room. He and others active in the alumni association shared their memories of attending the school and growing up in the area. Ronald Grosswiler, the first purchaser of *The Spirits of South Broadway*, gave me his perspective on the area as one raised at the State Home for Dependent and Neglected Children, an institution I examine extensively in volume three. Bettina Basanow highlighted her husband's activities in Washington Park and introduced me to many longtime backers of the Washington Street Community Center. Harold and Carol Williams also talked about the Community Center and numerous neighborhood events.

Dean Nye gave me the perspective of one who grew up close to the park in the 1960s and 1970s. He additionally arranged for me to talk with others knowledgeable about the neighborhood. Paul Kashmann of the *Washington Park Profile* allowed me to use the paper's rich store of South Denver photos. South Broadway booksellers Nina and Ron Else were also most supportive, especially in plugging *The Spirits of South Broadway*.

John Davoren and Sonja Leonard helped publicize *The Spirits of South Broadway*. Davoren further assisted in proofreading along with Dinah Land, Lisa Jones, Mike Davenport, David Wetzel, and Maxine Lankford. Thanks also go to those who have taken my tours and bought my books, signs that residents are committed to a prosperous future by an appreciation and understanding of the past.

Phil Goodstein
Halloween 2009

Chapter One

The Gem of
South Denver

South Denver burgeoned in the 1970s. The decade saw the renovation of numerous houses. Within ten years, real estate values surpassed the modest character of many existing residences. Owners and speculators responded by drastically remodeling and expanding houses. Before long, contractors started tearing down the bungalows that had marked the neighborhood since the early 20th century. In their place they erected gigantic residences worthy of exclusive suburban enclaves. Nothing more fueled the popularity of the area than its main amenity, Washington Park.

Stretching for the mile between Virginia and Louisiana avenues from South Downing Street to South Franklin Street—a quarter mile—with an extension to South Gilpin Street from Arizona Avenue to Louisiana Avenue, Washington Park has been a defining South Denver institution from its beginnings in the late 19th century. Its origins go back to post–Civil War urban planning trends and the Town of South Denver. Most of all, the park is inextricably linked to the City Ditch.

No sooner had miners, traders, and real estate speculators created Denver in 1858–59 than they realized irrigation water was vital for the area's future. Without locally grown food, the region would be hopelessly dependent on outside suppliers. Given the community's location in the Great American Desert, a system was necessary to bring water to farmers. Toward this end, contractors started work on a wide array of canals.

The Platte Water Company was in the lead. It stemmed from the Capitol Hydraulic Company, a firm incorporated on November 30, 1859. Alexander Cameron Hunt, territorial governor from 1865 to 1867, headed it. Some of the early Denver elite were part of the effort, including Richard Sopris, Amos Steck, and William

7

MF

This aerial overview of Washington Park dates from the mid-1920s.

Newton Byers. Work began on the project in 1860. The undertaking quickly bogged down. In 1864, the successor Platte Water Company arranged for John W. Smith to dig a 25-mile-long irrigation ditch from Waterton Canyon at the Platte River near what is the modern Chatfield Reservoir to an area south and east of the fledgling city.

Born in Pennsylvania on September 24, 1815, Smith had made a fortune in Atchison, Kansas, in the late 1850s. He arrived Denver on June 3, 1860, with massive supplies and $20,000 in ready cash. By the time he took on the canal, he had already heavily invested in mining and milling operations in addition to running a grocery store. During the next two decades, he was a key figure in everything from operating the city's leading hotel of the 1870s, the American House, to investing in banks and the Denver, South Park, & Pacific Railway. In addition to the ditch flowing through Washington Park, he also dug a canal serving West Denver. Industrialist John Kernan Mullen eventually bought out Smith's West Denver interests. Along the way, Smith was among those who helped incorporate the forerunner of the University of Denver in 1864 while he served as an early president of the Board of Trade/Chamber of Commerce.

Smith poured $40,000 into the irrigation effort, coming to own the Platte Water Company by the time he completed the canal in 1867. Smith's Ditch or the Big

Ditch, as the project was originally known, flowed through modern Littleton and Englewood into South Denver. It provided irrigation water to the future grounds of the State Home for Dependent and Neglected Children (the modern Harvard Gulch Park near Iliff Avenue and South Clarkson Street) before meandering to the northwest of the University of Denver campus and flowing eastward along Buchtel Boulevard. From there it went through Veterans Park near Iowa Avenue and South University Boulevard and by South High School into land Smith had acquired in the northern part of what became Washington Park.

Taking advantage of a natural depression, an old buffalo wallow, Smith created Smith's Lake, the northern lake in the park. (In the course of the early 20th century, the name became simply Smith Lake.) Smith used it as a storage reservoir for ditch water. He designed the lake with a shallow bed so it would easily freeze in the winter. This allowed him to cut ice from it which he stored in a nearby cold house.

From Washington Park, Smith's Ditch flowed north along South Marion Street into the John J. Riethmann farm, land acquired by the Denver Country Club in 1902. Irrigating the golf course, the ditch crossed Cherry Creek on a flume near South University Boulevard and entered the Country Club neighborhood. With an elaborate design, artificially constructed banks, and an inverse siphon, the waterway climbed onto Capitol Hill, eventually terminating in City Park after delivering water to irrigate the grounds of the Capitol.

DMF

From the beginning, the City Ditch has been a foremost Washington Park amenity.

Besides irrigation, optimists hoped to use Smith's Ditch as a transportation arterial, complete with small flat boats. Nothing came of that. Farmers bought shares of water from the canal, cutting laterals to extend its reach. Before long, numerous extensions of the brook extended from Capitol Hill into the central business district. By 1882, numerous laterals branched off the waterway. One account insists that more than one thousand miles of such branches existed.

From the beginning, those buying water from Smith complained his Platte Water Company did not maintain the ditch properly. Disputes about Smith's stewardship and water rights were quickly part and parcel of the project. In the face of this and realizing that water from Smith's Ditch was vital to the city's future, on February 23, 1872, Denver agreed to pay Smith $2,500 a year as part of a 99-year lease for the use of Smith's Lake and the water from it. The deal gave the city the right to cut ice while the Platte Water Company promised to fill the lake annually in October-November and keep the lake full during the winter.

Smith still managed the ditch. The city, unhappy with his operations, pondered providing a rival source of water. When it found this impractical, in March 1875 community leaders called on voters to authorize a $60,000 bond issue, paying 10 percent interest for 20 years, to buy the waterworks. After the electorate said no, promoters convinced the populace to approve a lease-to-purchase agreement on May 19, 1875, by a margin of 14 votes.

Denver took charge of the canal on May 25. It paid the last of its debt to Smith and assumed complete ownership of the project seven years later after the Pennsylvania native had received $22,564.14 in interest in addition to the $60,000 purchase price. The administration thereupon redubbed the canal the City Ditch. In 1910, the city bought Smith Lake proper. Title problems popped up in 1915 when taxpayers found themselves socked with an additional $5,000 payment for the land they thought they already owned.

In poor health, Smith relocated to Oakland, California, in February 1883. For the next three years, he faithfully carried out doctors' orders as he sought relief from Bright's Disease. In 1886, he decided all physicians were quacks when he adopted Christian Science. He died in Oakland at age 80 on November 16, 1895. His son-in-law, Henry Miller Porter, had joined him in numerous real estate ventures. Porter Hospital recalls the latter. A legacy of Smith's presence in Denver is how he named a street in his Capitol Hill real estate development for his home state of Pennsylvania and another for his granddaughter Pearl. Washington Street was once known as Canal Street, the path of the waterway near 12th Avenue.

The Birth of Washington Park

Around the time the city obtained ownership of the canal, locals embraced the park ideal. Since the creation of Central Park in New York City in the mid-19th century, urban advocates had insisted that large, open, well-landscaped places were vital to the future of metropolitan America. After acquiring its first open space in 1868, Curtis Park at 32nd and Curtis streets, Denver pondered creating a park system. It began efforts to create what became City Park in 1880. Dreamers insisted the greenery must be part of an area-wide set of parks.

The Whitehead House, near the equivalent of Kentucky Avenue and South Humboldt Street in Washington Park, is still used as the park office.

Residents of the Town of South Denver hoped a large park would assure the community's destiny. In 1890, city fathers pondered obtaining real estate for a park near both Smith Lake and at Louisiana Avenue and South Franklin Street. On October 8 of the next year, the town acquired 20 acres of Edwin K. Whitehead's farm between South Downing and South Franklin streets from Kentucky Avenue to Tennessee Avenue. His farmhouse remains in place as park offices near the equivalent of South Humboldt Street and Kentucky Avenue.

With his brother Andrew, Edwin Whitehead ran Whitehead Brothers, a real estate firm offering mortgages and loans. Among its projects was South Capitol Hill, the slope south of Alameda Avenue near South Holly Street. Edwin and Andrew Whitehead had acquired their South Side farm from Alfred Miles, selling the property to the Town of South Denver for $170 an acre. The Whiteheads left the Washington Park farm around 1896.

(On retiring from business, Edwin Whitehead served as the longtime secretary of the Colorado Humane Society. It was a most politically active group. Charles Smith, the son of John W. Smith, was a foremost donor to it. In 1901, the agency gained state recognition as the Colorado Bureau of Child and Animal Protection. Whitehead ran the governmental agency until his retirement in 1936. As its head, he had intimate ties with many business and political leaders, especially Walter Scott Cheesman, the owner of the monopolistic Denver Union Water Company, and William Gray Evans, who ran the city's streetcar system, Denver Tramway.

Simultaneously, Whitehead bitterly clashed with Denver Juvenile Court Judge Ben Lindsey as to which of them truly represented the interests of children in the region. The original Washington Park settler died at age 79 in September 1940.)

Even before the Town of South Denver purchased the Whitehead farm, an 1894 proposal for an area park system had a park around Smith Lake, linked to another proposed park where the Denver Country Club emerged via a parkway along South Gilpin Street. The Town of South Denver aimed to transform the Whitehead land into the suburb's central park. Before much of anything happened, the economy collapsed in 1893. In the wake of Denver's consequent annexation of the Town of South Denver, the administration vowed the city would maintain and enhance existing Town of South Denver park lands.

As the region recovered from the financial downturn, promoters eyed the real estate near Smith Lake as a possible amusement park or resort. South Broadway interests urged that the land surrounding the mostly abandoned Rosedale Sanitarium at the old Broadway Park at South Broadway and Jewell Avenue become the major South Denver greenery. Not until 1898 did city hall commit itself to making Washington Park a reality when it commissioned Reinhard Schuetze (1860–1910) to design an open space stretching from Smith Lake to the Whitehead House.

A European-trained landscape architect from Holstein, Germany, Schuetze had come to Denver in 1890 to lay out Fairmount Cemetery. He also drafted early plans for City and Cheesman parks and the Capitol grounds. His proposal for Washington Park called for a considerable grading of the land to link the Whitehead House with Smith Lake. Most of all, he pushed a heavy planting of trees, including hauling in mature pines from the mountains. Until then, the land around Smith Lake was extremely barren with few trees or shrubs.

On August 7, 1899, Denver observed the centennial of the death of George Washington by dubbing the greenery "Washington Park." Before then, suggestions for its name included Broadview, Ramona, Ouray, or Sylvan Park. (The South Denver greenery was Denver's second Washington Park. The first Washington Park was at the northwest corner of West Colfax Avenue and the Platte River in the early 1870s. A private park/beer garden, it never succeeded as an idyllic resort and constantly changed ownership and name, also being known as Denver Garden, Olympic Park, and Olympic Gardens. It was long gone by the 1890s. For a while, the area which became Roxborough Park southwest of Denver also was known as Washington Park.)

Schuetze envisaged Washington Park as a scenic, romantic park in the grand Victorian manner, complete with a sweeping central meadow, a lily pond, countless trees, and numerous formal flower gardens. To help make it a reality, John B. Lang took charge as park superintendent in early 1899. Years later, he recalled his first days on the job were during bitterly cold weather.

Born in Bavaria in 1861, Lang came the United States on February 2, 1881. Before long, he was in Denver. The gardener went to work for the city in 1892. Under his direction, work finally was fully underway in transforming the farmland

A lily pond was part of Reinhard Schuetze's design for Washington Park. Saco R. DeBoer landscaped it and the rock garden in 1913.

into a park in 1902. Lang occupied the Whitehead House as his home and as park offices. In 1904, he oversaw the construction of a new barn by the residence for park horses. The next year, workers completed a tool shed near Smith Lake.

In 1905–06, Lang supervised the erection of a pump house on the southwest bank of Smith Lake. It was a vital improvement. Until then, landscapers had struggled to irrigate the greenery. A gasoline engine initially powered the pump.

Among his many duties, Lang was responsible for policing Lovers Lane. This was the tree-embowered section along Kentucky Avenue between South Humboldt and South Franklin streets. Lang left his Washington Park post at the end of 1906 to oversee City Park. He was subsequently superintendent of Cheesman Park from 1917 to his retirement in 1931 after a stint in Colorado Springs from 1912 to 1917. He died on September 10, 1936.

In August 1902, the city acquired an additional 35 acres between the park proper and Smith Lake, bringing the open space to 80 acres. About this time, the city created the South Denver Park District to finance park acquisitions south of Cherry Creek and east of the Platte River. Property owners paid extra assessments for the city to procure additional land for Washington Park. Commissioners oversaw the acquisition of other South Denver real estate for open spaces. The district continued to add land to Washington Park until, by 1916, the greenery was up to its current 160.8 acres. It is the city's third largest municipal park after City Park and Sloans Lake.

Park Improvements

*D*uring the early 20th century, three prominent landscape architects played major roles in implementing and modifying Schuetze's original Washington Park plans. George Kessler was in the forefront. The city brought him to Denver in 1906 to draft an overall park plan.

Kessler, who had designed the elaborate Kansas City parkway system, emphasized Denver should have a comparable series of romantic, lushly landscaped drives connecting parks. He suggested the city acquire the land adjacent to the City Ditch north of Washington Park for the Marion and Downing street parkways to link the gem of South Denver with the emerging Denver Country Club and Speer Boulevard. The city took possession of the property for the Marion Street Parkway in 1909. Kessler's landscape design emphasized the City Ditch in the center of the median where it was lined by quaint street lamps. The parkway extends to the alley of South Downing–South Marion streets. Original proposals were for the planting of a lush urban forest between the road and alley.

(As a pressurized water system emerged in the late 19th century while the importance of urban farming declined, workers continually filled in City Ditch laterals while they modified the course of the canal, a utility increasingly used exclusively for landscape irrigation. Already in 1895, efforts were underway to bury much of the brook in a pipe system. A 1914 modification saw the City Ditch flow down the Downing Street Parkway from South Marion Street from which it crossed Cherry Creek in a pipe and flowed up Corona Street. In the 1930s, Works Progress Administration crews buried most of the remaining exposed sections of the City Ditch in a 30-inch concrete conduit, including along the South Side parkways. The sluice gate where some of the canal's waters continue to flow into the Country Club is visible on the south side of Bayaud Avenue where it intersects with South Marion Street.)

In 1913, workers planted trees on the parkway. Saco R. DeBoer oversaw the job as city landscape architect. Born in Friesland, Holland, on September 7, 1883, he attended prestigious Dutch, German, and English schools before coming to the Rocky Mountain West to recover from tuberculosis. Arriving in Denver in 1908, he went to work for the city's park department. DeBoer eventually settled at 501 Iliff Avenue near the city nursery at the southwest corner of South Logan Street and Iliff Avenue. He planted his own model garden on the block between South Pennsylvania and South Pearl streets to the north of Iliff Avenue.

In the 1920s, DeBoer especially emphasized planting crabapple trees. He did so after severe weather frustrated Mayor Benjamin Stapleton's effort to make Denver mirror Washington, D.C., as the home of numerous ornamental Asian cherry trees renowned for their blossoms. Crabapple trees, DeBoer explained, had beautiful flowers and could withstand Colorado springs. The Downing Street Parkway between Cherry Creek and Bayaud Avenue is sometimes informally known as Blossom Drive for the many crabapple trees park crews installed there in the 1920s and 1930s.

The Dutch landscaper helped make Schuetze's design for Washington Park come alive. In 1917, he laid out the perennial flower garden along the western

DPL
The Marion Street Parkway looking toward Washington Park around 1920.

edge of Washington Park near Ohio Avenue. He designed the Martha Washington Mount Vernon Garden in 1926 on the north bank of Grasmere Lake, emulating the garden of the estate of George Washington. Park superintendent Adam Kohankie arranged to get shoots and seeds from the Virginia garden for the Washington Park plantings.

DeBoer continued to take a close interest in Washington Park until his death at age 90 in August 1974. For a while, he had collaborated with Frederick Law Olmstead Jr. in plans for the South Denver greenery. The son of the man who had designed New York's Central Park, Olmstead came to Denver in 1913 to consult on how to enhance the city's park system. When his recommendations concerning public rights-of-way, fencing parks, and emphasizing public transit over private auto roads to the emerging mountain park system rubbed the city's elite the wrong way, Olmstead found himself dismissed from his Mile High post. He left behind Evergreen Hill, the northern section of the park between Smith Lake and Virginia Avenue with its lush planting of pines and conifers designed to give park users a feeling of being in the foothills.

In 1913, DeBoer and Olmstead collaborated in creating the lily pond and a rock garden around the open-flowing City Ditch in the northeast corner of the park. Children used to walk at the edge of the pond despite warnings that if they stepped in the wrong place one of the lilies would swallow them. In the 1960s, after the creation of lily ponds in the Botanic Gardens, the city ceased to maintain the Washington Park lily pond. Not only was it too costly, but city hall lamented that its efforts went for naught in the face of the vandals who continually targeted the beauty spot.

Photo by Phil Goodstein
The Colorado Miner *sits to the north of Smith Lake.*

The *Colorado Miner* sits just to the west of the lily pond in a clearning on the southern edge of Evergreen Hill. Sculptor George Carlson designed it in 1980 with money from the estate of Samuel D. Nicholson (1859–1923). A prospector who accumulated a fortune as a mining engineer in Leadville in the 1880s, Nicholson subsequently went into politics. After serving as mayor of Leadville and failing in his quest to gain election as governor in 1916, he won the United States Senate contest as a Republican in 1920. He died in office two-and-a-half years later. His will specified that half of his $950,000 estate go for a monument in Washington Park depicting "an early-day miner with a pack burro, drill, pick, hammer, spade, and shovel."

Nicholson's gift came at the tail end of the "give while you live" campaign, an effort launched by Mayor Robert Speer in 1916 to decorate the city with monumental sculptures financed by the wealthy. The drive had mostly petered out by the time of Nicholson's passing. The late senator's family disputed the will. The Washington Park statue, his son argued, was an inappropriate use of the money.

A protracted probate ensued. Not until 1938 did the court resolve the controversy when it ruled that $375,000 of the statue money was to go for new wings of Presbyterian and Denver General hospitals. The other $50,000 was placed in a trust to pay for a sculpture costing no more than $100,000 following the deaths of

Nicholson's son and daughter-in-law, Edward D. and Amelia Nicholson. By the time funds became available following Edward Nicholson's death in 1976, the sum provided for the modest monument of the sitting miner in tribute to the men who originally dug Colorado's wealth.

Washington Park once featured the George Washington Elm to the north of Grasmere Lake near a picnic ground dominated by an ornate grill given by the Camp Fire Girls. In the mid-1910s, John L. Russell, a veteran landscaper who had been active in the politics of the Town of South Denver, served as city forester. As Denver sought to be a city of trees, he gathered a sprout from an elm near William Shakespeare's grave which he planted in City Park. Simultaneously, he got an elm seedling from the tree under which George Washington took the oath as commander of the Continental Army on July 3, 1775.

In a pious patriotic ceremony, locals dedicated the tree on May 3, 1917. Dutch elm disease killed the tree in the 1970s. The Peace Pipe Chapter of the Daughters of the American Revolution planted an oak tree, rather than the seemingly appropriate cherry tree, in its stead in May 1983. A mostly neglected DAR-sponsored flagpole, dating from 1907, stands close to the tree.

The Camp Fire Girls added the grill in 1924 as a way of encouraging members to learn to cook in the park. It complements the barbecue pit Nell's Service Club installed in 1914 along the northern edge of the park near South Humboldt Street. At that time, barbecue was considered a special dish, ideally prepared during a park picnic. Nell's Service Club was part of Sertoma.

Photo by Phil Goodstein

The ruins of the short-lived Ecology Pavilion in 1990, a year before its demolition. It stood near the Camp Fire Girls' barbecue pit. The slab foundation remained in place into the 21st century.

Various structures have come and gone in the park. In 1906, workers placed a shelter near the corner of South Downing Street and Louisiana Avenue. The Ecology Pavilion went up in 1973 near the Camp Fire Girls Grill and the George Washington tree. The bottling industry sponsored it in response to complaints that discarded cans and bottles besmirched the greenery. To show a creative new use for its products, it had workers construct the shelter from recycled bottles. By 1990, the pavilion had fallen apart. Crews removed the waste the next year. Careless park users have continued to litter the open space with their cans and bottles.

The Washington Park Garden Club

No group more decried park litter while working with landscape architects to enhance the beauty of the greenery than the Washington Park Garden Club. Edith Wheeler of 1169 South York Street took the lead of forming it in the spring of 1925 when she asked her neighbors to join her in creating a society to add to the beauty of the area. The response was overwhelming when the women gathered at the community room of Washington Park Community Church at South Race Street and Arizona Avenue on April 6. After a couple of exploratory sessions, Wheeler emerged as the founding president of the society on June 1, 1925. Its 24 charter members limited the organization to 45 members, all of whom were women. Applicants had to promise they would be active in the club while assuring their good character by receiving the recommendation of an existing member. The petunia was the sorority's official flower.

Originally, the Washington Park Garden Club gathered twice a month. Before long, its meetings were on the second Thursday of the month from February to November. The affairs were usually dessert receptions. For the most part, the sessions were at the homes of members. At least once a year, the group had a banquet when the club gathered at such a prestigious spot as Writers' Manor at South Colorado Boulevard and Mexico Avenue, the Cherry Creek Inn at 600 South Colorado Boulevard, or the Park Lane Hotel at South Marion Street Parkway and Virginia Avenue. From the beginning, the organization was as much a social group as it was an association focusing on Washington Park. Members were mostly married women. The organization listed their birthdays in its annual directory.

The Washington Park society was part and parcel of the city's garden club scene: primarily upper-middle-class women calling for a beautiful city, complete with efforts to spruce up residential sections on an annual day each spring for the cleaning and painting of structures. The society sponsored flower shows and tours of home gardens. At a time when much of the land along Arizona Avenue east of Washington Park was still undeveloped prairie land, it pushed the planting of grain on it to keep down weeds.

(During World War I, Washington Park neighborhood groups launched a frenzied campaign to fill vacant lots with victory gardens. Nobody more emphasized this than attorney Charles J. Munz of 1192 South Gaylord Street, who was long president of the South Denver Improvement Association. A few of the victory gardens remained in place until after World War II.

A plaque highlights the Mount Vernon Garden to the north of Grasmere Lake, a flower display arranged by Saco DeBoer based on the Mount Vernon estate of George and Martha Washington. The Washington Park Garden Club sponsored the unveiling of the marker in November 1934.

(Early Washington Park plans called for making Arizona Avenue into a grand parkway, linking the park proper with South University Boulevard, another road planned as an impressive romantic drive. The proposal included lining Arizona Avenue with ornamental lighting. Work on the effort got underway in 1908. Simultaneously, crews placed entry pillars at Arizona Avenue and South Gilpin Street. In 1984, the city totally rebuilt University Boulevard, widening the street by two feet on each side of the road.)

At times, the Garden Club had special events at the Washington Park Pavilion. Often, its flower shows were at the Garden Center at the southwest corner of West Alameda Avenue and South Kalamath Street. That location had initially been planned as a public swimming pool. In 1936, the city gave the property to the Colorado Federation of Garden Clubs as the headquarters for the flower group— the Washington Park Garden Club was a member of the organization. The Garden Center was the site of the predecessor of Botanic Gardens. Eventually, the South Kalamath Street real estate became part of the Valley Highway. From the start, the Washington Park Garden Club was among those eagerly encouraging the formation and growth of Botanic Gardens.

The club worked closely with Washington Park superintendent Adam Kohankie to place a bronze tablet atop a granite boulder in the Martha Washington Mount Vernon Garden. Kohankie had selected the boulder in the mountains. City officials helped unveil it in November 1934. Over the years, the Washington Park Garden Club donated trees and benches to the Mount Vernon Garden. It additionally pushed the landscaping of Washington Park School at South Race Street and Mississippi Avenue, the planting of a tree at South High School, and another tree at the Temple of Youth at Third Avenue and Logan Street. The association heartily endorsed a program for the reforestation of the mountains. On Kohankie's retirement as park superintendent in 1936, the club made him an honorary member.

During and after World War II, the Garden Club worked closely with the USO, receiving many appreciations of thanks from that organization. The sorority annually donated to a worthy cause such as the Denver Children's Museum, Red Cross, and seeing-eye guide dogs. While it focused on such charities, it had little direct involvement in Washington Park controversies. At the most, it worked to keep open the Colorado State University extension agent's office in the park in 1981 when budget pressures threatened to terminate the program. Minutes of club meetings lack any mention of problems with drugs, alcohol, and traffic in the park.

At one time, the club was something of an exclusive social organization. Generally, it hovered near 40 members. By the 1980s, it was down to around 20 backers. Supporters were increasingly dying off and new blood did not replace the old. In October 1987, the society could not find anyone willing to serve as officers during the next year. In the face of this, it unanimously voted to disband. It gave the remnants of its small treasury, $90.24, to the Washington Park Community Center at South Washington Street and Ohio Avenue.

Since its demise, other groups have worked to preserve the beauty of Washington Park. Typical is the Friends and Neighbors of Washington Park. Lovers of the greenery created it in 2006 as a volunteer effort to help in gardening, maintenance, and funding. The city, it hoped, would draw up a master plan for the park while Friends and Neighbors of Washington Park educated users on the heritage and history of the open space. The group pushed for the restoration of the rock garden by the lily pond. By the time it was in operation, the greenery was home of the city's largest flower garden, including 54 separate large flowerbeds.

Grasmere Lake

Smith Lake remained an important reservoir for irrigating the flower gardens with water from the City Ditch through the 20th century. Storm waters from the area east of the park mostly drained into the lake and canal. This was already obvious during a very rainy spring in 1900. The flow of water was so heavy that the City Ditch broke its banks on Sunday, April 15. A 12-foot-high dike went up by the lake to try to contain ditch waters and those produced by the storms. At one point, Smith Lake overflowed, sending water rushing down the hill to the west. Storm waters continue to drain into the lake and the City Ditch. Now and then, during extremely heavy cloudbursts, runoffs from the East Washington Park area have cascaded through the park and flooded houses west of the greenery.

Flooding problems with the City Ditch occurred elsewhere. The canal overflowed following a downpour on June 14, 1914. The torrent broke the banks of the canal at Harvard Avenue and South Corona Street. The flood tore away about 100 yards of the embankment, sending waters surging to South Broadway between Evans and Harvard avenues. Employees and the older boys at the State Home for

Dependent and Neglected Children near Iliff Avenue and South Clarkson Street managed to stave off the flood by spending all night building dikes.

In 1906, to balance Smith Lake and highlight the southern half of Washington Park, landscapers created Grasmere Lake. The water filled a depression which engineers had once used as an overflow reservoir for the City Ditch and Smith Lake. The name recalls the village of Grasmere in the Lake District of northwestern England. In the 18th and 19th centuries, Grasmere, England, was a literary center, home to, among others, Samuel Taylor Coleridge and William Wordsworth. Denver hoped Grasmere Lake would become a comparable cultural magnet. To emphasize this, plans called for a Grasmere Parkway to connect the lake and park with the University of Denver along South Race Street. Ideally, the pleasureway would mirror the Marion Street Parkway at the southeast corner of the park. Nothing ever came of this.

Bizarre events have occurred at Grasmere Lake. In some ways, given its name, this has been apropos. Besides being a literary enclave, Grasmere, England, was a center of drug abuse. Among those living there was Thomas De Quincey, the author of the *Confessions of an English Opium Eater*. Other members of the Grasmere circle experimented with and became addicted to narcotics.

In 1998, a caiman scare swept Grasmere Lake. A reptile, the media asserted, was on the loose in the lake, threatening pets and wildlife. Before long, television crews were omnipresent as part of a caiman hunt. Park workers drained the lake,

Photo by Phil Goodstein

Between 2004 and 2007, the city kept draining Grasmere Lake, claiming that too much water was seeping into the ground from it which the Denver Water Department could profitably sell to enhance suburban sprawl. Here the pier juts over the empty, weed-filled lake bed in May 2007.

Algae grew on Grasmere Lake once the city filled it with recycled sewage water.

finding nothing. (A drain from the lake flows into the storm sewer system and the City Ditch.) Some speculated that Albert the Alligator, a supposed phantom that fled the City Park Zoo in 1981, had somehow made his way via the City Ditch to Washington Park. Others insisted the whole affair was a hoax.

Park crews had already drained Grasmere Lake in September 1959 at the behest of the police department. The authorities were looking for a gun the suspect claimed he had dumped in the lake after murdering pharmacist John B. Lacey at 1744 Evans Avenue. They also hoped to find abandoned safes—Denver was then the burglary capital of North America. The thieves specialized in stealing and breaking safes. It later came out that most of the safecrackers were members of the Denver Police Department. Not only did the men in blue need cleansing, authorities explained, so did Grasmere Lake which suffered from all the litter park users had dumped into it since its last cleaning before World War II. The lake has an average depth of six to nine feet.

Beginning in 1988, the city frequently drained Grasmere Lake. Time and again, planners announced they had come up with a marvelous new means of stabilizing its banks and cleaning its pollution. Promises, seemingly, were never kept. In 1988, for example, after the lake had been drained, nothing happened. Before long, the empty lakebed was a weed-filled eyesore. After months of delay and massive complaints from residents, the city dismissed the contractor, realizing the company it had hired had insufficient expertise and equipment to clean the lake. This was only the beginning. During the first decade of the 21st century, rather than being a park amenity, Grasmere Lake was something of a swamp.

Though waters from Grasmere Lake had saturated the ground for nearly 100 years, the Denver Water Department (DWD) insisted too much water was seeping from the lake into the soil. Such water, it announced, was vital. Without it, the region could not keep growing. On this basis, the agency insisted on draining the lake and lining the bed with a special coating to prevent water loss. No sooner had the city announced that work was finally done in restoring the lake than crews drained and dug up Grasmere Lake anew the next year.

By the 1990s, DWD more operated as a utility selling water to the suburbs than as a city agency providing water to residents at as low a cost as good service allowed—its city charter mandate. The agency especially hated the City Ditch. The 19th-century technology, it declared, was not only an obsolete embarrassment, but it wasted too much water. Toward this end, and as part of installing a wastewater irrigation system for other city parks, DWD essentially destroyed the oldest working landmark in the community. It did so despite the Water Department having previously agreed to have the City Ditch in Washington Park listed in the National Register of Historic Places in 1976. The next year, on October 27, DWD proudly placed a medallion on a rock by the canal in the middle of the greenery to the west of the Washington Park Recreation Center to highlight that the City Ditch had become a Denver landmark district. Local preservationists were mute in protesting the water company's action. Water, they pointed out, still flowed in the ditch through the park.

With the massive disruption of I-25 as part of the T-REX program to rebuild the freeway in the early 21st century while adding light rail, DWD disconnected the City Ditch to the south of the Valley Highway where much of the canal south of the city line was still a scenic remnant of yesterday—DWD dismissed it as "a sewer." In place of ditch water from the Platte, the utility pumped water from a recycling plant near 56th Avenue and York Street to Veterans Park at the northwest corner of the freeway and South University Boulevard. There the water flowed back into the City Ditch, irrigating Washington Park and areas down the canal. Included was a dechlorination plant in Veterans Park.

Meanwhile, Denver water subscribers heeded the utility's injunction to save water. When they did so, they found DWD raised its fees: homeowners had saved so much water that the operation claimed it lacked the revenue necessary to further irrigate the suburbs while undermining the City Ditch and Washington Park amenities. Rumors flew about massive sweetheart deals between DWD and contractors while the utility's construction projects were seemingly unending and continually over budget.

At times, the refilled Grasmere Lake suffered from algae problems. The nitrogen-rich recycled water did not have the same quality as had the Platte River water previously brought in via the City Ditch. The sewer water was also polluted by the runoff from city streets, complete with petroleum-based products. Critics branded the irrigation fluid "purple water," a liquid on which the administration had failed to conduct an environmental impact study. (DWD placed the recycled water in purple pipes.) Some of the liquid, friends of the park charged, included effluvia from the Lowry Landfill Superfund site, complete with possible radioactive wastes. They observed that once the recycled water was the prime means of park irrigation, city park lawns were besmirched by extremely noticeable and sizeable brown spots while they charged the wastewater was killing trees.

At least locals could see the mountains when looking westward from Grasmere Lake. In the early 1980s, Washington Park advocates called for a mountain-view ordinance. The statute stipulated that nothing could be built blocking the vista of the Rockies west of a point in the park, about 130 feet north and 130 feet west of the intersection of South Franklin Street and Arizona Avenue. Gates Rubber, whose land was impacted by the suggestion, bitterly opposed the measure. So did the Chamber of Commerce. Showing its staff could not see anything, the Denver Planning Office also urged the rejection of the measure. The mountains, it explained, were not visible from the east of Grasmere Lake. Despite such opposition, under the guidance of Gertie Grant, an activist in the South Central Improvement Association (later the West Washington Park Neighborhood Association), the mountain-view ordinance became a reality.

Just to the northeast of Grasmere Lake, along the City Ditch, is the Washington Park Bowling Club. This refers to an illuminated, fenced-off section used for lawn bowling. The square, 120 by 120 feet, is regulation size, dating from around 1920. Members of the club added a small adjacent octagonal storage shed in 1925. At one time, when lawn bowling was a rage at the Denver Country Club, that organization eagerly competed against those playing on the public facility in South Denver. Not until the 1970s did a fence go up around the bowling green which essentially became the private property of the Bowling Club. By the 21st century, members were rarely visible participating in their sport.

Croquet players used the green after the Denver Croquet Club relocated from City Park to Washington Park in 1986. (A space for croquet was already in place as early as 1909 near the tennis courts to the northwest of Grasmere Lake. Nearby were pits for enthusiasts to play quoits, a variant of horseshoes. The city had

Photo by Phil Goodstein

Lawn bowling and croquet are part of the Washington Park mix on a small green to the east of Grasmere Lake.

installed the tennis courts the previous year. More tennis courts followed to the south of Grasmere Lake in 1922, the year before workers sodded the south lawn along Louisiana Avenue.)

Boating and Fishing

Virtually from the time John W. Smith created his lake, people put boats on it. Already in 1872, a small ship, *The Dolly Varden*, sailed on the lake as a pleasure boat. Sailors have taken to the water in a wide variety of crafts ever since. The fire department has taught those training for the force water rescue skills by having them float on and dive into Smith Lake while wearing wetsuits.

Even before the city acquired the Washington Park land, Smith Lake had been a neighborhood fishing hole. As the administration developed the park, the Colorado Division of Wildlife stocked Smith and Grasmere lakes. Beginning in 1954 to around 1979, the *Denver Post* had an annual summer fishing derby for youngsters up to age 14 in the park. It awarded prizes to those who caught at least three fish. Youths pooled their catches to get the rewards. The American Legion prominently cosponsored the event.

Opposed to the American Legion and the *Post*, the *Rocky Mountain News* worked with the Veterans of Foreign Wars to host an annual Huck Finn Day. The event began in 1949 as an effort to emphasize the park as an old-fashioned fishing hole. For the occasion, boys and girls, 15 years of age and below, dressed up in Tom Sawyer and Becky Thatcher costumes. While they were supposed to use only stick and string fishing poles, some brought fancy rods and reels to the event. At times, upwards of 7,500 were at the park for the festivities. The Division of Wild-life dumped so many fish into the City Ditch for the occasion that it was hard for some early fishermen not to pull them out.

Youngsters found they had to get to the park early—the crowds were so intense that it was virtually impossible for latecomers to get close to fishing spots. Some of those descending on the greenery were not there to go fishing. They saw Huck Finn Day as a summer Halloween where they got to dress up in fancy costumes. Judges gave awards to those whom they believed were in the most imaginative outfits.

Huck Finn Day came to an end in 1987 after the Division of Wildlife had awarded sponsorship of the fishing derby to a commercial outfit which soon walked away from the festival. The city subsequently reserved the lily pond for a Young Fishing Program, for "kids 15 and under." Not only did that effort never come close to matching Huck Finn Day, but few young anglers tried their luck in the pond. For the most part, park fishermen concentrated on Smith Lake. Back in the 1930s, neighborhood youths often sold the fish they caught in the lake to Rabb's, a store on Broadway.

Fish tales abound. Foremost is the legend of "Old One Eye." Supposedly, some monstrous fish, possibly a bass but most likely a carp, has swum in Smith Lake. On occasion, fishermen have snagged it, only to find their lines broken or themselves nearly pulled into the water. One time, a fisherman caught the denizen

Photo by Mort Karman, *WPP*

Huck Finn Day at Smith Lake in 1984.

of the deep. As he fought the leviathan, his hook broke, ripping through the plum-sized eye of the sea monster, leading to the "Old One Eye" moniker.

The Bathing Beach

*I*n 1911, the city transformed the northern edge of Smith Lake into a bathing beach. Included was a bathhouse at the northwest shore which went up in 1911–12, overseen by architect James B. Hyder at the cost of $10,000. The city's parks draftsman, Frederick W. Ameter, assisted him. Ameter also designed some of the bridges over the City Ditch in the park. Workers laid eight concrete traffic and five wood-and-iron bridges over the canal in the course of 1909–12.

Besides locker rooms, the bathhouse included showers and private baths twelve months of the year. Such a facility was a vital public amenity for those living in dwellings lacking bathtubs and showers—a common deficiency until well after World War II. Neighbors also came to the bathhouse for meetings in a public room. The men's locker room complemented the latter. Park employees could transform the changing area into a gathering space holding 300 people. The public room featured two fireplaces. They were lit in the winter when the hall served as a warming house for ice-skaters.

At the same time construction was underway on the bathhouse, crews hauled in sea sand which they placed on the north bank of the lake. A couple of piers, added in 1914, jutted into the lake from which swimmers jumped into the water. Those leaping into the swimming hole sometimes found themselves briefly sinking into the mud above their ankles. Two hundred locals swarmed to the beach on opening day in 1911. The beach was directly between the bathhouse and the lake.

Not everything worked out ideally at the Washington Park beach. Early Washington Park was a very strict, middle-class puritanical park. Originally, two beaches existed: one for men and the other for women. The men's section opened in 1911. Not until the next year were women allowed to go into the lake. A rope separated the two areas. Guards were on the alert for so-called mashers who slipped under the barrier to the women's side.

The sexual division immediately caused problems, especially for families with children. The city relented, adding a third, family beach. Moralists were scandalized when unmarried boys and girls mingled together on it. The park ended the segregation when no untoward events occurred from the mixing of the sexes. Even so, puritans insisted that the lake's waters not be contaminated by people from East Asia. In 1913, the city ruled individuals of Japanese heritage could not use the swimming hole despite state civil rights laws outlawing racial discrimination at all public facilities.

A separation sometimes existed between locals and those who made special trips to Washington Park to use the bathing facilities. Neighborhood boys and girls rarely went to the bathhouse, usually dressing at home. Sometimes, the boys skinny dipped across the field in a grove of trees near the City Ditch, a place they

Photo by Otto Roach, Roach Photos

A high-diving platform was at the end of a pier at the Washington Park bathing beach on the northern edge of Smith Lake.

insisted that was off limits to girls. In the process, they had to keep their eyes open for Adam Kohankie who took over as park superintendent on March 1, 1906. They remembered him as a tall man in a light blue uniform who wore a badge and carried a billy club. He was simultaneously a friend of children and a policeman checking adolescent pranks.

Born near Cleveland on March 31, 1864, Kohankie arrived in the Mile High City in January 1884. Before long, he made South Denver his abode. During the late 1880s and early 1890s, he worked for John L. Russell when the latter had a landscaping business and greenhouse near South Broadway and Alameda Avenue. For a while, Kohankie was a member of the volunteer fire department of the Town of South Denver. The superintendent was among those affiliating with the Ku Klux Klan, being applicant 4463 of 1924. He remained as the head of the park until his retirement in 1936. During his tenure, he lived in the Whitehead House. By the time of his death on February 10, 1945, he was dwelling at 1112 South Gilpin Street.

Among other problems, Kohankie had to deal with explosive conditions on New Year's Eve. For the occasion, teenagers and individuals in their 20s gathered near the pavilion. After building a large bonfire, they shot off guns and fireworks, sometimes throwing firecrackers into the blaze. On occasion, they pranced about naked, only to discover their fellows had stolen their clothes.

Over the years, the city made assorted improvements to the beach. In 1919, it proposed adding a small "plunge pool" between the bathhouse and the lake. It was never built. Nor did anything come of a simultaneous suggestion to add a swimming pool on the banks of the Platte River at Overland Park. Still, workers resanded the shore and lake bed that year. In the 1930s, Works Progress Administration crews replaced the piers and added a 10-meter-high platform—it lacked a diving board. A second tower was about 12- to 15-feet high; a third, on the east end, was five- to six-feet high. The South High swimming team long made the beach its home.

The Washington Park beach remained for whites only. Civil rights groups were not happy about this. On August 17, 1932, a group of about 50 blacks, encouraged by white members of the Young Communist League, attempted to use the beach, resulting in a race riot. The beach remained segregated.

The city frequently shut the swimming hole in the 1940s and 1950s in the face of polio scares: physicians realized polio spread through contaminated waters though they were not quite sure how. Around 1950, to clean the lake, park workers drained Smith Lake. They discovered an amazingly wide array of junk at its bottom. Missing was the carcass of a cow. For years, a favorite urban tall tale was that the body of a cow occupied the bottom of the lake. The cleanup also exploded another park myth. Over the years, the pond's depth had mysteriously grown whereby locals insisted it was so deep that its bottom had never been discovered. It is about eight to twelve feet deep.

Citing low water, the city sealed the lake to swimming during the summer of 1952. It permanently closed the beach in June 1957. By that time, the parks department was spending $5,600 a week on chlorine. During the summer, lifeguards constantly sailed the lake during swimming hours, dumping load after load of chlorine into the water. Not only was the cost excessive, city hall explained, but the chlorine was killing aqualife and polluting the City Ditch. The lake was so filthy that lifeguards could not see swimmers who were more than a foot down in the water. A swimming pool, the administration promised, would replace the bathing beach. The latter did not open until 1971 as part of the Washington Park Recreation Center.

Volunteers for Outdoors Colorado

*A*fter the city closed the swimming hole, the bathhouse became offices and storage space. For some years, it was the Mile High headquarters of the Colorado State University extension service. That agency worked with the federal Department of Agriculture in educating city dwellers on landscaping and crops. It issued a newsletter, *Gardener's Forum*. For the most part, the facility had no direct outreach to park users. Passersby simply saw an isolated building painted an ugly industrial green. In the spring of 1985, the city forester's office moved into the structure after the college program lost its funding.

When the city forester exited the bathhouse in January 1991, the structure badly needed renovation. Park lovers differed widely as to how it should be used. Some called for transforming it into an elite restaurant. Others insisted that, as a public building, it should be open to all regardless of their ability to pay. The department of parks and recreation announced it could not conceive of any park use for it. This opened the door for a private group to gain possession of the bathhouse.

Photo by Phil Goodstein

The Volunteers for Outdoor Colorado has transformed the Washington Park bathhouse into its headquarters.

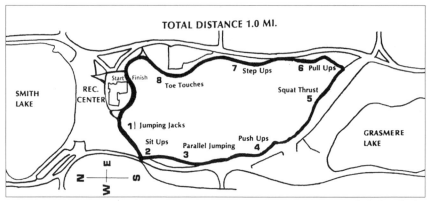

Before the Volunteers for Outdoor Colorado installed a jogging track around the perimeter of Washington Park in 1993, the YMCA had created an exercise trail in the center of the park in 1974.

In the course of 1995–96, the Volunteers for Outdoor Colorado (VOC) oversaw a $600,000 reconstruction of the building. In exchange for financing the improvements, the society gained a 32-year rent-free occupancy of the facility—it was the only organization to submit a bid after a compromise allowed private groups to occupy park buildings. VOC agreed to maintain the bathhouse for the duration of its tenancy.

Robert Root & Associates was the architect; Paragon Builders the contractor. Other than maintaining the architectural integrity of the exterior, workers more or less gutted the interior, transforming the bathhouse into offices. Included were a reading room and a research library. The fireplaces remained in place. The renovation saw the installation of a sprinkler system, new roof, heating and cooling system, basement, windows, and floors. Exterior signs stated there were no public facilities within.

By the time it moved into the bathhouse, VOC was a powerhouse among affluent friends of active park use and mountain camping areas. Those appreciating the state's natural wonders and mountain recreation opportunities formed it in 1984 out of the Public Lands Council created the previous year. Citizens, its leaders argued, must be active stewards of public spaces. "Show Colorado you love her" was VOC's early motto. Members worked to add facilities to campgrounds, parks, and other public lands.

Typical of VOC was its call for 1,200 volunteers to turn out on September 18, 1993. That day, with donated materials, it led friends of Washington Park who installed a trail around the perimeter of the greenery. Locals had pondered this improvement for decades. In the course of the 20th century, the city had eliminated many of the original pedestrian paths. Landscapers had never bothered to place sidewalks along the park's boundaries. At the most, over the years crews installed a few asphalt slabs in the park. Among them were spaces it deemed bicycle paths as part of a stillborn effort in the mid-1960s to make Denver an easier place for people to get around on two wheels.

The lack of pedestrian routes especially told with the rise of jogging in the 1970s. Runners then created their own well-beaten paths as they ran around the greenery. Before long, joggers were omnipresent. Combined with individuals out for a stroll, dog-walkers, mothers pushing strollers, bicyclists, roller-skaters, and many others, they helped make the greenery into a prime people-watching place. By the early 1980s, as many as 10,000 people descended on the park during week-end afternoons.

The VOC track more or less followed the route blazed by the joggers. On October 9, 1999, 600 or so volunteers worked to completely refurbish the trail which was badly eroded in places. At that time, they extended the path north of the park along the South Marion Street Parkway to connect with Cherry Creek.

By the time the bathhouse effort got underway, VOC claimed a membership of around 2,500. It recruited them and others to help make the building improvements a reality. The organization hosted a grand reopening of the facility in July 1996.

To pay for the renovation, VOC sold commemorative bricks on a plaza between the facility and Smith Lake where part of the bathing beach had once been. It also marketed such merchandise as duffel bags, coffee mugs, and backpacks. VOC additionally managed to get numerous monetary donations from various foundations while it maintained a volunteer clearing house and published a catalog listing the opportunities whereby concerned citizens could lend their hands and donate their money to make the outdoors a better place.

Delos "Dos" Chappell was VOC's driving force. A fifth generation Coloradan, he had been born out of state in New Haven, Connecticut, on November 14, 1946, while his father was in college. After graduating from the private Colorado Academy in the southwestern suburbs and serving in the air force at the peak of the Vietnam War, Chappell made his way through the University of Denver. He subsequently worked in sales and marketing while being an outdoors enthusiast. In 1988, Chappell joined VOC. Before long, as its executive director, he was a whirlwind of energy. Seemingly everywhere, he radiated his passion to others, getting them to join him in assorted efforts. When possible, he opened the bathhouse to tour groups. At times, it hosted art shows.

Chappell suddenly collapsed and died at age 52 during a VOC retreat at Empire on February 19, 1999. To commemorate his work, VOC christened its home the Chappell Bathhouse. Kate Boland, a former Denver County Court judge, succeeded Chappell as VOC director.

The Pavilion

*T*he park pavilion dominates the south shore of Smith Lake. Park planner Reinhard Schuetze proposed it in 1907 as something of an amphitheater, complete with a stage for concerts. Nearby were comfort stations, complete with indoor plumbing. (Toilets with functioning plumbing have remained in operation to the north of Grasmere Lake and by the tennis courts south of that lake. For the most part, park planners have preferred replacing comfort stations with portable toilets, claiming that "undesirable" activities occur in real restrooms in parks.)

Photo by Phil Goodstein

The pavilion, on the south bank of Smith Lake, is a foremost Washington Park amenity. Over the years it has been used as a picnic shelter, boathouse, warming facility, and gathering place. Architect Jacques Benedict designed it to accentuate Denver as a city of lights.

In 1913, architect Jacques Benedict designed the $20,000 boathouse in emulation of the 17th-century pavilion of Kara Mustafa Pasa at the Topkapi Palace in Istanbul. The latter, the residence of the sultan, contained a wide variety of structures. Denver's miniature version of the sultan's seaside resort opened when the community projected itself as the Paris of America, a city of lights. To make this a reality, the building shone after dark with numerous electric bulbs placed in exterior sockets. The edifice included storage space, toilets, a concession stand, and a winter warming room. The upper level was an informal gathering spot and picnic shelter with a fine view of Longs Peak. On the lower level, people rented boats and purchased tickets for rides around the lake.

As was the case with much of Washington Park, the city systematically neglected the pavilion during the 1960s and 1970s. The more Denver sprawled, the less attention the administration paid to existing park amenities. By the late 1980s, the building was in sorry shape, drastically in need of renovation.

Nobody recognized this more than the Park People. The organization dated from April 1969, established by friends of the city's parks who raised money to maintain and restore the city's open spaces, fountains, and monumental statuary when city hall claimed it lacked the funds to maintain this part of the community's heritage. Before long, the Park People was a foremost charity, receiving numerous donations from a wide array of sources. In 1987, it arranged a $90,000 restoration of the pavilion. Architect Jennifer Moulton, a leader of Historic Denver, oversaw the job. The aim was to return the pavilion to its 1913 charm. (Moulton was subsequently planning director under Mayor Wellington Webb.)

The administration sealed off the renovated pavilion to everyday park users. The department of parks and recreation made the top floor available only on a rental basis. Before long, the pavilion was the site of elite receptions. The edifice simultaneously emerged as the symbol of Washington Park. A local winemaker and realty featured the pavilion on their logos. The early 21st century saw the emergence of a concession stand directly west of the pavilion which rented bicycles, boats, and other craft to park users. Money from a 2007 bond promised new renovations of the boathouse.

The main park playground is adjacent to the pavilion. Originally, Washington Park had no specific area for children. In the early 20th century, reformers argued that if children did not have well-supervised places in which to play, they would get into mischief. The result was the addition of playgrounds to numerous parks and schools. Directors oversaw them to prevent bullying while they taught the children games and craft skills. Modifications of the playground have been constant. The 1980s saw a total redesign. Further alterations assured it was handicapped accessible. An additional playground is near the Camp Fire Girls' grill.

The main playground has blended with the pavilion in making folk dancing part of Washington Park. In 1915, two young women charged with overseeing the playground, Ruth Holland and Gertrude Strickler, introduced children to various international shuffles. Before long, adults joined the action. The effort soon faded. Schukr "Sugar" Basanow unwittingly reincarnated it in 1971.

A native of Belgrade of Kalmuck origins (a Mongolian people), Basanow survived World War II in Yugoslavia and in German labor camps. With 900 other Kalmucks, he came to America in 1951. Settling in Philadelphia, he was involved with the Fellowship House, a human relations training center, while he worked as a machinist.

Those running the Fellowship House observed Basanow's mettle as a dancer. Before long, drawing on his Kalmuck heritage, Basanow established himself as a performer, teaching others his jigs at the facility. Between 1956 and 1960, he occasionally worked as an acrobatic dancer in New York. He passed on offers to be on the "Ed Sullivan Show" and go to Hollywood.

While teaching dance in Philadelphia, Basanow met Richard "Dick" Barnes, becoming extremely close friends. The latter, who had been eased out of the Fellowship House, moved to Denver in June 1969, soon becoming the director of the Washington Park Community Center. Basanow followed Barnes to Denver the next year, brought to the state by his daughter's respiratory problems. He immediately got a job teaching folk dance at the Community Center. For a while, he held the dances in the sanctuary of the old church forming the heart of the Community Center's complex.

With the sponsorship of the Community Center and city funds, Basanow began the Washington Park dances in 1971. On Thursday evenings, the Yugoslav native encouraged locals to participate in a wide array of steps directly south of the pavilion. For a brief moment in the early 1970s, he also hosted folk dances at the Greek

Theater in the Civic Center. Opposition from the Steele Community Center at West 39th Avenue and King Street, which claimed a purview of folk dancing in the area, killed the latter program.

At times, more than 200 people participated in Basanow's Washington Park jigs. His goal, he explained, was "to teach people to come together with dance." Mayor Federico Peña saluted the effort when he declared August 9, 1990, "Sugar Basanow Day." The mayor hosted a party at the park for Basanow, dubbing a nearby tree across the City Ditch the "Sugar Basanow Tree." It had no plaque, but Basanow fiercely hugged it as his own.

The city provided Basanow with a free permit to conduct the dances—it paid him for his efforts during his first couple of years. He sought to convince bystanders to join the action, telling them they could easily learn to dance. Many of the Washington Park jigs were highly stylized and demanded a great deal of skill.

The Belgrade native continued to oversee the shuffles on Thursday evenings from May until October into the 21st century by which time, he observed, he had a third generation of families participating in the hops, including many who had first met through the Community Center. Some of the seniors participating in the jigs had patronized such popular South Denver dance halls in the 1940s and 1950s as the Rainbow Ballroom at Fifth Avenue and Lincoln Street and the Crystal Ballroom at 220 Broadway. Basanow's students emerged as leaders of numerous other folk dance ensembles. He styled himself as the "guru" of the dancers, being widely known throughout the city.

Photo by Phil Goodstein

Folk dancers have gathered at the pavilion every Thursday evening in the summer since 1971.

Ice-skating was once most popular on Smith Lake.

Ice-skating

Washington Park was also very much a winter sports center. Into the 1980s, youths found whatever hills they could in and around the park and used them for sledding runs. Before World War II, the city sometimes closed Dakota Avenue west of the park, especially between South Ogden and South Washington streets, allowing youngsters to coast down it after snowfalls. In other places, children went down Tennessee Avenue west of the park on anything from fancy sleds purchased from Montgomery Ward to pieces of cardboard. Those living northeast of the park went sledding on Dakota Avenue west of South Williams Street and on Alameda Avenue to the east of South Gaylord Street.

Early on, the parks department flooded the tennis courts northwest of Grasmere Lake in the winter to provide for an ice-skating rink. During the early 20th century, ice-skating was a foremost winter pursuit. For a while, the city flooded an empty lot at the southeast corner of Cedar Avenue and South Pennsylvania Street, so it would freeze over for the sport. In early 1921, the Sherman School PTA arranged for ice-skating on the lot at the northwest corner of Third Avenue and Grant Street across the street from the school.

Smith Lake was eventually the main ice-skating area in the park. To test the thickness and safety of the ice, during deep freezes a park worker drove and parked a pickup truck on the ice near the middle of the lake. If the ice showed no sign of cracking under its weight, crews cleared snow from parts of the lake, placed barrels and bales of hay as barriers, and opened the lake for public skating. Each day at noon, a park official inspected the truck. If there was too much melt by its tires or any sign of cracking, he drove it off and closed the lake to skating.

Weather permitting, skating during dusk and the evening during December and January was most popular. Sometimes, music piped from the pavilion serenaded the skaters. The bathhouse and pavilion were open as warming houses. Skaters could get hot chocolate, hot dogs, and hamburgers at the pavilion. A booth provided for skate sharpening and repairs.

The more Denver progressed in the late 20th century, the less favorable city hall was to ice-skating. In 1981, citing budget pressures, the administration prohibited ice-skating. While it permitted the activity after the Christmas blizzard of 1982, the city forbade locals from gliding atop the lake the next winter after a storm dropped 22 inches of snow over Thanksgiving weekend, followed by a severe stretch of freezing weather. Skating, explained newly elected mayor Federico Peña, was not safe. He also prohibited sledding as too great an insurance liability. The mayor simultaneously was nonpareil in championing skiing.

By the late 1990s, observing that Houston had a year-round public skating facility, locals again hoped to ice-skate in Washington Park. A series of warm winters, combined with bureaucratic snafus kept anything from happening. A 1968 plan for an ice-skating complex near South University Boulevard and Iowa Avenue never materialized. Eventually, the University of Denver provided a community ice rink as part of its Ritchie Center. The city made no effort to open Washington Park to ice-skating following extremely snowy weather during the winters of 2006–07 and 2007–08. By that time, it had no plans to reintroduce ice-skating to the open space.

The Eugene Field Connection

*T*he Eugene Field Cottage is at the southwest corner of Exposition Avenue and South Franklin Street, next to a statue, *Wynken, Blynken, and Nod*. These are Denver's tributes to Eugene Field (1850–1895). Highly acclaimed at the time of his death as the "children's poet," Field was the author of "Little Boy Blue," "Wynken, Blynken, and Nod," and other verses designed to wet the eyes of lovers of childhood. Field spent two pivotal years of his life in Denver from July 1881 to August 1883 as managing editor of the daily *Denver Tribune*. During part of his Denver days, Field lived in a simple frame cottage dating from 1875 at 315 West Colfax Avenue, near the northwest corner of West Colfax and Court Place. He shared the five-room dwelling with his wife and three children.

Robert W. Speer idolized Field. Mayor from 1904 to 1912 and 1916 to his death in 1918, Speer presented himself as a friend of children. Opponents blasted him as a crook who gave away numerous public concessions to private interests while the city's corrupt and incompetent milk inspection practices led to the deaths of children. During a visit to Dusseldorf, Germany in 1911, Speer espied a fountain depicting the joys of youth. He arranged to have a copy of it made and presented to City Park as *The Children's Fountain*.

Shortly before his death, Speer came across a miniature statue celebrating "Wynken, Blynken, and Nod" in a Chicago gallery. Inquiring as to the sculptor,

The city moved the Eugene Field Cottage from the northwest corner of West Colfax Avenue and Court Place to the southwest corner of South Franklin Street and Exposition Avenue in 1930. It was the Washington Park library from 1930 until 1970.

the mayor learned it was crafted by Mabel Landrum Torrey, who had grown up in Sterling and whose father was a Colorado judge. Her husband, Fred Martin Torrey, had created statues of Abraham Lincoln.

The mayor arranged for Mabel Torrey to sculpt a larger than life version of *Wynken, Blynken and Nod*. Frank Woodward donated ten $1,000 World War I Liberty bonds to pay for it. The city dedicated the artwork in a 25-foot-wide circular pool along the City Ditch in the middle of Washington Park between Smith and Grasmere lakes. Children immediately flocked to *Wynken, Blynken, and Nod*, splashing around it in the fountain during the summer. The city and newspapers frequently called it *The Lullaby Fountain*.

The Field Cottage joined *Wynken, Blynken and Nod* in Washington Park in 1930. Real estate pressures threatened the house in the mid-1920s. In response, Joseph G. Brown, an old friend of Field who had worked with him on the *Denver Tribune*, urged saving the building. He convinced the Colorado chapter of the American Penwomen to support the drive to transform the residence into a museum/memorial to the poet. The Penwomen received financing for the project from the Unsinkable Molly Brown. Not related to Joseph G. Brown, she claimed Field was her favorite poet who had given her inspiration at key moments in her life.

On this basis, on May 1, 1927, the Penwomen dedicated the cabin as the Eugene Field Memorial House. Newspapers referred to it as "The Children's Garden," a combination of a playground with kindergarten equipment and a shrine to the poet. The trauma of the Depression again endangered the house in 1930. Molly Brown thereupon bought it that spring for $350—she could not gain possession of the land. She gave the cottage to the city based on the promise the administration would move it to a park and maintain it as a memorial to Field.

Joseph G. Brown, who was then the head of the newspaper room of Denver Public Library (DPL), suggested Washington Park was the ideal site. Given Field's literacy, he was sure that a branch library would be the best possible way of recalling the poet. In July 1930, the house found its new bearings at Exposition Avenue and South Franklin Street where workers added a new porch to it. DPL opened its Washington Park branch there in mid-September 1930.

One person disgruntled by this was Molly Brown, then in Paris, who did not think it an appropriate way to remember Field. Denver leaders, she decried, were "such utilitarians" who should have had the good sense to simply make the house a permanent memorial to the poet. She had not said anything when DPL first informed her of its library plans. (Field had almost drowned in Smith Lake when he suffered cramps while swimming in it in June 1882.)

Besides packing the house with books, the librarians retained remnants of Field's living quarters, particularly where he used to nail his slippers into the wall when he sat back and read. The library featured a collection on the poet, complete with a copy of his family bible. After the construction of a new Eugene Field Library at the southeast corner of Ohio Avenue and South University Boulevard in 1970, designed by Oluf N. Neilsen, DPL abandoned the Field Cottage. The department of parks and recreation arranged for the Park People to use it as a meeting space and offices. As such, it is rarely open to the public.

After Field's death, his family and champions suppressed some of the poet's Denver writings. This was particularly the case with his *Children's Primer*. Far from being a doting champion of childhood, Field was a sarcastic critic of the gooey, meaningless tripe which he believed dominated children's readers. He accentuated this by writing a somewhat macabre version of what children's books might say:

> This is a gun. Is the gun loaded? I do not know. Let us find out. Put the gun on the table and you, Susie, blow down one barrel, while you, Charlie, blow down the other. Bang! Yes it was loaded. Run quick Jennie, and pick up Susie's head and Charlie's lower jaw before the nasty blood gets over the new carpet.
>
> The cat is asleep on the rug. Step on her tail and see if she will wake up. Oh, no; she will not wake. She is a heavy sleeper. Perhaps if you were to saw her tail off with the carving knife you might attract her attention. Suppose you try.
>
> Can you see the mouse trap? I wonder if it is set? Put your finger in one of the holes and see. There is a little mouse caught in one of the holes on the other side. Pull him out by the tail. He appears to be dead. Perhaps the trap was not well enough ventilated for him. Take poor little dead mouse and put him in Sister Dora's bed where she can see him when she pulls back the sheet tonight.

Some Denver adolescents sought to live up to Field's poor expectations of children. They were aided and abetted by city hall. By the 1960s, the *Wynken, Blynken, and Nod* statue was badly disfigured. The fountain rarely functioned. As the administration ignored Washington Park, vandals defaced the sculpture, ripping off some of the children's toes and part of Blynken's bonnet. After years of such neglect, in 1982 the Park People undertook a $9,000 renovation of the sculpture. Believing that the statue was no longer at home in the middle of the park by the City Ditch, the group moved it directly north of the Field Cottage. No effort was made to install a new fountain around it.

The Hazel Gates Woodruff Tribute Garden is on the west side of the Eugene Field Cottage to the south of *Wynken, Blynken, and Nod.* The Park People dedicated it in September 1996 in memory of a member of the Charles Gates family who had been a whirlwind of energy in park causes. (The Gates family was the namesake of Gates Rubber, long a privately held concern located near South Broadway and Mississippi Avenue.) The Gates Woodruff Garden includes brick pavers, honoring those who have given money to fund the Park People's tree conservation program. The ornately landscaped area, designed by Jane Silverstein Ries of the Park People, is hidden away from the rest of the park even as a popular jogging path goes right by it.

MF

Wynken, Blynken, and Nod *sail in a fountain in the middle of Washington Park. In 1983, the Park People moved the statue to near the Eugene Field Cottage at the southwest corner of Exposition Avenue and South Franklin Street.*

Music and Noise

Music was another premier Washington Park attraction. In 1911, the greenery hosted its first free concerts. Before long, the Innes Denver Band, a private ensemble led by Frederick Innes, performed sporadically in the grand meadow. During the summer of 1915, it gave weekly Saturday afternoon performances there. Around 1920, to accommodate various musical events, workers erected a bandstand near the gazebo. The latter is a 12-sided structure dating from 1912. For a while, the South Side YMCA sponsored community singing in the park on Saturday evenings in the summer. On occasion, the Denver Municipal Band played at the pavilion. Eventually, the bandstand came down.

For the most part, Washington Park was second fiddle to the Civic Center, Cheesman Park, and City Park as a public music spot. Not until the 1980s, after the Denver Municipal Band fled its old home in City Park, did Washington Park come to the fore as the city's main summer music center with the Denver Municipal Band playing one to two concerts a week from a temporary bandstand near the gazebo during July and early August. At the peak of its popularity, the band attracted upwards of 5,000 to its concerts; it was lucky to draw 500 listeners to its Washington Park recitals to which members of the audience had to bring their own chairs. (For many years, John S. Leick of 1325 South University Boulevard directed the Denver Municipal Band along with the band of the Highlander Boys. He died in January 1951. South High music director Ed Lenicheck subsequently took the baton of the Denver Municipal Band.)

The Denver Symphony and its successor, the Colorado Symphony, have given summer park concerts. More than 10,000 locals frequently flocked to them. The affairs were sometimes more beer bashes/wine tastings, with an extremely heavy consumption of alcohol than programs to appreciate the performances. With the symphony placing its stage on the western edge of the meadow, listeners sometimes could not literally face the music since the setting sun glared into their eyes during the first half of concerts.

Others provided their own music with blaring car radios and boom boxes. The omnipresence of such cacophony sometimes meant that, far from being an urban oasis and escape from the city, Washington Park was a reflection of the problems of urban living. This stood out during the 1960s, 1970s, and 1980s when rowdiness, alcoholism, and traffic jams were part and parcel of the open space.

During the late 1960s and early 1970s, Washington Park was something of a hippie park. Four thousand young men and women flocked to the greenery on Sunday, July 30, 1967, for the city's pioneer be-in, an anti-climactic event where not much of anything happened. Even so, adolescents gathered at the greenery, seeing it as a meeting spot. For a while, the island in Grasmere Lake had the reputation of being "Monkey Island" where monkey business occurred. Not only was it a necking spot, but it also became a drug-use area. The summer of 1970 saw a riot in the park when the police charged hippies hanging out around Grasmere Lake, clubbing and gassing them. To keep adolescents off of Monkey Island, the city destroyed the bridge between the island and the mainland. For a while, some locals did not want to go to the southern part of the park, fearing it as a center of

The city cut the bridge between Monkey Island and the mainland in the early 1970s so no monkey business would occur there. The ghost of a rebellious young woman, around 20 years old, who called herself Miss B. Haven, supposedly haunts it. The bridge over the City Ditch is in the foreground.

crime, alcoholism, and drugs. Now and then, undercover policemen found themselves arrested by other officers for suspected involvement in drug deals near Monkey Island.

Allegedly, the ghost of Beatrice Haven haunts Monkey Island. A rebellious young woman who was born at Porter Hospital in 1949, she called herself Miss B. Haven in the late 1960s. After getting out of high school, she hung around Washington Park, partying with boys while she studied to become a nuclear technician at a local hospital. Something happened to her whereby she disappeared in a glow. Supposedly, late at night her specter suddenly seems to shine for boys on Monkey Island before quickly disappearing amidst the squawking of birds. (Park personnel know something is wrong on the island when they hear the birds being much louder than usual.)

By the early 1980s, Washington Park had emerged as a cruising ground for young motorists who endlessly circled the park's 2.3-mile roadway with blasting sound systems. Some stopped to make drug and sex deals. This outraged other park users who insisted Washington Park had to be a center of peaceful relaxation, not a reflection of the worst of motor car culture. Besides the racket, car users often left behind piles of rubbish.

Complaints about traffic were not new. Landscapers designed Washington Park right when the automobile was beginning its ascendancy. Under Mayor Robert Speer, the city insisted that the amenities of motorists were a foremost concern. In the 1930s, manager of improvements and parks George Cranmer got New Deal money to have Works Progress Administration crews put in the parking lot to the west of the bathhouse. A drab asphalt lot subsequently occupied the southeast and southwest shores of Smith Lake. Cranmer also pushed the widening of park roads to make it easier for motorists to drive through the greenery.

The city has periodically modified the Washington Park road system. Once, for example, streets in the park connected the oval loop with the intersections of Louisiana Avenue and South Downing Street and Louisiana Avenue and South Gilpin Street. During World War II, the parks department closed an entry at Arizona Avenue and South Downing Street. Early on, neighbors fought a proposal to extend the Marion Street Parkway into the park as a thoroughfare. In 1921, residents vetoed a merchant's effort to put a filling station directly west of the greenery at the southwest corner of South Downing Street and Kentucky Avenue.

Fifty years later, members of a concerned neighborhood group, the Washington Park Action Council, called for sealing the park to motor traffic in the summer while providing a shuttle between the South High parking lot and the northern edge of the greenery. For the most part, nothing happened. As traffic got ever worse in the 1970s, the city experimented with making the loop around the park a one-way street. When this failed to produce the desired results, police raids and road closures ensued in 1982. Shutting most of the open space to automobiles proved quite successful in cutting down traffic, noise, and litter, leading some to argue that cars did not belong in the park, period.

No sooner were roadways closed to automobiles in most of the park in 1983–84 than a new menace appeared—bicyclists. Far from being peaceful, relaxed nature lovers using alternative forms of transportation, some of the bicyclists claimed the park oval as their personal racing arena. They ruthlessly tore through the greenery, intimidating those out for a peaceful stroll or a simple ride. The upshot was a new series of battles over which roads should be opened to bicyclists, where they could ride in the park, which way they could go, and how fast they could travel. The imposition of a one-way bike route counterclockwise on the loop meant that Washington Park was not necessarily a good place which bicycle commuters could cut through.

Despite turmoil about the bicyclists, Washington Park flourished once it was mostly free of motor traffic. In the process, it benefited by being a predominantly white park. At the same time locals complained about automobile cruising, noise, crime, and litter, comparable problems plagued City Park, Cheesman Park, and Sloans Lake. When the city tried comparable measures in those parks, civil rights advocates complained that the administration was discriminating against blacks, homosexuals, or Hispanos. Nobody argued the police were specially persecuting rowdy young heterosexual white men at Washington Park.

During the middle of the 20th century, members of the Young American League, a youth baseball and football program, played their games in the meadow. The greenery emerged as a premier volleyball spot in the 1980s. During the previous decade, tennis players had flocked to the open space, playing under the lighted courts virtually until the park's 11:00 PM curfew.

Locals have used the grand meadow in the center of Washington Park for a wide range of activities including volleyball and soccer. Here fishermen seemingly cast for worms in it.

The park has also hosted numerous special events. Various groups have used it for a wide array of "athons," marches, walks, runs, and affairs for pets, to raise funds for numerous worthy goals. The soccer craze accentuated the park's popularity. In 1983, the 37-year-old Nieves McIntire gained election to city council from West Washington Park, partly running in frustration that her son lacked a place to play what was becoming a highly popular game for the children of affluent settlers. Before long, the city installed numerous soccer fields in the grand meadow. (Sue Casey, elected to council in 1995 from Washington Park East, later claimed she was the original "soccer mom," writing McIntire's achievements off the books.) By the early 21st century, not as many people descended on the park for either soccer or volleyball.

The Washington Park Recreation Center

*I*ndoor sports became another dimension of Washington Park after the 20,850-square foot, $550,000 recreation center opened to the southeast of Smith Lake in the early summer of 1971 where a picnic shelter had once stood. It included the long-promised swimming pool as the replacement for the bathing beach. In some ways, the facility was tied to the urban upheavals of the 1960s when city experts urged more recreation centers as a means of calming a disgruntled population. Dignitaries broke ground for the hall on October 15, 1970.

In addition to the swimming pool, the Recreation Center included a gymnasium, arts and crafts room, and weight room. It had a kiln for firing ceramics while it promised to provide neighborhood-oriented programs for all age groups. A game room featured ping-pong and billiards tables. Initially, use of the center, including the swimming pool, was free. Not until 1981 did the city impose a charge for plunging into the pool.

The hall immediately attracted those committed to physical culture. Non-athletes shied away from it. The center emerged as the most heavily patronized city-owned recreation complex, drawing 900 to 1,100 people a day. Even those who could afford private athletic clubs preferred the Washington Park complex. If nothing else, it was a place to be seen. Individuals traveled for miles to use it, usually driving since they found long walks and runs to it unseemly.

After voters authorized a bond issue in 1989 for park and recreation improvements, the city closed the Recreation Center for remodeling in 1991. No sooner had the hall reopened in May 1992 than greater crowds than ever flocked to it. But something was wrong. The swimming pool lost 2,500 gallons of water a day through an open underwater light fixture. Lifeguards got sick from too great an exposure to chlorine. The water heating system did not work, leading to cold showers. The air conditioning similarly failed to meet expectations. Employees further found glitches in the electrical system and problems with the gym and locker room floors. The city, consequently, had to shut the center for more repairs in August 1992. The center was frequently closed on Sundays.

Residents fiercely guarded the integrity of the Recreation Center. No sooner had the shoddy renovation been redressed than Mayor Wellington Webb announced in the summer of 1994 that the city planned to keep the facility open all night as a place to detain youthful curfew offenders. This meant using the park after its legal closing hour of 11:00 PM. Locals argued the mayor's program was no solution at all. If the city needed a place to hold those suspected of breaking the curfew, the logical site was the nearby district #3 police station at Iowa Avenue and South University Boulevard. The mayor, conceding that his program primarily targeted

DPL

The Washington Park Recreation Center displaced a picnic shelter to the northeast of Smith Lake.

low-income members of minority groups, gave in to the protests when Good Shepherd Lutheran Church at 770 South Federal Boulevard agreed to allow the police to incarcerate curfew offenders there.

The Firehouse

*F*ire station #21 is at the northeast corner of the park at Virginia Avenue and South Franklin Street. It is a product of the rapid development of the area east of Washington Park after World War I. The city announced plans for it in 1921 as the city's first postwar firehouse. The Denver Fire Department (DFD) occupied it in August 1924. The building included ornate brickwork. Locals, especially visiting schoolchildren, remembered it for its shiny brass pole and the big boat it had to rescue people from park lakes.

The administration placed the fire station in the park to save money. Parks, city hall insisted, were more than just recreational facilities; they were ideal places for other city services. The station quickly emerged as something of a de facto outpost of city hall in the area. It was long the place where locals went to vote. The administration continued to believe park land was its for the taking when it concluded the 50-year-old, one-truck facility was obsolete in 1974.

That year, with money available from a 1972 bond issue, the fire department announced its intention to combine station #21 with station #13 in a sprawling new home at the southeast corner of Virginia Avenue and South Downing Street. (Station #13, at the southeast corner of South Broadway and Center Avenue, dated from the days of the Town of South Denver when it began operations as the John L. Russell Hose Company in 1891–92. After Denver took over the Town of South Denver, DFD reorganized the firehouse into station #13.)

Many residents and park lovers objected to the fire department's plans. The new fire station, they pointed out, would tear away valuable acreage from Washington Park. Manager of parks and recreation Joe Ciancio agreed. This opposition forced DFD to scale back its new station which it erected directly west of the old firehouse, dedicating it on July 31, 1975.

Simultaneously, neighbors pushed for preserving the old station. They managed to obtain a $100,000 federal grant from the Community Development Agency to renovate it into a senior citizens center. Right when they thought they were moving ahead, the city destroyed the landmark with the blessing of local city councilmen. In the hasty demolition job, the wreckers bulldozed some of the artifacts of the old firehouse into what became the parking lot of the new facility.

Members of station #21 have acted as guardians of Washington Park. This not only included assisting distressed park users, but the firefighters promised to look after the safety of ice-skaters should the city ever again allow that form of recreation in the park, especially on the lily pond. Those at the station have helped in the landscaping improvements at Steele School while being part of picnics of neighborhood associations. The facility hosted park gatherings of retired firefighters. The firehouse experimented with environmentally friendly technologies.

Besides referring to the greenery, by the 1980s the label "Washington Park" had become a state of mind, a term used to describe the best of South Denver.

Denver Firefighters Museum

In 1975, the city destroyed the original firehouse #21 at the southwest corner of South Franklin Street and Virginia Avenue for a modern facility.

Newcomers usually referred to it as "Wash Park." This name had already been in currency in the early 20th century when Tramway put "Wash Park" signs on its streetcars headed to the destination. Nonetheless, the modern title separates recent settlers from longtime South Denverites. Many of latter called the open space "Warshington Park," with a very distinctive "r" in the name. They lived in the surrounding neighborhoods, a story in themselves.

A Note on Sources:

Overviews on the history of South Denver are my *South Denver Saga* (Denver: New Social Publications, 1991), *The Spirits of South Broadway* (Denver: New Social Publications, 2008), and Millie Van Wyke, *The Town of South Denver* (Boulder: Pruett, 1991). Nancy Widmann, *Washington Park* (Denver: HD, 2007), is part of a superficial set of guides to the city. It mentions key points around the park, but lacks any color about the evolution of the greenery, primarily focusing on architects and architecture. On p. 76, she mentions Blossom Drive. Mundus Bishop Design, *Washington Park: Cultural Landscape Assessment and Preservation Plan* (Denver: Mundus Bishop, 2003), is a consultant's report.

DPL holds an immense store of information on the area in a variety of places, including clipping files in the Western History Department on neighborhood schools, churches, and individuals, planning and park documents in the Government Publications section, and books written on the city's schools and churches. The University of Denver Archives have scattered materials on the neighborhood, especially University Park and individuals associated with the college. The library of the Colorado Historical Society is a gold mine of old newspapers, brochures, and collections that relate to the section. The South High Historical Room has uneven materials on Washington Park and the surrounding neighborhoods.

Extremely different accounts of the drowning of Chester Sirkle are in *DX*, *DT*, and *DP*, all June 22, 1914. The *Post* told of the impact of the drowning on city safety measures, June 23, 1914, p. 6. *DT* criticized the city's unsafe lifeguard practices on June 23, 1914, p. 1.

Louisa Ward Arps, *Denver in Slices* (Denver: Sage Books, 1959), 61–73, is a short history of the City Ditch; cf. Rebecca Herbst, *The History of City Ditch* (Denver: Colorado Department of Highways, 1983), which emphasizes the thousand-plus miles of laterals. The NRHP nomination also discusses the evolution of the canal, especially in Washington Park. So does the file on the landmark district at the DLPC. Also see the July-August 1977 SCIA newsletter. Earl Mosley, "History of the Denver Water System, 1859–1919" (Denver: Unpublished Manuscript, 1966), looks at the city's early waterworks, paying attention to the irrigation canal.

The late Don Winters recalled growing up in a house where the City Ditch flowed through its backyard. In conversations in 1992 and 1995, and in memoirs provided by his widow Joyce, he also recalled fishing in Washington Park, selling the fish he caught there, ice-skating on the lake, and working at fire station #21. Members of his family shared stories about the role of the fire department in the greenery.

CHS holds the minute book of the Smith Canal & Ditch Company, John W. Smith's West Denver venture. Portraits of Smith are in Frank Hall, *History of the State of Colorado* (Chicago: Blakely, 1889), 1:428, 3:221–24, William B. Vickers, *History of the City of Denver* (Chicago: O. L. Baskin & Company, 1880), 589–91, *The Trail*, 4:8 (January 1912), 5–8, and Jerome Smiley, *History of Denver* (Denver: Denver Times, 1901/Old American Publishing Company, 1978), 375, 461, 793. There are also references to Smith in Mark Foster, *Henry M. Porter: Rocky Mountain Empire Builder* (Niwot: University Press of Colorado, 1991), esp. 43–45, and Bill Convery, *Pride of the Rockies* (Boulder: University Press of Colorado, 2000), 27–28. *Colorado Prospector*, November 1994, contains articles critical of John W. Smith and his election manipulations in 1868.

Van Wyke, *The Town of South Denver*, 97–100, traces the links between the Town of South Denver and the origins and evolution of Washington Park. The Frances Melrose column in *RMN*, April 23, 2000, p. 23D, discussed Roxborough Park as Washington Park. Ben Draper, director, "A History of Denver's Parks" (typescript by the Denver Museum Collection, 1934), 207–13, tells of the land procurement for Washington Park and gives a chronology of the development of the greenery. Park documents in the Government Documents section of DPL include official statistics on Washington Park.

Newspaper articles on the negotiations over the acquisition of Smith Lake and the development of the park include *RMN*, September 5, 1897, p. 5, and October 24, 1897, p. 4, and *DT*, August 8, 1899, p. 2, January 18, 1900, p. 6, and December 30, 1900, p. 2, part 2. *SDM*, August 26, 1949, reviewed the history of Washington Park as did *DP*, August 8, 1936, and *WPP*, July 1980, pp. 8–9.

Don Etter, *Denver's Parks and Parkways* (Denver: CHS, 1986), a brochure based on his nomination of the Denver park system to the NRHP, includes a history of Washington Park, 47–53, and the South Marion Street Parkway, 53–54. In the process, he mentions the role of such landscape architects as George Kessler, S. R. DeBoer and Frederick Law Olmstead Jr. With his wife Carolyn, Etter reviewed the career of Reinhard Schuetze, *Forgotten Dreamer* (Denver: Western History Department of DPL, 2001), esp. 30–31, on Washington Park. They are also the authors of *City of Parks: The Preservation of Denver's Park and Parkway System* (Denver: DPL, 2006), 6, 8, which reports the 1894 park plan.

My "Monumental Denver," *CH*, 3:1987, 34–43, covers the assorted plaques and statues in the park. "Thirty-seven Points Every Denver Resident Should Be Familiar With," *Denver Daily Doings*, 6:5 (January 29, 1927), 43, perpetrates the myth of the bottomless Smith Lake. *Greenthumb*, 15:10 (December 1958), 374, celebrates Evergreen Hill. *Colorado Prospector*, February 1983, p. 2, "Art in Denver," *Lookout*, 1:2 (January 1928), 29–30, and Agnes Wright Spring, *Denver's Historic Markets, Memorials, Statues and Parks* (Denver: CHS, n.d.), 35, are also apropos.

My *In the Shadow of the Klan*, 394–96, 399, looks at Edwin Whitehead and his wars with Ben Lindsey. Jack E. and Patricia A. Fletcher, *Colorado's Cowtown* (Yuma, AZ: Jack E. and Patricia A. Fletcher, 1981), 5, 10, mentions real estate investments of Whitehead Brothers, especially South Capitol Hill. DPL includes a clipping file on Sam D. Nicholson and the controversy over his estate. *The Glory that Was Gold* (Denver: Central City Opera House Association, 1936), 109, highlights Nicholson. *WPP*, May 1980, p. 1, covered the dedication of the *Colorado Miner*; cf. *RMN*, May 8, 1977, p. 14Now, August 15, 1977, p. 23C, and August 10, 1980, p. 6.

DPL holds the S. R. DeBoer papers. He reflected on his career and Washington Park in "Plans, Parks, and People," *Greenthumb*, 29:5 (December 1972), 142–212, and *Around the Seasons in Denver* (Denver: Smith-Brooks, 1948). Tom Noel and Barbara Norgren, *Denver: The City Beautiful* (Denver: Historic Denver, 1987), 146–50, heralds him. *MF*, May 1928, p. 4, outlined the nature of the Washington Park flower garden. On p. 5, it featured the views of S. R. DeBoer. Jane Silverstein Ries recalled DeBoer in various informal conversations in the mid-1980s. The February 1983 *Colorado Prospector* was filled with articles on the history of Denver open spaces, DeBoer, and Washington Park. *The Ghosts of University Park* will discuss DeBoer's estate on Iliff Avenue.

An undated February 1964 column from *RMN* on DeBoer is in scrapbook two of the papers of the WPGC at DPL. That collection, WH 1149, has one box of records, including club minutes, and four scrapbooks. The latter are filled with stories about area gardening efforts. They have only limited amounts on Washington Park proper. *DP*, August 22, 1926, p. 5, celebrated the installation of the Mount Vernon garden. *SDE*, February 26, 1916, p. 1, August 18, 1917, p. 1, and February 22, 1919, p. 1, told of the plantings sponsored by the South Denver Improvement Association. I briefly mention the victory gardens in *Robert Speer's Denver*, 442. *WPP* highlighted the efforts of the Friends and Neighbors of Washington Park, August 2006, p. 17, January 2008, p. 1, and November 2008, p. 7. In its October 2008 issue, p. 1, *WPP* observed Washington Park's 54 large flowerbeds.

RMN, September 12, 1936, recalled the life of John B. Lang. *WPP*, February 1981, p. 10, were the memories of Lang's son about growing up in Washington

Park. *RMN*, February 16, 1936, p. 6, told of the retirement of Adam Kohankie. It reported his death in its February 12, 1945, issue. Scrapbook one of the papers of the WPGC has clippings on Kohankie. A report about the Ecology Pavilion was in *RMN*, January 19, 1973, p. 97. *WPP*, July 1984, p. 1, mentioned the widening of South University Boulevard to the east of Washington Park.

Margaret O'Neill, *The Original Eight* ([Denver]: n.p., [c. 1986]), includes tales about skinny dipping in Washington Park, and New Year's Eve festivities. Dianne Clark shared her father's memories of prancing around nude in the park on New Year's Eve in discussions in 1989. Those attending the South Denver history seminar of February 17, 2008, remembered the revels on New Year's Eve, the police in the park, the rowboat dumping chlorine into the lake, and sinking in the mud after jumping into the lake. John Davoren also recalled the mud and the diving platforms in a discussion on March 7, 2009.

DT, April 17, 1900, p. 1, and *DR*, April 18, 1900, p. 7, reported the flooding associated with Smith Lake. In an August 4, 2008, interview, Harold Williams recalled his house at South Corona Street and Virginia Avenue suffering flood damage from the waters east of Washington Park during a cloudburst in the 1970s. *DT*, June 15, 1914, p. 12, reported the flood after the City Ditch burst its banks at Harvard Avenue and South Corona Street.

I participated in Huck Finn Day events as a youth. Jim Peiker shared his experiences of fishing in the park during a discussion on September 16, 2008. Randy Wren recalled the costume contest as part of Huck Finn Day in an interview on January 14, 2009. He also remembered the hot chocolate at the warming houses when ice-skating in the park. The *Post* had an annual article touting its fishing derby, especially the many corporate sponsors, e.g., August 29, 1976, p. 28, and August 15, 1977, p. 11. Also see *DP*, August 31, 1959, p. 44. Bill Good told of fishing antics in the park before World War II in informal discussions in 1990. Paul Hutchinson wrote up the legend of Old One Eye, *WPP*, June 1998, p. 8.

SDE, October 29, 1921, reported plans for the Grasmere Parkway. *WPP*, September 1998, p. 29, reviewed the search for the caiman in Grasmere Lake, including discussing whether the whole affair was a hoax. *RMN*, September 15, 1959, p. 5, told of the draining of Grasmere Lake. I look at the police burglary scandal in *The Seamy Side of Denver*, 207–15.

Representative articles on the Grasmere Lake cleanup, shore stabilization, and water projects were in *WPP*, August 1988, p. 1, December 1988, p. 1, June 1993, p. 3, April 2004, p. 14, and July 2006, p. 10. Mick Spano, a former Adams County state representative, shared his thoughts about DWD as an arrogant, monopolistic utility in a series of conversations in the mid-1980s. I deal with the politics of DWD in *DIA and Other Scams*, 379–97.

In the October 2003 *WPP*, p. 21, councilman Charlie Brown promised work on Grasmere Lake would be done by the spring of 2004. *WPP*, May 2007, p. 10, and September 2007, p. 9, were other stories confidently predicting that the lake's problems were past. Dale Behse recalled the hideous weeds that grew in Grasmere Lake during various cleanups in a discussion on July 5, 2008.

WPP, November 2001, p. 2, and March 2002, p. 17, *LCH*, April 2001, p. 6, and *RMN*, January 28, 2004, p. 14A, were among many articles on the wastewater plant and the essential end of the City Ditch. Diana Bray took exception to the effort in a letter in *WPP*, April 2002, p. 18. She shared her views with me in a personal discussion in 1999; cf. *WPP*, May 2007, p. 16. Dave Felice ripped "purple water" and its possible poisonous waste in an Internet article of August 8, 2008, "Bureaucracy Leaves Urban Wildlife in Limbo." Bruce Field, a former employee of DWD, discussed his views of the recycling system, complete with its inflated costs, in a phone interview on November 12, 2008. *RMN*, November 1, 2008, p. 15N, was an article about possible fraud in DWD contracts, a piece primarily apologizing for the utility.

WPP, January 1983, p. 1, told about the debate on the mountain-view ordinance. Don Etter stressed it in a talk about the city's parks on April 20, 1983, at DPL—the Western History Department has an audio tape of the session. Charlotte Winzenburg emphasized Gertie Grant's role in making the mountain view ordinance a reality in an interview on February 13, 2009. SCIA newsletters for 1980–82 chronicle the campaign for the law.

MF, July 1927, p. 5, *UPN*, August 31, 1961, p. 3, and *WPP*, May 1982, p. 8, looked at the Washington Park lawn bowling club. *WPP*, April 1995, p. 4, plugged the Washington Park croquet club. Widmann, *Washington Park*, 20, 22, mentions the early croquet court, quoits facility, and lawn bowling club.

DMF gave an overall view of Washington Park, June 4, 1910, pp. 3–4. It celebrated the beach, August 5, 1911, p. 10, March 30, 1912, p. 5, and April 20, 1912, p. 5. So did *MF*, June 1920, p. 10. *CD*, December 12, 1914, p. 6, and *MF*, December 1918, p. 3, highlighted the pavilion. *MF*, January 1919, p. 7, and November 1920, looked at ice-skating. I probe the Washington Park race riot in *From Soup Lines to the Front Lines*, 305–06; cf. Ruthanne Johnson, "The 1932 Washington Park Incident," *Urban Spectrum*, September 2007, pp. 9–10.

WPP, June 1979, p. 3, featured the role of the Colorado State University extension division at the Washington Park Bathhouse. There is passing reference to the program in scrapbook four in the WPGC papers. *WPP*, April 1985, reported the city forester occupying the bathhouse. Ibid., July 1992, p. 13, mentioned the possibility of a restaurant in the bathhouse. The paper reported the YMCA-sponsored jogging trail, October 1981, p. 10.

Dos Chappell shared his vision of VOC and the role of the bathhouse with me during a tour I conducted of Washington Park on May 3, 1998. His death was in *DP*, February 21, 1999, p. 1B, and *WPP*, March 1999, p. 29. *DP*, July 20, 1999, p. 1E, told of Kate Boland taking charge of VOC.

WPP reported the VOC meeting to ponder a Washington Park trail, August 1991, p. 6. It announced the call for volunteers for the path, July 1993, p. 1, August 1993, p. 11, and September 1993, p. 1. Ibid., August 1994, p. 5, and February 1995, p. 1, looked at debates over the fate of the bathhouse. The renovation of the trail and its extension along Marion Street were in *WPP*, March 1999, p. 20, September 1999, p. 22, and December 1999, p. 9.

WPP, July 1981, p. 6, May 1986, p. 3, June 1986, p. 1, August 1994, p. 18, and August 2004, p. 14, heralded the Park People and the renovation of the pavilion. It mentioned plans for upgrades from the 2007 bond issue, September 2008, p. 18.

Jane Silverstein Ries gave me her glowing account of the Park People in a set of chats in 1984–86. Also see *Denver Magazine*, September 1987, pp. 70–71.

RMN, September 21, 2000, p. 6D, *WPP*, August 1979, p. 12, July 1980, p. 17, July 1982, p. 6, July 1992, p. 5, August 1995, p. 7, and July 2008, p. 15, featured Schukr Basanow and the Washington Park folk dances. Bettina Basanow told me stories about her husband in an interview on July 24, 2008. Besides reviewing the text, she chatted about the changing character of Washington Park since the early 1970s, including the decline in the number of volleyball players in the open space.

Russ Nye reflected on the dances and living close to Washington Park for 50 years in a discussion on July 24, 2008. His wife Ila shared area photos and tales with me. Their son Dean remembered growing up in the neighborhood as did his close associate Darrell Schwartzkopf.

Harold and Carol Williams discussed their longtime residence near the park in an interview on August 4, 2008. He especially recalled sledding runs in the area. Chuck Woehl informed me of the sledding on Alameda Avenue during an interview in 2000. *SDE*, January 4, 1919, p. 1, mentioned sledding on Dakota Avenue. It told of ice-skating at Sherman School, January 8, 1921, p. 1.

DP, November 20, 1968, p. 43, celebrated ice-skating in the park. *WPP*, January 1982, p. 1, reported the ban on ice-skating. George Youngren gave me his memories about ice-skating in discussions in 1987–88. I covered Denver city politics in 1983–85 at the time of Peña's war on ice-skating. City councilwoman Sue Casey talked about her unsuccessful efforts to bring ice-skating back to Washington Park at a meeting of the Washington Park East Neighborhood Association in the late 1990s.

Robert Conrow, *Field Days* (New York: Scribner, 1974), is an outstanding biography of Eugene Field. It especially treats his writings, activities, and legacy in Denver. Arps, *Denver in Slices*, 228–45, is an excellent portrait of Field's Mile High presence. Eugene Parsons, "Eugene Field in Denver," *The Trail*, 14:6 (November 1921), 3–10, is mostly fluff, containing some of the poet's Denver verses. *MF*, July 1918, p. 10, and January 1919, pp. 1, 20, featured *Wynken, Blynken, and Nod*. *DP*, August 4, 1919, p. 6, reported the installation of the artwork. Ibid., July 17, 1966, p. 61, observed the disrepair of the sculpture. *DP*, May 25, 1983, p. 4, reported the relocation of *Wynken, Blynken, and Nod*. Frances Melrose discussed the origins of the statue in *RMN*, July 15, 1990, p. 10M. Also see Widmann, *Washington Park*, 26.

Discussions of how the Field House was saved and moved include *DP*, April 6, 1924, p. 15, and April 10, 1927, p. 10, and *RMN*, March 29, 1927, p. 1, and February 3, 1983, p. 22. City librarian Malcolm G. Wyer, "An Interesting New Park Attraction," *MF*, November 1930, pp. 12–13, tells of the transformation of the house into a library. *DR*, June 19, 1882, p. 4, reported that Field had almost drowned in Smith Lake. Kristen Iversen, *Molly Brown: Unraveling the Myth* (Boulder: Johnson, 1999), 226–27, has a most superficial glance at Molly Brown's involvement with the Field House. *RMN*, September 3, 1930, p. 9, gave Molly Brown's critical appraisal of the transformation of the house into a library. *DP Empire*, July 28, 1974, pp. 26–27, glanced at the Field Cottage as the headquarters of the Park

People, outlining the origins of that group. Also see *WPP*, August 1994, p. 18, and the clippings in scrapbook three of the WPGC papers.

The Field Library has a special collection about the poet in Denver and the origins of the library. Also see [Fred Yonce], *The Denver Public Library: 100th Anniversary Celebration* ([Denver]: [DPL], [1989]). *DP*, October 5, 1996, p. 1E, told of the plans for the Hazel Gates Garden. I analyze the policies of Robert Speer in *Robert Speer's Denver*, including contaminated milk, 207–08, 354–55.

DMF, June 24, 1911, p. 12, heralded Washington Park concerts. *DP*, June 24, 1914, p. 8, and *SDE*, July 25, 1915, p. 1, reported on the Innes Denver Band. *SDE* highlighted the community singing on June 28, 1919, p. 1. Comments on symphony and Denver Municipal Bank park concerts are based on personal observations.

Carol Williams recalled the unsavory reputation of the southern section of the park in the late 1970s and early 1980s in an interview on August 4, 2008. Karen Freml informed me of the doings of Miss B. Haven during a tour of Washington Park on May 16, 2004. Vern Howard talked about how park personnel listen to the birds to judge if something is amiss on the island in informal discussions from 1998 to 2006. R. Laurie and Thomas H. Simmons, *Denver Neighborhood History Project: East Washington Park* (Denver: Front Range Research Associates, 2000), tells of problems in Washington Park, including the 1970 riot. Richard Turner recalled participating in Washington Park hippie happenings during chats in the winter of 1988–89.

DP Contemporary, August 8, 1982, pp. 28–30, reviewed the heavy usage of the park and laments over drugs and traffic. *WPP*, April 1979, p. 1, July 1980, p. 4, June 1981, p. 6, April 1982, p. 12, May 1982, p. 1, June 1982, p. 1, and April 1983, p. 1, were typical of complaints about traffic and crime in Washington Park. Also see *UPN*, March 25, 1971, p. 19, *RMN*, June 24, 1979, p. 46, May 9, 1982, p. 4, and May 10, 1982, p. 4. Other articles about traffic problems, including the bicyclists, were *RMN*, June 23, 1978, p. 8, July 31, 1987, p. 8, July 14, 1989, p. 11, July 26, 1989, p. 10, and July 27, 1989, p. 19, *Up the Creek*, August 7, 1987, pp. 4–5, and *DP*, July 26, 1989, p. 1B. The July-August 1978 SCIA newsletter emphasized the traffic closing experiments.

DP, October, 15, 1970, p. 19B, reported the groundbreaking for the recreation center. The facility's first director, JoAnne Dunham, outlined plans for it, *UPN*, March 25, 1971, p. 19. *WPP*, January 1981, p. 11, mentioned the imposition of a 25-cent fee for swimming at it. The *Profile* told of the problems with the renovation of the building, April 1992, p. 1, May 1992, p. 1, August 1992, p. 1, and September 1992, p. 1. The debate over its use as a center to hold curfew violators was in the *Profile*, August 1994, p. 1, September 1994, p. 1, and December 1994, p. 21.

Denver Fire Department, 1866–2003 ([Denver]: [DFD], 2003), 231–32, includes a history of station #21. It mentions station #13, 179–82. I look at the latter in *Spirits of South Broadway*, 50–51, 161–62. *DP*, February 17, 1974, p. 42, told of protests about plans for the new firehouse. The monthly SCIA newsletter during 1975 was filled with laments about the destruction of the old station.

Chapter Two

West of
Washington Park

*T*he residential areas surrounding Washington Park have waxed and waned with the greenery. They have ranged from farming areas and simple working-class quarters to stolid middle-class enclaves. At times, sections have been slightly dilapidated rental districts. Other parts have always been most prestigious neighborhoods.

Since well before World War II, those living east of the park considered themselves socially and economically better than individuals dwelling west of the greenery. Residents on the eastern side of the park dismissed those off toward the Platte River as blue-collar workers who labored at places like Gates and Samsonite, factories near Mississippi Avenue and South Broadway. The section north of the park, in turn, blends into the Country Club. South High School defines the region directly south of the open space.

Early houses west of Washington Park were a mix of elite country houses and modest farm residences. Often they were one- or one-and-a-half-story cottages erected in the late 19th and early 20th centuries. Some had only 600–800 square feet. Even at that, the homes were frequently well built of brick and included leaded glass, hardwood floors, and a Victorian flair.

Numerous simple duplexes were part and parcel of the Washington Park fabric. In addition to them, prior to the planting of Washington Park, a few isolated mansions stood on the hill west of South Downing Street. On May 15, 1882, brothers George W. and William M. Clayton platted the land between Exposition and Kentucky avenues from South Clarkson Street to South Franklin Street as Bryn Mawr. (William Clayton was mayor of Denver in 1868–69; on his death in 1899, George

Photo by Phil Goodstein

Developers sometimes built duplicates of the same house near Washington Park as illustrated by these residences at 1101–05–09–13 Alameda Avenue.

Clayton left his $3 million estate to the city to establish Clayton College at 32nd Avenue and Colorado Boulevard as home for white orphan boys from good families.) They projected their South Denver investment as a premier area emulating the Scottish Highlands. On March 23, 1888, the Town of South Denver authorized the resubdivision of part of the section by Charlotte Gallup, the wife of South Denver promoter Avery Gallup.

The eastern half of Bryn Mawr became part of Washington Park. The same was true of the real estate to the south, Joseph P. Farmer's Addition of January 22, 1889. It covered the ground to Mississippi Avenue between South Clarkson and South Franklin streets. Farmer had originally grazed sheep and cattle on the spread. His wife, Elizabeth F. Farmer, officially staked claim to the real estate.

For a while, Center Avenue west of the park was Lakeside Avenue, paralleled by Lakeview Avenue, the name of Virginia Avenue. Lakeside was the name of another addition, parts of which were likewise incorporated into Washington Park— the city recorded its plat on April 14, 1888. Elizabeth Smith, the wife of John W. Smith, filed the claim to Lake View from Alameda Avenue to Virginia Avenue between South Clarkson and South Franklin streets on February 28, 1881. The Craig Subdivision subsequently included parts of Lakeside from the north of Washington Park to Bayaud Avenue.

Lore surrounds many of the residences west of Washington Park. The house at 500 South Ogden Street, for example, is secluded from the neighborhood by high walls and lush landscaping. Burt Rhodes was the brother-in-law of Charles Gates of Gates Rubber and the company's chief architect. He built the house as a Mediterranean-style villa in 1920. A closet door on the main level led to a pole by which someone could slide down into the basement party room. Owners hid illicit liquor during Prohibition in secret panels behind revolving bookshelves and concealed compartments underneath the stairs. Supposedly, a resident once stashed loot in the latter taken in a bank robbery. So people in the house could make a quick escape, 500 South Ogden Street had a tunnel from the basement to the alley. The yard included a swimming pool. Neighbors viewed it as the Gates family's play palace.

Directly east of the Rhodes House was a residence Gates Rubber used to house visiting guests. The company built housing for employees on the 700 block of South Ogden Street. Some in the area long complained about the presence of Gates Rubber: the stench from its factory was occasionally omnipresent.

Given its seemingly shady side, residents of 500 South Ogden Street should have worried about their neighbor at 1195 South Ogden Street, Earl Wettengel. Voters elected him district attorney in 1928 as a fighting veteran of World War I who promised he would be a moralistic prosecutor. In office, Wettengel cracked down on fortunetellers, sham stock operators, and purveyors of information about birth control. The Vatican especially heralded him for the last activity. Voters returned the Republican Wettengel to office in 1932 in what was otherwise an overwhelming Democratic sweep. Four years later, the Colorado Supreme Court disbarred Wettengel. It ruled he had committed perjury and fabricated evidence as

Photo by Otto Roach, Roach Photos

The Montgomery Ward tower at South Broadway and West Virginia Avenue anchored the western end of the West Washington Park neighborhood. This 1933 photo shows the colonnaded house at the southwest corner of South Corona Street and Virginia Avenue in the left center, a place used by Gates Rubber to host visiting guests.

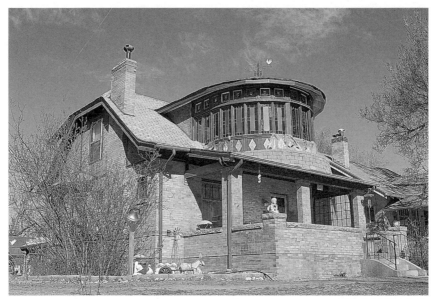

Photo by Phil Goodstein

Tales abound of the unusual origins of South Denver houses. Naval Captain William Ray Harrison built 1051 South Downing Street in 1911, modeling it on the cabin of a riverboat. Locals have called it the "Captain's House," "Riverboat House," and "Wheelhouse."

district attorney to cloak his close ties with those conducting illegal gambling operations. Nonetheless, it allowed him to remain in office. (Wettengel had lived at 326 Cedar Avenue at the time he became district attorney. Charles Prentice, a Republican politician who unsuccessfully sought his party's nomination for district attorney in 1920, lived at 1107 South Corona Street.)

Then there is the story of 950 South Corona Street. It dates from 1897. The Robert Smith family once occupied it—Robert Smith had been a teller at Denver National Bank. Supposedly, an owner subsequently lost it in a poker game. Nearby, at 1111 South Corona Street, was banker Harry L. Morgan, who was the state secretary of the Colorado war bond drive during World War I. Omar Garwood of 1301 South Corona Street was a wide-ranging attorney and politician during the first third of the 20th century who had ties to everyone from municipal reformers to neighborhood activists to champions of Prohibition to the Republican Party to the Ku Klux Klan. Rosaman L. Little of 618 South Corona Street wrote the words and music to "Denver," the official song for the Colorado Rush to the Rockies Centennial of 1958–59.

The most eye-catching house directly west of Washington Park is the so-called Captain's House at 1051 South Downing Street. William Ray Harrison was a retired naval captain who had previously commanded ocean-going vessels. In 1911, he bought Denver's version of beach-front property to the west of Grasmere Lake. Harrison oversaw the design and construction of the residence, modeling the front of the exterior of the second floor on the cabin of a beloved riverboat. He included 18 small pieces of stained glass in what he branded "the dome." Before long, locals had come up with tales that the residence had been brought into the city from a former Mississippi River paddlewheeler. They have also referred to it as the "Wheelhouse" and the "Riverboat House." Harrison, who was a military recruiting officer in Denver, did not stay in the dwelling long, moving out by the time of World War I. The Gary Johnson family acquired the residence in 1934, living there into the 21st century.

A couple of doors down at 1025 South Downing Street was the home of Isham P. Howze in 1918. He was a politically powerful Republican lawyer who ran for numerous offices with little success. Axel P. Johnson, another attorney and a failed candidate for city council in 1923, was to the south of the Captain's House at 1059 South Downing Street. A few blocks to the north at 811 South Downing Street was the residence of Robert J. "Bob" Stroessner. The curator of the Latin American collection at the Denver Art Museum from 1970 to 1991, he was a relative of the longtime notorious dictator of Paraguay, serving as that country's Denver consul.

In 1925, architects Willis Marean and Albert Norton designed a distinctive $35,000 Mediterranean-style villa at 555 South Downing Street for Mary Clark Steele. Her deceased husband, Everitt Steele, had been among the city's foremost musicians at the turn of the 20th century, heading the local Brahms Club. After teaching music at Miss Wolcott's School, an elite academy for young women at 14th Avenue and Marion Street which included a music conservatory, and running his own music school, he was among the victims of the flu epidemic who died on December 17, 1918. She stayed in the Washington Park house until her death on October 26, 1952, willing the residence to her daughter. Opera singer Orville Moore subsequently had the house, turning it into six apartments. After Paul Koby purchased the manor in 1979, he restored it as a single-family home. Lush landscaping mostly hides it from the road.

Rainbow Row

*T*he musical theme of 555 South Downing Street blends in with Rainbow Row, the west side of the 900 block of South Pennsylvania Street. It is among the many distinctive sections in West Washington Park. Altogether, the neighborhood embodies about 125 years of different housing patterns.

Singleton M. Morrison, the president of Denver Pressed Brick, developed Rainbow Row. In 1901, working with architect James B. Hyder, Morrison received a permit for an $8,000 mansion at the southwest corner of Kentucky Avenue and South Pennsylvania Street. Instead of erecting it, workers constructed four $2,000 houses there. The next year, Morrison and Hyder arranged to build another four dwellings on the block. Morrison marketed the residences as showplaces for his brick firm. He subsequently established the S. M. Morrison Investment Company.

As South Denver soared in popularity in the last third of the 20th century, locals embraced the name "Rainbow Row" to stress the variety on the block or that they lived at the end of the rainbow. It was a prestige address: homeowners insisted their residences were more distinguished than those of their immediate neighbors. The dwellers mostly fenced off their front yards, filling them with ornate gardens. Some added private street lamps as part of the decorations.

Antonia Brico was the most famous resident of Rainbow Row, living at 959 South Pennsylvania Street. Florence M. Wagner had taught piano in that house during the 1910s and 1920s. During Brico's Rainbow Row residence, supporters insisted the woman was the world's foremost woman symphony conductor. Music lovers polarized about her skills. Proponents, including her star pupil Judy Collins, argued Brico never got her chance because she was a woman. Critics insisted Brico was a novelty as a woman conductor who did not have the talent to hold the podium of a major orchestra.

A native of Rotterdam, Holland, born on June 26, 1902, Brico emerged as a musical prodigy at the University of California in the early 1920s. Before long, she knew everybody in the world of classical music as she aspired to become a conductor. In 1930, Karl Muck arranged for her to become the first woman to lead the Berlin Philharmonic. She called Finnish composer Jean Sibelius a good friend.

Back in the United States, Brico received numerous invitations as a guest conductor with the nation's leading orchestras. She failed, however, to obtain a permanent appointment. For a while, she was part of an all-woman orchestra in New York. In the face of poor health and the lack of opportunities during World War II, Brico moved to Denver in 1942.

Photo by Phil Goodstein

Rainbow Row is the name of the ornate early 20th-century houses on the west side of the 900 block of South Pennsylvania Street. In recent years, homeowners have decorated them with fences, gardens, and street lamps.

Originally, Brico was sure she would emerge as the first full-time professional conductor of the Denver Symphony. The orchestra bypassed her for Saul Caston in 1945. Staying in the Mile High City, she tutored musicians while leading a community orchestra. For some years, it was the Brico Symphony, an amateur ensemble which eventually evolved into the Denver Philharmonic. Brico frequently conducted the summer *Denver Post* Opera (actually a musical) in Cheesman Park and was active in the music program at Trinity Methodist Church. She stayed on Rainbow Row until shortly before her death at age 87 on August 4, 1989.

Lincoln School

*L*incoln School at 715 South Pearl Street illustrates the changing patterns in West Washington Park. The school's name not only celebrates Abraham Lincoln, but reflects the Lincoln Subdivision, a real estate filing covering much of the area south and west of the school platted on March 13, 1882. This was a project of the Denver Circle Railroad. Between 1882 and 1898, it and its successor, the Denver & Santa Fe, ran a steam-powered narrow-gauge passenger line along South Logan Street to the south of Bayaud Avenue.

From its beginning, the Denver Circle was as much a land developer as it was a transportation provider. In addition to the Lincoln Subdivision, its real estate arm was behind the adjacent Sherman Subdivision, filed on April 15, 1882, for the land between Mississippi and Florida avenues from South Broadway to South Clarkson Street. A Grant Subdivision followed on July 18, 1889, stretching from South Broadway to South Downing Street between Mexico and Jewell avenues.

By 1891, enough people lived in the modern West Washington Park neighborhood to lead Arapahoe County school district #2 to announce plans for the academy as Exposition School, a name soon changed to Lincoln School. (Until December 1, 1902, Denver was part of Arapahoe County, a jurisdiction including modern Denver, Arapahoe, and Adams counties. The establishment of the City and County of Denver saw the merger of local school districts into district #1 of Denver Public Schools [DPS]. Prior to that time, district #2 covered the area to the south of Cherry Creek and east of the Platte River to Mississippi Avenue to South University Boulevard. Exposition Avenue referred to where the National Mining and Industrial Exposition of 1882–84 had been located along that road to Virginia Avenue between South Broadway and South Logan Street.)

Architect Thomas D. Robinson designed Lincoln School with eight classrooms, one for each grade from first through eighth. In addition to spending $4,185 on the land, the school board paid $39,525 for the building. In no time, the school was overcrowded, leading to double sessions in 1899. The cause, parents believed, was students from the east side of Washington Park who flocked to the better section of the area—West Washington Park. The community lobbied for an expansion of Lincoln School, leading district #2 to acquire three-and-a-half lots south of the original building in December 1899 where an annex opened in 1904. By that time, Lincoln School was experiencing disciplinary problems.

Being close to Washington Park, students sometimes preferred playing in the park to attending classes. Teachers often found it difficult to handle the older students near the end of the school year. This was the situation on May 18, 1903, when more than 50 Lincoln School boys went on strike. Led by eighth-grader Willie Cahill, the pupils walked out of classes at noon, insisting the teachers had lied to them. A few weeks earlier, the instructors, knowing spring fever was in the air, had promised the boys in the upper grades a reward if they behaved for the next few weeks. When the grades for deportment were passed out, the boys claimed they had been betrayed. Consequently, they spent the rest of the day milling around Smith Lake rather than staying in school.

The administration learned the lesson of the student revolt by World War I. At that time, a frenzied patriotic hysteria swept the country. The White House deemed it impermissible to question the country's policies. So schoolchildren would join the crusade, Lincoln School assigned students the task of collecting tinfoil and filling pillows for the soldiers. Shortly before the American entry into the war, Buffalo Bill Cody died in January 1917. Lincoln students responded by donating their pennies to place flowers on his grave. They additionally worked to fill Red Cross Christmas boxes during the fighting.

Prior to American involvement in the European conflict, Lincoln School was embroiled in battles between its founding principal, John H. Dodds of 420 South Emerson Street, and school board member Ben B. Jones. The latter, a real estate attorney and a vehement anti-Catholic, lived at 508 South Pearl Street. On his election to the DPS governing body in May 1915, Jones treated Lincoln School as his personal bailiwick, seeking to dictate who its principal would be and how it should be run. In particular, he turned his wrath on Dodds, a man well liked by parents and faculty. Not only did Jones see the administration exile Dodds to Swansea School at 46th Avenue and Columbine Street, but the district slashed the principal's annual pay from $2,000 to $1,800. After protest meetings failed to gain the restoration of Dodds, the Lincoln community joined other disgruntled voters who recalled Jones from the school board on July 31, 1917. (On June 7, 1920, the Colorado Supreme Court ruled the recall illegal, leading Jones to return to the school board—his term expired in May 1921.)

Dodds, a native of Pennsylvania, had come to Denver in 1891 to take charge of Lincoln School. He was subsequently the head of Milton School at the northwest corner of Evans Avenues and South Bannock Street. After retiring from the system in 1923, he died at age 81 on October 12, 1932. By then he was living at 429 South Pennsylvania Street.

In the early 20th century, Lincoln School introduced a kindergarten program. For some years, Edwina Fallis (1876–1957) taught it. The year before her death, she published a memoir of growing up in the city, *When Denver and I Were Young*. DPS remembered her in 1960 with Fallis School at 6700 Virginia Avenue, an academy it shuttered in 2006.

The school system memorialized Lincoln principals Anna Laura Force (1915–24) with Force School at 1550 South Wolff Street, and Leon Slavens (1934–51) with Slavens School at 3000 South Clayton Street. The former, who lived from 1864 to 1952, was a Denver native and West High graduate who served as principal for other schools. She led Lake Junior High from the time it opened in 1926

The backside of Lincoln School, at South Pearl Street and Exposition Avenue, shows the landscaped playing field, the old wing on the right, and the new wing on the left. In the center is the smokestack. Over the years, some students have argued the chimney looks like a penitentiary watchtower. Such is the legacy of Willie Cahill, an eighth grader who led a walkout of students in May 1903.

until her retirement in 1941. The latter, 1894–1954, was also principal of numerous schools, including overseeing the establishment of Knight School at South Steele Street and Exposition Avenue in 1951. He retired the next year on account of poor health.

In 1929, workers added a gym and auditorium to Lincoln School. To make way for them, they tore down the 1891 wing. Enrollment remained high. Lincoln had 750 students during the 1933–34 school year. It included cooking and shop classes which drew in students from other elementary schools. Girls, for example, attending Washington Park School at South Race Street and Mississippi Avenue, traveled to Lincoln every Thursday morning for cooking classes. Those in the cooking school were responsible for preparing and serving refreshments at various Lincoln School functions.

The school had a capacity of 473 students by the 1970s. That decade saw its enrollment plunge with the passing of the baby boomer generation and the onset of court-ordered school busing for integration. It was down to 316 students in the early 1980s. Before long, with the massive closing of schools elsewhere, Lincoln had 350 neighborhood children joined by another 125 who were bused in. Among the latter were Hispanos from near Fairmont School at West Third Avenue and Elati Street and African-Americans from close to Stapleton Airport. They mixed with an overwhelmingly white student base from West Washington Park. Lincoln students were not bused out of the area.

By the 21st century, Lincoln School had an enrollment of about 320. "Lynx" was its nickname. When it first adopted a mascot in 1974, Lincoln students were the Pandas. Given the falling number of students, DPS pondered closing the historic academy. Lincoln School, the educators explained, might lack the crucial student base to remain open.

Lincoln suffered from the runaway price of neighborhood real estate. As politicians, business interests, and bureaucrats increasingly dominated DPS, the quality and character of the entire system were ever more suspect. Affluent families increasingly sent their children to private schools. Those with elementary-aged offspring who could not afford elite academies, in turn, increasingly found themselves priced out of the Washington Park area. The school responded with special offerings and outreach efforts, including a Montessori program. It provided, it told parents, as good an education as any private academy.

A remodeling of Lincoln School in 1995 saw the addition of a new entry along South Pennsylvania Street. The brick on it did not come close to matching the rest of the structure. Ironically, this is where the school placed a landmark medallion after the city listed Lincoln as a landmark on June 19, 1998.

South Pearl Street Businesses

$\mathcal{A}$ major telephone facility is directly west of Lincoln School at the southwest corner of South Pennsylvania Street and Exposition Avenue. Mountain States Telephone opened a switching station there in 1932 at the cost of $1.8 million. The West Washington Park building replaced a 1901-vintage phone structure at 30 West Bayaud Avenue designed by architects Willis Marean and Albert Norton. In 1947, Mountain States Telephone added a major wing south of the 1932 structure. Subsequent remodeling has obscured the original building. Well into the 1960s, many South High graduates, especially young women, took jobs with the phone company, working as clerks and operators.

For years, most South Denver phone numbers began with seven—the Pennsylvania Street facility was the complex through which all calls were routed beginning with seven. Before the adoption of such numeric exchanges as 722, 733, 744, 755, and 777, in the mid-1960s, the Pearl, Spruce, Race, Skyline, and Sherman exchanges were popular South Denver numbers. They replaced the South and Sunset exchanges on the opening of the South Pennsylvania Street station.

A business strip is along South Pearl Street by Lincoln School. During the heyday of the trolley, streetcars #7 and #8 headed south of the road from Alameda Avenue. (The #7 turned around near Jewell Avenue; the #8 continued to Evans Avenue where it went east to South Milwaukee Street.) As late as World War II, upwards of 90 percent of trips downtown were via public transportation. Merchants located near popular stops, providing locations where commuters could pick up needed goods. At one time, groceries and pharmacies were the defining institutions of such streetcar malls including a Piggly Wiggly at 714 South Pearl Street (part of a national chain of food markets), Pearl Street Meats at 716 South Pearl Street, and South Denver Drugs at 695 South Pearl Street.

Lincoln Drugs at 700 South Pearl Street rivaled the last. It occupied the ground floor of the Lincoln Hotel, the main entrance to which was at 620 Exposition Avenue. Between October 1, 1909, and October 4, 1920, a contract post office operated out of the pharmacy. The apothecary was subsequently Howell's before emerging as Hutchison's Pharmacy.

Everything from hotels to hardware stores to real estate agencies have been across the street from Lincoln School at the southeast corner of Exposition Avenue and South Pearl Street, a distinctive South Denver streetcar shopping area.

In 1970, Straight Johnson's, part of a hippie "food conspiracy," was catercorner from the Lincoln Hotel. A popular record store that became Twist & Shout was nearby. Lincoln Hardware was at 675 South Pearl Street in the 1920s. A bakery had once been down the street. The Lincoln Creamery was nearby. It claimed to have the best ice cream in South Denver. The northwest corner of the intersection was eventually the site of Listen Up, a company featuring electronics equipment. Stories circulate that a pickle factory once existed on the 700 block of South Washington Street, served by a railroad spur.

The Gwen Bowen School of Dance Arts at 714 South Pearl Street was a long-lasting establishment in the modern era. Its namesake opened her studio in 1953 at 387 South Pearl Street. It was across the street from a small apartment house which included the residence of iconoclastic preacher Frank Hamilton Rice at 386 South Pearl Street. From 1923 to his death in 1945, he led the Liberal Church, a downtown congregation reaching out to the "undeserving poor," i.e., bums, prostitutes, beggars, and street hustlers. As its self-ordained bishop, Rice readily mocked the pious hypocrisies of the religious establishment. The Holy Trinity, he proclaimed, were food, clothing, and shelter. At one point, he arranged for architect William Norman Bowman, a close friend, to design a $250,000 cathedral for the Liberal Church at South Logan Street and Virginia Avenue. The Liberal Church never came close to raising the funds necessary for the building.

Bowen relocated her studio across the street from Lincoln School in 1956. A onetime ballerina, she subsequently taught at McKinley School, 1275 South Logan Street. The dancer retired in 2005, selling her school to Lori Rickert who turned it into Arts for All at the Grant Avenue Community Center at South Grant Street and Cedar Avenue in Grant Avenue Methodist Church while putting her insurance agency in the old dance hall. (Rice had once been an assistant pastor at Grant Avenue Methodist. Shortly after World War I, the congregation ousted him for his advocacy of dancing.)

Numerous other dance studios and academies have come and gone from the South Side. James F. "Jimmie" Gallagher of 120 West Archer Place, for example, ran a school of dance at various locations including 7 Bayaud Avenue, 30 West Bayaud Avenue, 400 Broadway, and 110 West Alameda Avenue. He offered everything from tap dancing for "business girls" to a children's troupe which performed at various South Denver celebrations while he conducted his own band, the Colorado Royals. He died at age 55 in July 1960.

In the late 1950s and early 1960s, Arlene Garver conducted the Covillo–Park School of Ballet at 1923 Kentucky Avenue in what was once known as the Fine Arts Center, the stores at the northwest corner of South Race Street and Kentucky Avenue. The Andersen Ballet was at 1725 Evans Avenue in the early 1970s. A Platt Park church had hosted dance classes a decade previously. The Denver Ballet Academy long occupied 2 Broadway. That group evolved into the Denver Civic Ballet Academy which had its studio on the 500 block of Broadway.

A Lost Theater

Another streetcar business center is three blocks north of Lincoln School on the 300 block of South Pearl Street. In addition to once being home of a couple of groceries, a long-lived dry cleaners has been on the block. The section has included various dining and drinking establishments. Some have had unsavory reputations, especially the Alameda Tavern at 616 Alameda Avenue. Fights and stabbings, locals bemoaned in the mid-1980s, were all too common there. Nor were some of the neighbors happy about what they called the "Candle Fight" at 383 South Pearl Street. This was their name for the Candle Light, a bar dating from around 1958. Over the years, it had been everything from a gathering spot for railroad workers to Gates employees to self-proclaimed tough guys. Some patrons took ironic pride in an Internet publication branding it the "Best Dive Bar in Denver."

A movie theater once drew locals to this part of South Pearl Street. William Menheh, the owner of a chain of cinemas in Greeley, Fort Collins, Longmont, and Fort Lupton, opened the Majestic Theater at 312 South Pearl Street on January 3, 1926. He drew on the services of architect Charles M. Gates, the same man who designed the Washington Park D&R Theater at 1028 South Gaylord Street. The result was a virtual twin, a fact bitterly protested by the owners of the East Washington Park movie house.

Charles and Cora Kreiling soon ran the Majestic Theater. After they sold the building in 1935, it became the Amuzu Theater the next year before emerging as the Alameda Theater in 1937. The Ross Woolridge family operated it from 1938 until the cinema closed on December 9, 1958. Two years later, Western Cine occupied the space. Established in 1952, it was a specialty film processor that sometimes worked with Hollywood to restore vintage flicks. In 1998, Western

WPP

The Alameda Theater was at 312 South Pearl Street. It opened on January 3, 1926, as the Majestic Theater, closing on December 9, 1958. The South Pearl Street building was subsequently remodeled and became the offices of Western Cine, a film processing studio. The neighboring Royal Crest Dairy leveled the structure in June 1998. A private sanitarium, St. Philip's Hospital at 324 South Pearl Street, once stood between the theater and the dairy.

Cine relocated to 2735 South Raritan Street. Shortly thereafter, the block's dominant business, Royal Crest Dairy, tore down the remnants of the Majestic Theater.

Headquartered at 350 South Pearl Street, Royal Crest Dairy dates from 1927 when home milk delivery was the norm, Denver being the home of numerous independent dairies which had nearby farms. Sam and Dorothy Thomas established Royal Crest.

Before World War II, Dad's Cookie Company was down the block from Royal Crest at South Pearl Street and Alameda Avenue. The owner gave schoolchildren cookies. The youngsters thereupon went to Royal Crest, buying milk. Sometimes, they received a free quart of milk from the dairy.

After the death of Sam Thomas in 1964, his widow sold the plant to general manager John Garret and Paul R. Miller of the Owens Dairy. Miller, collaborating with his son Lynn, merged the Owens Dairy into the South Denver operation. They kept it going while most of its rivals disappeared and grocery stores came to dominate milk retailing. It survived as a delivery service, processing milk on South Pearl Street. Royal Crest advertised its product as the "aristocrat of milks." Over the years, it continually grew, swallowing and demolishing many surrounding properties.

Royal Crest Dairy has been at 350 South Pearl Street since 1927. Its headquarters building looks much the same in the 21st century as it did in this 1940 shot.

Nearby residents were not always pleased by the dairy, complaining it polluted the neighborhood. This was especially the case in August 1996 when 250 pounds of anhydrous ammonia leaked from Royal Crest onto the 300 block of South Washington Street for more than an hour. The fire department discovered that a Royal Crest safety valve had leaked since the 1930s. Royal Crest settled a lawsuit with locals stemming from the incident. It continued its South Pearl Street operations after it opened a new distribution center in Longmont in September 1999. The plant remained administrative offices and the home base for the milkmen who raced through the city before dawn, delivering Royal Crest products. The South Pearl Street business has also operated a chain of Farm Crest convenience stores.

David T. Garland's grocery store, on the south side of Alameda Avenue to the west of South Pearl Street, was another neighborhood business of the 1920s. The proprietor, who lived at 128 Pearl Street before relocating at 259 South Pearl Street, was a most active supporter of South Denver sporting and recreation programs. The city remembers him with Garland Park at Cherry Creek and South Holly Street, greenery dedicated on May 14, 1963.

In 1971, mayoral aspirant Dale Tooley occupied Garland's old space at 538 Alameda Avenue as his campaign headquarters. For a while, Tooley's father, Clifford, a veteran meatcutter, ran a grocery at the southeast corner of South Pearl Street and Kentucky Avenue. It was near another streetcar shopping center stretching, in spurts, to I-25. Among businesses lasting there into the 21st century was the Kentucky Inn, a tavern at 890 South Pearl Street. Until his sudden death on June 2, 2007, owner Al Anderson was something of a local landmark, known to acquaintances as "Moose." Around the corner at 614 Kentucky Avenue was Chuck's Donuts, a shop that closed in the early 2000s after about 50 years in business.

A wide variety of restaurants have come and gone from the area, including the Central One, a Greek establishment at 300 South Pearl Street, in what was a grocery run by Morris Weinberger in 1924. He had previously partnered with Otto W. Schultz of 264 South Pearl Street in operating Schultz & Weinberger, a market at 295 South Pearl Street.

A widening of Alameda Avenue from two to four lanes in the 1950s saw the destruction of the trees and most of the sidewalks along the arterial near South Pearl Street. Walking conditions became extremely poor with pedestrians right next to speeding traffic. In the face of this, most of the independent stores along Alameda Avenue soon closed. (Alameda Avenue is a four-lane road to Franklin Street. Since the time it was expanded in the 1950s, planners have pondered continuing it as a four-lane road to the east, complete with the installation of a bridge over Cherry Creek near South Cook Street—voters rejected that idea when they were first asked for a bond issue to make the bridge a reality in the 1930s. Those living south of the Country Club area have vigorously opposed increasing Alameda's carrying capacity. Engineers realize that the bridge would essentially do nothing to abate congestion. Even so, the idea pops up every few years.)

The Washington Park Community Center

*T*he transformation of Alameda Avenue was indicative of massive changes sweeping much of the West Washington Park area in the 1950s and 1960s. A 1971–72 Denver Planning Office survey branded the area between South Downing Street,

Photo by Phil Goodstein

Ohio Avenue Congregational Church at 622 Ohio Avenue became the Washington Park Community Center in 1967. A wing opened on Washington Street in 1978. Lush landscaping has followed.

the Valley Highway, Mississippi Avenue, South Broadway, and Alameda Avenue "endangered." As such, city hall argued it needed special government help and funds to revive as an ideal middle-class abode. Toward this end, the administration received $3.5 million from Washington as part of the Federally Assisted Code Enforcement program. The effort aimed to redress houses with unkempt lawns and broken windows. Boosters and urban experts moaned these were signs that the land was on the verge of disintegrating into a slum.

Many residents bitterly decried the program as an unwarranted governmental invasion of their homes. By this time, seeing the severe tensions in the area, locals had organized into the Washington Park Action Council to control their own destiny. They urged practical actions to check traffic and sprawl while nurturing the middle-income citizens who made the area their home. After it faded in the early 1970s, some of its backers supported the South Central Improvement Association (SCIA), a group dating from the mid-1960s. Neighbors formed the group to fight city policies to cut a freeway through South Denver.

Supporters incorporated the SCIA in November 1966. By the early 1970s, the organization had wide-ranging ties, mobilizing the neighborhood and sending out a lively monthly newsletter. At one point, it published a local business directory. The SCIA worked closely with Lincoln School. Beginning in 1976, it sponsored tours of neighborhood houses as a most successful fundraiser. Pushing cooperation with the people living east of the greenery, it has held annual picnics with the backers of the Washington Park East Neighborhood Association in the park, usually near the Fourth of July. In 1986, recognizing nobody knew exactly where or what the South Central Improvement Association was, the organization changed its name to the West Washington Park Neighborhood Association (WWPNA)

Most of all, the residential group had intimate links with the institution that helped define the area into the 21st century, the Washington Street Community Center at the southwest corner of South Washington Street and Ohio Avenue in the former Ohio Avenue Congregational Church. In 1902, locals created the congregation, dedicating their chapel at 622 Ohio Avenue six years later. The church was a quiet sanctuary for decades, more or less reflecting the calm, middle-class nature of most of the neighborhood. Ohio Avenue Congregational failed to get new blood after World War II. By September 1966, the dwindling congregation could no longer afford to maintain its building. This led it to merge into its daughter congregation, Washington Park Congregational Church at the southeast corner of Dakota Avenue and South Williams Street.

Not all of Ohio Avenue's congregants affiliated with Washington Park Congregational. Many had moved out of the area years earlier and had kept their allegiance to their old church. When Ohio Avenue shut down, they joined congregations closer to their new homes. By this time, the Congregational Church had become part of the United Church of Christ (UCC).

Under the leadership of Elizabeth Clark, Opal Johnson, and Carol Williams, the Washington Park congregation suggested transforming the Ohio Avenue structure into a community center. The decision came after canvassing the neighborhood. Locals agreed it was a good idea. The area lacked any comparable facility.

The Washington Street Community Center has worked closely with the West Washington Park Neighborhood Association in sponsoring tours of the area. Here are the sponsors of the neighborhood's inaugural tour in May 1976, standing on the South Washington Street side of the old Ohio Avenue Congregational Church, the core of what became the Community Center.

Ideally, the community center would emerge as a central meeting place, bringing together the people of West Washington Park.

Washington Park UCC, which owned the building in the wake of the merger, endorsed the proposal. So did the Colorado Conference of the parent United Church of Christ. The Rocky Mountain Methodist Conference and the Rocky Mountain Lutheran Synod also stepped on board. So did seven other neighborhood churches: the Kirk of Bonnie Brae (another member of the UCC), Washington Park Methodist, Epiphany Lutheran, St. Francis de Sales Catholic, South Broadway Christian, Salem UCC, and First Plymouth Congregational. The religious bodies provided funds to remodel the Ohio Avenue building into a community meeting house.

In April 1967, locals incorporated the Washington Park Community Center as a non-profit agency to administer the Ohio Avenue building and provide a wide array of programs. The purpose, backers declared, was "neighbor helping neighbor." Sponsors invited locals to take out memberships as a sign of their support. There was virtually no city involvement in creating the complex.

The Community Center offered activities for seniors, after-school outreach for elementary schoolchildren, instruction in crafts, and a place where locals could play cards and other games. Mental health counseling, dances, and art shows became part of its matrix. Over the years, it sponsored various theatrical performances. A preschool was another prime offering. The South Central Improvement Association met there, using the center's address as the return address on its mailings. The club frequently held candidate forums at the hall.

Nobody pushed the facility more than Harold and Carol Williams, longtime members of Ohio Avenue Congregational. When the church closed, they joked, they came with the building. Carol Williams served as a cook, especially for Friday afternoon soup lunches for members and financial supporters of the effort. The churches provided the desserts at such gatherings, which continued into the 21st century.

Members of sponsoring congregations volunteered for the Center's wide array of programs. The hall also attracted the backing of some local businesses. For a while, it had a monthly roundtable brown-bag luncheon that brought together business interests, representatives of neighborhood groups, officeholders, city officials, and others interested in shaping the destiny of the area. Along the way, the Center developed links with the University of Denver.

Soon money poured in from the United Way and the government, including the War on Poverty. Before long, United Way contributions financed about half of the Center's efforts. By 1970, the facility was doing well enough whereby it was able to hire a paid, full-time director, Richard Barnes, who oversaw its expanding operations until 1985. A most visible community figure, he had come to the city from Philadelphia where he had worked at the Fellowship House, a program that included job training and a commitment to civil rights. Barnes died at age 84 in 2007.

A 1974 federal grant through the Denver Community Development Agency allowed the facility to expand and upgrade the old church. Included was a new wing along South Washington Street. Upon its completion in 1978, the Center changed its address to 809 South Washington Street. The construction included filling in the basement of the church which engineers decreed was not stable. The public money led the city to take ownership of the agency in 1976 while the private group continued to administer it. Volunteers remained the heart of its programs.

While some neighbors immediately embraced the Center, attending numerous events, others stayed away. Some never returned after patronizing it once, finding themselves uncomfortable in a place they believed primarily catered to something of a clique. Backers of the Center vehemently sought to counter such illusions, emphasizing that they fervently welcomed newcomers. Even so, outreach efforts were not as successful as some wished in recruiting students from the nearby Lincoln Elementary School in the 1970s. (In 1910, the Ladies Aid Society of Ohio Avenue Congregational had been in the vanguard of forming the inaugural Lincoln School PTA. Backers of the Community Center collected history on Lincoln School.)

In the early 21st century, the presentation of the Jane Craft Good Neighbor Award was the highlight of the Center's year. It went to the individual doing the most to enhance the facility and the surrounding area. The honor memorialized a resident of Rainbow Row at 931 South Pennsylvania Street who coordinated the Center's senior efforts and served as head of its board. Her husband, Joe, joined her in making the neighborhood what it is. On the side, he was the driving force behind the Denver Public Schools' annual Shakespeare festival.

South Denver garages range from simple sheds for cars to old barns that included living quarters for grooms. This structure is on the alley between South Corona and South Downing streets on Cedar Avenue.

The Washington Park Community Center sometimes had a problem getting its message out. People often confused it with the Washington Park Recreation Center in the park proper. In the face of continual mix-ups between the two centers, in August 1999 the West Washington Park complex changed its name to the Washington Street Community Center.

Renovations and remodeling were constant. So were money problems. During the early 1990s, the Center cut back many efforts because of a lack of funds. It was able to upgrade its mechanical system in 1995 thanks to a city bond issue. A playground renovation was its 1998 project. A kitchen remodeling followed in 2000.

The Center faced a crisis in the early 21st century when the city decided to privatize most community centers. Instead of overseeing them through the department of parks and recreation, the administration decided in 2000–01 that politically well-connected organizations and charitable groups should run them. The Washington Street Center found itself forced to accept a lease-purchase agreement whereby the facility reverted to private status as of May 2004. In the process, it had to cut back on services to pay for maintenance and other impending costs associated with the exit of city ownership. A revised agreement had it buying the property from the city for $10 by 2009. The deal required it to have a $50,000 building reserve, leading it to launch a frenzied fundraising effort.

The social services agency managed to accumulate necessary funds, including the building reserve. By the early 21st century, the United Way provided a small portion of the Center's income. Programs included twice weekly breakfasts for those who wished to dine there. It had a monthly "I don't wanna cook" night on Thursday evenings. At times, it conducted bus tours of the area as fundraisers. The hall had an annual budget of around $350,000 by the end of the first decade of the 21st century.

As the Center established itself as a nucleus of West Washington Park, the neighborhood's supposed "endangered" status vanished. Opposed to city hall, many residents realized that old was not automatically bad. Owners renovated properties through the 1970s. Before long, the section pulled in newcomers, especially those who could not afford the ever soaring real estate prices east of the park. That enclave, in turn, found itself largely torn down and rebuilt at the turn of the 21st century.

A Note on Sources:

*I*nformation on the Washington Park neighborhoods is primarily drawn from institutional histories, clipping files, real estate records, and interviews. Participants at the South Denver history seminar of February 17, 2008, observed the divisions between those living east and west of Washington Park. *DP Contemporary*, August 8, 1982, pp. 28–30, reported that real estate prices were 10- to 15-percent higher east of the park than west of the greenery. A brochure pondering landmark status for the area by Barbara Norgren, Dianna Litvak, and Dawn Bunyak, *West Washington Park Neighborhood: Historic Report Reconnaissance Survey* (Denver: WWPNA, 2002), outlines the origins of the neighborhood, real estate developments, and architectural styles.

DP, September 12, 2000, p. 1C, and *WPP*, February 1980, p. 4, looked at the house at 500 South Ogden Street. Harold Williams recalled living near it and mowing its lawn in an interview on August 4, 2008. I highlight the impact of Gates Rubber in *Spirits of South Broadway*, 185–88. The Colorado History Museum has a lobby display featuring the Gates family. The April-June 2003 issue of the WWPNA newsletter glanced at Gates' houses on the 700 block of South Ogden Street. Patsy Vail recalled the hideous stench from the Gates factory in the West Washington Park area in an interview on September 18, 2008.

My *Seamy Side of Denver*, 135–37, and *From Soup Lines to the Front Lines*, 176–77, touch on Earl Wettengel. The Colorado Supreme Court disbarred him in *Melville v. Wettengel*, 98 Colo 529. I mention Omar Garwood in *Soup Lines*, 275, and *In the Shadow of the Klan*, 50, 166, 336, 429. *Robert Speer's Denver*, 78, 342, 345, touches on Isham Howze.

WPP, March 1980, p. 10, recalled Bryn Mawr and 811 South Downing Street. *DP*, April 1, 2007, p. 4K, told the story of 950 South Corona Street. Also see Van Wyke, *Town of South Denver*, 57–58, 133. The December 1978 *WPP*, p. 4, featured the Sea Captain's House. David Gerace shared his memories of it with me in letters and informal conversations in 2007. *WPP*, October 1980, highlighted 555 South Downing Street. Also see building permit #3180 of May 1, 1925, *DT*, February 9, 1902, p. 19, and December 17, 1918, p. 4, and *RMN*, November 1, 1952, p. 26.

An advertisement on p. 9 of the May 2006 *WPP* probes the origins of Rainbow Row. DPL has an Antonia Brico scrapbook. Judy Collins recalls Brico in *Trust Your Heart* (New York: Fawcett Crest, 1987), 27ff. She helped put together a PBS documentary on Brico. *UPN*, October 15, 1970, p. 10, featured Brico as the Business and Professional Woman of the Year. Irma Anzini, "Antonia Brico, Conductor," *Opera and Concert*, June 1950, pp. 22–24, 39–40, was a tribute to the maestra; cf. *RMN*, October 22, 1961, p. 1A. Ron Grosswiler shared his memories of Brico in an interview on August 13, 2008. Allen Young discussed her in informal chats in 1984–85.

DPS records are extremely uneven on Lincoln School and all its other facilities. Reports the system submitted to the United States District Court in the 1970s, 1980s, and 1990s as part of the busing order frequently had contradictory information about specific school enrollment and capacity. The Government Documents division of DPL has wide gaps in its collection of DPS reports. Many of the latter are extremely superficial. Specific numbers on enrollment and capacity are drawn from the *Finger Report* of April 5, 1974, the 1979 *Report on the Status of Pupil Assignment*, and *Pupil Assignment Plan, Unitary System* of October 14, 1981. At times, DPS personnel have been most helpful in opening its records to me; on other occasions, they have been completely uncooperative.

Edwina Fallis recalled her childhood in *When Denver and I Were Young* (Denver: Big Mountain Press, 1956). *DP*, July 17, 1952, p. 44, and *RMN*, July 18, 1952, p. 61, reported the career of Anna Laura Force. The obituary of Leon Slavens was in *RMN*, October 9, 1954, p. 32, and *DP*, October 10, 1954, p. 23C.

Kenton Forrest et al., *History of the Public Schools of Denver* (Denver: Tramway Press, 1989), outlines school districts and gives specific dates of buildings. An extremely diverse compilation about neighborhood schools is *Histories of the Denver Public Schools* (Denver: DPS, n.d.), a typescript assembled by the system in the early 1950s. DLPC files include information about the history and architecture of schoolhouses it has declared landmarks, including Lincoln.

The Spirits of South Broadway, 29–33, 41, 67–69, probes the Denver Circle Railroad and its land dealings. That volume also details many of the churches and other schools of West Washington Park, especially those near Broadway. The South High Historical Room has a file on Lincoln School. The collection includes a paper on "One Hundred Years of South Denver, 1891–1991," written for the centennial of Lincoln School. *DT*, May 19, 1903, p. 9, reported the revolt led by Willie Cahill. I touch on the controversies surrounding Ben Jones and the school in *Robert Speer's Denver*, 468. *SDE*, September 4, 1915, reported a community meeting to support keeping Dodds as principal. *DP*, October 13, 1932, p. 35, and *RMN*, October 14, 1932, p. 25, chronicled Dodds' passing.

SDM, December 14, 1928, p. 1 sect. 2, told of the planned expansion of Lincoln School. Dave Watson remembered his experiences as a Lincoln student in the 1970s in an interview on March 16, 2008. In passing, he commented on the problematic relations between Lincoln School pupils and the nearby Washington Street Community Center. *WPP*, January 1992, p. 4, mentioned the threat to close Lincoln School. Ibid., September 1993, p. 3, June 1995, p. 17, and December 2002, p. 4, emphasized the academy's innovative programs. The paper celebrated the school's centennial, February 1991, p. 5, and its becoming a landmark, April 1999, p. 6, and May 1999, p. 20.

SDM, January 9, 1931, p. 1, and April 10, 1931, p. 1, highlighted the coming of the phone exchange. Those participating in the South Denver history seminar of February 17, 2008, included former telephone operators who shared their immense knowledge of the system and the workings of phone exchanges. George Makulowicz and Herbert J. Hackenburg also informed me of this aspect of the phone system in personal conversations in 2001–04.

In an interview on August 4, 2008, Harold and Carol Williams recalled living near Lincoln School in the 1950s and 1960s when their children went to the academy. He focused on the wide array of businesses at the intersection of Exposition Avenue and South Pearl Street.

Howard M. Ham investigated the Liberal Church and Frank Hamilton Rice in chapter eight of the 1947 volume of *Denver Cults* at Taylor Library of the Iliff School of Theology. Also see Inez Hunt, and Wanetta W. Draper, *To Colorado's Restless Ghosts* (Denver: Sage Books, 1960), 270–91.

The June 1998, p. 4, June 2003, p. 3, December 2005, p. 13, and October 2006, p. 4, issues of *WPP* told about the Gwen Bowen School of Dance Arts. Ibid., June 1981, p. 11, looked at various South Denver dance schools. The late Don Winters recalled the Jimmie Gallagher School in discussions in 1992 and 1995. *SDM*, May 1, 1931, p. 2, emphasized Gallagher's offering tap dancing for "business girls." On June 15, 1934, p. 1, it told of the performances of his students. *RMN*, July 13, 1960, p. 75, reported Gallagher's death. Paul N. Fiorino shared his memories of the Denver Civic Ballet Academy at 2 Broadway in a note in January 2008.

Bob Oblock recalled the rowdiness of the Alameda Tavern in discussions in 1986. Gertie Grant told me how neighbors have called the Candle Light the "Candle Fight," in a walk through the area on April 1, 2007. Britt Kaur shared his experiences drinking there in an informal chat on November 21, 1995. The owners, who had it from 1971 to 1997 and wished only to be identified as Patty and Floyd, discussed their experiences with me at the same time. DenverCitySearch.com labeled the Candle Light the "Best Dive Bar." *WPP*, September 2001, p. 10, mentioned neighborhood complaints about the tavern.

WPP, February 1983, p. 3, featured the history of the Alameda Theater. Ibid., November 1982, p. 13, and March 1999, p. 3, and *RMN*, February 24, 2004, p. 8B, looked at Royal Crest Diary. Don Winters wrote about Dad's Cookies and Royal Crest in memoirs provided by his widow, Joyce. *Denver Magazine*, September 1986, pp. 30–44, glanced at home-delivered milk service. The November 1982 *WPP*, p. 20, sketched the work of Western Cine. Doug Gerash gave me his version of it in chats in 1994.

In 2007, the WWPNA Web page highlighted the Garland family. *DP*, May 13, 1963, p. 9, reported the impending dedication of Garland Park. Dale Tooley told his story in *I'd Rather Be in Denver* (Denver: Colorado Legal Publishing Company, 1985).

WPP, July 2007, p. 4, reported the death of Al Anderson of the Kentucky Inn. The story of Chuck's Donuts was in the *Profile*, July 1980, p. 4, and the April 2003 newsletter of the WWPNA. *WPP*, May 2008, p. 4, and February 2009, p. 3, glanced at the changing nature of the intersection of South Pearl Street and Kentucky Avenue. Jim Peiker and Patsy Vail recalled growing up nearby in the 1930s and 1940s in conversations on February 17 and December 7, 2008. Volume three discusses South Pearl Street south of the Valley Highway. It also looks at the debate over the expansion of Alameda Avenue, the suggested bridge at Cherry Creek, and wars over one-way streets. The work additionally tells of the Pearl Theatre which was near South Pearl Street and Mississippi Avenue.

Articles on the Federally Assisted Code Enforcement program include *DP Contemporary*, November 28, 1971, p. 6, *DP*, January 30, 1972, p. 1, and February 2, 1972, p. 50, and *CJ*, December 20, 1971, p. 1, March 6, 1972, p. 12, and March 13, 1972, p. 10. Also see *Spirits of South Broadway*, 226–27. Charlotte Winzenburg praised the program in interviews on February 9 and 13, 2009, during which she recalled the evolution of the SCIA.

Virginia Greene Millikin et al., *The Bible and the Gold Rush* (Denver: Big Mountain Press, 1962), is a history of the Congregational Church in the region. Harold and Carol Williams shared their memories of being members of Ohio Avenue Congregational, the merger between it and Washington Park Congregational, and the origins and evolution of the Washington Street Community Center in an interview on August 4, 2008. Charlotte Winzenburg also talked about the facility and WWPNA on February 13, 2009. She shared with me her collection of neighborhood newsletters and memorabilia dating back to the early 1970s. The newsletter especially reported on the expansion of the Community Center.

CCN, April 4, 1967, p. 1, and April 19, 1967, p. 2, looked at the newly formed Washington Park Community Center. *DP*, December 5, 1970, p. 6R, and *DP Contemporary*, September 19, 1971, pp. 18–20, highlighted the facility during its early years. *DP Roundup* reviewed its theater productions, August 8, 1971, p. 8. Cf. *UPN*, March 25, 1971, p. 19, and June 3, 1971, p. 3B. Bill Himmelmann and David Akerson shared their views of the facility when they served on its board in the 1990s.

WPP, May 2006, p. 18, gave an overview of the work of the Washington Street Community Center and the Jane Craft Good Neighbor Award. Also relevant were its issues of February 1979, p. 10, January 1998, p. 6, April 2004, p. 10, and May 2007, p. 21. The *Profile* had numerous other articles on the facility, e.g., February 1983, p. 7, June 1983, p. 7, September 1991, pp. 5, 17, October 1991, p. 2, February 1992, p. 10, May 1992, p. 1, January 1993, p. 4, July 1993, p. 1, November 1995, p. 5, and August 2000, p. 14, and June 2004, p. 6.

Frances Bechtold sounded a bitter note about the Center in a letter to the editor in the February 1993 *Profile*, p. 14. Bettina Basanow recalled working as secretary at the hall between January 1971 and December 1973. She also shared her memories of Dick Barnes, in a chat on November 28, 2007. Mark Miller informed me of doings and welfare activities in the West Washington Park region in discussions in June 2005 and January 2006. Sheila Corwin discussed her experiences living in the area during informal conversations in 2006–08. On July 23, 2008, Duane Duff recalled growing up at 862 South Grant Street.

Chapter Three

Myrtle Hill

*O*riginally, the location east of Washington Park was more modest than the land to the west. In the course of the late 19th century, the section east of South Franklin Street emerged as Myrtle Hill. This related to the area's foremost pioneer, George Bohm. He staked the land between approximately Alameda and Mississippi avenues from South Franklin Street to South University Boulevard in 1872. So everybody would know and remember this, he named the area's central street for himself, Bohm Avenue, today's Exposition Avenue. He platted the northern half of the area on May 22, 1883, as Broadway Heights Second Filing. (The inaugural Broadway Heights of January 20, 1882, was a joint project of John L. Dailey and Arthur E. Pierce which never made it off the drawing board.) Bohm developed the land between Exposition and Kentucky avenues from South Franklin Street to South University Boulevard as Bohm's Subdivision, submitted on March 25, 1889. His family settled at the southeast corner of Kentucky Avenue and South Franklin Street where, by the 1890s, Bohm listed himself as a gardener/farmer or a simple carpenter.

Initially, Bohm sold divisions of his land in five-acre chunks—five acres is the average size of a South Denver block, including streets. Before long, he expanded his operations, selling off lots and encouraging residential development. His agents plugged Broadway Heights as the "Capitol Hill of South Denver," i.e., the premier section of the South Side.

Advertisements for Bohm's land asserted the subdivision was fully connected with the nascent South Denver water system, a dysfunctional effort that helped bankrupt the Town of South Denver. To promote the area, Bohm paid a streetcar operator $9,000 to link Broadway Heights with South Broadway. The region, he told buyers, had great educational possibilities, being close to the emerging cam-

76

The home of Myrtle Hill pioneer George Bohm remains standing at 900 South Franklin Street.

pus of the University of Denver. Industrialist Charles Boettcher, a fellow German immigrant, was a quiet partner in Bohm's real estate ventures.

Nobody more plugged the area east of the future Washington Park than Carrie Bartels, the daughter of a Bohm business associate. She focused on the land which had once been part of Bohm's holdings between Tennessee and Mississippi avenues from South Williams Street to South University Boulevard. On August 9, 1888, the young woman platted it as Myrtle Hill, denoting the myrtle plants she treasured and grew. Prior to her efforts, the real estate included a nursery, alfalfa fields, and an apple grove. Nearby was a highly productive truck garden on South Vine Street owned by another German settler, John Gonner.

Before long, Myrtle Hill was the name of the East Washington Park area. To boost the section's fortunes, in July 1892 Carrie Bartels donated the land where Myrtle Hill School arose at South Race Street and Tennessee Avenue. This was four years after she married Frank A. Bailey, a local investor and promoter, on October 3, 1888. His F. A. Bailey & Company of 1509 Arapahoe Street was the firm promoting Myrtle Hill and handling land sales for Bartels. Bailey also pushed the development of Bohm's Addition and Broadway Heights.

After living at 32 West Ellsworth Avenue, Frank and Carrie Bailey settled in a house at the northeast corner of South York Street and Mississippi Avenue. Generations of the family subsequently dwelt at 901 South Williams Street. Frank Bailey threw himself into politics, winning election to the board of aldermen, the lower house of Denver's bicameral city council. He died in May 1929. She passed away at age 67 in December 1936.

(Carrie Bartels Bailey was related to another real estate plunger, Louis F. Bartels Jr. He also served on city council while coming to be a major figure in Capitol Hill property development, living in a commanding mansion, since demolished, at 1144 Pennsylvania Street. To confuse matters, Bartels married Carrie Crandell who became the second Carrie Bartels.)

Within a few years, numerous projects and developments took the Myrtle Hill moniker. In 1908, for example, newspapers described St. Thomas Seminary as being on Myrtle Hill when it opened a new facility near South Steele Street and Louisiana Avenue. Myrtle Hill Drive was a U-shaped road from South Colorado Boulevard at Amherst Avenue to the 4100 east block to the 2850 block of South Colorado Boulevard prior to the emergence of the University Hills Shopping Center. At one time, Evans Avenue west of Clarkson Street was Myrtle Avenue. The Denver Water Department initially called its facility at South University Boulevard and Jewell Avenue the "Myrtle Hill Pump Station."

The Lort family joined the Bohms, Baileys, and other Myrtle Hill pioneers. In 1891, painter and paperhanger Frank J. Lort built a house at 725 South High Street. For a while, with Albert B. Beattie who lived at the corner of South York Street and Ohio Avenue, he ran Lort & Beattie, a home decorating store at 121 Broadway. (Beattie later moved to 119 West Ellsworth Avenue.)

Born in Maryland in 1862, Lort relocated to Manitou Springs in the 1880s, working in the booming construction industry. In January 1891, seeing great opportunities in Denver, he settled in the Queen City. At the same time, he invited his sister Hattie to join him. She was badly afflicted with asthma. Colorado's enhancing air, he was sure, would cure her affliction. Their elder sister Ella likewise moved to the house.

In no time, the Lorts were a flourishing Myrtle Hill clan. To accommodate the growing family, Frank Lort expanded the residence, adding a second story. The dwelling emerged as something of a neighborhood gathering place. Ella and Hattie Lort opened a private kindergarten in the South High Street residence in 1894. They charged students 75 cents a week tuition, pulling them in from as far west as South Logan Street. The sisters transported their charges in a converted milk wagon.

Another sibling, Thomas H. Lort, shared the 725 South High Street house. He was the father of three girls and one boy. The three daughters all became Denver Public Schools teachers, none of them ever marrying. During the early 20th century, the Lort sisters rode through the city on streetcars, advertising their neighborhood, shouting out "C-O-L-O-R-A-D-O, we're from Myrtle Hill by jingo." In 1951, one of them, Lydia Terrell Lort, wrote a sketch of the development of Myrtle Hill, *A Church Bell Rings in Denver*. The Lort women were subsequently at 1165 South Williams Street. The rumor mill insisted that Colorado Symphony Orchestra conductor Marin Alsop made her home at 725 South High Street in the 21st century.

For a while, members of the Lort family were at 416 South High Street and 2375 Mississippi Avenue. Joseph M. Lort, who came of age at 725 South High Street, subsequently lived at 993 South University Boulevard. Born on November 12, 1895, in Wilmington, Delaware, he moved to Denver to join the rest of the

This 1894-vintage stone-faced house at 1017 South Race Street survives in the East Washington Park neighborhood, dating from the days when the area was known as Myrtle Hill. Owners thoroughly renovated the structure in the modern era, getting it designated a city landmark on February 17, 2004.

family when he was seven. After graduating from South High in 1914, he received his bachelor's and master's degrees from the University of Denver. In 1921, Lort went to work for Denver Public Schools, serving 39 years in the system as a coach, teacher, and administrator. The South Denver resident was principal of South High from 1950 to 1960 after holding the same post at North High from 1947 to 1950. Upon his retirement, he threw himself into the Young American League (YAL). This was an effort to provide organized baseball and football competitions for boys which he helped create in 1927. The Redskins was the name of the YAL team for the Washington Park area. The junior team feeding into it was the Papooses. Lort, who married Ethel Bailey on August 27, 1919, passed away in March 1973.

Myrtle Hill Community Church started at 725 South High Street. With the help of South Denver Methodist missionary John Collins, locals founded the congregation as the neighborhood Sunday school in February 1893. The Lorts created the religious center when they found the commutes to Trinity Methodist and Grant Avenue Methodist extremely slow and inconvenient. (Alternative accounts have the congregation first gathering at the home of George Bohm at 900 South Franklin Street.) Frank and Carrie Bailey gave the congregation five lots at the southwest corner of Tennessee Avenue and South High Street where Frank Bailey had the honor of breaking the ground. Worshippers consecrated "the little old church on the corner" on September 3, 1893. Reverend William F. McDowell, the chancellor of the University of Denver, led the services. It was Myrtle Hill's inaugural institution and public building. Martha and Lydia Lort were the first babies baptized there.

Though officially Methodist, during its early years the congregation had a Baptist minister. This was apropos. As a community church, it reached out to all Protestants on the rather isolated Myrtle Hill. The prayer center, it told the faithful, was "a center of Christian friendliness." Initially, the church had a high turnover of pastors. Adam Kohankie, superintendent of Washington Park, was a firm supporter. He sometimes gave the congregation flowers from the park while he allowed it to use park equipment to clear its paths in the winter. His daughter married the son of pastor George Nuckolls.

The Lorts knew everybody. Virginius Ellett, for example, ran a nursery, complete with a greenhouse, at the southeast corner of Exposition Avenue and South Race Street. He specialized in growing cantaloupes. On February 5, 1890, he established Ellett's Subdivision for block five of Bohm's Second Filing on the land bordered by Exposition and Ohio avenues and South Race and South Vine streets. This action was not unusual. Into the 20th century, developers carved numerous small new plats out of land that had once been part of the Bohm estate. The 1910s and 1920s were especially the boom time when the area filled in with numerous middle-class bungalows.

Edmund Siebers of 648 South Williams Street was a neighborhood actor and musician. Daniel H. Plaisted and his wife of 1317 South University Boulevard were an elderly couple in the early 20th century who were something of the informal neighborhood grandparents. Then there was the tragic story of William P. Stephens of 777 South Williams Street.

Stephens occupied an 1889-vintage dwelling on a sprawling property at the northwest corner of South Williams Street and Ohio Avenue. On June 15, 1901, he gained appointment as an associate to the Denver Police Department. His duties included running a South Side animal pound on his property. Dogs, cows, and horses constantly came and went from his lot. Horses were common in the area, both to pull carriages and work on farms.

After he gained a full position on the police department in 1903, Stephens specialized in animal control. This was especially important in the summer of 1908 when a wave of horse thefts outraged residents of Myrtle Hill and University Park. With Nathaniel Hunter, the city herder (the official in charge of animals), the police assigned Stephens to track down those responsible for the crimes. This was the situation on the evening of August 25, 1908, when the 44-year-old Stephens, then at police headquarters at 14th and Larimer streets in the old city hall, was ordered to take a report of a burglary at 2324 South Emerson Street.

As he alighted from the streetcar at around 9:00 PM at the corner of Evans Avenue and South Emerson Street, Stephens, the father of four, espied a suspicious character on horseback leading a riderless horse. When Stephens confronted the horseman, whom he apparently knew, the suspect opened up on the patrolman, badly wounding Stephens. The latter fired a couple of shots at the fleeing rider. Neighbors who witnessed the encounter carried Stephens to the office of Dr. Daniel

Photo by Phil Goodstein

Patrolman William P. Stephens once lived in a farmhouse at 777 South Williams Street. He used the surrounding land to corral animals as part of a city pound. A horse thief murdered him on August 25, 1908. His drastically modified home retains part of its spacious yard.

F. Richards at 1590 South Pearl Street. Stephens died about the time he arrived at the physician's quarters.

An all-out search pinpointed H. Baxter Portis, the owner of a poultry ranch at Mexico Avenue and South Jackson Street, as having some connection with the crime. Meanwhile, a suspicious horse-buyer near Sullivan (approximately the site of the Cherry Creek Dam) observed he had purchased a horse from a bloodied cowboy, John Bradley, a man riding a horse that had recently been shot—Stephens' dying words claimed he had wounded the horse of the man who had fired at him. This led to Bradley's arrest. No sooner was he in custody in the Denver city jail than police officers led by Sergeant Thomas P. Russell started viciously beating Bradley. Before long, they pulled the suspect outside where they planned to lynch him. Other officers, under the command of Chief Hamilton Armstrong, drew their guns on their fellow policemen, hauling Bradley to the safety of the Denver county jail. The courts convicted Bradley of murder; he died at the state penitentiary in 1930. The Fire and Police Board, the body overseeing the police department, briefly suspended Russell without pay for his role in the attack. The Stephens family remained at 777 South Williams Street until 1983. New owners popped the top of the farmhouse.

(An aura of crime seemed to haunt parts of South Emerson Street. This especially came out shortly before midnight on February 12, 1933, when Verne Sankey of 2292 South Emerson Street kidnapped industrialist Charles Boettcher Jr. at the latter's home at 777 Washington Street. The crime shook the nation. In no time, Sankey was the first man Washington labeled "public enemy number one." After he was captured in Chicago in 1934, he committed suicide in a South Dakota jail cell while awaiting trial—he had held Boettcher for ransom in South Dakota.)

Washington Park Community Church

After the city christened the nearby greenery Washington Park in 1899, the label Myrtle Hill started to fade. Myrtle Hill Community Church recognized this on January 31, 1912, when it changed its name to Washington Park Community Church. Four years later, it launched a $30,000 building program. Asking donors to "help us over the hill," it raised $14,000 to complete the effort in a whirlwind campaign beginning on January 2, 1917. The goal was to place an Italian Renaissance-style home at the northwest corner of Arizona Avenue and South Race Street where the congregation already had its Sunday school.

Architects Willis Marean and Albert Norton designed the building. The interior matched the exquisite exterior. Ivory and mahogany decorated the sanctuary which seated 600. The congregation used the courtyard for outdoor services. The complex included a public gymnasium designed as a community recreation center.

The father-and-son team of William Gray Evans and John Evans II helped the congregation procure the land. Besides their control of Tramway, William Gray Evans and John Evans were Methodists. Over the years, William Gray Evans collaborated with Frank Bailey in real estate dealings. Henry Buchtel, the chancellor of the University of Denver and a close cohort of the elder Evans, oversaw the laying of the cornerstone at the church. Governor Julius Gunter, Supreme Court Justice S. Harrison White, and city attorney James A. Marsh prominently

Washington Park Community Church, at the northwest corner of Arizona Avenue and South Race Street, about the time of its dedication in January 1919.

participated in the ceremony. On January 5, 1919, Bishop Francis McConnell preached the dedicatory sermon.

Bond dealer James Causey of 1190 South Franklin Street was a foremost figure in paying for the effort. In 1916, he had recruited George L. Nuckolls as the congregation's pastor. A dynamic preacher, Nuckolls oversaw the church until 1920. After briefly serving a congregation in New York, the parson returned to the Washington Park pulpit in 1922. Before long, he was among the clerics who heralded the Ku Klux Klan at the peak of its power in the mid-1920s. Nuckolls left Denver for a position in Detroit in 1926. This was a year after he had turned down a call of First Methodist Church of Wichita in exchange for the promise that Washington Park Community Church would launch an expansion campaign. While Nuckolls was in charge of the church, the congregation acquired a pastor's house for him at 1312 South Gaylord Street.

From the beginning, Washington Park Community Church sought to live up to its name. Its 500 members, the dedication program asserted, represented 11 different denominations. Most of all, it was a neighborhood institution bringing residents together. The church housed a reading room of the Denver Public Library until the Eugene Field Library opened in 1930. The Washington Park Woman's Club long met at the church. The congregation also hosted the Tuesday Community Club, an organization attracting women living east of the park. The building included a five-room headquarters for the Camp Fire Girls. In January 1931, the congregation sponsored the area's inaugural pack of Cub Scouts. The Methodists added an organ in December 1934.

Eight years previously, the church had acquired six lots to the west where two houses stood. For years, the congregation used the one at 1194 South High Street as the janitor's quarters. The church tore down the dwellings for a parking lot and an annex/school building on which it broke ground on March 19, 1950. During the course of construction, a worker was buried and killed when the organ chamber collapsed atop him, leading to rumors of strange organ sounds being heard in an isolated wing of the annex. The faithful dedicated the $165,000 hall on April 8, 1951. The church ran Camp Rosalie as a summer retreat near Bailey. At one time, a couple of camp directors urged renaming it Camp Wa-Pa-Co-Chu for Washington Park Community Church.

The congregation eventually changed its name to Washington Park United Methodist Church. For years, the Lort family seemingly ran the place. The three Lort sisters were omnipresent as Sunday school teachers. They looked so much alike that children were sure the three women must be triplets. Living close to the Lorts at 1157 South Williams Street was Reverend Arthur Ragatz, a Methodist divine who was the secretary of the American Bible Society while his wife Ruth was a soloist in the Washington Park Methodist Church choir.

Across the street from Ragatz at 1150 South Williams Street was the home of Minoru Yasui (1916–86). The Oregon-born son of Japanese immigrants, he had joined the bar shortly before World War II. Unsuccessful as a lawyer in Portland, he was holding a job with the Japanese consulate in Chicago at the time of Pearl Harbor. The army scorned his professions of loyalty after that attack when he reported for duty as a junior officer in the reserves. A firm believer in constitutional law, Yasui protested the exclusion of people of Japanese heritage from the West Coast during World War II. For his efforts, he found himself imprisoned and stripped of his citizenship. After the United States Supreme Court reversed that decision and Yasui was allowed to seek work in Chicago, he was frustrated with his job opportunities. Relatives drew him to Denver in September 1944 by which time he strongly urged interned Japanese-American young men to join the military despite no apology from Washington for its unconstitutional attacks on their citizenship rights.

After the war, Yasui worked as a lawyer. Eventually, he had strong political connections, heading the city's Commission on Community Relations from 1967 to 1983. Supporters cited him as the epitome of the American dream. Detractors claimed he was a flack catcher who apologized for the dirty deeds and the brutality of the police under mayors Thomas G. Currigan and William H. McNichols.

Greek-Americans have also been part of the East Washington Park mix. None stood out more than Pete Contos of 692 South Gilpin Street. He arrived in Denver in the 1950s at the behest of a relative. By 1962, he had worked his way up in the restaurant/bar business from a janitor and dishwasher to the ownership of the Satire Lounge at 1920 Colfax Avenue. In the 1970s, Contos introduced Greek fast food into Denver, especially gyros. During the next couple of decades, he built a chain of diverse restaurants around town, all named "Pete's."

Myrtle Hill School

Washington Park School was directly north of Washington Park Methodist at the southwest corner of Mississippi Avenue and South Race Street. It stemmed from the two-room Myrtle Hill School a block to the north at Tennessee Avenue and South Race Street. District #2 opened the academy in January 1893 at the cost of $3,396. Originally it was for grades one through four. Students in grades five through eight went to Lincoln School west of the park.

As the area's population boomed and Myrtle Hill School expanded through eighth grade in the early 20th century, parents became increasingly unhappy with the administration of the academy's inaugural principal, Philip A. Lynch. In 1901, at the behest of Harry F. Barnard of 1090 South York Street, who operated a real estate agency and investment house, the school board replaced Lynch with Barnard's neighbor and friend George McMeen of 1190 South York Street. On the side, Barnard was the superintendent of the Myrtle Hill Community Church Sunday school; McMeen succeeded Barnard in that post. The latter was subsequently the secretary of the church board.

A native of Illinois, born in 1875, McMeen arrived in the Denver area in 1897, teaching in Jefferson County. Before long, he oversaw grades one through four at Myrtle Hill School. He remained as principal of the academy until 1917. McMeen subsequently lived at 600 South Williams Street before moving to a 1922-vintage house at 1800 Arizona Avenue. After leaving Myrtle Hill School, he served as principal of Grant School, supervising the move of its elementary classes to Thatcher School in 1920. He was later head of Swansea School and oversaw the dedication

DPS

Upon its expansion in 1922, Myrtle Hill School, at the southwest corner of Mississippi Avenue and South Race Street, became Washington Park School.

of Adams Street School at 38th Avenue and Adams Street in 1926. (After McMeen left 1190 South York Street, the address became politically charged, being the home of both the director of the election commission, James H. Hamilton, in 1918, and city councilman Joseph Rees who unsuccessfully ran for mayor while living there in 1919.)

In 1941, McMeen retired, moving to Los Angeles with his wife Margo. She died there in July 1946, shortly after their golden wedding anniversary. He passed away at age 80 in Beverly Hills, in June 1955. DPS remembers him with the 1959-vintage McMeen Elementary at 1000 South Holly. (Dorothy Roems, a close cohort of the Lort sisters, incidentally, occupied 1800 Arizona Avenue into the 1960s.)

In 1906, DPS constructed a new Myrtle Hill School at the southwest corner of South Race Street and Mississippi Avenue. This simple five-room structure had no electricity or sanitary sewers. A year after it opened for classes, the administration sold the Race and Tennessee edifice, a structure new owners demolished.

Myrtle Hill School became a modern academy with first-class fixtures and utilities in 1922 when workers completed a major addition to it. On September 1 of that year, the facility officially became Washington Park School. The title indicated the waning of the Myrtle Hill moniker. A massive 1928 expansion designed by architect Harry Manning brought Washington Park School to a capacity of nearly 850 pupils. The kindergarten room included both a mantel with the busts of famous figures and a mural highlighting nursery rhyme characters.

During the 1970s, busing and the maturation of the baby boom generation saw a precipitous decline in the school's enrollment. DPS went from 96,848 pupils in 1968 to 57,503 in 1987. Under court orders, Washington Park School was home of kindergarten and grades four through six, paired with Stedman School at 30th

Avenue and Dexter Street which had a kindergarten and grades one, two, and three. In 1979, DPS announced the old Myrtle Hill academy did not have enough students to remain open. Locals yelped. The move, they complained, would destroy Washington Park East as a middle-class area where parents of young children could comfortably send them to a walk-in school.

After activists managed to convince the school board to keep Washington Park School open, the administration stated it would review the whole matter in 1982. Already in 1980, it once more targeted the facility. DPS shuttered it at the end of the 1981–82 school year. After pondering using the abandoned building as a community center—a suggestion bitterly opposed by the Washington Park East Neighborhood Association as causing too much traffic and commotion—in the summer of 1983 the administration leased the structure to Denver Academy.

Paul Krott founded Denver Academy as a private school in 1972 for the "learning impaired." It provided services for the children from affluent families who had had problems in the educational system, offering the young men and women special programs and tutorial clinics. Incorporated the next year, Denver Academy was originally located at 2797 South Logan Street. It occupied the former St. Francis de Sales High School at 235 South Sherman Street before settling in at Washington Park School. Denver Academy's main focus was on the 15 percent of the students having learning disabilities or who had failed for other reasons in the regular schools.

Locals sometimes had problems with Denver Academy students. On occasion, they branded them nothing but privileged juvenile delinquents. Had those going

Photo by Phil Goodstein

Trips to the principal's office were not what they used to be in the completely remodeled Washington Park School, a building transformed into 10 lofts in 2008.

to Denver Academy been poor and African-American or Hispano, cynics asserted, they would be in Juvenile Hall, not the school in the center of Washington Park East. Denver Academy headmaster Jim Loan complained that such views were a vestige of the primitive way society once scornfully treated youngsters with learning disabilities.

Denver Academy continually grew in the Washington Park location. It added a new gym, sodded the playing field with grass, and added modular units. The school opened its doors for meetings of community groups. By the beginning of the 21st century, it had 340 students when the annual tuition was $13,300. The institution found itself increasingly cramped at Washington Park School while it realized it sat on extremely valuable real estate.

In the course of 2001–02, Denver Academy relocated to the 21-acre campus of the former Bethesda Sanatorium at 4400 Iliff Avenue. This was a onetime tuberculosis facility for individuals of Dutch heritage which had been a mental health center between 1950 and its closure in 1998. Moving to the Bethesda site, Denver Academy expanded its programs to cover grades first through twelfth.

Denver Waldorf School, a private academy seeking to provide students with a thorough grounding in classic mythology while having a mystical Christian orientation, eyed Washington Park School. It had outgrown its premises in the former Denver Christian School at the northwest corner of South Clarkson Street and Florida Avenue where it taught 280 students from kindergarten through 12th grade. Its effort to obtain the Myrtle Hill space collapsed in March 2001 when Waldorf did not receive as much as it expected from the sale of its Florida Avenue building.

Soon thereafter, Denver International School acquired Washington Park School. Marcel Arsenault, the owner of a property management firm, bought the Myrtle Hill edifice for $4.1 million, leasing it to Denver International School for 30 years. Denver International School was yet another private academy—the more DPS declined with the onset of court-ordered busing in the 1970s, the more private schools emerged, draining enrollment from places such as Washington Park School.

The French government helped establish Denver International School in 1977. The goal was to educate children of French nationals in Colorado. The academy had a curriculum modeled on that in Paris, complete with accreditation from French educational authorities. Starting out with classes from preschool through fifth grade, the school expanded to focus on the sons and daughters of other Europeans living in the Mile High City while attracting a sizeable percentage of American pupils. It had previously occupied space at 2690 South Holly Street. The school, which then had 220 students, hoped to more than double its enrollment to 500 within five years while adding a middle school. Included in the complex was Star Dance Center, a private dance school.

Denver International School never comfortably settled in at Washington Park School. Costs were greater than it expected. Neighborhood real estate developments sent the value of its land skyrocketing. Enrollment declined rather than increased at its new location—the campus opened in the wake of 9/11 which saw some Europeans return to their home countries.

Mortgages and convoluted real estate transactions also bogged down the academy. By early 2005, the school faced a severe economic crisis, needing $2 million immediately. The boiler required replacement, the city mandated a new sprinkler system, and other maintenance bills soared. Denver International School conceded it could not afford the facility while it had failed to develop a rapport with the neighborhood. The result was the academy's exit. After relocating to the former home of Machebeuf High School at 1958 Elm Street, Denver International School announced a merger in late 2008 with Montclair Academy, moving to the former Lowry Air Force Base the next year.

Developer Jonathan Miller of Colorado Land & Home got hold of Washington Park School for $6.9 million in June 2005. He announced plans to demolish the landmark for 16 to 18 single-family houses which, he promised, would blend in with existing neighborhood structures—the zoning permitted only single-family houses. His announcement set off a firestorm. Many liked the presence of Washington Park School. They feared the noise and clutter of the construction and new traffic more residences would bring. Toward this end, they formed the Friends of Washington Park School. There was no reason, the group observed, that Miller could not creatively reuse the school as condos comparable to developments at the old Byers and Thatcher schools which had been transformed into dwellings. To make it a reality, the organization backed Miller in a zoning change. The result was an agreement in 2006: Miller saved the core of the 1928 building, tearing down the rest of the complex as part of Myrtle Hill at Washington Park Place. Included were ten lofts in the old schoolhouse, eight attached brownstones (built of brick), and nine high-priced single family houses which were ready for occupancy in the fall of 2008. The interior of the school was virtually all new, complete with additional construction while the facade stayed in place along South Race Street. A remnant of the kindergarten remained in unit 104.

Elite Housing

*T*he new dwellings arising at Washington Park School were comparable to what much of the neighborhood had become since the 1980s. From the days of Myrtle Hill, bursts of development had swept the area. Besides the Bohm and Bailey families, numerous others filed claim to real estate in the late 1880s and early 1890s. After the city had recovered from the Panic of 1893, building resumed. Promoters continually staked land near the park such as the Washington Park Addition between Mississippi and Arkansas avenues from South Race Street to South University Boulevard, filed on January 23, 1902, and Washington Park Place and Washington Park Place First Addition, land from approximately South Franklin and South Gilpin streets to Mississippi Avenue to South Race Street to Louisiana Avenue, filed in 1906 and 1907. Washington Park View is the area between Kentucky and Tennessee avenues and South Williams Street and South University Boulevard. The city authorized the plat on January 25, 1909. A slight jog in the streets at Tennessee and Kentucky avenues is indicative of the changing real estate sections. Developers continued to eye the land after World War II which included open agricultural fields.

Sidewalk patterns reflect the evolution of the area. Original sidewalks were often flagstone. Concrete squares became popular in the early 20th century. By the 1940s, the city dismissed sidewalks as a needless luxury from the horse-and-buggy era whereby sidewalks are often narrow streetside embankments in many of the postwar developments south of Arkansas Avenue. Sidewalks are often missing altogether in areas east of South University Boulevard.

As Washington Park emerged in the early 20th century, prestigious houses especially popped up on South Franklin Street between Ohio and Arizona avenues. Settlers had already built some houses there in the 19th century such as 918 and 932 South Franklin Street, both of which dated from 1885. A developer demolished them in 2008.

Attorney Clarence Bailey, the son of Frank and Carrie Bailey, erected his house at 974 South Franklin Street in 1902 for $6,000 on what was then unplatted land. Members of the Bailey family stayed there for generations. The George Dunklee family, which had a wide-ranging influence in political and legal circles, was at 1025 South Race Street. Among other ventures, George Dunklee was a leader of the Steele School Improvement Association around the time of World War I. In 1921, his son won the most perfect baby award in an infant beauty contest. Journalist Thomas F. Dawson, a Republican insider, biographer of United States Senator Edward Wolcott, personal secretary of United States Senator Henry M. Teller, and curator of the Colorado Historical Society, lived his later years at 925 South Gaylord Street. He was killed in a car crash in June 1923. On the side, Dawson had been president of the Sons of Colorado, a group composed of those settling in the region before statehood.

Photo by Phil Goodstein

This dwelling, dating from 1885, was directly east of Washington Park at 932 South Franklin Street. A developer destroyed it in 2008.

Attorney Joseph Sterling, previously of 2332 South Emerson Street, occupied the villa at 800 South Franklin Street. He erected it in 1906, about the time he carved Sterling's Park Front Home Addition out of Bohm's Addition for the half block south of Ohio Avenue between South Franklin and South Gilpin streets. Before long, Sterling ran the Sterling Lumber & Investment Company while he served as a leader of the Republican Party. He died in the early 1910s, his family remaining in the house until about 1920.

Abner Endsley, a politically active figure who joined the Ku Klux Klan in the mid-1920s, was subsequently at 800 South Franklin Street. At one time, he was the clerk of the county treasurer's office. William H. Burnett lived in the house in the 1950s, 1960s, and 1970s. After serving as a Democrat in the Colorado House of Representatives in 1953–54, he became a municipal judge. Eventually he served on the Denver County Court and Denver District Court. A friend of Mayor Thomas G. Currigan, Burnett headed a 1966 effort to redevelop the Platte River in the wake of the previous year's flood. He suddenly died of a brain tumor at age 49 in September 1973. Edward C. Day Sr., the managing editor of the *Denver Post* in the 1930s whose son was long a member of the Colorado Supreme Court, lived across the alley at 811 South Gilpin Street for many years.

Far and away the most impressive villa directly east of the park is the James Causey Manor at 1190 South Franklin Street. The partnership of Willis Marean and Albert Norton designed it in 1920 for a most powerful municipal bond dealer. It included an ornate garden landscaped by Irvin J. McCrary.

For a while, Marean (1853–1939) lived next door at 1150 South Franklin Street. He and his wife Charlotte had moved into that residence, the first house on the block, in 1908. Marean and Norton were responsible for such structures as the Cheesman Park Pavilion, what became the Governor's Mansion at Eighth Avenue and Logan Street, and the Greek Theater of the Civic Center. The 1150 South Franklin Street house cost Marean $5,000.

The architect subsequently moved a block north to 1074 South Franklin Street, a residence he designed in 1925 for oilman Frederick A. Van Stone for $7,000. Laundry king Harry Goodheart, whose establishment was at the northwest corner of West Dakota Avenue and South Broadway, dwelt for many years at 1150 South Franklin Street. Charles Lomonaco followed Goodheart as the occupant of 1150 South Franklin Street, subsequently moving to 1074 South Franklin Street. He ran the Colorado Blueprint Company.

In 1911, Marean and Norton oversaw the erection of the $6,000 house at 1100 South Franklin Street for attorney Theodore M. Stuart. The latter's son, after a stint as an assistant Colorado attorney general, emerged as a most successful railroad attorney for the Denver & Rio Grande. (Dr. John Roe, the chief surgeon for the railroad, lived nearby at 1168 South Gilpin Street. Stuart's onetime partner in the firm of Stuart and Murray, Charles A. Murray, was at 1234 South Gilpin Street.) All these residences pale in contrast to the Causey Manor.

James Causey was born in Baltimore on June 27, 1873, to a cabinetmaker. At age 17, he moved to New York City where he entered the apparel business. Before long, he ran a tie factory in Brooklyn. Right when his career was about to take off,

The James Causey House is at 1190 South Franklin Street.

tuberculosis laid him low. He came to Denver in 1901 to recover his health, complete with a letter of introduction to William Sweet.

No figure was more omnipresent in securities and religious charities in early 20th-century Denver than Sweet. In addition to being something of the father of the YMCA Building at 16th Avenue and Lincoln Street, Sweet arranged the underwriting of numerous 17th Street projects. Simultaneously, he actively collaborated with Progressive reformers and was most active in the Democratic Party. He was governor between 1923 and 1925.

Sweet's bond house was Sweet, Causey, and Foster with Alexis Foster. The last dwelt in a Cherry Hills mansion designed by brothers William E. and Arthur A. Fisher at the southeast corner of South University Boulevard and Hampden Avenue. It included an ornate garden landscaped by S. R. DeBoer. Architect Temple Buell, the developer of the Cherry Creek Shopping Center, subsequently dwelt in that manor which eventually came down.

During World War I, Causey was a YMCA representative in Europe. After the fighting, he was extremely disturbed during a visit to Germany in 1923 by that country's political and economic collapse. To redress it and learn why capital and labor continually fought, he approached the chancellor of the University of Denver, Heber Harper. The latter convinced Causey to donate considerable sums to the college to create the Foundation for the Advancement of the Social Sciences, the forerunner of the university's Graduate School of International Studies. (In 2008, DU renamed the facility the Josef Korbel School of International Studies after its founding dean and longtime head who was the father of Madeleine K. Albright and the teacher of Condoleezza Rice. When he first came to Denver after World War II, a refugee from Czechoslovakia, Korbel lived at 995 South Williams Street.)

Causey personally did his part to promote international understanding, being a friend of leaders in Latin America. After his first wife passed away in 1923, he married the daughter of an executive of Colorado Fuel & Iron. For a while, he operated a chain of furniture stores. Causey suffered financial reverses in the 1929 stock market crash. During the 1930s, he mostly lived in Cuernavaca, Mexico. He died there in April 1943.

Utility magnate William C. Sterne occupied the Washington Park villa between 1929 and his death in 1948. Born in Peru, Indiana, on December 13, 1869, Sterne attended Harvard and worked as a journalist in Europe and a fertilizer manufacturer in Indianapolis before coming to Denver in the late 19th century to recover from tuberculosis. Once his health was restored, Sterne was most active in Littleton where he directed numerous suburban utilities. In 1898, he married Orian Shepperd of Littleton, a community in which he lived prior to his South Denver days. While in the suburb, Sterne was president of Littleton Lumber Company and a member of the Littleton Rotary. On the side, he was a college football referee.

Denver native Alfred J. Ryan, the president of a consulting and engineering firm, lived in the rustic-styled, cedar-shingled Causey Manor during the 1950s and 1960s. At one time, Ryan was a partner in Crocker & Ryan, the company that designed the Denver–Boulder Turnpike and parts of the Valley Highway. A special favorite of Mayor Quigg Newton (1947–55), Ryan received numerous city contracts. He died at age 59 at the Washington Park house on October 28, 1967.

Jerome D. "Jerry" and Ellie Mae Sutherland moved into the landmark in 1969. A foremost radiologist and native of South Denver, Jerry Sutherland raised his family there. In 2000–01, he arranged for workers to create a matching house to the south of the Causey Mansion for his son Jason, a pathologist. Included was a new gazebo while the estate retained its distinctive, rural flair. (Beginning in the early 1950s, owners sold off land from the Causey estate east of the alley where architects Jared B. Morse, Paul R. Reddy, and Daniel J. Havekost built their modern-style homes at 1171, 1187, and 1195 South Gilpin Street. A huge postmodern edifice has replaced 1171 South Gilpin Street.)

Other well-known residents lived directly east of the park. Among them at 1130 South Franklin Street was Howard L. Johnson with his wife Bonita. A onetime South High School teacher, Johnson won the favor of the administration during the 1930s as an outstanding football and baseball coach. This qualified him for advancement in the DPS hierarchy which drew many of its principals from coaches. After serving as assistant principal at West High, Johnson took charge of Emily Griffith Opportunity School. In that post, he helped launch Channel Six, KRMA, as the DPS television station in 1956. In May 1960, he emerged as assistant superintendent. Ten years later, he took charge of the entire school system, right when school busing controversies were tearing DPS apart. The South Franklin resident failed to give the system firm guidance during that period of chaos. The school board convinced him to retire in the fall of 1973, just before his 65th birthday. He died on July 6, 1986.

Car dealer Finley MacFarland lived at 1717 Arizona Avenue in the 1920s and 1930s when he was a foremost civic figure.

Before Johnson moved in, 1130 South Franklin Street had been the home of auto dealer L. Kent Robinson who served on the school board from 1929 to 1947. The latter was the brother-in-law and assistant of another neighborhood figure, Finley MacFarland of 1717 Arizona Avenue. Architect Jacques Benedict designed that neo-Tudor house at the northeast corner of Arizona Avenue and South Gilpin Street house in 1919. MacFarland moved in the next year. (Jane Peet originally occupied 1717 Arizona with her son Creighton, a man who emerged as a leading children's author. She subsequently lived in houses at 1164 and 1284 South Gilpin Street.)

MacFarland was literally a wheeler-dealer, running a Buick dealership near the Capitol. Additionally, he was a preeminent figure in the Chamber of Commerce and the Real Estate Exchange, the coalition of the city's landlords and property speculators. During the 1910s, he helped establish the Denver mountain parks system. In 1918, MacFarland was among the corporate leaders seeking to build a monument to memorialize the city's recently deceased mayor, Robert W. Speer. The same year, he emerged as the first president of the city-owned, corporate-dominated Denver Water Department.

A staunch advocate of Prohibition, in 1927 MacFarland initially sought to fill the place of deceased Republican Congressman William Vaile. Before long, he withdrew from the race. He and his wife moved into the Park Lane Hotel at Virginia Avenue and South Marion Street Parkway in 1936. He died at age 75 in June 1937 after a long illness.

The Scottish-born Roderick Reid and his wife Grace made 876 South Franklin Street their home. From 1911 until his retirement in 1943, he was the general auditor of Mountain States Telephone, a firm headed from 1924 to 1943 by his younger brother, Frederick H. Reid. Roderick Reid was eventually vice president of the phone company and a member of its board of directors until his death at age 68 in December 1947.

South of the Reid House, at 880 South Franklin Street, is a modern structure. Larry Pozner, a leading trial attorney, lived there. In 1984, as part of a tour of the neighborhood, the League of Women Voters featured the erection as being on the cutting edge of the new style of Washington Park—at that time, the residence was completely out of place with the historic homes of the area. Since then, numerous other contemporary houses have followed.

Down the block to the north of the Reid House was another most colorful figure, Charles D. Spivak, at 850 South Franklin Street. Born in Russia in 1861 as Chaim Spivakovsky, as a youth Spivak joined the revolutionary movement seeking to overthrow the tsar. After imprisonment in Siberia, he made his way to the United States in 1882. As a mill hand in Maine, he emerged as a socialist militant against capitalist exploitation. Eventually, he graduated from Jefferson Medical College in Philadelphia. Before long, he was in Denver where he helped establish and oversee the Jewish Consumptives Relief Society near Pierce Street and West Colfax Avenue—its mailing address was Spivak, Colorado. His medical specialty was intestinal disorders. Spivak pushed for a strong Yiddish culture, supporting the city's religious and secular Jewish communities. By the time of his death in 1927, he was an internationally renowned authority on the Yiddish language and an activist in countless community pursuits.

Spivak was a bibliophile. In addition to compiling an impressive political library, long housed at the Charles Spivak Educational Institute, 1453 Lowell Boulevard, his medical library became the core of the library of the Denver Medical Society. For years, the volunteer librarian overseeing the latter collection was Dr. Frank W. Kenney, of 1140 South Franklin Street, a pioneer in anesthesiology. Peter Dominick Jr. (1946–2009), a foremost architect, occupied the Spivak House in the 1970s when he helped oversee the renovation of parts of lower downtown.

In the 1920s, builder Arthur J. Anderson of 1324 St. Paul Street, often collaborating with Frank B. Croft of 1851 South High Street, built numerous houses directly east of Washington Park. Among them were residences at 840, 842, 942, 966, 1048, and 1080 South Franklin Street. Many were modest. The poptop boom beginning in the 1980s saw the destruction of some of them; many others have been remodeled beyond recognition.

The commanding houses on the 1200 block of South Gilpin Street, directly east of the dogleg of Washington Park, have largely retained their architectural integrity. Among them is the home architect Edwin H. Moorman built for himself at 1286 South Gilpin Street. It is a couple of houses down from where South Denver city councilman Harry Risley lived at 1274 South Gilpin Street. Emory Afton, the manager of the Ford assembly plant at South Broadway and Kentucky Avenue, occupied 1248 South Gilpin Street until 1931 when it became the residence of J. Stewart Potter, the president of Shattuck Chemical at 1805 South Bannock Street. His firm processed radioactive materials.

Lauddale Shotwell, a general contractor, built the houses at 1200 and 1220 South Gilpin Street. The former went up in 1929 at the cost of $13,000 for investor and real estate plunger Frank Snow. The latter cost $9,000 in 1946. At times, Shotwell lived in both of them with his wife Florence. He also constructed the house at 1260 South Gilpin Street in 1936 for Harry Burkhardt of Burkhardt Steel, the manufacturer of structural steel at 787–95 South Broadway.

The 1100 block of South Gilpin Street also stands out. Besides distinguished homes, it had famous residents, many of whom succeeded in public service and engineering. Phillip Kinzie, for example, was at 1101 South Gilpin Street. He was a mechanical engineer with the Bureau of Reclamation. Next door at 1111 South Gilpin Street was Louis Puls, another Bureau of Reclamation engineer who helped design the Glen Canyon and Flaming Gorge dams. Across the street at 1120 South Gilpin Street was John Hatton, a high-ranking figure in the United States Forestry Service. George Lewis of 1125 South Gilpin Street, a former superintendent of the Portland Mine in Victor, worked on engineering the Moffat Tunnel. Thomas Fitzsimmons of 1136 South Gilpin Street was superintendent of the Griffin Wheel Company at the southwest corner of West Evans Avenue and South Navajo Street, a manufacturer of wheels for railroad cars. The president of the company, Herbert Rosen, was at 1178 South Race Street. The residence at 1137 South Gilpin Street was built in 1933 at the cost of $8,000 for internationally

Photo by Phil Goodstein

Federal-style houses were popular east of Washington Park such as 1080 South Franklin Street which contractor Arthur J. Anderson built in the early 1920s.

Photo by Phil Goodstein

Numerous Mediterranean-style homes, with tiled roofs, are east of Washington Park. Among them is the villa Jacques Benedict designed in 1926 at 1168 South Gilpin Street for Dr. John F. Roe, the chief surgeon of the Denver & Rio Grande Railroad.

renowned brain surgeon J. Rudolph Jaeger. Marean and Norton designed the house at 1243 South Williams Street for Joseph Blee in 1913, the auditor of the Victor-American Fuel Company, a major supplier of coal which operated extensively in southern Colorado.

The Secret Gold Mine

Orville Harrington operated a much different kind of mine than those run by Victor-American. He lived in a sprawling farmhouse at 1485 South University Boulevard. A graduate of the Colorado School of Mines, he had a gold lust which he was never able to fulfill. He walked with a limp, the result of suffering a gunshot wound during a hunting accident when he was 11. It led to the amputation of his foot and lower leg, and he hobbled around on a stump. Harrington never as successful as he wished to be as a mining engineer. Over the years, he had worked at the Mint.

During World War I, Harrington traveled widely as a mining engineer. He resumed his job at the Mint in 1919. Shortly thereafter, the Secret Service became convinced there was something more to Harrington's gait than his old injury. In particular, gold disappeared from the section of the Mint where Harrington worked.

Surveillance showed that Harrington made frequent trips to the backyard of his house at the northwest corner of South University Boulevard and Florida Avenue, complete with a spade. The homeowner explained he loved his garden. His spread included ten lots. In addition to a lush planting of flowers, Harrington filled it with fruit trees and vegetables.

Hearing that a fellow worker had stated Harrington might be stealing gold, the Secret Service baited him with $1,400 worth of the metal on February 6, 1920. He fell into the trap, leading to his arrest. Within hours, he confessed all. At times, he had fitted gold bars, seven by three-and-a-half by one inch into his wooden leg. On other occasions, when he took amounts too large to conceal in the pegleg, his limp prevented guards from observing any bulky packages Harrington stashed under his clothes near his prosthesis.

The Secret Service searched 1485 South University Boulevard. Harrington showed them where he had dug bricks out of the basement behind which he had concealed some of the $81,400 in gold he had embezzled. He had planted other ingots beneath his concrete sidewalk near the garden. The mining engineer explained he planned to melt the bars and mix them with gold he had in a mine in Victor.

After pleading guilty to the theft, Harrington served three-and-a-half years in Leavenworth of a ten-year term. Back in Denver, he worked for a city paving crew until 1930 when he deserted his family. His wife, Lydia Melton, never forgave him.

She was working as a nurse at St. Luke's Hospital where she met Harrington when he was being treated for pain from his leg injury. At the time of his arrest, Lydia Harrington was the mother of a four-year-old daughter and an 11-month-old

The Korean Christian Church, Kyo Yuk Kwan, at the northwest corner of South University Boulevard and Florida Avenue, went up in the late 1950s as the University Boulevard Church of Christ. It occupied the land where Orville Harrington buried the gold he stole from the Mint in 1920.

son. To keep the house while he was in prison, she placed her children in an orphanage and rented out the dwelling while she occupied a large chicken coop in the yard before getting the job as the governess to a wealthy family. Despite her faith in her husband, he never contacted her after he quit his paving job for an adventure in Arizona. Eventually, he died while living with a sister in New York. Lydia sold the house at 1485 South University Boulevard, never wanting to have anything more to do with him.

Around 1958, University Boulevard Church of Christ opened its home at 1495 South University Boulevard where the Harrington House had stood. A Korean congregation, Kyo Yuk Kwan, occupied the land after University Church relocated to South Milwaukee Street and Asbury Avenue in about 1974. Rumors insist gold is still present somewhere under the parking lot while, at midnight under a full moon, the shade of an old prospector limps through the area.

Old South Gaylord Street

Old South Gaylord Street, the block of shops, offices, and restaurants between Tennessee and Mississippi avenues on South Gaylord Street, is a foremost neighborhood destination. It dates from the early 20th century, right about when Myrtle Hill was becoming Washington Park East. By the 1910s, the road was emerging as a streetcar shopping area, served by route #5 which made its way east from Washington Park before turning around at Louisiana Avenue and South Gaylord Street. (Originally, route #22 served the area, heading east on Alameda to South Franklin Street. One branch headed up Virginia Avenue to South University Boulevard, terminating near Mississippi Avenue; another, the forerunner of route #5, went up Kentucky Avenue to South Gaylord Street.)

During the first half of the 20th century, South Gaylord was the site of numerous groceries. At least three or four markets were on the street during the 1920s and 1930s. The 1932 city directory lists seven such businesses in addition to a couple of butcher shops. Some of the food stores, such as Miller's at 1004–06 South Gaylord Street and later 1010–12 South Gaylord Street, and Piggly Wiggly at 1065 South Gaylord Street and then 1092 South Gaylord Street, were part of chains. Others were locally owned. None stood out more than Chrysler's at the northwest corner of Mississippi Avenue and South Gaylord Street.

Jeremiah Chrysler came to Denver from Kansas with his wife and six children in 1896. Before long, he plunged into the grocery business, running Chrysler & Sons at 1419 South Broadway, a shop that was subsequently at 1388 South Broadway and 1451–53 South Broadway. He lived at 1831 South Pennsylvania Street. Around 1910, Chrysler moved to 1381 South Gaylord Street, transferring Chrysler & Sons to 1093–95 South Gaylord Street. Five years later, he relocated the business to a new building at 1075–83 South Gaylord Street. The store provided delivery service. Residents found it a crucial source of sustenance in December 1913 when a vicious blizzard completely isolated Myrtle Hill from the rest of the city for more than a week. The family operated the store until 1943. (The William Reed family ran Myrtle Hill's first grocery around the turn of the 20th century.)

The Old South Gaylord Street shopping strip is between Tennessee and Mississippi avenues. A former filling station on the right has emerged as a flower shop while a one-time house has become a bicycle business.

Before long, the Chrysler family expanded into real estate, building and renting stores on South Gaylord Street. Most of all, members of the clan were politically active. Jeremiah Chrysler, a dedicated Republican, ran for city council in 1919. He was a key figure in Washington Park Community Church where he headed the finance committee. On the side, he arranged for his father-in-law, James H. Hunter of 1157 South Bannock Street, the superintendent of the zoo, to bring animals to the church for a special pageant.

In the 1920s, Jeremiah Chrysler's son, Harry F. Chrysler of 1283 South Gaylord Street, affiliated with the Ku Klux Klan. In 1927 and 1929, the younger Chrysler won election to city council. Harry Chrysler went on to serve as a Republican in both the state House of Representatives and Senate. He was seeking re-election to the latter chamber at the time of his death at age 73 in 1956. (Another local politician tied to the Klan was James McInroy of 1284 South High Street. Besides operating a real estate agency, he pushed the successful gubernatorial campaign of Democrat Ed Johnson in 1932 and was on the state Tax Commission for 14 years.)

For a while, Harry Chrysler served in the legislature with his brother, W. Roy Chrysler of 1225 South Williams Street. Over the years, the latter was president of the Colorado Retail Merchants Association and the Denver Retail Grocers Association. Roy Chrysler won election to the Colorado House in 1938, 1942, 1946, 1950, and 1958. A major figure in the Masons, he died at age 90 in December 1971. By the 1930s, as the Chrysler boys were increasingly involved in politics, the grocery had become Chrysler & Brunner. Eventually, Andersen's Market had the space. It was part of the Red and White chain, an outfit controlled by Morey Mercantile to distribute its Solitaire brand.

Drugstores complemented the South Gaylord groceries, complete with soda fountains. None stood out more than Washington Park Pharmacy at 1096 South Gaylord Street. Leo Charney long ran it. A refugee from Russia who arrived in the United States in 1911, at one time he lived above the store. Eventually, he had a house at 667 South Vine Street. He was still going strong on his 100th birthday in 1995. The pharmacist passed away in April 1999.

During the shop's heyday in the 1940s and 1950s, Washington Park Pharmacy was a hangout for South High students. On the surface, Charney treated them gruffly. Deep down, he greatly appreciated them and welcomed them to his soda fountain. Young people recalled him as always chewing a cigar. After his retirement, he regularly visited the restaurant that subsequently occupied the space of his apothecary.

The pharmacies filled the prescriptions of nearby doctor and dentist offices. The road included barber shops, beauty salons, creameries, bakeries, a hardware store, and other neighborhood-oriented businesses in addition to remaining the site of some residences. A Greek woman had a tailor shop renowned for her skillful alterations. Mr. Fix-It or the Fix-It Shop was at 1088 South Gaylord Street where locals could get a wide variety of household goods repaired, including bicycles. W. N. Twist ran it whereby patrons often called it "Oliver Twist."

Photo by Phil Goodstein

Belmont Plumbing at 1076 South Gaylord Street is the site of the oldest continuously operating business on Old South Gaylord Street, dating from Braconier Plumbing which opened there in 1906. The building long included apartments upstairs. The location of what was Washington Park Pharmacy is on the far right.

Mapelli Brothers had a branch of their meat market on the street, specializing in Italian sausages. Bob's Grocery was another landmark. Candymaker Jolly Rancher had an outlet store on the road which included a soda fountain. Belmont Plumbing at 1076 South Gaylord Street provided hardware and help for the area into the 21st century. The presence of the latter is indicative. Ben J. Braconier of 1370 South Gaylord Street was among the first to have a business on the block, opening his doors at 1076 South Gaylord Street in 1906. On the side, he constructed wire seats for South Denver streetcar stops. Braconier Plumbing & Heating continued to operate at a different location in the 21st century. During the mid-20th century, Bonnie Brae Plumbing was at 1076 South Gaylord Street.

When Cecil's Supermarket moved out of 1004 South Gaylord Street in 1970 to 785 South University Boulevard in the Bonnie Brae shopping strip, the Myrtle Hill road lost its last major anchor. Within a few years, most of the shops had closed or were on the verge of failing. The old streetcar shopping area could not compete with modern malls and supermarkets.

Entrepreneurs plunged in during the mid-1970s, believing they could revive the street as a second Larimer Square, a destination where old buildings were transformed into distinctive boutiques for affluent customers. New restaurants opened. Landlords and tenants remodeled businesses. Before long, South Gaylord had a new élan, pulling in shoppers from far and near. A merchants' group marketed it as "the small town in town." The block, it told patrons, combined urban sophistication with small town charm. An annual Memorial Day street fair highlighted South Gaylord's activities.

At times, questionable real estate operations have impacted Old South Gaylord Street. So have escalating rents. Typical of how these have affected the strip was the fate of its movie house at 1028 South Gaylord Street.

On August 12, 1925, partners Dick Dickson and Frank Ricketson Jr. opened the Washington Park D&R Theater—the D&R stood for their initials. It was part of a chain they ran through Western Enterprises. The cinema, they promised, would be a "community playhouse," a facility designed for both live performances and films. Even while locals heralded the coming of the cinema (they had previously viewed movies at Washington Park Community Church) labor bitterly protested it. The D&R chain, unions insisted, was a scab outfit depending on child labor.

Contests were a central part of the operation of the D&R chain. Ricketson went on to make an immense fortune by developing and promoting grocery night giveaways at movie houses in the 1930s. The Washington Park cinema emphasized prizes on opening night when it gave away a couple of Shetland ponies. Friday night, it promised, would be family night. Not only were the films viewable by the entire family, but, it insisted, they had a valuable educational dimension.

Before long, Carl E. Adler of 1045 South High Street owned the cinema. He got involved in the theater through his bakery which was adjacent to the facility. Under his management, the Washington Park D&R emerged as a second-run movie house. Local youth attended Saturday matinee cowboy movies at it. The cinema

The Washington Park D&R Theater at 1028 South Gaylord Street opened in 1925 and was long a central destination for those coming to the shops on the 1000 block of South Gaylord. A new owner transformed it into a miniature shopping mall in 1983.

was never financially secure and changed names on a number of occasions, also being known as the Washington Park Theater and the Park Theater. For a while in the 1950s it was the home of Sunday services of the Calvary Bible Church.

The facility became the Trident Theater in 1965 when, in addition to movies, it also hosted experimental live theater ranging from Shakespeare to the avant garde. The Denver Players Guild, led by Charles Ault, acquired the building in 1968, christening it the Guild Theatre. The company sought to be a professional outfit. Even so, it included numerous amateurs and volunteers. To supplement income from live performances, the house continued to show motion pictures. It was also the home of live musical performances, mostly by folk artists. On occasion, other theater troupes rented it.

The Guild Theatre never took off as Ault hoped. Frequently, it presented shows only three days a month. Given the escalation of South Gaylord property values, he sold the 235-seat hall to David Billings in 1982. The new owner had previously run Hovey–Billings Real Estate which had restored the Evans Store at South Milwaukee Street and Evans Avenue as its office. After he sold the brokerage in 1979, he operated the David Billings Company out of Cherry Creek North when he invested in South Gaylord Street, buying and renovating properties. The onetime movie house, he declared, would be no more. Under his direction, workers gutted the structure, transforming it into a miniature shopping mall. About this time, suffering financial reverses, Billings left the area while rumors percolated about his confused love life.

A literary theme popped up at a couple of South Gaylord restaurants. Hemingway's opened in late 1977 at 1052 South Gaylord Street. That site had been the home of various diners since the 1920s, especially the Marine Bar & Grill which lasted from 1947 to 1965. Doc Roberts, the self-proclaimed "mayor of South Gaylord," ran Hemingway's, admiring the famous author. After the eatery closed in 1985 and the building had been vacant for some years, complete with a colony of alley cats, a new proprietor opened Hemingway's Key West Grille at the location in 1996. A decade later, a letter from the Hemingway family complaining about the unauthorized use of the name led the restaurant to become the Max Gill & Grill for owner Max Barber.

Down the road at 1085 South Gaylord Street was Reivers. F. W. "Billy" Jones opened it with Will Frothingham in 1977. They titled it after a William Faulkner novel, *The Reivers*, about three young adventurers setting out on a wild car trip in the early 20th century which became a Hollywood feature starring Steve McQueen. Across the street, the old Washington Park Pharmacy was home of such eateries as JR's Malt Shop, the Big D Diner, Falcone's, and the Washington Park Grille.

In 1992, with the goading of the city, South Gaylord merchants found themselves assessed new fees and taxes for a massive landscape remodeling of the block. Included were diagonal parking spots. Some store owners, faced with the extra charges to pay for the maintenance district, complained that the assessments did not bring in new revenue.

The redesign of the street failed to redress the constant reproach of storeowners and neighbors alike about parking. The former moaned that demand exceeded supply; the latter argued shoppers created too much noise, traffic, and congestion on residential streets. The city imposed various parking restrictions on the area outside of the 1000 block of South Gaylord, with controversy over the subject remained unending. Many stores rapidly came and went from the shopping strip.

Neighborhood Churches

A small neighborhood commercial area remained at Virginia Avenue and South Vine Street in the 21st century. Another group of shops were at South Race Street and Kentucky Avenue. The corner of South Clayton Street and Louisiana Avenue was also a commercial enclave. A grocery store was once at the northeast corner of South Gilpin Street and Center Avenue. Here and there, stores predating the zoning code of the mid-1920s lingered amidst houses until well after World War II. Such a survivor remained operating at 620 South Logan Street into the 21st century. The prevalence of markets illustrated that, prior to the coming of refrigerators as part and parcel of middle-class homes, many residents daily patronized stores for fresh bakery goods, dairy products, meats, and produce. Even after ownership of automobiles had become widespread, many women did not drive. They required shops within walking distance of their homes.

In places, residences replaced old stores. After World War II, a grocery at 1001 South University Boulevard emerged as the dentist office of Carryl M. Becker in a modern building. This was part of a city push to relocate medical offices in residential sections, a program which never succeeded as planned. Eventually, the structure became a private home.

Churches are also present in the neighborhood. Besides Washington Park Methodist, St. John's Lutheran at 700 South Franklin Street and Washington Park United Church of Christ at 400 South Williams Street have been defining bodies.

St. John's occupies the block directly east of Washington Park between Exposition and Ohio avenues from South Franklin Street to South Gilpin Street. Until the church obtained the real estate in the 1950s, this land had escaped development. Early on the Masons purchased the real estate, hoping to put a temple there. The group encountered financial problems, leaving the property as a weed-filled patch with one farmhouse on the block. Many neighborhood children loved the acreage as a vacant lot. They played in the field without the formal restrictions imposed on them in Washington Park. Some dug underground hideouts, now and then linking them via a series of tunnels. Others enjoyed bicycling on what was hilly ground.

(Stories of tunnels and caves permeated the neighborhood in the years before World War II. Neighborhood youths targeted vacant lots—virtually every block had such an open space. There they created their hideaways, complete with clubhouses burrowed under the dirt while they blazed bicycle trails. On occasion, with no ventilation, the youngsters roasted potatoes in the caves.)

St. John's, the area's pioneer congregation for German Lutherans, is part of the Missouri Synod. Members incorporated the church on December 21, 1879. After holding services at 1846 Arapahoe Street, the faithful moved to a simple house of worship at West Fifth Avenue and Cherokee Street in December 1886. The church subsequently made its home at the northeast corner of West Third Avenue and Acoma Street. After World War II, not only was St. John's outgrowing that space, but many communicants relocated near Washington Park. The congregation dedicated its day school on the land east of the greenery on December 21, 1959.

Nine years later, St. John's occupied its impressive new basilica, designed by architect Charles E. Stude of Illinois. Mayor Tom Currigan helped dedicate the plant which included numerous facilities besides the sanctuary. By that time the congregation had upwards of 1,700 members.

The church came across as an innovative assembly with numerous outreach programs. Among them was the "School for Fulfilled Living" for God-seekers desiring to change their lifestyles. In addition to traditional services, it had worship sessions featuring rock music. St. John's led annual Christmas caroling at the Washington Park Pavilion. At times, it opened its doors to community festivals and concerts. Most of all, by the 21st century it emphasized its school as among the 50 best performing academies in the country. Only a minority of the students were children of church members. Some were the offspring of atheists who appreciated the highly structured, achievement-oriented school which promised a "Christ-centered education."

Opposed to St. John's, which is theologically quite conservative, insisting that it strictly follows the teachings of the scriptures, Washington Park United Church

In 1927, Washington Park Congregational Church occupied its new home at the southeast corner of South Williams Street and Dakota Avenue. A 1958 remodeling drastically changed the exterior of the temple.

of Christ has been part and parcel of liberal modern mainstream Christianity. The congregation at the southeast corner of Dakota Avenue and South Williams Street is a spin-off of Ohio Avenue Congregational at 622 Ohio Avenue. Shortly after believers consecrated that church in 1908, they established a branch for those living north and east of Washington Park. The group initially gathered at the house of George W. Hewitt at 1121 Alameda Avenue. Before long, worshippers assembled in a tent on the grounds of Steele School at South Lafayette Street and Dakota Avenue. With the encouragement of the Missionary Society of the Congregational Church, in 1925 Reverend William O. Rogers of 401 South High Street took charge of the effort, working with supporters to transform the assembly into Washington Park Congregational Church. He served as the congregation's minister until about the time of the 50th anniversary of his ordination in 1950. He subsequently led a congregation in Lyons until his retirement in 1957. Rogers was serving as the volunteer pastor of a senior citizens' home at the time of his death at age 88 in November 1963.

Rogers quickly established himself as a community figure. In no time, he had a Sunday school class of 170 that met at a temporary church which was a combination of a tent and a dugout at the southeast corner of South Williams Street and Dakota Avenue. The minister was among the area's pioneer radio preachers, broadcasting on KOA. Under him, the nascent congregation began a building drive, asking Denverites to build Reverend Rogers a church of his own so he and his followers would not have to squeeze into a cramped 36-by-72-foot basement. Toward this end, the congregation raised $20,000 in 1927 to erect its permanent home. Architect Glen Huntington designed the edifice in the style of a New England meeting house—the Congregationalists proudly call themselves the descendants of the New England Puritans. A remodeling in 1958 by architect William G. Muchow, completely transformed the exterior look of the church.

After the Congregationalists helped create the United Church of Christ (UCC) in 1955, Washington Park Congregational emerged as Washington Park United Church of Christ. The neighborhood religious center flourished in the 1960s. It acquired adjacent property as it continually expanded and came to have retreats near Dillon and the Black Forest. For a while, the congregation hosted the Agape Coffee House in a residence directly south of the church. A hippie-style establishment geared to neighborhood youths, Agape (the Greek word for spiritual love) featured black light and day-glow paint. Adolescents flocked to the coffeehouse, including many who had no affiliation with the church. A new minister in the 1970s did not like the gathering spot. With no notice to its supporters, he called in a bulldozer to wreck the hangout, leaving behind extremely bad feelings.

For many years, the congregation sponsored a Boy Scout troop. Members of the youth group had a small printing press in the church basement which they used to print cards and advertisements for local businesses. The church assisted in establishing the Washington Park East Neighborhood Association and often hosted its meetings. The improvement association long took pride in having a hand-delivered newsletter as a way of mobilizing volunteers and keeping in contact with all who lived in the area. It dropped that program near the end of the first decade of the 21st century.

During the second half of the 20th century, Charles Milligan, a professor at the Iliff School of Theology, was a staunch member of Washington Park Congregational. He served as interim pastor in 1959–60, 1970–71, and 1977–78. For a while, he lived at 864 South University Boulevard before relocating to 2266 South Columbine Street. On the side, he was on the board of the American Civil Liberties Union and the host of a Sunday morning talk radio show.

Corine Younger, a nearby resident, was something of a neighborhood grandmother supporting the congregation. A talented artist, she pulled her red wagon down alleys, picking up junk which she took to the church where she showed children how to transform the cast-off items into arts and crafts goods. During Christmas season, she produced distinctive decorations.

A large red-brick house once stood at the northeast corner of South Williams Street and Dakota Avenue which became the church's parking lot. When the residence was vacant in the early 1930s, youngsters explored it, being convinced a ghost was present. The discovery of a gun there increased their fears.

A specter seemingly haunted a house a block to the north at 298 South Williams Street. In 1951, the Ralph W. Leavitt family occupied the bungalow. A

Photo by Phil Goodstein

For years, sisters Virginia and Shirley Leavitt lived in a bungalow at 298 South Williams Street. Virginia killed herself in the house in 1989 after Shirley left her. The latter was mugged in San Francisco and lost her memory for some years. A new owner popped the top of the residence around 2001.

longtime employee of the Morey Mercantile Company, Leavitt committed suicide at age 69 in 1965. His two never-married daughters, Virginia and Shirley, thereupon quit work to take care of their mother, Stella. After she died in 1977, the two sisters withdrew from the world. Before long, they only left the house to go shopping on Saturday mornings, having virtually no communication with their neighbors or anybody else.

Locals realized something was wrong in early November 1989 when newspapers started to accumulate at the house. The police responded to their queries, breaking into the residence where they found the body of the 62-year-old Virginia. The house was a cluttered mess with everything from old meat wrappers to empty cracker boxes. The authorities could find no trace of Shirley. Rumors floated that she had been kidnapped or had fled after killing her sister. The coroner's office ruled Virginia's death a suicide caused by carbon monoxide inhalation.

The case remained a mystery until the missing persons bureau discovered Shirley living in a senior citizens center in Gilroy, California, in June 1994. For years, she had deeply resented being endlessly bossed around by her older sister. Nothing she did was good enough for Virginia. Shirley snapped in November 1989 and walked out on Virginia. The latter was so despondent about this development that she killed herself. Meanwhile, no sooner had Shirley gotten off the bus in San Francisco than she was mugged. The trauma led her to lose her memory and she wandered homeless around northern California. A social services worker assisted her in recovering her memory as part of an effort to get her Social Security benefits. When contacted by the Denver police, Shirley stated she had no wish to return to her personal house of horrors at 298 South Williams Street. A new owner remodeled the Leavitt House into a poptop in the early 21st century.

Poptops

*T*he fate of the Leavitt House was indicative of massive transformations sweeping Washington Park East. In many ways, Myrtle Hill was built anew at the turn of the 21st century. Beginning in the 1970s, houses near the park became increasingly popular. Young couples often purchased them. Among them were individuals who had grown up in the suburbs and wanted something different and far more distinctive than the generic houses and neighborhoods they had known.

In response to a severe housing shortage in Denver in the 1940s, landlords turned many single-family houses, particularly to the west of Washington Park, into apartments. In other places, owners added mother-in-law units, converted garages, basements, and attics into living quarters, and divided large lots for new building sites. The 1950s saw the filling in of the many empty fields to the east of Washington Park. For the most part, the heart of South Denver remained a stolid middle-class enclave.

The Washington Park neighborhoods were increasingly in transition as baby boomers graduated from college and entered the workforce. This was a time when Denver was rediscovering its old neighborhoods and Victorian charm. Instead of fleeing to the suburbs, young couples eyed historic properties. At times, they

Photo by Phil Goodstein

Even as poptops and McMansions have displaced the historic housing stock of Washington Park East, modest units, such as this duplex at 445–47 South Gilpin Street, have survived into the 21st century.

Myrtle Hill 109

Photo by Phil Goodstein

A former bungalow has grown into a veritable mansion at the southwest corner of Mississippi Avenue and South Vine Street, typical of the massive transformation of the residential stock of the East Washington Park neighborhood since the 1980s.

projected themselves as veritable homesteaders who sought to take over and change what had become primarily poor areas populated by members of ethnic and racial minorities. Such gentry often encountered severe turbulence in reshaping such districts as Curtis Park, North Denver, and Capitol Hill.

In contrast, Washington Park flourished because it was mostly a white, rather homogeneous area—observers joked that the section east of the greenery was a "blond" enclave. Initially, housing prices were relatively low. Much of the section had aged; elderly homeowners were ready to sell. The area was more diverse than ever during the early 1970s, being a hodgepodge of the old and the young, renters and owner-occupants, low-income individuals who had been in the enclave for decades, assorted hippies, and the men and women who would soon be known as yuppies.

The oil boom of the 1970s accelerated the transformation of Washington Park neighborhoods. Some people attracted by the "Rocky Mountain High" desired to live in the city. Looking for something different from the faceless areas in which they had been raised or had previously dwelt, newcomers were attracted by the beauty of the park, the charm of the old houses, and the mature tree cover. No sooner had they settled in than they started to remodel the houses. Property values soared as living in "Wash Park" became a mark of distinction.

By the 1980s, real estate prices and homeowner aspirations started to outpace the Myrtle Hill housing stock. Liking the location but dissatisfied with the simple cottage cabins and bungalows of yesterday, owners started drastically to expand the residences. Many became "toppers": contractors cut off the roofs of existing

At the turn of the 21st century, it was rare to go for more than a block or two in Washington Park East and not see what locals derogatorily called "particleboard palaces" going up such as this unit at 568 South Gilpin Street.

one-story houses, adding a second and sometimes a third story. (The term "poptop" rapidly replaced "topper" in describing such dwellings.)

Scrapeoffs followed. Also known as scrapes, they described where owners destroyed the existing houses for mini-mansions, structures often emulating those touted in leading architectural magazines and which were the hallmark of sprawling, upscale suburban areas. Many mocked the new houses as "McMansions." Huge fences surrounded some of the palaces, especially those directly east of Washington Park. The walls symbolically sealed the imperial homes from the rest of the neighborhood.

By the late 1980s, despite a general real estate slump in the region stemming from the oil crash, it was rare to go down a Washington Park East street and not see at least one house in the process of being built anew. By that time, commercial developers supplanted homeowners, buying properties, completely remodeling them or building new houses in their places, and selling the residences for substantial profits. In the process, Washington Park East evolved into an upper-middle-class enclave if not the city's ultimate yuppie village.

The prevalence of the poptops and scrapeoffs provoked a crisis by the 1990s. Many residents objected to the drastic remake of the section they had long called home. All too many of the toppers and new houses, they complained, were completely out of scale with the area. Not only did the mini-castles block the sunlight of their neighbors and destroy the views from them, but they often gobbled up entire lots, leaving little open space between the sidewalks and the houses. Some were architectural monstrosities built with no sympathy for the existing structures.

Tensions exploded with the completion of a veritable palace at the northwest corner of South Williams Street and Mississippi Avenue in the early 1990s. Dennis Schlachter of 801 South Race Street owned a design firm and underwrote various poptops. He replaced an existing house with a structure occupying 4,791 square feet at 1089 South Williams Street. Detractors branded it "The Cathedral." In contrast to its size, many historic Washington Park bungalows were around 1,000 to 1,200 square feet.

Complaints led city council to ponder a modification of the building code to assure that new residences matched existing homes. After a two-year study by a citizens' group, council adopted a zoning amendment on July 10, 1993. It imposed a 30-foot height-limit on dwellings on sites that were 50 feet or less in width. The statute further required that at least 3,000 square feet or half of the lot be open space.

Many vehemently opposed the law. Former city councilman John Silchia observed that among the "citizens" behind the effort were members of the Denver Planning Office. Developers and architects, he and other critics insisted, would easily get around the law. The way new castles continued into the 21st century confirmed his fears. Already in 1999, a *Rocky Mountain News* review reported

Photo by Phil Goodstein

In the early 21st century, city laws were a lot tougher about saving trees than the architectural heritage of South Denver. Statutes required the preservation of street trees amidst construction projects when yesterday's homes were replaced with McMansions. In the process, contractors fenced off trees at work sites such as at the northeast corner of Cedar Avenue and South Marion Street Parkway.

that the regulation had little impact. The board of zoning adjustment had approved 84 percent of the requests for structures violating the ordinance since the law had gone into effect. Those unhappy with the poptops and scrapes observed that many of the new buildings, though in compliance with the zoning regulations, were as objectionable as those put up before the amendment went into effect.

Toppers and scrapeoffs sometimes harmed existing homeowners, especially those living in small houses on tiny lots. They could not easily sell their properties since their real estate was not large enough for the houses desired by those wishing gigantic homes. Because of the presence of the new castles, small homeowners complained that they faced higher property taxes while the relative value of their properties declined. Developers could build out-of-code houses on small lots with the consent of the board of zoning adjustment or by receiving a planned-unit development zoning clearance from city council.

Typical of the less than sterling quality of city officials in overseeing building ordinances was a new double house at 381–83 South Franklin Street. It replaced the structure at 381 South Franklin Street which had been the residence of Arthur R. Ochs, a member of the Ku Klux Klan during its heyday in 1924. After the house sold for $318,000 in 2002, it came down for an upscale duplex, half of which sold for $688,000 in 2006. The planners authorized the contractor to build 20 feet from the sidewalk despite the requirement of 28 feet in the zoning code.

As the palace went up, Ginny Bayes objected. A former real estate reporter for the *Denver Post* who lived nearby, she protested the McMansion was in violation of the building ordinance. Pointing out that the city had twice approved his plans, developer Edward Fitzgerald Jr. went ahead with the effort. The administration backed him. If city hall makes a zoning error, it explained, the error will stand without need for correction or compliance. Legal action ensued. The courts stated the city could not arbitrarily waive the law—such action hinted at malfeasance if not corruption. A settlement followed in which the city paid $43,500 of Fitzgerald's estimated $65,000 cost to modify the building to conform with the ordinance.

This case was not alone. Signs requesting a waiver sometimes went up on new houses in the midst of construction. At times, locals, hating the way the castles were destroying their area, reported building violations—in more than one instance, contractors sought to take more space than was legally allowed.

By the time of the South Franklin Street controversy, efforts at historic preservation in Washington Park East had more or less collapsed. In 2000, locals received a $10,000 grant from the Colorado Historical Society via Historic Denver to finance Progress and Preservation Together. The Myrtle Hill organization aimed to review the area in the name of creating a landmark district to preserve the existing ambiance of the neighborhood.

Despite the grant, Progress and Preservation always begged for money. Most of its funds, apparently, went to those who raised the revenue. It presented various plans to the Washington Park East Neighborhood Association, but nothing came of its suggestions.

Residents on the west side of the park launched a comparable survey. Little resulted. Poptops and scrapeoffs continually invaded that section. In response,

While in some places poptops and scrapeoffs have emerged as gigantic palaces out of scale with South Denver neighborhoods, in other cases, architects have creatively blended the old and the new as is illustrated by 1067 South Race Street.

locals urged a downzoning of the area from R-2 to R-1, denoting single-family houses. (Myrtle Hill is mostly R-1.) In this manner, they hoped to check the destruction of existing structures and their replacement with gigantic multiplexes.

Members of the West Washington Park Neighborhood Association had advocated downzoning since at least the mid-1970s. A neighborhood plan of around 1990 said all the right things and had no impact. Developments, including McMansions and poptops, continued. City planners responded with numerous documents, none of which redressed the issues which so provoked passions about the destruction of the historic housing stock of the area.

Not all homeowners embraced downzoning. Opponents argued it threatened property values. Others stated an intense distrust of the government generally, observing that the area had flourished since the 1970s largely outside of the purview of city hall. They also pointed out the longtime incompetence of the planning office. Its previous efforts, they observed, had allowed the problems with monster houses to develop. Worst of all, they found city planning documents filled with bureaucratic gibberish and cute names like "Blueprint Denver" and "Quick Wins Two."

Public officials questioned downzoning schemes because they interfered with the jargon-filled city plan. The latter divided the West Washington Park neighborhood at South Clarkson Street, urging a zoning change only for the area east of that road. On December 15, 2008, after a six-and-a-half-hour public hearing, neighborhood pressure led council to adopt an 18-month moratorium on combining lots for multi-unit residences while it downzoned 208 acres in the area between South Downing Street and the alley of South Clarkson and South Washington streets from Cedar Avenue to Mississippi Avenue. Among those whose residence was rezoned was city councilman Chris Nevitt who backed the measure—prior to taking office, he had been active in pushing the downzoning of the neighborhood. All the while, the South Side's commanding landmark, South High School, was the place next to the park where residents from all parts of South Denver have come together.

A Note on Sources:

Nancy Widmann, *Washington Park* (Denver: HD, 2007), mentions some of the houses east of the park. Her nomination for landmark status for Washington Park Place is on file with DLPC. R. Laurie and Thomas H. Simmons look at part of greater Myrtle Hill in *Denver Neighborhood History Project: East Washington Park* (Denver: Front Range Research Associates, 2000). Commissioned by the city, it discusses 19th-century real estate developments. Along the way, it chronicles the evolution of South Gaylord Street. The LWV 1984 tour booklet, *Washington Park Promenade*, highlights some of the area's early history and modern architecture. Eleanore Cramer recalled her residence on the 800 block of South Gaylord Street since 1958 in an interview on December 15, 2005.

A History of the Washington Park Community Church (Denver: Washington Park Community Church, 1943), is another valued source on the area. The chapter on Washington Park Elementary School in *Histories of the Denver Public Schools* (Denver: DPS, n.d.), touches on the origins and evolution of Myrtle Hill.

Colorado Exchange Journal, October 1889, pp. 42, 74, 77, heralded Bohm's Addition, Myrtle Hill, and Broadway Heights; cf. *DR*, January 2, 1882, p. 4, on the last-named section. *RMN*, December 14, 1936, p. 5, reported the death of Carrie Bailey. Ibid., June 18, 1929, p. 5, stated Frank Bailey had left an estate of about $40,000. *RMN*, July 22, 1930, p. 30, and *DP*, July 21, 1930, p. 8, reviewed the life of Louis Bartels.

UPN, June 29, 1961, p. 3, featured the Lort family saga. Those at the South Denver history seminar of February 17, 2008, recalled the Lort sisters and Joseph Lort. Lydia T. Lort wrote about her girlhood, Lort family lore, and how her family was central to the establishment of Washington Park Methodist in *A Church Bell Rings in Denver* (Denver: Otto J. Stockmar, 1951). Ellen and Hattie Lort had an article on early Washington Park and Myrtle Hill in *South Denver News* in 1978, copy in scrapbook 3 of the WPGC papers at DPL. *South Confederate*, May 25, 1960, p. 1, reported the impending retirement of Joseph Lort as the school's principal and reviewed his career. *RMN*, March 13, 1973, p. 95, and *DP*, March 13, 1973, p. 20, observed his death.

Harold Williams remembered the Redskins and the YAL in an interview on August 4, 2008. Bob Sheets told of playing for the Papooses in a discussion on December 7, 2008. At the same time, Jim Peiker informed me of Marin Alsop's presence in the Lort House.

Besides the 1943 history of Washington Park Community Church, also see J. Alton Templin et al., *The Methodist, Evangelical and United Brethren Churches in the Rockies, 1850–1976* (Denver: Rocky Mountain Conference of the United Methodist Church, 1977), 139, 309–10. *WPP*, February 1993, p. 1, saluted Washington Park Methodist on its one hundredth year. *MF*, September 1920, p. 5, and *DP*, January 5, 1919, p. 5 sect. 3, highlighted its new building. Jerre Conder called my attention to Camp Wa-Pa-Co-Chu in an undated letter in September 2008. My *In the Shadow of the Klan*, 231–33, looks at George Nuckolls and Washington Park Community Church. *RMN*, December 6, 1925, p. 16, mentioned the Wichita offer to him. It reported his resignation, August 15, 1926, p. 1. Also see Widmann, *Washington Park*, 70, 78–83. *SDM*, April 22, 1927, p. 7, told about the Washington Park Woman's Club.

DP, August 26–28, 1908, and *RMN*, August 26–28—all stories page one— detailed the shooting of William Stephens. Lort, *Church Bell Rings*, 24, 46, mentions the police officer. Also see *Denver Police Department History Yearbook, 2003* (Evansville, IN: MT Publishing, 2002), 30. LWV, *Washington Park Promenade*, 17, looks at 777 South Williams Street. Timothy W. Bjorkman, *Verne Sankey, America's First Public Enemy* (Norman: University of Oklahoma Press, 2007), tells the story of the Sankey kidnapping of Boettcher, compete with its South Emerson Street dimension. He inadvertently lists the address as 2922 South Emerson Street.

The Minoru Yasui papers are at the Auraria Archives. Barbara Annette Upp analyzed his career in "Minoru Yasui: You Can See the Mountain from Here" (Ph.D. dissertation, University of Oregon, 1997). I glance at Yasui's political role in *DIA and Other Scams*, 7–8, and *From Soup Lines to the Front Lines*, 444–46. Richard Gould, *The Life and Times of Richard Castro* (Denver: CHS, 2007), 52, 199–200, mentions controversies about Yasui's work on the Commission on Community Relations. Also see Widmann, *Washington Park*, 72.

Pete Contos informed me of his experiences in numerous chats during the 1990s. Nicola Psyllas recalled growing up in the East Washington Park neighborhood and its Greek community in various conversations in the spring of 1993.

Besides the chapter on Washington Park School in *Histories of the Denver Public Schools*, DPS has a clipping file on the academy. Widmann, *Washington Park*, 66, mentions the George McMeen House. *RMN*, June 3, 1955, p. 74, and *DP*, June 2, 1955, p. 63, reported the death of the educator. Dianne Clark shared her memories of growing up a block from the South Gaylord commercial strip in a set of conversations in 1989. She further recalled attending Washington Park School in the 1960s. Participants at the South Denver history seminar remembered both attending Washington Park School and being parents of students there.

WPP, April 1979, p. 1, May 1979, p. 1, December 1980, p. 1, January 1981, p. 1, May 1981, p. 9, January 1982, p. 3, and February 1983, p. 4, dealt with the closing of Washington Park School. The same paper looked at Denver Academy, April 1981, p. 14, August 1983, p. 1, and January 1998, p. 4. Delia K. Armstrong, a veteran DPS educator, shared her views on the problems of the learning-impaired and places like Denver Academy in various informal conversations in the late 1990s and early 2000s. Denver Academy's takeover of the Bethesda campus was in *WW*, April 20, 2000, p. 73, *WPP*, February 2000, p. 1, and *DP*, September 16, 2004, p. 2B. Volume three further probes that development and the history of Bethesda Hospital and Waldorf School. The latter's negotiations to buy Washington Park School were in *WPP*, February 2000, p. 1, November 2000, p. 15, and April 2001, p. 3.

DP, August 15, 2001, p. 8C, and July 26, 2005, p. 1A, and *WPP*, May 1998, p. 3, August 2001, pp. 4–5, August 2002, p. 4, February 2005, p. 10, April 2006, p. 7, September 2006, p. 10, and May 2007, p. 5, looked at Denver International School, its problems, and the fate of Washington Park School. The *Profile* told of the International School's merger with Montclair Academy, January 2009, p. 27. In October 2007, p. 4, *WPP* hyped Myrtle Hill at Washington Park Place. It reported the opening of the Myrtle Hill Lofts, October 2008, p. 3, and November 2008, p. 4. Also see *RMN*, October 18, 2008, p. 1R.

CD, October 10, 1914, p. 13, and Widmann, *Washington Park*, 38, feature the Theodore Stuart House at 1100 South Franklin Street. David Wetzel recalled Thomas Dawson in *Colorado History Now*, February 2002, p. 3. Ellen T. Ittelson reviewed the career of Willis Marean in Noel and Norgren, *City Beautiful*, 211.

The DU Archives hold immense materials on the Foundation for the Advancement of the Social Sciences. DPL has a clipping file on James Causey. CHS and the Colorado State Archives have holdings on William Sweet. I look at the activities of Causey in passing in *Robert Speer's Denver*, 47, 89, 91, 286, 288, 529, and *In the Shadow of the Klan*, 105–07, 112, 194–96, 232. Widmann, *Washington Park*, 32, highlights the house.

The 1931 *Who's Who of Denver*, 185, includes William Sterne. *CJ*, September 24, 1959, p. 23, listed the many city contracts Alfred Ryan received. *DP*, October 30, 1967, p. 25, reported Ryan's death. Jerry Sutherland discussed the Causey House with me during a phone conversation in mid-November 2001. *RMN*, November 5, 2000, p. 6G, focused on the Jason Sutherland House. Jan Thomas, "Remembering Joe," *University of Denver Magazine*, Fall 2008, pp. 26–31, emphasized the impact of Josef Korbel. The DU Archives have a file on him.

DP, February 24, 1947, p. 22, and *RMN*, February 25, 1947, p. 11, recalled Roderick Reid. LWV, *Washington Park Promenade*, 16, heralded the Pozner House. Jeanne Abrams shared her research about her new book, *Dr. Charles David Spivak* (Boulder: University Press of Colorado, 2009), during a conversation on February 2, 2009. I glance at Spivak in *Exploring Jewish Colorado*, 19–21. Also see Ida Uchill, *Pioneers, Peddlers, and Tsadikim* (Denver: Sage Books, 1957), 231, 242–58, and Allen duPont Breck, *A Centennial History of the Jews of Colorado* (Denver: DU/Hirschfeld Press, 1961), 116, 191, 205–06. Members of the Spivak family, especially Ruth S. Oppenheim and Adele Karsch, recalled him in informal conversations in 2004 and 2005.

Widmann, *Washington Park*, 40–58, examines houses on the 1100 and 1200 blocks of South Gilpin Street, and in her nomination of Washington Park Place. She mentions the MacFarland House on p. 50. FF 26 of the Robert Speer collection at DPL, WH 434, briefly refers to MacFarland. Also see *RMN*, November 1,

1931, p. 16, *DP*, June 16, 1937, p. 8, *RMN*, June 17, 1937, p. 5, and *Mile Higher*, December 2008–January 2009, pp. 1, 3.

Orville Harrington's embezzlement of gold is in Arps, *Denver in Slices*, 120, and David J. Eitemiller, *The Denver Mint* (Frederick, CO: Renaissance House, 1983), 21–22. Lisa Ray Turner and Kimberly Field, *The Denver Mint* (Denver: Mapletree Publishing, 2007), is trite and contains a disclaimer stating readers cannot believe the statements in it. Features on the robbery were *DP Empire*, November 13, 1966, pp. 20–25, and *RMN*, December 26, 1982, p. 6N.

Lort, *Church Bell Rings*, 63–64, recalled Jeremiah Chrysler. Obituaries trace the story of the Chrysler family, including *DP*, March 7, 1936, p. 5, and December 30, 1971, p. 12, and *RMN*, September 30, 1956, p. 72, and October 18, 1958; cf. Widmann, *Washington Park*, 66. Ibid., 88, mentions James McInroy. The Klan membership books at CHS list members of the McInroy family as holding cards 26169–70.

Those at the South Denver history seminar shared memories of patronizing South Gaylord Street shops in the 1930s, 1940s, and 1950s, including the tales of Washington Park Pharmacy and Leo Charney, the Greek tailor, Mr. Fix-It, and the Jolly Rancher store. Lort, *Church Bell Rings*, 57, mentioned Ben Braconier. Alvan Morrison analyzed the real estate decline of South Gaylord and the exit of Cecil's in a letter of November 11, 1991. Jim Peiker talked about other South Gaylord groceries and explained the workings of Red and White to me in an interview on December 7, 2008.

Over the years, *WPP* has contained promotional articles and advertisements for Old South Gaylord. Typical were August 1979, p. 4, May 1994, pp. 11–17, and May 1995, pp. 15–19. Also see *GCCC*, April 2009, pp., 32–33. In November 2004, p. 10, *WPP* told about mediation between the merchants and neighbors over parking problems and the impact of traffic. The monthly heralded the South Gaylord landscaping program, April 1991, p. 3, and June 1992, p. 3. Pat Hodapp discussed the activities of the Washington Park East Neighborhood Association and the trials and tribulations of South Gaylord Street in discussions in 1990. Mike Costello, who for some years operated Project Earth, an excellent bicycle shop at 1004 South Gaylord Street, gave me his impressions as a small merchant on the road about how developments affected him in assorted conversations from 1990 to 1996.

WPP, May 1982, p. 3 June 1982, p. 6, September 1982, p. 18, and March 1983, p. 5, traced the history and transformation of the Washington Park D&R Theatre. Resolution #4 of the 1926 convention of the Colorado State Federation of Labor condemned D&R theaters as scabherders. Ralph Batschelet, *The Flick and I* (Smithtown, NY: Exposition Press, 1981), talks about the city's movie scene in the mid-20th century, including the omnipresent operations of Frank Ricketson.

Pat Hodapp shared gossip about the problems of David Billings during chats in 1990. *WPP*, July 2006, p. 6, and August 2006, p. 8, glanced at the evolution of Hemingway's. Reviews of Reivers include *DP*, July 20, 2000, p. 2C, and *WPP*, November 1997, p. 3.

I trace the origins of St. John's Lutheran in *Spirits of South Broadway*, 124–27. DPL has a clipping file on the congregation which includes a copy of the December 1962 *St. John's Lutheran*, an anniversary edition of the church newsletter outlining the history of the congregation. Carl Albert Gieseler, *Golden Jubilee Book of St. John's Lutheran* (Denver: St. John's, 1929), is an official history. Gieseler also touches on the congregation in "The History of the Colorado District of the Missouri Synod Lutheran Church" (Ph.D. dissertation, Iliff School of Theology, 1947). Lyle L. Schaefer, *Faith to Move Mountains* (Denver: Colorado District, Lutheran Church–Missouri Synod, 1969), emphasizes the vital role of St. John's in the evolution of the Missouri Synod in Colorado.

WPP, September 1992, p. 14, glanced at St. John's School for Fulfilled Living. It looked at the church's school programs, September 2000, p. 4. Also see *RMN*, February 18, 1967, p. 61, and June 3, 1972, p. 141. Reverend Michael Eckelkamp of the church shared his thoughts about the congregation in an interview on September 27, 2007. Participants, led by Bob Sheets, Patsy Vail, and Jim Peiker, at the South Denver history seminar talked about the vacant lot that became St. John's and the many other empty spaces and caves in the area before World War II.

Virginia Greene Millikin et al., *The Bible and the Gold Rush* (Denver: Big Mountain Press, 1962), 100, 119, 258, 263–64, 271, traces the growth of Washington Park Congregational Church. Articles on the congregation include *DP*, September 26, 1949, p. 2, March 5, 1950, p. 18D, and April 5, 1958, p. 5, and *RMN*, February 8, 1959, p. 44. Obituaries of Reverend Rogers were in *DP*, November 14, 1963, p. 64, and *RMN*, November 14, 1963, p. 25. Harold and Carol Williams recalled their longtime affiliation with Washington Park UCC. They told of the role of Corine Younger and shared the story about the rise and fall of the Agape Coffee House in an interview on August 4, 2008. Dianne Clark remembered growing up in the congregation during the 1960s in conversations in 1989. Carl Ott told me the story about the haunted house and the gun at Dakota Avenue and South Williams Street in 1991.

DP, April 8, 1965, p. 50, mentioned the passing of Ralph Leavitt. Ibid., November 12, 1991, p. 1A, chronicled the death of Virginia Leavitt and the disappearance of Shirley Leavitt. It reported Shirley's California odyssey on June 30, 1994, p. 1B.

Newspapers looked at the controversies over poptops and council's rezoning efforts, especially for the meetings of June 28, 1993, and July 10, 1993. *WW*, April 1, 1992, p. 4, and *DP*, June 9, 1993, p. 1B, highlighted "The Cathedral." Compare *WPP*, July 1991, p. 2, August 1991, p. 1, June 1993, p. 1, May 1998, p. 1, January 1999, p. 21, June 1999, p. 44, August 1999, p. 1, and November 2000, p. 1.

Mike Davenport and Harold and Carol Williams shared tales in various conversations about contractors erecting poptops and McMansions larger than the building code allows. Davenport, an architect and city planner, also gave me his views about the incompetence and bungling of the planning office in numerous discussions stretching back to the mid-1980s. He also shared his memories of being active in the Washington Park East Neighborhood Association and delivering its newsletter. Henry Johns talked about "particleboard palaces" in personal conversations in the late 1990s and early 2000s. He put together, *Harman and Its People* (Denver: Harman Neighborhood Reunion Group, 1992), a look at Cherry Creek North. Realtor Ann Atchison informed me of how architects and developers get around the city restrictions on poptops in a discussion around 1999.

RMN, March 21, 1999, p. 21A, reviewed the impact of the law on poptops. *DP*, May 5, 2005, p, 2B, *WPP*, April 2005, p. 13, and May 2005, p. 30, reported the imbroglio over 381–83 South Franklin Street. *WPP*, April 1999, p. 44, told of problems with a new house violating the zoning code at 1161 South Clayton Street.

WPP, December 2000, p. 1, mentioned the grant for historic preservation of the Washington Park East neighborhood. Also see *WPP*, September 2001, p. 10, November 2001, p. 8, October 2002, p. 12, November 2002, p. 10, and May 2007, p. 6. I had assorted discussions with Terry Andrews during the turn of the century about Progress and Preservation Together in which she always complained about poverty despite getting grants. The organization's Web site has a good basic introduction to the history of the Washington Park area. *WPP*, November 2001, p. 8 and March 2002, p. 1, told about efforts at historic designation for West Washington Park. Ibid., April 2002, p. 6, featured Sarah McCarthy, a major figure in South Denver historic preservation efforts.

WPP, August 2008, p. 1, and December 2008, pp. 1, 8, mentioned the downzoning debate in West Washington Park. The area's councilman, Chris Nevitt, gave his analysis of the proposal on p. 12, including his worship of the city plan "Blueprint Denver." Councilman Charlie Brown, who opposed Nevitt on the matter, questioned downzoning in the September 2008 *Profile*, p. 9. Ibid., September 1996, p. 25, January 1999, p. 30, and May 2007, p. 6, reported the WWPNA's embrace of downzoning. *WPP*, July 2006, p. 7, and January 2009, p. 17, contained letters criticizing the downzoning campaign. Letters supporting the effort were in August 2006, pp. 13–15, and September 2006, p. 13. Also see the letters in its October 2008 number, pp. 27, 29. *Denver Daily News*, December 17, 2008, p. 1, and *WPP*, January 2009, p. 38, reported the downzoning debate and city council action. The January-March 2009 newsletter of WWPNA heralded the action, pp. 1, 2. Charlotte Winzenburg shared it with me along with copies of the association's sheet which had articles on downzoning in the 1970s, 1980s, and 1990s.

Chapter Four

South
High School

South High School emerged simultaneously with Washington Park. In the 19th century, the prime task of South Denver educators was creating a system of elementary schools. Before long, in addition to school district #2, covering the area south of Cherry Creek and east of the Platte River, the region was home of district #7. The latter emerged on September 6, 1871, out of the reorganization of an earlier district dating from at least 1869.

District #7 initially covered a rural area between Mississippi and Yale avenues from the Platte River to approximately South University Boulevard. During its early years, it opened and closed a number of widely scattered and short-lived one-room schools. With the emergence of the Town of South Denver in 1886, it was at the heart of that community's school system. On December 1, 1902, upon the establishment of the City and County of Denver, district #7 merged into district #1 of Denver Public Schools (DPS).

In 1890, district #7 opened Grant School at the northeast corner of South Pearl Street and Colorado Avenue. Located in the Grant Subdivision, it honored President Ulysses S. Grant, holding classes from grades one through eight. (An original designation simply called the academy the Pearl Street School.) Administrators set aside two Grant rooms for high school classes in 1893, marking the essential start of South High School.

By this time, East, West and North high schools were already in place. Prior to the creation of South High, South Side students who had made their way through eighth grade went to West High School, the prime institution of school district #2. It dated from 1880, initially occupying space along West Colfax Avenue between

Photo by Roy Hyskell, DPL

Grant School, at the northeast corner of South Pearl Street and Colorado Avenue, was the original home of South High School. This picture was taken in 1924, just before South moved to the south of Washington Park.

Lipan and Mariposa streets. West High was subsequently at West Sixth Avenue and Fox Street before moving to West Ninth Avenue and Elati Street in 1926. Into the 21st century, it has pulled in South Denver residents, especially those living in the Baker neighborhood.

Typical of South High's tortured beginnings was the way the administration cut the academy from grades nine, ten, and eleven to just grades nine and ten in 1903 when South had 39 students and two teachers. The educators reinstalled 11th grade in 1905. The first 12th grade graduating class was of six students in 1908. Until 1923, the academy was South Denver High School or South Side High School. At one time, athletes wore a "D" on their jackets denoting they were part of the greater Denver High School.

In 1906, DPS added a wing to Grant on South Washington Street for high school purposes. An independent survey of the school system ten years later blasted the South plant as "cheaply constructed." At Grant, the report observed, the high school lacked space for manual training, domestic science, or physical education. Teachers used the library all day for classroom instruction. The typing room was in a converted hallway, 40 feet by six feet. The atmosphere was not conducive to learning.

By the time South had occupied the annex, the original Grant building included both elementary and high school classes. In 1920, elementary students left Grant for the newly opened Thatcher School at South Grant Street and Colorado Avenue. DPS thereupon divided Grant into two separate schools. South High was for grades ten through twelve. Grant Junior High School emerged for students in grades seven through nine. Principal John J. Cory oversaw both the junior high and high school. By this time, upwards of 1,500 pupils packed the building.

Locals agreed that South Denver needed a separate high school structure. Talk about such an edifice was heard immediately after World War I. Socked by the soaring cost of living, voters then rejected a bond issue for new high schools. But new schools were urgent. Or so the Denver Chamber of Commerce argued. The city, the booster group announced, had to expand from 250,000 residents in 1920 to 500,000 by 1930. To make this a reality, the organization called on voters to approve bond issues so Denver would have the capacity to educate the sons and daughters of the half-million residents.

Before long, the slogan "500,000 in 1930" was omnipresent. The electorate backed it by approving funds, including an $8.6 million bond in October 1923 for three new high schools and various junior highs. Voters authorized additional money in October 1925. The decade, consequently, saw a major school-building program. The effort also aimed to advertise Denver as the city beautiful. School buildings, DPS announced, had to be distinguished landmarks close to parks and boulevards. These temples of education, promoters believed, would assure top-notch learning.

New South

$\mathcal{A}$ new South High was a foremost accomplishment of the campaign. Initially, DPS eyed the undeveloped land from Mississippi Avenue to Arizona Avenue between South Ogden and South Downing streets where South Corona Street did not cut through for the campus. Realizing that the property was too small for a modern high school, in 1922 the school system acquired 72 acres of rolling, vacant land from the Colorado & Southern Railway whose tracks were adjacent to what became Buchtel Boulevard. On January 26, 1940, during the excavation of a rifle pit, workers discovered bones of a prehistoric camel buried on the school property.

South High Historical Room

The architectural drawing of South High by architects William E. and Arthur A. Fisher. Missing is the gargoyle above the main entrance.

Photo by L. C. McClure, DPS
South High School was appropriately located near South High Street

Scientists from what became the Denver Museum of Nature and Science excavated them, adding the fossils to the research institute's collection.

Masons laid the new school's cornerstone on October 31, 1924. They placed a memorial casket in it, including a bible, flag, copy of the constitution, and South High memorabilia. The school, the administration promised, would last a century while having space to educate 1,600 students. The edifice cost $1,252,000.

During the break between semesters in January 1926, South teachers, students, and staff marched from Grant School to their new home. Walking together, they carried their books and supplies to the recently completed structure. Within a few years, this became something of an epic-mythic event where South pioneers heralded their participation in it. The Washington Park school hosted its first classes on January 26, 1926, with an enrollment of 1,010 pupils taught by 44 faculty members. The complex included a manual training wing. The community dedicated the new South High on March 25, 1926.

The partnership of brothers William E. and Arthur A. Fisher designed South in the style of the Italian Renaissance. The exterior features elaborate brick work to create a mosaic effect of lights and shadows. Rome's Santa Maria Cosmedia inspired the main tower which Fisher & Fisher called the campanile—the bell tower which was part and parcel of Italian churches. The architects copied the five-arched loggia over the main entrance from the San Ambroggio Cathedral in Milan.

Striped poles on the western exterior of South are based on the cathedral in Siena, Italy. The main entrance frames a series of grotesque creatures and friezes. Robert Garrison created them, an artist who worked closely with Fisher & Fisher

on many projects. Foremost of the sculptures is a three-and-a-half-foot-high griffin perched above the main west entrance, its eyes peeled for truants, ready to
pounce upon them. At least that is how Garrison explained the beast's symbolism.
Some South High boosters viewed it more fondly, naming it "Gertie Gargoyle"
who looks after and protects South students. (In the modern era, the administration has mounted a couple of surveillance cameras beneath Gertie.)

A gargoyle on the Spoleto Cathedral in Italy was the model for Gertie. Original architectural drawings did not include the griffin. Besides Gertie, the building
was topped with a weather vane. After lightning struck and damaged it, patriots
pulled it down during World War II and ceremoniously gave it to a scrap metal
drive.

Two bizarre creatures sit below Gertie, resting on the backs of students. They,
Garrison asserted, symbolize the weight of knowledge and the final examinations
bearing down on South scholars. A bas-relief, *Faculty Row*, of squabbling creatures is on the arch above the main entrance, Garrison's interpretation of a teachers' meeting. It includes the principal, assistant principal, and dean of girls trying
to contain the instructors. Below it is a frieze, *Animal Spirits*, depicting such evil
student activities as chewing gum and shooting rubber bands. Should a bewil-
dered learner look up to see what time it is on the tower, he is apt to observe not
that it is half past eight, but Aquarius after Sagittarius. Instead of numerals, the
hours on the tower clock are marked with the signs of the zodiac. Aries is one
o'clock with the signs running counterclockwise.

A frieze at the north entrance is a parable on the workings of the school system.
First an eager, healthy student sets out on a winged horse to conquer the world.
Soon he is dismounted. Finally, he arrives weary and belatedly. Four griffins
guard the gateway to the northern courtyard where the school had its bicycle racks.
Squabbling cats and reptiles dominate a frieze near the south exit. A school expan-

Photo by Phil Goodstein

*Students are supposed to parrot what they hear—it will give them the knowledge
of owls. Such is the message of the owl and parrot near the ceiling of the South
High library.*

Photo by Phil Goodstein

Gertie Gargoyle looks down over the beasts of knowledge at the main entrance of South High School.

sion has mostly cloaked it from view. A reflecting pool in a formal Italian garden was never installed as planned in the south courtyard. Seniors always claimed that space as their own, complete with Senior Hall to the south of the Auditorium.

Decorations are throughout the school. In places there are figures of monks, hermits, doves, and winged seraphs. Four birds are near the ceiling of the library to illustrate the grind of education: a cock to keep students awake; a parrot burlesquing memory; a penguin exemplifying deportment; and an owl standing for knowledge and the long hours of burning the midnight oil to complete homework. Terra cotta reliefs of the parrot and owl are next to the doors of the auditorium.

The auditorium includes a frieze, *Protection of the Tree of Knowledge*, on both sides of the proscenium arch. Here scholars bravely guard the tree of knowledge from serpents of ignorance so students may emerge from South as learned adults. The cornices of the auditorium feature angels symbolizing good students; Grecian lamps for the studious; and stylized monkeys representing fools. To provide natural light, the sun shone through windows on the south side of the auditorium. Custodians drew velvet drapes to darken the hall. In the name of modernizing South, the administration filled in the windows after World War II.

The City Ditch originally flowed through the west lawn which extended to South Franklin Street. Supposedly, a rite of initiation was for upperclassmen to dump sophomores into the stream. (A different account has the juniors and seniors throwing the tenth-graders into Grasmere Lake.) During fights, opponents sometimes forced adversaries into the stream. On occasion, bullies pushed the unsuspecting into it, sometimes pulling off the pants of their victims in the process. A rope hung by a tree adjacent to the stream which students used to swing across the canal.

During World War II and the Korean War, the lawn west of the stream was victory gardens. Workers buried the City Ditch by the school in the 1950s. Shortly thereafter, crews paved the ground between South Gilpin and South Franklin streets for a student parking lot. Walter Pesman designed the original landscaping of South.

Gargoyles are supposed to scare away ghosts and evil spirits. Nonetheless, a lore exists about hauntings at the school. In July 1965, for example, a girl supposedly jumped from the tower whereby some occasionally see a body falling from it. In reality, during a summer school session, a 16-year-old woman from southwest Denver, who had previously attempted suicide by slashing her wrists and had threatened to kill herself on other occasions, made her way to a ledge beneath the tower, 40 feet over the north courtyard. After a long standoff, the police, firefighters, and two priests coaxed her to safety. A 1931 South graduate who was an assistant fire chief, John De Jong, led the rescue.

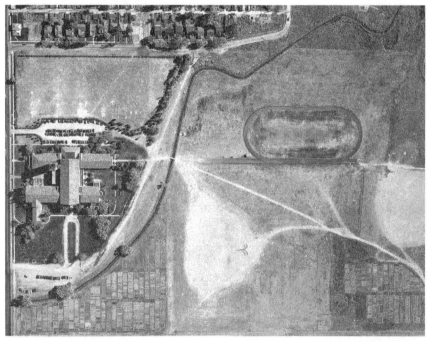

South High Historical Room

The open City Ditch flowed through the grounds of South High School until the 1950s. Land to the west of the canal (bottom), subsequently the student parking lot, was used for victory gardens during World War II and the Korean War. The location of the oval on the right became the site of All City Stadium. This photo dates from 1948.

A mural decorates the south wall of the main entrance to South High School.

Despite the successful resolution of the crisis, psychics in the tower have felt strange vibrations and various hot and cold spots. They are often hypnotized by an endless, repetitive ticking—the beating of the clock. Daydreaming students in the library have been sure that they have heard the birds squawking at them or at least flapping their wings and turning their heads.

As part of a Civil Works Administration project to create jobs during the Depression, Allen True painted twin 100-inch by 170-inch murals inside the main entrance in 1934. They depict the promise of youth, the advancement of science, the world of music, and the challenges facing graduates. Eventually, the South administration placed two pay phones in the middle of the south panel. With help of alumni and a grant from the Colorado State Historical Fund of the Colorado Historical Society, conservators restored the murals in the late 1990s.

South Rebels

*T*hough stemming from a school named for Union general and president Ulysses S. Grant, early on South adopted considerable Confederate symbolism. The school's fighting nickname became the Rebels, the student newspaper the *Confederate*, and its yearbook *Johnny Reb*. Athletes played at Rebel Field.

The first yearbook in 1920 was the *Aeronaut*, celebrating aviation. To launch the project, a pilot dropped a copy of the first annual from his plane to parachute into Washington Park. The bombardier missed his target and the book plunged into Smith Lake. Beginning in 1921, *Aeronaut* was the title of the student newspaper, a moniker that switched back and forth to the *Confederate* into the 1930s. As an April Fools' Day stunt, the students sometimes published the sheet as the *Counterfeit.*

On occasion, the yearbook was known as *Southern Lights,* the *Southerner,* the *Rebel Loco,* the *Cotton Kingdom,* the *Gargoyle,* and other titles. Not until 1950 was it *Johnny Reb.* A 1933 charter for the student government was known as the "Confederacy Constitution." The girls' reserves during World War II were the "Southern Belles." The young women learning to shoot guns with the help of the ROTC program were the "Rebelette Riflers." The school saluted outstanding seniors as "Rebel Rousers."

During the 1950s and 1960s, amidst the civil rights revolution, the *Confederate* featured the Confederate battle flag on its masthead. Students proudly flew the banner of slavery during sporting contests and pasted copies of it on their cars. In response to controversy, on November 21, 1967, the student body voted by a five-to-one margin to adopt the Stars and Bars as the official school flag. Rebels continued to fly it, marching with it at football games, well into the 1970s. On occasion, black students were at one with white students in waving the pennant.

The class of 1965 placed a terrazzo mosaic of Johnny Rebel in the main lobby—that was the South insignia displayed at DPS high school gyms. At one time, numerous Confederate flags were around the auditorium. The school also included statues of a winged Mercury and the Little Mermaid which disappeared in the late 1950s. A pedestal for a statue to the north of the main entrance was once supposedly reserved for a sculpture of Robert E. Lee.

The presence of Johnny Rebel and symbols celebrating the Confederacy became extremely problematic during controversies over school busing in the late 1960s. Crowds of up to 1,500 then flocked to highly contentious school board meetings. To accommodate the crowds, the school board moved its sessions from its downtown administrative headquarters to South High.

In September 1968, blacks protested the meetings at South. The school, they stated, was a living embodiment of racism and the worst of the Civil War. The

South High Historical Room

During the 1950s and 1960s, the Confederate, *the South student newspaper, included the Confederate battle flag on its masthead.*

A terrazzo of Johnny Rebel dominates the main entryway at South. It has been hidden under a rug for some years. The administration has continually disciplined students who have rebelled against school policies. In the 1960s, it was also intolerant of young men, like Johnny Rebel, who had beards.

administration reacted by covering Confederate symbolism which was highly offensive to advocates of civil rights.

The name *Johnny Reb* disappeared from the cover of the yearbook in 1991. Political correctness saw the *Confederate* become the *Gargoyle* in the fall of 1995 with a good deal of controversy. Eventually, a rug was usually over the Johnny Rebel mosaic in the main lobby. Rather than the seemingly appropriate gray, the school colors are purple and white. On February 19, 2009, at the behest of black students, the school board agreed to make a griffin, rather than Johnny Rebel, the official symbol of the school.

Despite being "Rebels" in name, South High students were rarely rebels in deed. A student handbook, *Southern Customs*, informed new pupils about the school's conservative, respectable traditions. Typical of South's reputation was a December 1948 *Life* magazine article praising South High student body leader Earl Reum as a model and hero for youth. The Moscow *Literary Gazette* noticed it, labeling Reum a "hooligan" who personified the dead end facing American high school students. Reum went on to become a nationally respected expert and consultant on programs for student leadership.

Far from agreeing with the Soviets, South High students thought themselves special. This was especially the case with the Hi-Y, an elite boys social organization which had a clubhouse in the tower, a place closed to girls. Hi-Y was part of a national fellowship that promised to set "high standards of Christian character." For a while in the late 1930s and early 1940s, the South High radio club gathered in the school's campanile. The space eventually became part of a museum operated by the South High Alumni and Friends Incorporated.

During the late 1960s, some South students acted as rebels. In February 1968, seven students were suspended for selling an unauthorized student newspaper, *The Activist*. A mimeographed letter-sized monthly, it included articles opposing the draft while denouncing the South dress code as "forced conformity." Most of all, *The Activist* advocated "student power," including a student bill of rights, student representatives on the school board, and something comparable to what became the Parents, Teachers, and Student Association. Those backing *The Activist*, about ten seniors, insisted the sheet was a vitally necessary alternative to the stale, censored, pro-Vietnam War *Confederate*.

To assure there would be no rebels at South, the administration staunchly turned back about 20 members of the radical Students for a Democratic Society (SDS) in January 1969 when they sought to get South pupils to join a citywide strike against the crude disciplinary measures the DPS administration was imposing against black students at Cole Junior High School—the "Rebels" failed to respond to the SDS plea.

Under principal Joseph Peonio, who served briefly in the late 1960s, the South administration was especially intolerant of boys who dared show too much facial hair or grew their hair too long. It ordered boys to get a haircut or face suspension. In October 1969, the school board upheld the principal's expulsion of South student John Brick of 2010 South Downing Street because he let his hair grow well over his ears. Discipline and order, the authorities insisted, trumped education and self-expression. While it was fine to celebrate the slaveholders' rebellion of 1861, students were not to rebel against the South administration.

Photo by Phil Goodstein

The South Alumni Association has transformed the school's old basement ROTC firing range into a historical room/museum. Nearby are a series of utility tunnels beneath the school.

Racial tensions socked South during the fall of 1970. Final plans for court-ordered busing were completed only at the beginning of the school year. Assignments were confused and many new black students found the administration completely unresponsive to their pleas for assistance—it preferred to discipline them rather than redressing their bafflement and problems in getting to South on time. To protest what they believed were discriminatory policies, many African-American students refused to attend classes on October 2. Principal Erik Holland responded by calling in uniformed police and ordering a severe crackdown against all rebels. This led to new upheavals on October 28–30. Once more, uniformed police were present while plainclothes officers patrolled the hallways. Amidst the tensions, students formed a chapter of the National Association for the Advancement of Colored People. Latino students organized La Raza de Aztlan whose members described themselves as being Christian "by the grace of God."

Tensions about race, censorship, and discipline continued at South in the 21st century. This came out in December 2004 when the administration ordered the removal of a new mural, *In Transition*. The Mayor's Office of Education and Children presented it to the school, believing the canvas, created by local artists, highlighted what keeps students from succeeding. Included were a swastika, drugs, and weapons. Protesters argued *In Transition* created a negative image of minority youths while it distracted pupils from preparing for standardized tests. Around the same time, the school allowed student artists to paint the handball courts in a graffiti style.

Eventually, the South upheavals of the hippie era became part of South nostalgia. The South High Alumni and Friends Incorporated emerged in October 1991 as a foremost advocate of the school. It took charge of the tower, paying for the maintenance of the clock. The alumni association came to operate a "historical" room in the basement in what had been the firing range of the school's ROTC program. In the process, it raised a great deal of money for South. The alumni association sponsored everything from reunions to golf tournaments to baseball games while creating its own choir. At times, it criticized the operations of the school. Many alumni took out subscriptions to South's student newspaper while they backed the South Booster Club to provide extra funds for their alma mater. The society hoped to replace the original weather vane with a replica.

In the fall of 1991, the South High Alumni and Friends saw the city officially declare South a landmark, celebrating the installation of a medallion on February 20, 1992. The group thereupon arranged to get South placed in the National Register of Historic Places. It has issued a lively newsletter, the *Alumni Confederate*, filled with memories about South and the surrounding area.

All City Stadium

South emerged as the center of DPS athletic competitions in 1957–58 with the opening of All City Stadium. A facility with baseball and football fields, it occupied the land between South High School and the new Valley Highway. The complex was the fulfillment of a long-sought dream.

For years, prep athletics had been a foremost city sporting venture. The five teams in the Denver Public School League—South, West, North, East, and Manual—usually played key games at privately owned fields such as Broadway Stadium near West Sixth Avenue and Broadway and Merchants Park at South Broadway and West Exposition Avenue. After the University of Denver opened its Hilltop Stadium at Asbury Avenue and South Race Street in 1926, Denver high schools had many of their crucial grid encounters there.

DPS planned a high school sports facility in 1938–39 in partnership with the New Deal's Public Works Administration. Washington promised to pay 45 percent of the cost; Denver would pick up the rest of the tab. Before the issue went on the ballot, the University of Denver vetoed the playing grounds: the college feared it would lose revenue from its field if the new venue opened—the college was deeply in debt in trying to pay off the bonds for Hilltop Stadium. Voters subsequently rejected the school issue anyway.

Prior to the erection of All City Stadium, the land between South High and the University of Denver was a weedy, undeveloped area that sometimes flooded after heavy rainstorms. It was a natural drainage area that was usually quite wet. A small shack stood in the middle of it, the home of the caretaker of a nearby dump.

With the sports complex at South, students from other high schools usually made their way to the Washington Park school to view or participate in various events. Among the agencies eyeing the field in the early 1970s was the Denver Organizing Committee (DOC) for the 1976 Winter Olympics. Denver won the games in May 1970. The DOC concocted all sorts of fantasies about exactly where competitions would be staged. Among them was adjacent to All City Stadium where it planned to install an oval for speed-skating events. As was typical of the extremely arrogant, corporate-dominated outfit, it originally failed to inform DPS or the South administration of this venture. The effort to add the speed-skating track collapsed with the Olympics when voters said no to them in November 1972.

A $1 million, federally financed improvement to All City Stadium saw the installation of new lights and seats at the baseball field in the summer of 1978. A major renovation and expansion of facilities followed in 1993–95 when All City Stadium held competitions of the United States Olympic Festival, an event hosted by the University of Denver. In the wake of this, DPS pushed for an $8 million to $12 million mass upgrade of the facility in 1998. It retreated when voters showed hesitations about approving more money for the school system. The complex includes a softball field.

Besides the usual social and sports activities, South emphasized academics. In part, this was a response to claims that it was second rate. At least East High insisted as much. That school and its backers always viewed East as city's most distinguished academy. South forever sought to upstage East. Observing that East's colors were red and white, South backers asked: "What's red and white? What's red and white? Horsemeat! Horsemeat! East High, horsemeat!"

South was overcrowded by the 1930s when 2,000 South Denver youths enrolled. Not only did the city's population increase, but so did the percentage of

All City Stadium is directly south of South High School.

adolescents who attended high school. This was even more the case after World War II when Denver finally started to approach its dream of being a community of 500,000 residents.

By the late 1950s, nearly 3,500 students attended South in grades ten through twelve. Among them were young men and women living outside of Denver in Cherry Hills. To handle the crowds, South was on split sessions. Group activities at South were huge. The school's symphony, for example, had 120 members. They practiced on the fourth floor at the base of the tower.

In 1959, South awarded 896 diplomas, the most it ever granted in one year. In contrast, 660 had won degrees from South in 1940 and 653 in 1950. South generally tended to graduate about 10 percent more girls than boys.

DPS opened George Washington, Thomas Jefferson, and Abraham Lincoln high schools in 1960. All were in the southern half of the metropolis, pulling many students who would have previously attended South. Even so, the Washington Park school remained vastly overcrowded. While DPS listed the school as having a capacity of 2,100, South had more than 2,400 students in the fall of 1961. The administration added new wings to the school in 1962–63.

Students continued to pour into South through the 1960s when baby boomers started to enter high school. During these years it had more than 2,500 pupils. The number plummeted in the 1970s as the baby boomers graduated and school busing saw the massive exodus of families with school-aged children from the City and County of Denver. By the time a new South gymnasium went up in 1987–88, the school's student body was less than 1,200 students in ninth through twelfth grades in a building with a capacity for 2,460 students. (The school added ninth grade in

1982. A 1981 report listed the much expanded school as having a capacity of 1,724 when its enrollment was 1,374.)

The academy stabilized at around 1,400 students in the early 21st century. More than half of its enrollment were those with "limited English proficiency." South served as the "newcomer orientation" school for DPS. As such, it not only attempted to educate pupils, but to Americanize them. It produced between 175 and 235 graduates annually.

Veterans Park

Veterans Park is southeast of All City Stadium. It covers the area from the school land to South University Boulevard between I-25 and Iowa Avenue. The city acquired the property, once a set of brickyards, around the time it pondered the freeway in the late 1930s. Numerous brickyards were in the area. Town of South Denver marshal Alexander Miller, for example, had his pit on the land that became Veterans Park. Robinson Brick also once dug up clay and manufactured its product there. Schreimer Brick was at 1846 South Race Street. The headquarters of Excelsior Brick were at 1800 South York Street. By the time work got underway on the Valley Highway after World War II, rain water accumulated in the gouged out sections of the land. Floods followed cloudbursts, washing debris down into the depression of what became I-25.

Photo by Phil Goodstein

In 1990, members of the American Legion installed a flag pole and small garden on the northern edge of Veterans Park near Iowa Avenue and South Gaylord Street.

After World War II, the South Denver Civic Association, a booster organization promoting the South Side as the area's best business environment, beat the drum for the property next to the emerging freeway as the ideal location for a new Denver Municipal Auditorium. For the most part, engineers used the land as part of the flood control system for the Valley Highway. Not only did the City Ditch flow under the freeway into the open space, but the land was designed to absorb much of the runoff from the speedway.

A flood holding pond is directly south of police station #3. The latter facility, at the southwest corner of South University Boulevard and Iowa Avenue, opened in 1966, moving from 20 Center Avenue. On March 3, 2005, the police dedicated a massive new hall there that had seven times as much square footage as had the old. It came complete with a community meeting room as the force reached out to neighborhood leaders. An abstract sculpture, *Aegis*, went up outside the precinct station. Jonathan Stiles designed it with a mobile and a bench as part of the city's commitment to beautify public buildings. Another work of art by Stiles, *Gratis*, is in the police fortress.

For years, the city called the land the Vine and Iowa Ballfield, complete with a baseball diamond to the southeast of All City Stadium. In 1987, the administration committed itself to landscaping parts of the 14 acres as a park. Toward this end, it asked for suggestions for names. John Perich, a veteran of the Korean War and an activist in American Legion Post #1, took the lead. Under his impetus, the organization insisted the open space should be named in honor of veterans. The city thereupon dubbed the acreage Veterans Park. The Legion raised $5,000 for a plaque and flagpole. It helped dedicate the greenery on Memorial Day, May 28, 1990. The organization subsequently held Flag Day observances in the park which usually drew only a few dozen spectators.

Shortly after the christening of Veterans Park, Denver finally got Major League Baseball. To build rapport with the populace, the Colorado Rockies donated a community baseball field on the grounds of Veterans Park. At times, the greenery, which has few trees or picnic facilities, is virtually empty. This includes on beautiful weekend afternoons when Washington Park is jammed.

In 2006, the city committed itself to enhancing the landscaping of Veterans Park. The flood-control measures associated with ending the City Ditch on the other side of I-25 had not worked as planned. The administration further sought to install a three-hole "frisbee" golf course where players threw their disks at the destinations. The area north of Washington Park, in turn, has remained a most prestigious section, the land south of the Denver Country Club.

A Note on Sources:

Histories of the Denver Public Schools (Denver: DPS, n.d.), includes chapters on Grant School and South High. Library clipping files and DPS records have also been consulted on the evolution of South. *WPP*, December 1994, p. 4, celebrated a century of South High. Gene Vervalin, *West Denver: The Story of an American High School* (Boulder: EHV Publications, 1985), is the story of West High.

Alumni Confederate, a publication of the South alumni association, has had numerous articles on the history of the school and South Denver. The 1994 number was a special historical edition. The archives of the South Alumni Association include copies of the *Catalyst*, the newsletter of the school's Parent, Teachers, and Students Association. *The Helmsman*, a special pamphlet put out for the fiftieth anniversary of the class of 1938, contains South High stories.

DT, August 17, 1903, p. 4, reported a protest against cutting out 11th grade at South. Lewis M. Terman, *Building Situation and Medical Inspection*, vol. 5 of Franklin Bobbitt et al., *Report of the School Survey—District One* (Denver: School Survey Committee, 1916), 49, emphasized the miserable, inadequate space at Grant School. *RMN*, January 8, 1922, p. 9, told of the purchase of the land for new South; cf. *DP*, December 16, 1922, p. 1.

The 1970 issue of *Johnny Reb* reviewed fifty years of South's yearbook and touches on the history of the school, including the discovery of the camel bones, 64. *MF*, January 1926, pp. 4–7, contained a detailed architectural description of the school and the meaning of its symbolism. It also featured South, June 1926, pp. 4–5, and May 1930, p. 3. "Art in Denver," *The Lookout*, 1:2 (1928), 30–31, talks about the school's sculptures and friezes. *RMN*, November 1, 1924, stressed the laying of the cornerstone. DPL has Fisher & Fisher records, including its design of South. *DP*, January 24, 1926, p. 13, highlighted the opening of new South.

Life, December 20, 1948, pp. 72–73, heralded Earl Reum. *DP*, June 1, 1949, p. 1, reported the Russian attack on him as a "hooligan." *RMN*, August 19, 1961, p. 24, *CJ*, February 8, 1967, p. 1, and *DP*, February 25, 1967, p. 24, featured Reum's work on student leadership programs. Bob Sheets remembered the Hi-Y Club in a discussion on December 7, 2008. *Southern Customs*, p. 21, a copy of which is in the educational clippings at CHS, reports Hi-Y's vow of "high standards of Christian character." (The CHS file also includes the dedication program of South.) *Alumni Confederate*, June 2008 p. 8, mentioned the South High radio club.

UPN, September 14, 1961, p. 1, and September 28, 1961, p. 1, reported complaints about overcrowding at South. *WPP*, November 1995, p. 4, included a discussion of the Historical Room. The *Profile* looked at the expansion of the school, December 1987, p. 1. A copy of the dedication program of the gym, on April 10, 1989, is in the DPS clipping file on South.

Retired South history teacher Paul Ton recalled his many years at the school during numerous discussions in the early 1990s when we shared an office at the history department of Metropolitan State College. He informed me how some around South harkened back to the march from Grant School. Nancy Down remembered taking part in the trek in her interview at the DU Archives. Joyce Winters reminisced about attending South High School in conversations in 1992 and 1995. Members of the class of 1953 discussed their schooldays during their 55th reunion in September 2008.

DP, July 11, 1965, told of the suicide attempt at the ledge of the tower. The *Alumni Confederate*, June 2008, p. 1, reprinted it. Susie Woytek discussed the formation of the South Alumni group in a phone interview in 1990. Bill Wiederspan was most helpful in opening up the files at the South Historical Room to me and giving me his slant on the Alumni Association and the school. Other members of the group gave me tours of South and shared their memories of attending South. In an August 13, 2008, interview, Ron Grosswiler recalled attending the academy from 1952 to 1955 while living at the State Home for Dependent and Neglected Children. In passing, he mentioned how students would get thrown into the City Ditch. Jim Peiker, Patsy Vail, and Bob Sheets also remembered students getting shoved into the canal and the rope over it in a discussion of South Denver on December 7, 2008. The three also reminisced about the dump south of South High School and the flooding of the land that became the Valley Highway. Harold Williams gave me a different version of the flooding when he recalled the brick-yards in an interview on August 4, 2008.

SDM, June 8, 1934, p. 5, mentioned the installation of the Allen True mural at South. Alvan Morrison wrote me about his South days in a letter of November 11, 1991. He stressed the alumni's role in conserving the murals in a chat on July 5, 2008. *Alumni Confederate*, Fall 2001, p. 1, reviewed the problems with the tower clock.

Comments on *The Activist* are from reading the three copies in the CHS clipping files on South. *UPN*, January 23, 1969, p. 1, gloatingly reported the failure of SDS to invade South High. *RMN*, October 17, 1969, p. 8, and October 21, 1969, p. 8, told of the expulsion of John Brick. Eric Tagge, who graduated from South in 1969, recalled the extreme discipline at South in a discussion on September 24, 2008. Susan Bardwell chatted about her experiences as a South student in the mid-1970s during a phone conversation on December 5, 2008.

My *DIA and Other Scams*, chap. 2, analyzes the school busing wars, including the role of South. The 1971 *Johnny Reb*, 66, reviewed the racial upheavals at the school in the fall of 1970. On p. 198, it looked at La Raza de Aztlan. Also see *UPN*, November 5, 1970, p. 1, and *DP*, October 30, 1970, p. 3, and December 7, 1970, p. 93. The *Gargoyle*, October 1, 1995, stressed the new name of the student newspaper and the controversy surrounding it. *DP*, February 20, 2009, p. 1B, and *WPP*, March 2009, p. 8, reported the school board's authorization to change the South logo. A transcript of a December 10, 2004, broadcast of 9News in the DPS clipping file on South tells about the problem of *In Transition*.

The South Historical Room has a file on All City Stadium. *WPP*, November 1993, p. 4, mentioned the refurbishment of the field and the Olympic Festival. In October 1998, p. 29, the *Profile* told of DPS plans for an $8 million to $12 million upgrade of the facility; cf. *RMN*, August 24, 1998. I analyze the controversies over the city hosting the Winter Olympics in *Big Money*, chap. 5.

WPP, May 1990, p. 1, and June 1990, p. 1, heralded the dedication of Veterans Park. Mary DeGroot chatted about it with me during a Memorial Day conversation in 1991. In April 1998, p. 15, the *Profile* mentioned clashes over the use of the ballfield. The April 2006 issue, p. 13, looked at plans to renovate the greenery. *DP*, June 15, 2008, p. 1B, glanced at the origins of Veterans Park and reported the minuscule turnouts for Flag Day ceremonies.

Chapter Five

South of the Country Club

*P*restigious though the neighborhoods directly east and west of Washington Park have become, they do not compare to the section nestled between Alameda Avenue and the Denver Country Club. Much of the acreage is hidden away. East of the alley between South Williams Street and South High Street, high walls guard exclusive manors north of Alameda Avenue.

In 1902, a consortium led by future mayor Robert W. Speer acquired the bulk of the John J. Riethmann estate between Fourth and Bayaud avenues to the east of Downing Street for the new Denver Country Club. Those behind the effort immediately reserved the land north of First Avenue for residential development which became the Country Club neighborhood proper. Simultaneously Speer, who won the 1904 mayoralty contest, remained an active real estate investor. He kept 160 acres of the Riethmann estate to the south of the Country Club. He realized that the land stretching to Alameda Avenue, with its commanding view of Cherry Creek, had great potential as a super-deluxe section. Speer's prime policies as mayor encouraged real estate development near the Country Club, especially through a flood-control measure to channel Cherry Creek and place a grand parkway along the stream, Speer Boulevard.

Prior to the arrival of the Country Club, development had been sporadic in the area south of Bayaud Avenue. Much of the real estate was Shackleton Place, the land bordered by Bayaud and Alameda avenues between South Marion and South Race streets. Speculators initially staked it on November 3, 1874, platting the land on March 12, 1887. Some of the early houses were quite ornate, especially those stonemason George Endres constructed on the west side of the 200 block of South

138

Photo by Phil Goodstein

Ornate stone work is part of a duplex at 271–73 South Franklin Street in Shackleton Place, a development predating the mansions of the South Country Club area. Other modest units went up nearby in the 20th century, sometimes being the homes of Country Club employees.

Williams Street, including homes occupied by his family at 219 and 225 South Williams. Other structures were rather modest, including simple farm homes and a few duplexes. Some were subsequently quarters of Country Club employees.

The coming of the golf course drastically transformed land values and the nature of the housing stock. No place did this stand out more than at the estate of John Evans II at South Race Street and Cedar Avenue which had the official address of 2001 Alameda Avenue. Born in 1884, Evans was the grandson of Colorado's second territorial governor, John Evans I. Besides politics, the first Evans had wide-ranging real estate and railroad investments.

William Gray Evans was the father of John Evans II. In addition to running the monopolistic Denver Tramway Company during the early 20th century, the second Evans was the boss of the Denver Republican Party while simultaneously controlling the policies of Democratic Mayor Robert W. Speer. Detractors called him "Napoleon" Evans. On November 11, 1908, John Evans II married Gladys Cheesman, the only child of the recently deceased Walter S. Cheesman. The latter, a close compatriot of William Gray Evans, had been the kingpin of the monopolistic Denver Union Water Company (DUWC).

John Evans II followed in the footsteps of both his father and father-in-law. Among other posts, he was the head of First National Bank and the Denver & Rio Grande Western Railroad. As had his father and grandfather, he played a central role at the University of Denver, serving as president of its board of trustees from 1925 to 1943. Unlike them, he generally shunned the limelight. He hid from the city atop what was once called Tank Hill.

To get water to flow downhill, in the 1880s water providers selected high spots around the city on which they built reservoirs. Among the locations was the real estate north of Alameda Avenue to the east of South Race Street. The forerunner of DUWC acquired that land for its Hilltop Reservoir in the late 1880s. The 3.32-acre spread included the land to South Gaylord Street, occupying about half of the block north of Alameda Avenue. In 1890, the water company completed two red 660,000-gallon iron tanks at the southwest corner of Alameda and Gaylord. Wooden pipes with a 30-inch diameter brought water from Cherry Creek. The facility also had pipes pulling in water from the Platte River near West Alameda Avenue. A smokestack and standpipe were near the reservoir for the coal-fueled pumping station. Locals called the promontory Tank Hill.

The waterworks remained in place until 1911. The previous year, voters rejected the DUWC's application for a 20-year renewal of its franchise. The bulk of the citizenry called for a municipally owned and operated utility. DUWC, which never maintained its facilities well, responded by declaring the Hilltop facility superfluous. There was not enough water, it observed, in Cherry Creek to make Tank Hill part of the water-supply system. Besides, DUWC investor John Evans II wanted the land for his home.

Brothers William E. and Arthur A. Fisher designed the Evans Castle as a Northern Italian stuccoed villa with a red-tiled roof. Numerous big trees surrounded the mansion, transplanted from the mountains. The landscaping firm of McCrary, Culley, & Carhart oversaw the installation of various gardens and terraces to accentuate the hilly setting. For years, Gladys Cheesman Evans pushed civic beauty

Photo By Orin Sealy, DU Archives

The John Evans House was an Italian villa surrounded by pools, fountains, and lush landscaping at South Race Street and Cedar Avenue.

as the president of the Colorado Forestry and Horticulture Association, an organization which was something of the forerunner of Denver Botanic Gardens.

Privacy fences excluded outsiders. During the next few decades, a select group of businessmen, most of whom were John Evans' associates, settled the area between Bayaud and Alameda avenues from South Williams Street to South University Boulevard. By this time the name Tank Hill was forgotten; many called the location Evans Hill.

The Gerald Hughes Palace

Nobody was personally and politically closer to Evans than Gerald Hughes. In 1936, Hughes moved into a mansion directly west of Evans at 1900 Cedar Avenue. (The house also had the address of 1919 Alameda Avenue, the other side of the block.)

Like Evans, Hughes, born in Richmond, Missouri, on July 8, 1875, grew up in a politically and financially influential family. His father, Charles, was a foremost utility lawyer and a leader of the conservative wing of the Colorado Democratic Party. When Charles Hughes won election to the United States Senate in 1909, Gerald Hughes took over his father's law practice. Charles Hughes did not enjoy his role in Washington long, dying in office on January 11, 1911.

Two months after Charles Hughes passed away, David Moffat was found dead in his New York hotel room on March 11, 1911. The latter, the head of First National Bank, was closely linked to Walter Cheesman and the Evans family. During his last years, Moffat's goal had been to construct a direct railroad link between Denver and Salt Lake City through northern Colorado. His Denver, Northwestern, & Pacific Railroad, commonly known as the Moffat Road, was anything but a financial success. Moffat was constantly strapped for funds to pay for construction and to meet loan payments. In consequence, he juggled his personal finances while he committed the assets of First National Bank to the railroad. By the time of Moffat's death, not only was he for all intents and purposes bankrupt, but First National Bank was insolvent.

Gerald Hughes rescued the bank through a skillful set of political and financial maneuvers. In the process, he passed on the option of going to the Senate as his father's successor. With his Republican law partner, Clayton Dorsey, Hughes made the bank's opinions known on local political matters. Their firm of Hughes and Dorsey was the city's preeminent home of lawyer-lobbyists. Until virtually the time of his death in 1956, Hughes was an omnipresent voice in assuring that 17th Street exercised its clout over the community.

Architects Fisher & Fisher modeled the Hughes' Villa on the 16th-century Davarasotti Palace in Florence. Hughes' wife, Mabel, had espied the manor on a trip and made it known she wished to live in a comparable dwelling. Built on a 6.24-acre estate and costing upwards of $250,000, the 42–room house was decorated with numerous museum-quality pieces, reproductions of European antiques, tapestries, chandeliers, marble fireplaces, and travertine, parquet and terrazzo floors. The beamed ceilings included stenciling designed by acclaimed artist Vance Kirkland who painted murals in the drawing room and dining room. (At the time

A developer destroyed the Gerald Hughes House at 1900 Cedar Avenue in 1972.

Hughes erected the house in the middle of the Depression, a nice middle-class house cost $4,000 to $6,000.)

The Moore and Morey Houses

Real estate investor Hudson Moore Jr. married John Evans' daughter Alice on December 30, 1930. As a wedding present, Evans built the couple a house east of his castle at 2201 Alameda Avenue (near the northeast corner of South Gaylord Street). The firm of Fisher & Fisher designed the English Tudor manor. It featured oak interior paneling and a distinguished Italian Renaissance–style fireplace for the library.

A native of Atlanta, born on May 10, 1906, Moore was the son of a powerful attorney who came to Colorado Springs in 1919 for his health. Two years later, the family relocated in the Mile High City. After graduating from Denver Public Schools, the younger Moore went from the University of Colorado to Oxford University where he was a Rhodes Scholar. On getting his degree, he joined Public Service as an electrical engineer. Before long, he headed the Evans family real estate firm, Cheesman Realty. Eventually, he was president of the Denver Water Department while serving on the boards of Mountain States Telephone, Public Service, and the Boettcher Foundation. For years, he headed the Denver Museum of Natural History. He died at age 77 in October 1983.

John Morey lived close to Moore. His father, Chester Morey, had run the city's largest wholesale grocery, Morey Mercantile. In 1905, the elder Morey was a close associate of Charles Boettcher in establishing Great Western Sugar. Born in Denver in 1878, John Morey attended Yale before following in his father's footsteps as the president of Morey Mercantile. He also served as chairman of the board of International Trust, a financial institution interlinked with First National Bank. Additionally, he was a director of Tramway and the Denver & Rio Grande, other Evans family enterprises. In 1905, John Morey married Mable Feldhauser, the daughter of a foremost figure in the city's German-American business community.

The grocery heir commissioned brothers Merrill and Burnham Hoyt in 1925 to design a 14,000-square-foot Gothic-Victorian home on the hill overlooking the Country Club and South University Boulevard. The investor had a personal entrance to the house from 229 South University. (Its official mailing address was four blocks away at 1929 Alameda Avenue.) He occupied the palace in 1929. Inside, the house was filled with plenty of stained glass, damask, 17th-century Flemish tapestries, hand-woven rugs, and assorted international antiques. Outside, the manor included stables for horses and Morey's pet llamas.

In 1954, with neighbors Gerald Hughes and John Evans, Morey arranged for the Denver Country Club to acquire 32 acres of their land when the city began expanding First Avenue to the east of Downing Street from a two-lane to a six-lane road. The administration paid the Country Club $6,500 an acre for 5.6 acres along First Avenue. Additionally, the city agreed to landscape First Avenue by the Country Club as a parkway. The Country Club thereupon moved a section of its golf course south onto the Hughes-Evans-Morey land. It paid the three titans $6,920 an acre for 25 acres in addition to leasing seven more acres from them for 99 years. At that time, Morey sealed the South University Boulevard drive to his property. Soon thereafter, the city began work on widening University Boulevard east of the Country Club from a two-lane road.

The John Morey House is at 229 South University Boulevard.

*John G. Gates tore down this house at 300 South York Street in 1940 as not suffi-
cient for the aspirations of those living south of the Country Club. He replaced it
with an even more gigantic mansion.*

On Thursday, November 1, 1956, Morey announced his retirement and the sale
of Morey Mercantile to the Consolidated Food Corporation of Chicago. Two days
later, he attended a football game in Boulder where he saw the University of
Colorado take on national champion Oklahoma. As he was leaving the stadium,
he died in the parking lot from a stroke.

The grocer's only child, Katherine, occupied the house. On May 15, 1929, she
had married John A. Ferguson Jr. (1900–1980), the son of the founding president
of the Denver Country Club. The elder Ferguson made his money in life insurance
and in holding patents for brick-making tools used around the world. John Ferguson
Jr.'s two sons inherited the property on their father's death. Initially, they offered
the manor and the surrounding 3.5-acre estate to the Country Club for $1.5 mil-
lion. The organization declined after pondering transforming the castle into a second clubhouse.

In 1983, developer Stan Brooks acquired nine acres surrounding the Morey
Mansion for $2.2 million. After announcing plans to put up 12 custom homes, he
constructed eight houses adjacent to the golf course. Realtors touted them as standing atop "Morey Hill."

Parts of the South Country Club are rolling, hilly land. Much of the property
directly to the south, especially on the 300 blocks of South York, South Gaylord,
South Vine, and South Race streets blends in with the South Country Club. Quite
noticeable is the house of John G. Gates at 300 South York Street. The brother and
partner of Charles Gates, the head of Gates Rubber, in 1922 he moved into a commanding $18,000 manor on the northern half of the block bordered by South Uni-
versity Boulevard, Alameda and Dakota avenues, and South York Street. By 1940,
it did not suffice when John Gates had workers tear down the house, replacing it
with a lushly landscaped palace designed by architect Burnham Hoyt. DU chan-

cellor Maurice Mitchell made the Gates Castle his home when he led the college from 1967 to 1978.

The Destruction of Landmarks

*B*y the 1950s, the South Country Club generation was growing old. The men and women who had settled there in their prime years were now in their 60s and 70s. John and Gladys Evans found their huge mansion too much for them. In 1961, the couple moved to more sedate quarters at 38 Polo Club Circle. The fate of the Evans Mansion is typical of what happened in the South Country Club.

Evans was past president of the Colorado Historical Society. In 1959, he helped save the Josephine Evans Memorial Chapel. Located at the southwest corner of West 13th Avenue and Bannock Street, it was catercorner from his father's and sisters' house. The sanctuary remembered his aunt. DU, having recently acquired the real estate, slated the church for demolition for a parking lot. Learning of this and lobbied by people around Iliff School, the Methodist Church, and the University of Denver, Evans helped arrange to move the building, stone by stone, to the DU campus. Preserving his South Country Club home, however, was too much for him.

When John and Gladys Evans moved to the Polo Club, the family real estate firm of Cheesman Realty, headed by Hudson Moore, put the Tank Hill house on the market. There were no takers. At that time, new suburban luxury houses were in vogue while the South Country Club was a forgotten area. Both the Denver Country Club and DU rejected the house when Evans offered it to them as a gift. The maintenance costs, the institutions explained, were prohibitive and they did not see an immediate use for it. Consequently, after the house had remained vacant for three years, Evans decided that progress dictated its destruction in 1964. His wife died a decade later. He passed away in 1978.

Demolition was also the fate of the Gerald Hughes House. At one point, fire badly damaged it. Hughes departed from the world on August 27, 1956, leaving an estate of $5,368,253, most of which went to his widow, Mabel Yates, whom he had married on April 2, 1907. For years, she had been an active society figure, especially supporting Children's Hospital. She stayed in the South Country Club castle until her death at age 93 on April 9, 1969.

As was the case with the Evans Mansion, no purchaser sought the Hughes Palace as a single-family residence. Locals had a final chance to peek at it when the Junior Symphony Guild, working with the area's interior designers, turned it into a show house to raise money for the Denver Symphony in 1971. (The previous year, the Children's Hospital Auxiliary Show House Tour featured it.) Shortly thereafter, the estate earned $200,000 from an auction of the mansion's fixtures. Hersh Lacker bought the castle, calling in the wreckers in June 1972.

Developers were convinced that mansions like those of Hughes and Evans were dinosaurs. In their place, they erected large single-family homes and townhouses identical to those found in suburbia. Development opportunities continued in the area into the 21st century.

Those with power and money flocked to the area. A short-term resident of the cul-de-sac where the Hughes Palace had stood was Neil Bush, the son of George H. W. Bush, who was involved in shady Mile High savings and loan operations during the 1980s. A neighbor was Del Hock at 250 South High Street. He was the head of Public Service. Wayne Brunetti, who succeeded Hock in the job, was at 205 South High Street.

Owen Bradford "Brad" Butler occupied a modern house at 1805 Cedar Avenue. Born into a devout Christian family on November 11, 1923, in Lynchburg, Virginia, he went to work for Proctor & Gamble. An outstanding soap salesman, he rapidly rose in the firm. As its head Butler pushed everything from Pampers to laundry detergents with enzymes. This provoked protests of environmentalists and college students in the late 1960s and early 1970s. Butler egged them on, explaining "the devil made me do it." Hearing this, a few religious fanatics claimed the Proctor & Gamble logo was a satanic symbol.

Butler retired to Colorado in 1989 to be near his adult children. Before long, he was a close associate of Governor Roy Romer, pushing various child welfare efforts. The soap salesman personally oversaw the construction of his South Country Club home. Included was his picture in a life-sized mural in the kitchen. This proved ominous when the wind once blew open a door, tripping the burglar alarm. Responding, the police initially thought the figure on the mural was the burglar, threatening to shoot it. After Butler died in 1998, his widow, Erna, sold the house for $1.8 million in 2002.

Photo by Phil Goodstein

Custom houses popped up on part of the John Morey estate after his family sold much of the land south of the Country Club in 1983. This residence is at 2303 Alameda Avenue, behind the privacy walls guarding the South Country Club from the city.

Photo by Phil Goodstein

The Weckbaugh Mansion is at 1701 Cedar Avenue.

The Weckbaugh Mansion

Not everybody in the South Country Club was directly linked with the Evans empire. Such was the case with the Mullen family which had land to the north of Cedar Avenue and the west of the Evans and Hughes properties. Dynasty founder John Kernan Mullen (1847–1929) was Denver's outstanding 19th-century miller. Eventually, he dominated all aspects of the grain industry while serving on various civic bodies. At the same time critics charged he was an unscrupulous monopolist, he contributed to a wide array of charities. He presented each of his four daughters with a mansion upon her marriage near his Capitol Hill home at 896 Pennsylvania Street. Following Mullen's death, his family started to disperse.

In June 1903, Ella Mullen married Eugene Weckbach. A dreamer, he never pleased his stern father-in-law. After failing in the Mullen milling empire, Weckbach devoted himself to leisure. Before long, he changed the spelling of his name to Weckbaugh. Tensions grew between him and his wife when the man's marital indiscretions became quite blatant. By 1912, conditions were so bad that Catholic Bishop Nicholas Matz, a close Mullen family friend, conceded that a divorce was tolerable in this case. Mullen arranged for Weckbaugh to leave town, paying him $15,000 in exchange for the promise never to return.

Ella Weckbaugh remained at her Capitol Hill mansion at 450 Ninth Avenue until her father's death. In 1933, she moved just south of the Country Club to 1701 Cedar Avenue. Oil heir Myron Blackmer, whose father had been a central player in the Teapot Dome scandal of the mid-1920s, had previously commissioned architect Jacques Benedict to design a huge mansion for the block bordered by Bayaud and Cedar avenues between South Gilpin and South Williams streets.

Benedict modeled the castle after the 1443-vintage house of Jacques Coeur of Bourges. The Depression killed the effort, Blackmer subsequently moving to South Colorado Boulevard and Quincy Avenue. Kent School eventually made the latter location its headquarters. Ella Weckbaugh, in turn, obtained the property south of the Country Club, hiring Benedict to oversee the construction of a 25-room, two-and-a-half-story palace in the 17th-century French Provincial style.

The residence has marble from Georgia, Alabama, and Italy. Weckbaugh arranged for veteran marble workers from Italy to oversee the stonework. The main room features four Tiffany windows depicting the seasons. Interior decorations include bronze chandeliers and 18th-century French furniture. Ornate gardens were a central part of the five-acre estate.

More than anything, the mansion was the home of Ella Weckbaugh's daughter, Eleanore, a woman known to one and all as Ellie. Born on February 21, 1905, the younger Weckbaugh grew up as the city's glamour girl, going around in high heels, wearing long, sleek gowns, and racing about in fancy automobiles. For nearly 50 years, she was a dominant and highly controversial community figure.

Ellie Weckbaugh helped design and decorate the mansion. She annually hosted a series of parties at it. During Christmas, a 15-foot-high tree was at the center of a winter wonderland setting. Another party was on the first Sunday after New Year's. Valentine's Day saw her place red hearts and white gardenias around the house. For the occasion, she had a "Valentine's Day Tree," her still-standing Christmas Tree. The playgirl often blended the mid-February affair with a party celebrating Washington's Birthday which she claimed as her birthday. White lilies were omnipresent on Easter. The society queen staged her own fireworks show on the Fourth of July.

Most of all, Weckbaugh had ornate bashes for those performing at the Central City Opera and the summer stock theater at Elitch's. Beginning in 1940, she met the Central City stars at the airport, chauffeuring them in her blue Packard convertible to the mountain town. Ellie drove at whatever speed she wished—a police escort accompanied her car. The roads approaching Central City were quite rough. Not until the 1950s did U.S. 6 directly connect with the mountain mining town.

For the opera crowd, Weckbaugh decorated her estate with a theme from one of that year's performances. At times, she had workers place artificial moons in the trees of her estate. Now and then, she had snow brought in from the mountains for the summer celebrations. Before long, her gatherings were a central part of national high society. Big-name stars often played at Elitch's and Central City as much to attend the Weckbaugh soirées as to earn extra money.

Weckbaugh never married. This did not mean she did not have time for men in her life. On the contrary, they constantly came and went. Urban folklore insists that the South Country Club queen was always looking for handsome young men whom she offered jobs as chauffeurs, gardeners, and butlers. Sometimes, late at night, she allegedly demanded other services from them. Neighborhood men reported her approaching them with various offers.

Telegrams to newspapers and politicians on any and every topic continually flowed from the Weckbaugh Mansion. Ellie additionally involved herself in community welfare efforts. Typical of her activities was her suit against the Denver Archdiocese in 1974 over its plans for a $400,000 remodeling of the Cathedral of the Immaculate Conception at Colfax Avenue and Logan Street. Since a great deal of Mullen money had gone into the erection of the church, she claimed her family had the duty to see the structure maintained its architectural integrity against the "incredible insanity" which Ellie asserted the remodelers wished to impose on the basilica.

Though she lost that battle, Weckbaugh was vindicated in 1993. That year the pope visited Denver for World Youth Day, staying at the Cathedral. To prepare it for him, the Archdiocese ordered a massive renovation of the church, trying to restore its original beauty which had been besmirched by the "incredible insanity" which Ellie had decried.

While her daughter was everywhere, Ella Weckbaugh generally shunned the limelight. Highly religious and the donor to numerous church programs, she received a medal from Pius XII, Pro Ecclesia et Pontifice (For the Church and the Papacy), on December 2, 1942. The senior Weckbaugh additionally was a major financial backer of the Denver Symphony. After breaking her hip in a bad fall on September 25, 1963, Ella Weckbaugh lived at Saint Joseph Hospital until her death at age 95 in February 1971.

Ellie Weckbaugh survived her mother by 6 years, passing away in April 1977 when she was 72. The one-time playgirl was already in poor health by the time of her mother's death. A heavy smoker with an omnipresent black cigarette holder,

Photo by Phil Goodstein

Ellie Weckbaugh is buried by her mother and grandparents, John and Catherine Mullen, at Mount Olivet Cemetery.

she suffered chronic pulmonary disorders. During her last years, she was intermittently in the hospital. Still, she was always kicking.

Typical is what happened when Ellie was the victim of an armed robbery on November 16, 1971, when she was living alone in the house. Around 10:30 PM, two men broke in through the kitchen, bound her to a chair, and tore out the phone lines. Ransacking the mansion, they made off with $35,000 in jewels and two television sets. They informed her they had been paid to pull the heist. After they left, she managed to crawl free and make it to an undamaged phone in the basement to let the police know what had happened. A few weeks later, the police received a parcel in the mail containing the stolen jewelry.

Neighborhood youths knew Weckbaugh would not call the police if they behaved. At least that is what boys and girls believed who frequently sneaked onto the grounds to plunge into the mansion's swimming pool on the edge of the Country Club. An artesian well provided water for it. Kirchhof Construction installed the 25-foot by 70-foot amenity at a cost of $4,000 in 1932. Usually, after parties, Weckbaugh welcomed children to the pool. When not entertaining, she frequently left it empty.

The Weckbaugh well seemed inexhaustible. In 1933, responding to the Country Club's longtime complaint that it did not have an adequate source of water for a swimming pool, Ella Weckbaugh agreed the high society organization could use water from her well. After drilling it another 300 to 400 feet deep, workers installed a 1,120-foot-long pipeline from the well to a swimming pool near the clubhouse. In exchange, the Country Club waived dues for the Weckbaugh family as long as the water flowed. It expected this was a permanent agreement since engineers claimed the Weckbaugh well had an "inexhaustible supply" of water. They were nonplussed when it suddenly went dry shortly after World War II.

In 1961, Ellie had so squabbled with other supporters of the Central City Opera that she found herself purged from the organization's board. Some complained she drank far too heavily—she never returned to the auditorium after the first act, they observed; rather, she spent the rest of the evening at a nearby bar. Historian Caroline Bancroft was frequently her companion at such Central City events. Weckbaugh's money, others on the opera board argued, was not worth all the havoc she brought to the festival.

The heiress also bitterly clashed with Helen Bonfils, the owner of the *Denver Post*, as to which of them was Colorado's true culture queen. The *Post* naturally highlighted Bonfils; the *News* reported the doings of Weckbaugh. Against Bonfils, who backed the Denver Civic Theatre, Ellie provided money for the Denver Players Guild as a semi-professional theater company. Eventually, Weckbaugh adopted the Denver Civic Ballet as her favorite charity. She installed a stage for it on the grounds of her mansion and invited dancers to perform there. Ideally, she hoped to will the house to the troupe as its permanent home.

Ellie never owned the mansion. She had a lifetime tenancy in it from the Ella Mullen Weckbaugh Benevolent Corporation. Soon after the playgirl's death, the philanthropy put the estate on the market, emphasizing it included 44 lots and "substantial vacated areas." Genesis Investments bought the land in 1979. It im-

Bill Rhodes, the chaplain of the University of Denver from 1955 to 1966 who was subsequently head of the Metropolitan State College philosophy department, occupied a house to the south of the Weckbaugh Mansion at 208 South Gilpin Street from the 1960s to the 1990s. It was indicative of the middle-class residences stretching between Cedar and Alameda avenues in the South Country Club.

mediately subdivided the northern section, right on the border of the Country Club, as the site for eight private residences. Members of the family owning Robinson Dairy were among those living there. So was Don Ringsby whose family had holdings in a trucking firm and real estate and had owned the Denver Rockets of the American Basketball Association.

Though deprived of its northern lawn, the Weckbaugh Mansion survived as a single-family house. Roger and Beverly Willbanks bought it in 1980 as their home. The president of Royal Publications, he grew up in very modest circumstances in the Washington Park East neighborhood, attending South High School. Besides participating in various South High alumni events, he emerged as a collector of antiques and classic automobiles. On the side, he had performed with Weckbaugh in the Denver Players Guild. Treasuring their privacy, the couple kept the mansion closed to outsiders.

Raymond Burr got in. When he was in Denver during the 1980s filming the "New Perry Mason" television films, he stayed at the mansion. Hollywood occasionally flashed pictures of the house as Perry Mason's home. The Weckbaugh Palace retained its eye-catching attraction as the most distinctive and visible of the South Country Club villas.

Next door at 1681 Cedar Avenue, hidden away behind a privacy fence, numerous trees, and a huge lawn, was the home Katherine Mullen O'Connor planned for

herself. The sister of Ella Weckbaugh, Katherine Mullen married corporate lawyer James Emerson O'Connor, in 1905. He handled much of the legal work of
Mullen's milling empire. The attorney died of syphilis at age 44 in 1918. The
couple had never gotten along well, experiencing endless marital troubles.

Nor was Katherine Mullen O'Connor on the best of terms with her father. Mullen
was a strict Prohibitionist, decrying liquor in any form. His daughter, in contrast,
liked to drink. This led to her arrest in June 1923. Prohibition authorities charged
she had colluded with Father Walter A. Grace, the chaplain of the Mullen Home
for the Aged at West 29th Avenue and Lowell Boulevard, in procuring Kentucky
whiskey under the pretext that it was being used for medicinal and religious purposes. John Kernan Mullen heartily supported the prosecution, most likely being
responsible for the crackdown and arrest. She received probation; Grace spent a
year in a federal penitentiary.

Already in 1922, to escape her father, Katherine Mullen O'Connor relocated
from 860 Pennsylvania Street to 701 Emerson Street, the residence which had
previously been the home of Claude Boettcher. Around the time of Mullen's death
on August 9, 1929, she arranged for a sedate 30-room house south of the Country
Club. The 24-lot building site overlooked Cherry Creek and the golf course. She
planned to occupy the $25,000-manor with a grand society bash on Thanksgiving
1930. As the house neared completion, O'Connor's health suddenly collapsed.
She died from a blood clot on the brain on August 9, 1930, at age 46.

Her two children, John, 23, and Katherine 19, took possession of the villa.
They joined with other members of the Mullen family in creating a home for boys
at 3601 South Lowell Boulevard in 1931, the origins of Mullen High School. Their

*Modest houses survive south of the Country Club such as 175 South Franklin
Street where a modern front is on a Queen Anne residence.*

South Country Club castle included a built-in pipe organ. A swimming pool followed in 1936.

Katherine O'Connor II did not stay at 1681 Cedar Avenue long, moving out after her marriage to William W. "Bill" Grant on June 10, 1931. He then represented the merchant banking house of Boettcher, Newton & Company in New York. Eventually, he lived down the road at 101 South Humboldt Street. That was long after their marriage had ended.

John O'Connor stayed in the South Country Club estate with his wife, Carol K. Sudler, the scion of another moneyed family. He came to head the J. K. Mullen Corporation while running Continental Construction Company. The heir additionally was president of American Standard Insurance.

In 1952, the John O'Connor family moved out, eventually relocating at 2975 Cedar Avenue. He sold the South Country Club palace to oil investor and broker Robert V. Hodge for $85,000. The price was exclusive of the organ which O'Connor sold separately for $4,000—it landed up in a Canon City church. The new owner remained only a few years, transferring to 4747 Belleview Avenue, where he died in 1958. In the interim, another oil man, Zachary K. Brinkerhoff Jr., who had made his money in Texas and Wyoming, leased the house. Brinkerhoff purchased it around 1965, dwelling quietly there for decades.

The Mary Grant House

The Mary Grant House at 100 South Franklin Street is just to the west of the O'Connor Chateau. Born Mary Matteson Goodell on July 9, 1857, to Mary Jane Matteson and Roswell Eaton Goodell, she grew up in Joliet, Illinois. On occasion, she visited Springfield, staying at the home of her grandfather, Joel Matteson, who had been governor of Illinois from 1853 to 1857. After a spell in France from 1870 to 1873, the Goodell family settled in Chicago. Her father made and lost fortunes in the Windy City. Raised an Episcopalian, she attended the Catholic Georgetown Academy of Visitation, an elite finishing school for young women in Washington, D.C.

The Goodell family, which included five girls and one boy, moved to Leadville in 1879. The oldest child, Annie, had married James Day Whitmore in Chicago the previous year. The newlyweds relocated to Denver where Whitmore headed an investment company. Annie Whitmore was subsequently among those leading the drive to create Mesa Verde National Park.

The eldest sibling set the pattern for her sisters. They won acclaim for their beauty and sophistication. Rumors widely flew that, with his four other eligible daughters, Roswell Goodell arranged financially suitable matches for them with leading, rich Leadville bachelors. All his daughters emerged as wives of prominent Leadville and Denver figures. None stood out more than Mary, the second eldest, upon her marriage to James Benton Grant on January 19, 1881.

Grant was from a leading Virginia family who had degrees in metallurgical engineering from Cornell and the Freiburg School of Mines in Germany. He came to Leadville in 1878 at the behest of eastern capitalists to invest in the silver boom. In the Cloud City, he oversaw the erection of the extremely profitable Grant Smelter while establishing himself as a leader of the Colorado Democratic Party. In 1882, at age 34, he won election as governor whereupon he moved to Denver. When he took office the next year, the 25-year-old Mary was the state's youngest first lady. Grant did not seek re-election in 1884; instead, he threw himself into banking and smelters. Before long, he was a personal and financial conduit between Leadville and Denver fortunes.

In 1902, the Grants moved into the "White House of Denver." Such was the nickname of their commanding mansion at 770 Pennsylvania Street. Mary Grant was extremely active in charity and social endeavors as she oversaw the local Daughters of the American Revolution (DAR) and the Colonial Dames in addition to helping found the Woman's Club of Denver and sponsoring the YWCA. Between 1917 and 1920, she was the vice president-general of the national DAR. She promoted other patriotic societies with exclusive memberships whose ancestors had lived in colonial America.

Six years after her husband's death in 1911, Mary Grant sold the White House of Denver to Albert E. Humphreys Sr. She lived in a couple of other Capitol Hill houses before commissioning brothers Merrill and Burnham Hoyt to design her $30,000 South Country Club villa in 1924. She moved in the next year. Until her death on April 12, 1941, Mary Grant hosted numerous high society functions at it. William T. and Minnie A. Diss spent 35 years in the residence, raising 11 children there. A major figure with Arthur Young & Associates, once part of the Big Eight of national accounting firms, he and his wife had wanted an even dozen offspring, but health problems forced her to forgo a 12th pregnancy.

Slowly, over the years, the owners neglected the lush landscaping around the mansion. By the early 1990s, it had something of a Sleeping Beauty-look, a place seemingly forgotten by time. In 1998, Jerold and Sandra Glick purchased the house. They undertook a massive renovation of it, winning awards for their efforts. The city declared it a landmark on July 17 of that year.

A block south of the Mary Grant House was the home of part of the other branch of the Grant family, the William West Grants at 101 South Humboldt Street. W. W. Grant was the brother of James Benton Grant. He came to Colorado from Iowa in 1889 at his brother's suggestion where he emerged as an outstanding physician. His son, William W. "Will" Grant (1881–1957), was a foremost corporate attorney who served on numerous boards and commissions and unsuccessfully ran for mayor in 1935. After occupying the Richthofen Castle at 12th Avenue and Pontiac Street, Will Grant eventually lived in the Norman at 99 South Downing Street.

Architect Langdon Morris designed 101 South Humboldt Street for William W. "Bill" Grant in 1954. Born in Estes Park on August 29, 1910, the third Grant very much followed in his father's footsteps as an attorney, businessman, and community activist. After attending an elite eastern preparatory academy in Connecticut, he graduated from Dartmouth in 1931. He thereupon joined the powerful Denver-based securities firm of Boettcher, Newton & Company, working in its New York office. After earning a law degree from Harvard in 1938, Grant returned to Denver where he joined his father's law firm.

Photo by Phil Goodstein

The Mary Grant House is atop a hill overlooking the Country Club at 100 South Franklin Street.

Most active in politics, after World War II Bill Grant teamed up with Quigg Newton. The latter was the son of James Q. Newton, the Newton of Boettcher, Newton. In 1947, Quigg Newton gained election as mayor with the help of Grant who managed the campaign. Grant oversaw Newton's re-election four years later. In the interim, he was a foremost city hall adviser, the first head of what became the Denver Commission on Community Relations, and the chairman of a 1947 city charter convention—voters rejected its suggestion to adopt a new city constitution.

An owner of KOA Radio, Bill Grant helped establish and run Channel Four which was originally KOA-TV. Former newswriter John Davoren remembered him as "a pretty good guy" for whom to work. In 1963, despite the endorsements of the *Post* and *News*, Grant came in third in his bid to gain the mayor's seat. Besides serving as the chancellor of the Colorado Episcopalians, the South Country Club resident chaired the state Democratic Party in the mid-1960s while he played a major role in Colorado National Bank and dabbled in shopping center development.

Bill Grant died on August 7, 1992. His widow, Helen Prindle, whom he married on June 6, 1938, remained in the house into the 21st century. The city declared the residence a landmark on July 17, 1998.

A daughter, Gertie Grant, was a community figure in her own right, helping lead the West Washington Park Neighborhood Association, Inter-Neighborhood Cooperation, and the Park People. Most of all, she was the power behind Denver Digs Trees. This was an ambitious effort to replant street trees after Dutch Elm Disease destroyed much of the city's mature tree cover. Eventually, under Grant's inspiration, the group was behind the planting of upwards of 20,000 trees. She was the person most responsible for pushing through the Washington Park mountain view ordinance. In 2008, the Washington Street Community Center honored her with its Jane Craft Neighborhood Award. Her brother, William W. "Pete" Grant, followed in his father's footsteps at Colorado National Bank. Close relatives played major roles in the National Western Stock Show.

A house directly connected with Bill Grant is directly south of the Mary Grant Manor at 140 South Franklin Street. It is a modern-style residence completely out of harmony with the existing architecture on the block. Victor Hornbein designed it in 1966 for Ralph Radetsky. Born in Denver on August 30, 1910, Radetsky worked as a reporter for the *Denver Post* through the 1930s. Around the time of World War II, he teamed up with a fellow journalist, Gene Cervi, in a public relations firm. After the return of peace, the two threw themselves into Democratic Party politics. They were most active in the 1947 Quigg Newton campaign. In the process, they developed close ties to Bill Grant. After Radetsky went to work at city hall and broke with Cervi, the latter branded his former partner the "silent mayor" of Denver.

After helping Newton gain re-election in 1951, Radetsky collaborated with Bill Grant in creating Metropolitan Television, the company owning KOA. Eventually, Radetsky was president and general manager of KOA Television and Radio. He left the post on September 1, 1967, shortly before his death on October 14 of that year. Radetsky had acquired the land for 140 South Franklin Street from Bill Grant. Until he moved into the South Country Club house, including during his years as Denver's "silent mayor," Radetsky had dwelt in Greenwood Village.

Radetsky's wife, Martha Fuller, whom he married in 1940, was a story in her own right. While her husband was alive, she behaved as if she were inspector

Photo by Phil Goodstein

Here and there, frame houses dating from the 19th century have survived south of the Country Club such as 140 South Lafayette Street.

general on visits to KOA. Active in numerous community concerns, she was a foremost advocate of school busing in the late 1960s and early 1970s. In addition to hosting fundraisers for the cause at her South Country Club home, Martha Radetsky served on a court-appointed supervisory board to oversee the implementation of the busing order. She also worked as a lobbyist for the American Civil Liberties Union. A native of the San Luis Valley, she died at age 71 in August 1985.

The Indian House

$\mathcal{A}$ block west of the Bill Grant residence is the Indian House at 1322 Bayaud Avenue. Romance surrounds it, especially its first owner, Cora Arnold. A Denver belle, she threw herself heart and soul into various civic activities in the late 19th century. The Pueblo Indians especially fascinated her. She studied their customs and worked with them. In 1896, she met a Santa Clara Pueblo, Albino Chavarria, who was in Denver as a performer at the Festival of Mountain and Plain. Despite the opposition of her family, love had its way and she married him.

Or so the story goes. At the time they met, Cora Arnold was 43 years old. He was 41 and did not speak English. She, an accomplished linguist, started regularly visiting him in New Mexico. Chavarria, in turn, made annual sojourns to Denver to see her. After a long courtship, they married in December 1907. They received building permit 3179 on December 11, 1909, to construct their $4,000, 58-foot by 33-foot Pueblo-style house at the southwest corner of Bayaud Avenue and Lafayette Street overlooking the Country Club. Following a Santa Clara custom, they planted two trees in the garden, separated by the width of Cora's waist. Ideally, the trees would grow around each other, marking the maturing of the couple's love. (Disease led to the destruction of the trees in 1961.)

On settling in Denver, Chavarria went to work as a gardener at Elitch's. The couple's romance remained a subject of gossip for years. In 1920, they relocated to 1266 Logan Street where he died in March 1930. She followed him to the grave in December 1939 at age 86.

James Grafton Rogers was the next inhabitant of the Indian House. A renaissance figure, he was born into a distinguished Denver family on January 13, 1883. When he did not do well at East High School, he transferred to the elite St. Paul's School in the East. He proceeded to Yale where he graduated in 1905, being the class poet.

After a stint as a reporter for the *New York Sun* in 1905–06, Rogers returned to Colorado. Upon making his way through the University of Denver Law School, he joined the bar in 1908. Two years later, he married Cora May Peabody, the daughter of the state's reactionary, union-busting Governor James H. Peabody (1903–05). By the time of the marriage, Rogers was an assistant Colorado attorney general. He specialized in water law, railroads, and utilities.

Most of all, Rogers was a mountain climber. Not only did he help form and lead the Colorado Mountain Club, but he named numerous peaks in the course of the 1910s and 1920s. Along the way, he composed songs about the West, including "The Santa Fe Trail" and "Old Dolores."

The Indian House overlooks the Country Club from 1322 Bayaud Avenue.

Beginning in 1910, Rogers taught part-time at DU Law School. He took the reins of the academy as its dean in 1927. The next year, he moved to Boulder as the dean of the University of Colorado School of Law. He sold the Indian House in 1929. Two years later, he moved to Washington when he became an assistant secretary of state under President Herbert Hoover.

A vehement opponent of the New Deal, Rogers returned to Yale as master of Timothy Dwight College after the inauguration of Franklin Roosevelt. During World War II, he was deputy director of the Office of Strategic Services. After the fighting, he represented bondholders against the new governments in eastern Europe. The lawyer eagerly joined the Cold War in combating communism and while he sought to protect the powers of the past. He was a leading Wall Street attorney who was most active in the Council on Foreign Relations.

Rogers retired to Georgetown at age 70 in 1953 where he emerged as police judge, a post equivalent to mayor. He used his powers to preserve the community as a quaint Victorian town. The onetime resident of the Indian House was also a major figure in the Colorado Historical Society, long chairing the organization while discussing the state's past. His son-in-law, Stephen Hart of the 17th Street law firm of Holland & Hart, followed in his footsteps in leading the historical society. Rogers died on April 23, 1971, preceded to grave by his wife who passed away in 1969. Subsequent owners retained the distinctive charm of the Indian House.

Minnie Love (1855-1942) lived down the block from Rogers at 175 South Lafayette Street. A pioneer woman physician, more than anybody she founded Children's Hospital in 1908. Already in the 1890s, she had been politically active in supporting Populism and feminism. At one point, she oversaw the State Detention Home for Women at 730 West Mississippi Avenue. An avid exponent of eugenics, Love served a couple of terms in the state House of Representatives in the 1920s in addition to being on the Denver school board from 1925 to 1931. Most of all, the decade saw her emerge as a foremost woman supporter of the Ku Klux Klan. (Another leading Klanswoman, Josie J. Jackson of 549 Kalamath Street, served in the legislature with Love.) By the time of her death, Minnie Love had also gained acclaim as the writer of short stories.

In the early 21st century, M. Stephen Ells constructed a gigantic manor directly west of the Indian House at 100 South Marion Street Parkway. He was the founder of the burrito chain Chipotle, opening the first store at the southwest corner of Evans Avenue and Gilpin Street around 1992. Ells destroyed two existing houses for his 5,763-square-foot spread that included a swimming pool and home theater. The entrepreneur sold the structure for $3.456 million in 2008 which had cost him $750,000 to build. His structure is right where the South Country Club meets the neighborhood that is northwest of Washington Park.

A Note on Sources:

*I*nformation on the South Country Club include materials on the key figures living there. John Evans II is the subject of Allen duPont Breck's fawning biography, *John Evans of Denver* (Boulder: Pruett, 1972). Sally Davis and Betty Baldwin, *Denver Dwellings and Descendants* (Denver: Sage Books, 1963), observes the family ties of the Evans, Hughes, Moore, Mullen, Grant, and Morey families and the houses in which they lived. Edith Eudora Kohl, *Denver's Historic Mansions* (Denver: Sage Books, 1957), also deals with this subject. James Bretz, *Mansions of Denver* (Boulder: Pruett, 2005), is a pale echo of *Denver Dwellings* and *Historic Mansions*. Stories about some of the families mentioned, such as the Evanses, Mullens, Grants, Moreys, and Rogerses, are on wall displays in the lobby of the Colorado History Museum—the families have been donors to CHS whereby the panels are something of official history.

Earl Mosley, "History of the Denver Water System, 1859–1919" (Denver: Unpublished Manuscript, 1966), chap. 4, discusses the reservoirs of the 1880s and 1890s, including Tank Hill. The Fisher & Fisher records at DPL include the specifications of the Evans and Hughes estates. Eugene H. Adams et al., *The Pioneer Western Bank* (Denver: First Interstate Bank of Denver, 1984), a history of First National Bank, chronicles the central role of John Evans and Gerald Hughes in the financial institution while mentioning Interstate Trust and John Morey, see esp. 117–58.

RMN, December 6, 1935, p. 1S, looked at Gerald Hughes' villa. I glance at the power of the Hughes family in *Robert Speer's Denver*, 191, 194, 297, *In the Shadow of the Klan*, 160–61, and *From Soup Lines to the Front Lines*, 72–73, 75. Joanne Ditmer, "Visit to the Hughes Mansion," *DP Empire*, April 26, 1970, pp. 64–69, highlighted the landmark on the eve of its destruction. George C. Gibson, "Gerald Hughes," *CL*, 18:7 (July 1989), 1304–06, emphasized Hughes' central role in the bar. CHS collection 960 features Hughes.

RMN, October 22, 1983, p. 13, and *DP*, October 22, 1983, p. 14A, recalled the life of Hudson Moore Jr. Kohl, *Historic Mansions*, 173–81, talks about the Morey family. *RMN*, November 4, 1956, p. 15, and *DP*, p. 21A, reported the death of John Morey. *DP*, June 12, 1983, p. 33F, focused on the subdivision of the land around the Morey Mansion. Robin Kassoff, "Anybody Have $2.2 Million?" *Denver Magazine*, March 1984, pp. 42–45, is a portrait of the Morey Villa.

Charles C. Bonniwell and David Fridtjof Halaas, *The Denver Country Club* (Denver: Denver Country Club, 2006), 29, 30, 35–36, emphasizes the development of the land south of the Country Club and the roles of Robert Speer and John Ferguson. The volume mentions the Country Club's rejection of the homes of John Evans and John Morey, 83. On 242–43, 255, the book looks at the widening of First Avenue and its impact on the Country Club. *DP*, February 15, 1998, p. 1A, featured Brad Butler.

Bill Convery, *Pride of the Rockies* (Boulder: University Press of Colorado, 2000), is a biography of John Kernan Mullen. The volume tells about the Weckbaugh family, 43, 147, 205–06. Bonniwell, *Country Club*, 106–07, relates the connections between the Weckbaugh artesian well and the Country Club swimming pool. *WPP*, July 1983, p. 3, glanced at the history of the Weckbaugh Mansion. DPL has a clipping file on the Weckbaughs, filled with many stories about Ellie and her parties and civic engagements.

Bill Rhodes, who long lived at 208 South Gilpin Street, recalled Ellie Weckbaugh as a neighbor in informal conversations in the late 1980s and early 1990s. He shared the stories about Weckbaugh approaching neighborhood men with various offers and the young men who constantly came and went from the mansion. Roger Willbanks participated in the South Denver history seminar of February 17, 2008, sharing stories about living in the Weckbaugh Mansion and his fascination with vintage cars. He also talked about the Denver Players Guild. Others at the forum remembered swimming in the Weckbaugh pool and tales about Ellie's drinking. *DP*, November 17, 1971, p. 3, reported the robbery at her house. The late Allen Young shared inside gossip about the Central City opera during personal conversations in 1984–85. His memories of the festival are in *Opera in Central City* (Denver: Spectrographics, 1993). Obituaries of Ellie Weckbaugh were *DP*, April 8, 1977, p. 3, and *RMN*, April 9, 1977, p. 6.

Davis and Baldwin, *Dwellings and Descendants*, 150–67, reflects on the Mullen family and its houses. Convery, *Pride of the Rockies*, 148, 158, 205–06, 247, mentions the O'Connor clan. He discussed his research on the family with me on November 20, 2008. My *In the Shadow of the Klan*, 85, 271, glances at the controversies concerning William Grace and Katherine Mullen O'Connor.

Helen Cannon, "Mary Goodell Grant," *CM*, 51:1 (Winter 1964), 27–33, recalled Mary Grant as Colorado's first lady. *DP*, April 13, 1941, p. 1, reported her death. *Taming the Silver Serpent* ([Denver]: Colorado Chapter of the DAR, n.d.), includes chapters on Mary Grant, 1–14, and Annie Goodell Whitmore, 43–50. Davis and Baldwin, *Dwellings and Descendants*, 49–61, and Kohl, *Historic Mansions*, 211–19, tell the epic of James Benton Grant and his family. I touch on the wide-ranging career of Will Grant in *From Soup Lines to the Front Lines*, 189–

193, 196–98, 523. He reflected on his career in *Such Is Life* (Denver: Privately printed, 1952).

DPL has clippings about Bill Grant's civic activism. George V. Kelly, *The Old Gray Mayors of Denver* (Boulder: Pruett, 1974), 19, 163–70, tells of Bill Grant's city hall connections. Gertie Grant briefly mentioned her family in informal discussions in 1984–85. John Davoren shared his memories of working at KOA in the 1960s and the characters of Bill Grant and Ralph and Martha Radetsky in chats on December 5, 2008, and March 7, 2009. He reviewed the text. Tom Noel, *Rocky Mountain Gold* (Tulsa: Continental Heritage Press, 1980), 211–13, has a paid history of KOA. Charlotte Winzenburg especially praised the role of Gertie Grant as a primary South Denver figure during an interview on February 13, 2009.

Glances at the Radetsky House are in Don Etter, *Denver Going Modern* (Denver: Graphic Impressions, 1977), 118, and Michael Paglia and Diane Wray Tomasso, *The Mid-Century Modern House in Denver* (Denver: HD, 2007), 140. The latter book also discusses the Bill Grant House, 45. Gene Cervi reviewed the life of Ralph Radetsky in *CJ*, October 18, 1967, p. 36. Also see *DP*, October 15, 1967, p. 3, and Mark Foster, *Citizen Quigg* (Golden: Fulcrum, 2006), 101, 112, 127–29, 150. Margaret Picher, "Eugene Cervi and *Cervi's Rocky Mountain Journal*" (Ph.D. dissertation, DU, 1986), glances at Radetsky in the context of the career of Cervi. *RMJ*, January 28, 1976, p. 31, was a brief profile of Martha Radetsky as a lobbyist. *RMN*, August 6, 1985, p. 15, reported her death.

Newspaper accounts of the romance of Cora Arnold and Albino Chavarria are *DR*, November 19, 1903, p. 7, *DP*, March 24, 1930, p. 1, and December 19, 1939, p. 8. Stephen H. Hart feted James Grafton Rogers, "A Humanist of the Deepest and Widest Tradition," *CM*, 50:3 (Summer 1973), 183–95. He repeated the tribute in *CL*, 18:7 (July 1989), 1294–97. CHS has an excellent tape of Rogers' reminiscences. *In the Shadow of the Klan*, 248–58, integrates Minnie Love into the KKK story. *WPP*, October 1999, p. 20, glanced at Steven Ells.

Chapter Six

Northwest of Washington Park

*D*istinctive structures stand between Washington Park and Cherry Creek near South Downing Street. This area brings together the exclusiveness of the Country Club with the middle-class character of West Washington Park. It was once the home of a distinguished hotel and the city's foremost apartment house while stores near Alameda Avenue and South Downing Street have served the neighborhood.

Illustrative of the mansions dotting the section is the Henry Wilcox Manor at 1134 Bayaud Avenue, also having the address of 101 South Downing Street. Born in Mississippi in 1858, Wilcox joined the Creede silver rush in 1890. There he represented eastern investors. Within a few years, having made his fortune, he moved to Denver where he operated a municipal bond house, Henry Wilcox and Son with Earl Wilcox. The latter occupied the house at 1112 Bayaud Avenue while his father dwelt at 112 South Corona Street.

The elder Wilcox was fascinated by the beauty of an adjacent dairy farm at the southwest corner of South Downing Street and Bayaud Avenue which had lush landscaping. Looking for a tranquil new home for his wife Mary, he oversaw the erection of a 3,700-square foot villa on five lots there in 1901. Included were lush gardens and a flock of peacocks and flamingos. The patio featured oriental carpets. "A world of strife locked out. A world of love locked in," declared a plaque on the patio wall. During the next decade, Wilcox continually remodeled and expanded the house.

In his new abode, Wilcox looked out at the streetcar stop across South Downing Street during the winter of 1904. Observing some women freezing as they

162

Photo by Phil Goodstein

The 1904-vintage streetcar shelter at the southeast corner of Bayaud Avenue and South Downing Street has survived into the 21st century as a place to wait for the bus.

waited for the trolley, he put up a simple shelter for streetcar passengers which matched his green-painted house. Wilcox oversaw the maintenance of the haven until his death in October 1918 at the start of the flu pandemic. Until he passed away, he had been a big World War I patriot, serving on the local draft board.

After Wilcox's death, owners transformed his residence into Green Gables Apartments. The son of an old friend, George Karstedt, adopted the trolley station. After Karstedt left Denver in the 1940s, no one cared for what was then a bus stop for route #73. The shelter increasingly suffered vandalism while it decayed. (Numerous streetcar shelters once dotted the city. Virtually all of them disappeared in the 1940s and 1950s.)

In 1980, the Regional Transportation District, as the successor of the trolley system, planned to demolish the shelter as an eyesore. Few knew much about the structure. A call for information about it in the *Washington Park Profile* led to an amazing outpouring of data. In the process, George Karstedt, who had long lived in Longmont, shared his memories of the erection. Wilcox's great-granddaughter also appeared, urging the preservation of the edifice. On this basis, led by Denver native, journalist, and gardener Julie Hutchinson who lived nearby, locals formed the Friends of the Downing Street Waiting Station. They oversaw its restoration, dedicating it anew on August 1, 1981. The renovated building included plexiglas windows and brick pavers from parts of the demolished Daniels & Fisher Department Store. October 1988 saw a refurbishment of the waiting house by members of Boy Scout troop #5.

With money from a bond issue for park and road improvements, in 2002 the city redesigned the intersection of Bayaud Avenue and South Downing Street. In the process, it decreed that the South Marion Street Parkway directly connected with South Downing Street at the shelter. As part of the effort, workers moved the waiting station away from the street, incorporating it into the parkway landscaping. (Some stories report that the shelter was originally located across the street.) While bus passengers continue to use the waiting station, they have constantly to get up to see if a bus is approaching. Maintenance crews spruced up the facility around 2006.

The effort relocating the shelter also saw the installation of a sidewalk/bike path along the west side of the Country Club. That organization had never placed a sidewalk there or along its southern boundary on Bayaud Avenue. The more the city helped the Country Club, the more the golf course emphasized its privacy walls. About the same time locals saved the streetcar station, a developer transformed the Wilcox Manor into 12 condominiums in 1981–82, adding new units and garages of frame construction. Far from keeping the green paint scheme of Green Gables, the condo association painted the complex gray.

Down the block, at 155 South Downing, is the 1909-vintage stone-faced Bradbury Elkins House. It includes a tunnel under the street, connecting with 152 South Downing Street, a residence with a concrete veneer designed to look like stone. (Members of the Elkins family were cement finishers.) All sorts of tall tales surround the Elkins residence, including that it was an old stagecoach stop, speakeasy, and bordello. None of the stories holds up on a close examination. The tunnel, incidentally, was sealed off years ago on the east side while remaining visible in the basement of the Elkins dwelling.

Across the alley, down the block, events could sometimes be explosive. At least that was the fate of the house at 186 South Corona Street. On the evening of March 5, 2005, a blast destroyed the residence, bringing down power lines. Such was the end of its owner/occupant Louis Nyiri. An artist with a gallery at 123 West Alameda Avenue, he had the house on the market. Badly suffering from depression and financial reverses, he blew himself up in it on his 40th birthday. Building inspectors ruled the remnants unsafe, ordering the demolition of the residence. By the summer of 2007, a new structure had replaced the ghost house.

The Norman and Country Club Gardens

At the same time the Country Club was emerging and Henry Wilcox was living in his idyllic villa in the early 20th century, a small farmhouse stood near the northwest corner of South Downing Street and Bayaud Avenue. Two elderly women occupied it, grazing a few cows and horses on their land. In the 1920s, the real estate became home of the "Aristocrat of Apartments." Such was the slogan of the Norman, the six-story apartment building which helped define the West Country Club.

William Norman Bowman designed the tower as his home. Born in upstate New York in 1868, he suffered a hard childhood after his father was badly injured in a sawmill accident in 1879. Apprenticing as a carpenter, he eventually landed up in Michigan where he studied under Elijah E. Myers, the architect who designed the Colorado Capitol. Bowman settled in Denver in 1910 after practicing his profession in Detroit, Cincinnati, and Indianapolis. During the next couple of decades, he achieved great success, being responsible for such structures as the

The vine-covered Norman at the northwest corner of Bayaud Avenue and South Downing Street has defined elite apartment living west of the Country Club since it went up in 1924.

Mountain States Telephone Building, Park Hill Methodist Church, the Colburn and Cosmopolitan hotels, Cole and Byers junior high schools, and the headquarters of El Jebel Shrine.

Bowman was among the very few who believed that the Barnum neighborhood, near West Sixth Avenue and Federal Boulevard, was slated to emerge as the city's prestige area when he built his idyllic home at 325 King Street in 1910. He called it Yamecila for his wife, Alice May Kniffin, a journalist from Grand Rapids, Michigan, spelling her name backward. In 1924, he set to work on the Norman as both its designer and developer.

The architect emphasized luxury and beauty in the West Country Club highrise. He enhanced the colonial revival building with marble entry walls, nine-foot-high ceilings, mahogany doors, and terrazzo bathroom floors. The Norman offered tenants carhop, laundry, and maid service. At a time when electric ice-making machines were a novelty, the apartment house provided residents with unlimited ice. The goal, advertisements announced, was to "surround its dwellers with more of an atmosphere of refinement." Before long, members of high society who did not desire to live in houses flocked to the Norman. For years, it was the city's most prestigious apartment address. Among those calling it home was the author of numerous westerns, William MacLeod Raine. Bowman financed the Norman with bonds paying 6.5 percent interest through a Chicago investment house.

Some units had more than 2,000 square feet. They included sunrooms, maid's quarters, and chromium-plated heat registers. Elevator operators assisted tenants with packages. The 55-car garage included a gasoline pump and a car wash. Rents were up to $225.00 a month at a time a nice, middle-class home rented for about $50.00 to $75.00.

Despite such opulence, Bowman did not do too well at the Norman. In 1935, he lost his interest in it when the courts auctioned it off for $164,000 to help pay the $313,132 in defaulted mortgage bonds on the structure. The architect stayed there as a tenant until his death on August 28, 1944, constantly trying to redeem his interest in the apartment house. Melvin Schlesinger, a retired army officer, owned and operated the building from 1949 to 1971, running it with a strict military discipline. On the side, Schlesinger was Santa Claus at the annual Children's Hospital Christmas party.

Country Club Gardens is the complex directly south of the Norman stretching to Ellsworth Avenue between South Downing and South Ogden streets. Built in 1939–40, it includes 187 units with 722 total rooms. The firm of Fisher, Fisher, & Hubell (the successor to Fisher & Fisher) designed it, claiming to follow the best of garden city planning principles.

The complex went up after quite a struggle with city hall. The developer originally proposed erecting Country Club Gardens with six-inch walls opposed to the building code which mandated 12–inch-thick exterior walls. The administration permitted the contractor to provide a 22–foot setback from the Downing Street

Photo by Phil Goodstein

A gazebo is on the lushly landscaped east lawn of Country Club Gardens, an apartment complex on the block south of Ellsworth Avenue between South Ogden and South Downing streets.

Parkway opposed to the required 35 feet. Boettcher interests owned the land and were part of a consortium of 12 local investors who financed the $1 million effort which the Federal Housing Administration guaranteed.

The first tenants moved into units in late 1940. Demand was less than supply. The city still suffered from the Depression. Only with the onset of World War II and the area's extreme housing shortage during and immediately after the fighting did the project fill to capacity. Before long, planners cited Country Club Gardens as a model of what modern, low-rise apartment design should be.

In the mid-1980s, residents of Country Club Gardens, along with those at the Norman and others in the area, complained about their new neighbor, Country Club Towers. Pat Broe built it in 1985–86 through his Broe Companies at the northeast corner of Bayaud Avenue and South Ogden Street where the parking garage of the Norman had stood. Controversy surrounded the owner and the project into the 21st century.

After starting out in small real estate investments in 1971, Broe greatly profited by syndicating Eagle Vail, a resort ski community. He eventually put together the deal that saw the erection of the Tabor Center on two blocks of prime 16th Street property in 1984 as the last part of the Skyline Urban Renewal Project. Broe further invested in railroads and came to own valuable properties which had once been part of the empire of Great Western Sugar.

In 1983, Broe's NewHeight Group bought the Norman, Country Club Gardens, and surrounding property from the Denver Real Estate Investment Association. The latter had acquired Country Club Gardens in 1963 and the Norman in 1971. The new owner immediately carved the Norman into 50 condominiums. In the process, NewHeight arranged to have the building listed in the National Register of Historic Places as a way of receiving tax credits for its renovation. Denver decreed the Norman a landmark on July 16, 2002.

The 183-unit, 22-story Country Club Towers cost $25 million. Those living nearby, especially in the Norman, immediately yelped that Country Club Towers did not fit in with the existing buildings. They observed it blocked the sun and interfered with their views of the mountains. A cultural clash also occurred between the sedate, upper-middle-class residents of the Norman and the younger, party-oriented renters at Country Club Towers. Some of those in Country Club Towers especially treasured Ogden Street South, a neighborhood bar at 103 South Ogden Street. The pub flourished beginning in the 1980s as a spot featuring live entertainment. Others bitterly complained about the presence of the tavern, finding it extremely noisy and a general neighborhood nuisance.

Country Club Towers was only the beginning of Broe's plans. His NewHeight Group hoped to put up three comparable highrises—that was the reason for the plural in the name of Country Club Towers. A downturn in the market stalemated such plans. In 1998, with South Denver real estate once more booming, Broe again sought to reshape the area. He announced his intention of tearing down Country Club Gardens for skyscrapers with a total of 750 luxury units.

Members of the Country Club joined those threatened with displacement by Broe's project. The former insisted that a tower did not belong west of the golf

Photo by Phil Goodstein

*Country Club Towers at the northeast corner of South Ogden Street
and Cedar Avenue literally towers over neighborhood houses.*

course which would block their view of the mountains. Despite such complaints,
a couple of skyscrapers went up in the late 20th century to the west of the Country
Club at 25 Downing Street at the behest of developer Stephen Owen. Still, residents protested Broe's suggestions as completely out of scale. To keep him from
tearing down Country Club Gardens, friends of the apartment complex asked the
Denver Landmark Preservation Commission to declare the garden city project a
landmark embodying the history, heritage, and architecture of the neighborhood.

A prolonged fight ensued. Broe modified his plans, cutting his proposal to 600
and then 400 units even while his lawyer observed that the existing zoning allowed for up to 1,000 units while pointing out there were other 20-story buildings
in the area. After 22 meetings in the course of the next three years, complete with
six continuances, in 2001 the Landmark Commission reached a seeming compro-
mise. Country Club Gardens, it ruled, was partially worthy of preservation. As
such, the body mandated that five of the project's buildings remain standing. Broe,
however, could tear down the parking structures, which dated from 1950, while
erecting three towers with a maximum height of 300 feet each (about 30 stories).
The developer further had the right to construct an additional five buildings of up
to six stories. Two existing midrise structures along South Ogden Street would
come down as part of the effort. The company had ten years to begin the effort.

By the time city council ratified the deal in December 2001, the economy was
in chaos in the wake of 9/11 and the collapse of many high-tech stocks. Nothing,

consequently, was immediately done about transforming Country Club Gardens. Five years later, Broe revived the effort. However, rather than proceeding according to the 2001 agreement, he wanted to modify it with two 26-story towers while demolishing two dozen to three dozen existing houses west of South Ogden Street. Among those pushing the amended effort was Tina Bishop, a landscape architect who had been a member of the Landmark Commission at the time of the 2001 agreement. After leaving the city agency, she worked as a consultant on the project for Broe. New disagreements followed, signs of how the extreme popularity of the West Country Club threatened the buildings which had made the area what it was.

The Park Lane Hotel

The Park Lane Hotel once linked the West Country Club with Washington Park proper. A vanished landmark, it occupied the block bordered by South Marion and South Lafayette streets between Dakota and Virginia avenues. The lodge was part of a building boom in the mid-1920s that saw the erection of the Norman. About the time the Aristocrat of Apartments was arising, Paul Stein eyed the real estate directly north of the park. An architect, developer, and hotel manager, he had recently arrived in Denver from Chicago. Emulating the Windy City where numerous skyscrapers were arising on Lake Shore Drive next to Lake Michigan, Stein figured Denver needed a palatial structure overlooking Smith Lake.

With the financial backing from the Zang family, Stein procured a building permit for the hotel on May 27, 1926. The 12-story, $2 million tower opened on June 16, 1928. The 225-room facility included 134 apartments ranging from one to five rooms. Many tenants leased suites for years on end. From the beginning, the Park Lane was more a residence for locals than a source of lodging for travelers. As was the case with the Norman, the hotel was an address of distinction.

In 1937, Stein installed a pipe organ in the lobby. By this time, the first and second floors were home to a lounge, barber and beauty shops, and other businesses. The Colonial Room on the first floor was the site of receptions and weddings. Limousine service took tenants to and from downtown on shopping expeditions and to theaters. The Park Lane billed itself as the "Friendliest Hotel in the West."

Twelve substantial bungalow cottages dotted the grounds of the hotel—they mostly predated it. The Park Lane modeled them on elite residences in the shadow of the Beverly Wilshire in Hollywood. The yard included two nine-hole putting greens, a swimming pool, two tennis courts, and a handball court. In addition to a large parking lot, the hotel had a garage at the southeast corner of South Lafayette Street and Dakota Avenue capable of storing 200 automobiles.

Among those living on the grounds were United States Senator Eugene Millikin (1942–57) and financier Courtland Dines. Sherman T. Brown, part of the Henry C. Brown family, was another Park Lane resident, having his quarters in a hotel bungalow at 401 South Lafayette Street. Broadway Department Store owner Joseph M. Cones occupied the house at 490 South Marion Street. An early resident of a Park Lane bungalow was Henry J. Arnold, mayor of Denver in 1912–13. He died at his home at 1312 Dakota Avenue on November 22, 1926. For a while, Major Fred W. "Freddy" Bonfils, a nephew of *Denver Post* publisher Frederick Bonfils, was in the house at 401 South Lafayette Street.

During her last years, Seraphine Pisko (1861–1942) lived in the Park Lane. A powerhouse in countless charity efforts during the late 19th and early 20th centuries, she was long the secretary of National Jewish Hospital and the president of the Jewish Relief Society of Denver. Both the South Denver Women's Association and the Park Lane Delphian Society met at the hotel, discussing politics, literature, and current events.

During the early 1930s, Park Lane manager Stein was most active in the South Denver Civic Association, the business organization projecting itself as the South Side chamber of commerce. He showed up on the board of numerous planning and improvement ventures. The hotel, however, never lived up to his expectations. Opened on the eve of the Depression, the Park Lane experienced endless financial difficulties. Creditors received 23 cents on the dollar after it plunged into bankruptcy in 1939. The court raised $470,000 when it auctioned off the hotel, $154,843 of which went to pay back taxes. Loyalty Group Insurance of New York, foreclosing on the mortgage, came to own the facility. It found no buyers when it offered it for $750,000.

When the hotel again faced foreclosure in October 1942, David Phillips, a veteran New York hotel operator, purchased the Park Lane for about $1 million. The lodge continued to have rough sailing until December 1948 when Benjamin F. Weinberg of Kansas City purchased it for $1.25 million. Weinberg bought it amidst a $300,000 remodeling effort. He specialized in taking over ailing hotels, restoring them to vigor, and selling them at a profit.

Weinberg made the Park Lane a destination for locals. In addition to emphasizing its services as a residential hotel, he arranged for radio station KTLN, 1280 AM, to begin broadcasting from the hotel in 1949. Its studio was on the ground floor with a glass booth whereby passersby could look at the radio personalities in action. Among them was Joe Flood who had the early morning show, complete with a 6:00 AM ringing of bells as part of his routine calling on listeners to wake up. (Flood was the son of the longtime principal of Englewood High School—that suburb remembers her with Flood Middle School at South Broadway and Kenyon Avenue.) In 1952, the Park Lane was the home of the city's first television station, Channel Two.

The same year Channel Two went on the air, Weinberg purchased the Swiss Haven, a mountain resort near Evergreen. Besides making it his summer home, he announced Park Lane guests could stay there at no extra charge. Shuttle service transported the Park Lane clientele to the mountains.

Already in May 1949, Weinberg had opened the Top of the Park. A fancy nightclub in the Park Lane's penthouse, it featured both fine dining and live entertainment, hosting some of the city's top dance and jazz bands—KTLN sometimes broadcast their concerts. During the next decade, the Top of the Park was the city's foremost destination night spot. High school groups sometimes arranged special ceremonies at it.

The Park Lane Hotel stood on the east side of South Marion Street Parkway between Dakota and Virginia avenues.

A roof garden, the Marine Deck, complemented the Top of the Park. The luxury spot dated from 1936. It had an ocean-going theme that included lifeboats, fishing equipment, and a pilot's wheel. During the summer, the Marine Deck encouraged locals and visitors to patronize it where they could dance under the stars. After the Marine Deck opened, the Denver Naval Officers Club occupied space on the first floor which had been the hotel's cocktail lounge.

Though he had no connection with the Top of the Park, Vincent Youmans (1898–1945) made the Park Lane his home. Starting out as a highly skilled pianist on Broadway, he wrote numerous pop songs including "Tea for Two." Most of all, he achieved acclaim for his score of the 1925 musical hit *No, No Nanette*. After convalescing in Colorado Springs from a breakdown, Youmans moved into the Park Lane in 1935 with his wife, a former star in the Ziegfeld Follies. He drove through the area in a wide array of fancy sports cars, staying at the Park Lane until his death.

On occasion, entertainment at the Top of the Park was extremely rancorous. At least it was on the night of October 2, 1959, when Eddie Bohn and his wife Janet dined there with Elwood Edwards and his wife. During the 1920s, the six-foot-four, 210-pound Bohn had been the state heavyweight boxing champion and the sparring partner of Jack Dempsey. That was when he met Edwards, a car dealer who had also been in the ring.

In addition to serving in the state Senate in 1937–38, Bohn was an irremovable fixture on the Colorado Athletic Commission from 1934 to 1979. The body regulated boxing. Proponents praised Bohn as a most knowledgeable administrator who knew and prohibited every dirty trick of boxing promoters. Critics argued that he gave special favors to boxers and promoters who patronized his Pig 'n Whistle, a combination bar, restaurant, motel, and filling station he ran at the northwest corner of West Colfax Avenue and Wolff Street. At times, Bohn was extremely insensitive, using derogatory terms to identify members of ethnic, racial, and religious groups. Eventually, Governor Richard Lamm got the legislature to abolish the Athletic Commission to get rid of Bohn as its head.

As the Bohn-Edwards party listened to a jazz band at the Top of the Park, it was disturbed by a party of drunken, obnoxious chiropractors. Janet Bohn approached them, asking them to keep it down so she could enjoy the music. One of them insulted her. The 57-year-old Bohn thereupon told the chiropractors that he just hoped he had not heard what he thought he had. Saying that, he settled back at his table. The party of seven or so young men, believing they would have no trouble against a couple of middle-aged men, thereupon jumped Bohn. With the help of

DPL

This aerial of the Park Lane Hotel, near Virginia Avenue and South Marion Street Parkway, shows the cottages surrounding it.

Edwards, Bohn systematically pulverized the drunks. (A different account had the fight between two rowdies and Bohn and Edwards before upwards of 20 others joined the fray.) In the wake of the commotion, the Park Lane banned Bohn for life from the premises. Before he died in 1990, he liked to recall that he was still around; the Park Lane was not.

Nothing came of Weinberg's 1953 plan to build a second Park Lane tower with 150 rooms. The promoter sold the revitalized Park Lane Hotel in May 1955 for $1.75 million to Joseph Massaglia Jr. of Santa Monica, California. In May 1960, W. L. Tooley of San Diego purchased it. He announced plans for an ornate expansion, including a convention hall holding 1,000 to 1,200 people, and a bubble over the swimming pool.

Before anything happened, Tooley discovered that Massaglia and the Park Lane were in severe financial trouble. The sale did not help. In July 1961, Weinberg began foreclosing on the hotel. His $365,935 offer was the sole bid at the bankruptcy auction.

Weinberg once more dedicated himself to modernizing the Park Lane. A $250,000 remodeling included adding the 24-hour-a-day Stage Coffee Shop in the lobby. He transformed the Top of the Park into the Sky Room, featuring touring national singers and comics. The Playgirl Lounge was the name of the ground-floor bar.

No sooner had Weinberg completed these changes than he sold the Park Lane for a second time in December 1962 to Marion Limited for around $1.3 million. The new owner was a local real estate syndicate led by veteran broker Lloyd C. Fulenwider in association with Charles Anema Jr. The purchaser planned to convert the Park Lane into condominiums, adding 12-story residential towers to the north and south of the hotel. Around this time, demolition crews destroyed the adjacent cottages. The new management converted the Sky Room back to the Top of the Park, emphasizing its food service. It poured about $300,000 and $400,000 into the complex. In the process, it dropped live entertainment at the Top of the Park on March 11, 1963.

Marion Limited encountered problems in transforming the hotel into condos. After it walked away from the project, Weinberg repossessed the hotel in 1965. By this time, the Junior League of Denver made the Park Lane its home, complete with a room where it stored costumes and props for its Children's Theater. As Weinberg resumed ownership of the hotel, Fulenwider sued Anema over disputes stemming from their failed Park Lane venture.

Upon resuming control of the Park Lane, Weinberg claimed the hotel had the finest kitchen in town. He sold the Park Lane for the last time in 1966 to a group headed by Doug Bell of Bell Plumbing and H. W. "Bill" Hewson of Hewson Construction of Texas. Not wishing to fail with the hotel, the new owners resolved to demolish it. They began by auctioning off furniture, fixtures, and memorabilia, including sheets upon which the Beatles had once supposedly slept.

This was part of Park Lane lore. In 1964, when the Beatles came to Denver during their inaugural American tour, they stayed at the Brown Palace. To get away from the groupies, they secretly relocated to the Park Lane—or so South

Denver mythology insisted. (The mid-1960s saw members of another popular rock group, Herman's Hermits, stay at the Park Lane. Fans descended on the lodge to see them.)

In March 1966, Bell and Hewson invited the Denver Fire Department to assist in tearing down the Park Lane by setting it afire. The force agreed, seeing the wrecking of the building as an ideal way by which firefighters could practice high-rise rescue skills while learning how to put out blazes in towers. For a couple of weeks firefighters were omnipresent in the scorched landmark, setting and extinguishing numerous blazes.

After pondering a zoning change to put in a commercial development, in 1968 developers started work on a replacement for the Park Lane. Originally, they planned a $14 million complex of four 20-story residential towers and a 16-story office building. They christened it Park Mayfair South after Park Mayfair near Hale Parkway and Eudora Street. Workers topped off the first monolith at 480 South Marion Street in May 1970 when promoters celebrated the 20-story, 205-foot-tall edifice as the highest brick structure of its type in the world. The two buildings directly to the north followed in the mid-1970s.

While locals complained that the highrises were inappropriate for the area, being visible for miles around, the apartment houses filled rapidly as prestige units. Seeing this and the growing popularity of condominiums, the office building never arose. The northernmost part of the Park Lane project, Marion Park, went up as a condo tower in 1976. It is more ornate than its southern neighbors. The last project did so well that the owner of the Park Lane apartments converted the three other towers, the home of 342 units, to condos in 1979.

Steele School

*D*irectly north of the Park Lane complex is Steele School. DPS acquired the land between South Marion and South Lafayette streets from Alameda Avenue to Dakota Avenue in 1910 where it planned Lake View School. Before work got underway, Colorado Chief Justice Robert Wilbur Steele suddenly died in October. Many mourned him. At a time when extremely dubious rulings and ethics were the dominating themes of the state Supreme Court, they heralded Steele as "the just judge," a man who frequently dissented from the rest of the court. His widow, Anna, lobbied the school board to dedicate the building in her husband's memory, donating a plaque, his portrait, a flag, and 600 books to the facility. (There was no connection between Justice Robert Wilbur Steele and an earlier Robert Wilbur Steele who was governor of the forerunner of the Territory of Colorado, Jefferson Territory, in 1859–61.)

Prior to the erection of the school, a section of the City Ditch flowed through the land. A grove of cottonwood trees lined the waterway. Locals, especially before the completion of the Washington Park beach, sometimes used the canal as a swimming hole. In the course of the excavation for the school, workers piled a mountain of dirt near the corner of South Lafayette Street and Dakota Avenue which was a favorite play place for children. Architect David W. Dryden designed the $116,030.98 building which opened in September 1913.

The original Steele School was a beaux-arts building opened in 1913. Architect Merrill Hoyt completely remodeled it in 1930.

Besides pulling in neighborhood children, Steele included an open-air school for consumptive youths. At a time when tuberculosis was a ravishing killer, many physicians argued the best treatment of the disease was plenty of fresh air and sunshine. Toward this end, DPS arranged for students with the TB to attend classes in rooms with huge screens. McKinley (1275 South Logan Street) and Park Hill (19th Avenue and Elm Street) schools were the other inaugural DPS facilities for tubercular students. Ideally, the well-ventilated classrooms would not only help stricken children recover from tuberculosis, but they would also prevent sickly youths from getting the disease. Soon Cheltenham School (the northwest corner of West Colfax Avenue and Irving Street) became the system's primary TB facility. Within a few years, Steele ended its open-air school. Together with Park Hill and McKinley, the city had at a peak nine open-air classrooms.

As the Washington Park neighborhood burgeoned in the 1920s, ever more pupils attended the increasingly overcrowded Steele School. On April 23, 1930, dignitaries dedicated an addition that was part of a total remodeling of the schoolhouse. As part of the job, architect Merrill Hoyt completely redesigned the building, placing southwestern motifs on the exterior and adding a new kindergarten. Allen True decorated the latter with a mural depicting the joys of childhood. At times, students used the kindergarten room as the lunchroom.

From 1930 to 1967, Mary Lou Spelman ran the kindergarten. Supporters saw her as something of a neighborhood godmother. Detractors, especially by the 1960s, were uneasy about her, thinking she had been at the school far too long.

For decades, Steele staged extravagantly costumed Christmas programs. The school was packed during the 1960s, having an official capacity of 480. Enrollment was less than 200 by the 1970s. During the era of court-ordered busing for integration, Steele was paired with Crofton School at 2409 Arapahoe Street. That academy, recalling educator Mary Crofton, was next to a housing project, having an official capacity of 240 students. Most who walked to it were of Hispanic heritage.

Initially, children spent half a day at Steele and half a day at Crofton. Before long, Crofton was the home of kindergarten and grades one through three; Steele also had a kindergarten and grades four through six. (Until the late 1980s, elementary schools were from kindergarten through sixth grade.) The enrollment of the South Denver school went from 172 in 1974 to 146 four years later once the impact of busing had been fully felt. It gained a surge of enrollment when Washington Park School closed in 1982. (The administration's numbers about Steele's capacity changed constantly. At one point, for example, it listed Steele as being able to educate 585 pupils. At another time, it stated the school could handle 494 learners. The confused numbers were illustrative of the system's extremely problematic reports about itself.)

Steele supporters sought to counter negative community perceptions of busing. Parents, teachers, and friends of the schools formed SCOPE, the Steele–Crofton Organization of Parents and Educators. While Steele and Crofton were supposedly twins with joint activities, the contrast between them illustrated how busing did not work. While Crofton children were usually bused to Steele for the upper grades, many Steele students never attended Crofton during first, second, and third grades. Rather, their parents arranged for them to attend private schools during

Photo by Phil Goodstein

Simple one-story cottage cabins were prime housing stock near Steele School during most of the 20th century. Some such units survive, such as this house at 211 South Downing Street.

those years. Steele-based students recalled the equipment at Crofton was defi-nitely inferior to that in their Washington Park school.

The concerned parents of the Steele School neighborhood flocked to PTA meet-ings and other school functions. The poverty-stricken parents of many Crofton students, in contrast, were usually invisible. Many of those attending Crofton were from families desperately seeking to survive, some of whom were in home-less shelters. The parents of the Crofton children lacked the time and wealth of their Washington Park counterparts. This does not mean that the Steele parents were all affluent—many were also trying to make ends meet in the extremely economically diverse area near Washington Park in the 1970s. Most of the latter, however, were part of the upward-achieving ethos which was central to the school-busing ideal that equal education would transform all graduates into successful middle-class citizens. This was not necessarily the case with the families of those living by Crofton.

An annual Steele-Crofton house tour began in 1988 to raise money for the academies. Invariably, it focused on distinctive Washington Park houses. Spon-sors never ventured to the historic houses of the Curtis Park neighborhood close to Crofton. Besides students from Curtis Park, DPS also bused youngsters from Lowry Air Force Base to Steele School.

The Steele School house tour continued after the end of busing with Crofton in 1995. This was a year after the city declared Steele a landmark on March 23, 1994. Those committed to children, the school, and the neighborhood undertook a major landscaping project in 1997, "The Greening of Steele." Under the slogan "from gravel yard to play yard," the effort included adding trees, a hedgerow, mulch, and a rock garden. Most of all, it saw the playing fields sodded with grass. Ideally, the nature-friendly design taught students about science and the environ-ment.

Led by Anne Witwer, sponsors sold bricks to help pay for the Greening of Steele. Denver Urban Gardens joined the effort, complete with a locked-off com-munity garden near the eastern edge of the school grounds along Alameda Avenue. At one point, Steele arranged for a chef to turn its garden-fresh produce into meals for students in the lunchroom. Major remodelings of the school followed in 2002 and 2006. The latter year also saw a redesign of the landscaping, including the replacement of some of the "Greening of Steele" effort.

The school offered distinctive programs in the hope of attracting students who had a choice. Included was a British primary model and a planetarium. The latter emerged after DPS discontinued its planetarium at North High School in 1972 which had been in place for about ten years. Steele gladly accepted what was called the Apollo Model Planetarium, remodeling room 103 for it.

After the space program's popularity faded, fifth-grade teacher Ralph Sodano reintroduced the planetarium in 1989. Many students came to share his interest in astronomy. While the DPS administration was not completely happy with the effort since it was not part of the standardized testing routine, the community ap-preciated it. Students from other schools often made field trips to Steele to view the planetarium which had a 14-foot-high dome. In the 1999–2000 school year,

Steele counted 6,000 students attending programs at the planetarium. Plaques of the signs of the zodiac were installed near the main entrance while pictures of phases of the moon were along the Dakota Avenue fence. By the early 21st century, the school had classes from early childhood education through the fifth grade, having an enrollment of about 350 students instructed by 19 teachers. It adopted the Stallions as its nickname.

Aladown

Youths living close to Steele School found numerous gathering spots and play spaces. Among them was a large barn near South Humboldt Street and Virginia Avenue owned by the Blamey family. Locals, especially adolescents, used it as a theater before World War II, complete with a wooden stage and heavy curtains. During the summer, young people performed there for each other and neighbors with song-and-dance routines. Down the street was the home of a woman residents called Mrs. Newlywed: every year, she had a different husband.

Such were the memories of members of the Ott family. George and Margaret Ott were German immigrants who built a simple farmhouse around 1891 at 369 South Humboldt Street. They raised eight children there who were active through the 20th century in countless South Denver ventures. In some ways, the house reflected the evolution of the area as a whole.

The Ott family did not get natural gas until 1941. As the fuel became available and the water service of the area improved—for years, residents complained about inadequate and weak flows out of their pipes—the land around the Ott House continually developed. By the 1990s, elite Washington Park palaces had mostly displaced the first and second waves of residential units. Typical was how 369 South Humboldt Street became part of a triplex.

For years, the intersection of Alameda Avenue and South Downing Street was a center of neighborhood commerce. Competing drugstores stood at the northeast and northwest corners. The latter, abbreviating the name of the intersection, was Aladown, 295 South Downing Street. It was in a shoppette dating from 1928. Originally, a Safeway stood at 291 South Downing Street, next to Powell's at 295 South Downing Street, a branch of an apothecary that operated at South Pearl Street and Louisiana Avenue. The partnership of James A. Early and J. Clifton Levin long ran the West Country Club pharmacy as Aladown. Eventually, a filling station/convenience store replaced the shoppette.

While Aladown had its loyal patrons, others preferred the drugstore across the street, Jackson's, at 290 South Downing Street. It started out in the early 20th century as Aspen's Pharmacy, operated by Charles B. Aspen of 364 South Franklin Street. By the 1920s, it was Ulley and Jackson Drugs. Arthur C. Jackson of 555 South Corona Street ran it as Jackson Pharmacy until 1935 when he sold it to the unrelated Robert L. Jackson of 665 South Gaylord Street who renamed it Jackson Drugs, an apothecary sometimes calling itself Jackson's Cut Rate Drug Store. It included a contract post office and a soda fountain. Liquor sales were a major part of its revenue. Ellie Weckbaugh ordered the booze for her parties from it.

A shoppette at the northeast corner of Alameda Avenue and South Downing Street was once the home of Jackson Drugs, a neighborhood pharmacy.

Jackson Drugs had a close working relationship with South High School. It employed South students as soda jerkers and delivery drivers. Many South graduates stayed at the store as they worked their way through the University of Denver. Robert Jackson presented returning veterans from South with new suits after World War II.

Sherman Rich bought the store in 1967 from the widow of Robert Jackson. The new owner eventually relocated the pharmacy to a suburban-style shoppette to the north where the store operated at 266 South Downing Street until March 1992. Its closing came amidst the shutdown of numerous independent drugstores. A new Walgreen's next to the Mayan Theatre near Second Avenue and Broadway took much of the business which had once been Jackson's. Numerous other businesses came and went from the shoppette around the second Jackson's, including nightclubs that patrons entered via the alley of South Downing/South Marion streets.

From 1949 into the 1980s, Busy Corner at 284 South Downing Street complemented Jackson Drugs. The Earl Johnston family, the owners of the shoppette, helped establish Busy Corner next to its real estate agency at 280 South Downing Street. For some years, Meredith W. and Clara L. Druif ran the store. Eventually, Jesse and Velma Decker were the proprietors. Busy Corner was something of a neighborhood convenience store, including the post office contract station after it left Jackson's. A creamery and a jewelry and watch repair store were nearby.

Between February 16, 1913, and August 31, 1918, the neighborhood postal station was at 939 Cedar Avenue. That was once the home of another pharmacy, Ager-Tabell Drugs, which dated from the early 20th century. Eventually, the apothecary evolved into a liquor store amidst an otherwise residential district.

The post office placed a contract station in Jackson's on September 5, 1929. A new owner closed the post office at Busy Corner in 1980. The hardware store did not survive long thereafter. The contract post office subsequently operated out of an antique store at 1211 Alameda Avenue between August 20, 1981, and June 10, 1988. That location was once a Piggly Wiggly which was the center of a milk boycott in 1945 during a bitter union dispute. The post office subsequently moved back to Jackson's, not surviving the drugstore.

Starbucks eventually had a branch in the old Piggly Wiggly. This was apropos. For many years, James "Jim" Sunderland Jr. was a most active, outspoken Jesuit priest who crusaded against the death penalty. He grew up just to the north of the coffee chain at 234 South Downing Street where his father, James Sr., was in the coffee business. The elder Sunderland often roasted coffee in the garage of the house whereby the aroma of the beverage was omnipresent near the Alameda and Downing intersection. Before settling in the West Country Club location, the elder Sunderland had run the Alameda Grocery at 316 South Broadway with his wife Anna when the family lived at 260 South Lincoln Street. For a while, Alameda Grocery operated the South Broadway Theatre at 281 South Broadway.

Until the 1950s, a grocery store was also at the southwest corner of Alameda Avenue and South Downing Street. For years, it was part of a chain, Red and White. Various owners came and went from it including Charles R. and Hazel Milliken who lived directly south of it at 309 South Downing Street. Eventually, the Milliken family had a set of other stores around the metropolis. Neighbor-

Photo by Phil Goodstein

A Starbucks occupies an art deco building at 1211 Alameda Avenue, a structure that was once home of the neighborhood grocery store. An antique store made the 1211 Alameda structure its quarters in the 1990s before the building was redeveloped in 1998.

hood-oriented shops lined Alameda Avenue to the alley of South Downing/South Corona streets.

In the 1960s, a hamburger stand, Scotty's, replaced the grocery. A franchise which aspired to rival McDonald's, its building included a fallout shelter. The structure was subsequently the home of the Park Lane Cafe. The owner tore it down for a replacement shoppette in 1996. Mike Morris, a bicycle racer, obtained the restaurant the next year, turning it into a bicyclist bar, the Handle Bar & Grill. The interior featured numerous bicycle bodies hanging from the ceiling. Before it was sold to a restaurant group in 2006, the eatery had a sign declaring "We ain't no chain."

A Note on Sources:

DP, October 24, 1918, reported the life and death of Henry Wilcox. *WPP*, August 1981, p. 1, mentioned the proposal to turn the Wilcox House into condos. The same issue, p. 3, looked at the history and renovation of the streetcar shelter. Also see LWV, *Washington Park Promenade*, 19, and clippings in FF 1 of folio four of the WPGC papers at DPL, including undated columns by Frances Melrose in the *News* and Jack Kisling in the *Post*.

Sue Grant of 152 South Downing Street discussed her house with me in a phone conversation about 2000. *WPP*, August 1997, highlighted the tunnels at 155 South Downing Street. *DP*, March 6, 2005, p. 2C, reported the blast at 186 South Corona Street.

Margaret O'Neill, *The Original Eight* ([Denver]: n.p., [c. 1986]), 81, recalls the Wilcox Manor and the adjacent farm that became the Norman. Artha Pacha Frickel glances at the career of William Norman Bowman in Noel and Norgren, *City Beautiful*, 191–92. *RMN*, August 29, 1944, p. 16, was his obituary. The Office of Archaeology and Historic Preservation of CHS has issued a short brochure on him. Also see Sharon R. Catlett, *Farmlands, Forts, and Country Life* (Boulder: Westcliffe, 2007), 65–67, and *RMN*, October 25, 1941. *RMN*, October 15, 1935, p. 8, told of the foreclosure sale of the Norman. *DP*, April 29, 1946, p. 4, reported that the Bowman estate lost a court case seeking to redeem the foreclosure. NRHP and DLPC files outline and history and architecture of the Norman. LWV, *Washington Park Promenade*, 18, reported the $225.00 rent. Alvan Morrison reminisced about the building and Melvin Schlesinger in a letter of November 22, 1991. *DP*, September 1, 1949, p. 2, mentioned Schlesinger's purchase of the property; it told of his sale of the Norman, December 9, 1971, p. 49. A copy of the bond prospectus for the Norman is in Jim Turosaugh, *Neighborfest 2007*, a brochure printing historic photos of the area.

RMN October 7, 1998, p. 2B, highlighted developments at 25 Downing Street. DLPC files treat the many controversies about Country Club Gardens. Alvan Morrison related its real estate history in a letter of November 22, 1991. *Denver Business Week*, August, 1, 1983, p. 4, observed NewHeight's acquisition of the Norman and Country Club Gardens. *HD News*, February 1984, p. 1, and *Rocky Mountain Business Journal*, May 21, 1984, p. 1, featured the tax credits in the renovation of the Norman.

WPP had far and away the best coverage of the continuing fights about Broe and Country Club Gardens, e.g., August 1985, p. 1, March 2000, p. 1, July 2001, p. 10, September 2001, p. 1, October 2001, p. 19, August 2006, p. 16, October 2006, pp. 3, 13, and June 2007, p. 20. Also see *LCH*, September 2001, p. 8, and July 2007, p. 3, and *DP*, May 30, 1999, pp. 31A, 39A. *DP*, August 17, 2008, p. 1K, looked at Pat Broe's controversial business practices. Charlotte Winzenburg talked about problems with the Ogden Street South during a February 13, 2009, interview. She provided me with copies of the SCIA newsletter, reporting complaints about the bar, especially the September and October 1981 issues.

DPL has a clipping file on the Park Lane. *SDM*, August 25, 1933, p. 1, September 15, 1933, p. 1, and September 22, 1933, p. 8, heralded Paul Stein's activities in the SDCA. *RMN*, June 15, 1939, reported the bankruptcy auction of the Park Lane. *DP*, October 4, 1942, looked at David Phillips' purchase of the lodge. *RMN*, December 6, 1935, p. 5S, told of women's clubs at the hotel. Jim Peiker recalled KTLN at the Park Lane, the Joe Flood show, and high school dances at the Top of the Park in an interview on September 16, 2008. Steve Leonard discussed the Flood family and its importance in Englewood in a chat on December 26, 2008.

Ida Uchill, *Pioneers, Peddlers, and Tsadikim* (Denver: Sage Books, 1957), 146, 190, 201, 266–67, 290, chronicles the wide-ranging activities of Seraphine Pisko. Forrest Johnson, *Denver's Old Theater Row* (Denver: Bill Lay Litho, 1970), 47, 49, and Douglas R. McKay, *Asylum of the Gilded Pill* ([Denver]: CHS, 1983), 122–23, glance at the career of Vincent Youmans. Stories about Eddie Bohn were in *RMN*, February 16, 1986, p. 18M, and June 5, 1990, p. 24, *DP*, June 4, 1990, p. 1B, and *Denver Magazine*, June 1983, pp. 74–75. Bohn shared his memories of the city and the affair at the Park Lane in personal conversations at the Pig 'n Whistle in 1986–87.

SDM, September 25, 1936, touted the Marine Deck. Reviews of the Top of the Park and Weinberg's involvement with the Park Lane include *SDM*, May 6, 1949, *DP*, July 20, 1952, February 17, 1962, p. 52, January 6, 1965, p. 16, and May 19, 1963, p. 1D, *RMN*, April 17, 1948, p. 5, April 22, 1955, p. 5, February 18, 1965, p. 82, and July 30, 1965, p. 92, and *CJ*, February 21, 1962, p. 9, and September 25, 1963, p. 42. *RMN*, May 28, 1961, p. 28, emphasized the role of W. L. Tooley at the Park Lane. Dianne Clark informed me about the Beatles supposedly staying at the Park Lane in informal discussions in 1989. Harold and Carol Williams remembered the visit of Herman's Hermits to the Park Lane in an interview on August 4, 2008.

RMN, October 20, 1968, p. 60, reported the Fulenwider suit. Ellen Fisher, *Junior League of Denver* (Denver: CHS, 1993), 56, mentions the presence of the Junior League at the Park Lane. *CCN*, January 13, 1966, p. 1, told about a possible shopping complex at the hotel site. *WPP*, June 1979, p. 3, reviewed the conversion of the modern Park Lane into condos. Rudi Hartmann gave me his impressions about living in Marion Park in August 2007.

SDE, April 30, 1910, p. 1, reported DPS's plans for Steele School. I glance at Robert W. Steele in *From Sand Creek to Ludlow*, 441, 443. Walter Lawson Wilder, *Robert Wilbur Steele: Defender of Liberty* (Denver: Carson-Harper, 1913), is a biography of the justice. Also see Walter A. Steele, "Robert W. Steele," *CL*, 13:7 (July 1984), 1179–81.

UPN, October 16, 1969, plugged Steele School. Carl Ott shared his memories of early Steele School in a set of informal conversations in 1991–92. He gave me a copy of a book by his sister, Margaret O'Neill, *The Original Eight*, about the Ott family. Included are stories about the Blamey Theater and the play areas near Steele School. Ott's widow, Cathy, recalled her experiences in phone conversations in 2008. Lewis M. Terman, *Building Situation and Medical Inspection*, vol. 5 of Franklin Bobbitt et al., *Report of the School Survey—District One* (Denver: School Survey Committee, 1916), 73, mentioned the open-air school.

WPP, May 1992, p. 1, reported neighborhood concerns when DPS pondered closing Crofton. Dean Nye and Darrell Schwartzkopf recalled being bused between Crofton and Steele in a joint conversation on July 24, 2008. Nye's mother Ila reflected on parents' role at Steele in the 1970s. Carol Williams, the mother of a Steele kindergarten student, gave me her less-than-pleasant memories of Mary Lou Spelman during an interview on August 4, 2008.

DP, May 29, 2000, p. 1B, and *WPP*, January 1983, p. 3, and February 1994, p. 15, focused on the Steele School planetarium. The *Profile* saluted SCOPE in January 1983, p. 7. *DP*, August 20, 2000, p. 2B, and *WPP*, March 1997, pp. 1, 27, stressed the Greening of Steele. *WPP*, January 1997, p. 6, looked at the British primary school at Steele. Also see *Alumni Confederate*, February 2007. *DP*, October 17, 2008, p. 5B, emphasized the school's garden-lunchroom link.

Alvan Morrison remembered Jackson Drugs, Ellie Weckbaugh procuring liquor from it, the store's ties to South High, and the way Robert L. Jackson gave returning veterans suits in a letter of November 22, 1991. *WPP*, March 1992, p. 1, told of the end of the pharmacy. The same issue reported the coming of Walgreen's as did the November 1992, issue, p. 3. Ibid., November 1979, and December 1980 highlighted Busy Corner hardware. Bob Wiederspan recalled Jackson's and Aladown in a discussion on July 10, 2008. Bob Sheets gave me his version of the two stores during a conversation on December 7, 2008.

Jim Sunderland shared his experiences growing up in Denver in a few informal discussions in the mid-1990s. Gene Amole highlighted the Sunderland family's coffee business in *RMN*, January 29, 2002, p. 6A. Harold Williams reminisced about the Alameda Avenue and South Downing Street grocery in an interview on August 4, 2008. He emphasized the fallout shelter at the hamburger stand. *WPP*, June 2006, p. 6, reported the sale of the Handle Bar Grill. Other mentions of the corner are in the *Profile*, July 1994, p. 1, and October 1995, p. 11.

Chapter Seven

Bonnie Brae
and Beyond

*B*onnie Brae is off the grid. The neighborhood from South University Boulevard to South Steele Street between Exposition and Mississippi avenues emerged in the 1920s when city planners and landscape architects were beginning to reject a rigid, compass-oriented road system that ignored the topography and the natural beauty of the land. Curvilinear roads, sponsors proclaimed, would reduce outside traffic while giving residents a special sense of place.

The Kansas Pacific Railroad originally owned the real estate, receiving it from the federal government in 1870 as an incentive to build its line from Kansas City to Denver. The company sold the property as farm land. George Olinger (1882–1954) obtained the spread in the early 1920s, eyeing it as a prestigious automobile-oriented suburb.

In the early 20th century, Olinger emerged as the city's foremost mortician. Besides arranging funerals, he had his own casket factory at 15th and Platte streets and ran Crown Hill Cemetery. On the side, he sponsored the Highlander Boys, a paramilitaristic youth group long located at Fourth Avenue and Logan Street. Most of all, Olinger plunged into real estate. His land development firm was Associated Industries, an outfit which included a realty, fuel company, and clay/brick interest. The outfit was involved in the development of Wellshire, Indian Hills, and Bonnie Brae.

Engineer Frederick C. Steinhauser, a former superintendent of the Denver parks system, oversaw the development of Associated Industries projects. Landscape architect S. R. DeBoer laid out Bonnie Brae streets in 1923. The goal was to recreate the aura of a peaceful Scottish village on a rolling countryside. Gaelic for "Pleasant Hill," Bonnie Brae actually more emulated a development in Kansas City than anything found in Scotland. A close Olinger associate, Cornelius Tho-

George Olinger promoted Bonnie Brae as an exclusive, elite neighborhood, one laid out with twisting streets to emulate a romantic Scottish highlands village.

mas Flynn of 1044 South University Boulevard, helped promote and supervise the development.

Olinger grew up in North Denver near a development known as Scottish Village, close to North High School. It included twisting streets with Scottish names. Bonnie Brae gave him the opportunity to add a comparable area to South Denver. To assure its high-class orientation, Olinger insisted on restrictive covenants barring blacks, Jews, and other "undesirable" elements from the South Side settlement.

Associated Industries promised buyers a virtually self-contained community. Besides Bonnie Brae Park in the middle of the development at Kentucky Avenue and Bonnie Brae Boulevard, the promotional map showed a planned school and ballfield near the southeast corner of Exposition Avenue and South University Boulevard, land which subsequently became Bonnie Brae Baptist Church. De-Boer slated a business center for Tennessee Avenue and South Columbine Street, complete with an automotive garage. The developer set land aside near South St. Paul Street to the north of the equivalent of Tennessee Avenue for a public building. An esplanade was to link the latter with a set of fountains and pools, connecting with a church and another park along Ohio Avenue close to South Milwaukee Street. The developer never came close to following this scheme.

Associated Industries placed stone pillars at Tennessee and Kentucky avenues along South University Boulevard as entryways. In April 1925, the company gave the city title to the land that became Bonnie Brae Park. The diagonal .71-mile-

Ornate landscaping fronts some Bonnie Brae houses such as 848 South Josephine Street.

Bonnie Brae features numerous art moderne houses such as this residence at 930 Bonnie Brae Boulevard. Architect William J. Boorman designed the dwelling which went up in 1939.

long Bonnie Brae Boulevard cut through the area. In 1960, the city officially added the road to its parkway system.

Residents moved into the first Bonnie Brae houses in 1923–24. The area's twisting streets were a challenge for locals. When a conflagration broke out in the neighborhood, the fire department took quite a while in responding. The problem, it told the aggrieved homeowners, was that it had gotten lost. This led Laurence O'Neill, the department captain responsible for Bonnie Brae, to tour the neighborhood and map it so firefighters would know where to go when called.

Before Bonnie Brae could take off as an idyllic enclave, the fate of Associated Industries badly impacted the project. Olinger sold his interest in the company in 1925 to three men who had worked closely with him on it: Richard M. Crane, Errett B. Dill, and Cornelius T. Flynn. They divided the company into numerous divisions, each of which had a most convoluted financial mechanism. The whole outfit collapsed in bankruptcy in December 1928. In no time, it faced 13 separate legal actions while Dill fled to escape prosecution. The district attorney's office charged that Crane, Dill, and Flynn had looted the firm of at least $5 million. In June 1930, a jury convicted Crane and Flynn of fraud while stating that the absent Dill was the biggest scoundrel of all. Judge James C. Starkweather sentenced Crane and Flynn to four-to-six years in the penitentiary.

By the time the leaders of Associated Industries were locked away, the Great Depression had stalemated development. Few Bonnie Brae houses existed. Property owners found fees and taxes excessive to pay for street and sidewalk improvements. With the onset of the financial crisis, construction ceased. Some houses were left with excavated basements and boarded-over windows. Through the 1930s, Bonnie Brae grew on a house-by-house basis. On the positive side, this resulted in a very diverse and distinctive architecture, including residences in the trendy art moderne style of the day.

A key turning point was the planting of Bonnie Brae Park in 1936. (It is also known as Ellipse Park for Ellipse Way, the road on the west side of the elliptical-shaped greenery.) Until then, the area's slow growth combined with water short-ages had kept the city from improving the open space as the center of the neighbor-hood. DeBoer landscaped Ellipse Park. Residents moved into new houses as the economy picked up with the approach of World War II. Only after the war did Bonnie Brae come of age. Contractors completed most of the houses east of the park in the 1950s. Building sites continued to be available into the 1970s.

James G. "Jim" Patton (1902–86) was among those making Bonnie Brae his home, living at 954 Bonnie Brae Boulevard. During the 1940s, 1950s, and 1960s, he was a commanding community figure as the president of the Denver-based National Farmers Union. It promoted cooperative marketing ventures and educa-tional programs among family farmers while it pushed the fortunes of Franklin Roosevelt and liberal Democrats. Patton seemingly knew everybody. On occa-sion, pundits mentioned him as a candidate for high elective office.

The Neighborhood Radio Station

Merrie Lynn was another well-known Bonnie Brae resident. Born Mary Frances Knott, she grew up at 1636 South Downing Street, working as a teenager in the mail-order department of Montgomery Ward at South Broadway and Virginia Av-enue. After attending Asbury School and serving as head girl of Grant Junior High, she was the editor of the South High *Confederate*, graduating in 1947. She proudly recalled that three generations of her family made their way through South High. For a while, her father had been the South band director.

The young woman earned a degree in journalism from the University of Den-ver in 1951. Shortly thereafter, she signed on with a new Englewood-based radio station, KGMC, serving as both a disc-jockey and a reporter. Given that the sta-tion was close to the old community of Cherrelyn, she took the radio personality of Cherrelyn Wood.

Moving over to KVOD, the broadcaster became Merrie Lynn. Getting a daily show on KHOW, her on-the-air persona was Kay Howe, named for the initials of the station. After seven years, she transferred to KOA in 1964 where she resumed the moniker Merrie Lynn for her popular mid-morning show, "Hello Neighbor." Before long, she also had various television shows on what was then KOA-TV, Channel Four. Along the way, she emerged as KOA's manager for community service.

On February 21, 1973, Merrie Lynn married Lieutenant Governor John Vanderhoof. The couple settled in a suite at the Park Lane apartments near South Marion Street and Virginia Avenue. She became Colorado's first lady on July 16,

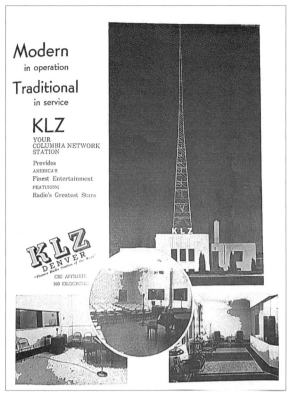

Modern
in operation
Traditional
in service
KLZ
YOUR
COLUMBIA NETWORK
STATION
Provides
AMERICA'S
Finest Entertainment
FEATURING
Radio's Greatest Stars

CBS AFFILIATE
560 KILOCYCLES

Denver's first radio station, KLZ, started at the home of its owner, Doc Reynolds, at 1124 South University Boulevard. For years, its broadcast tower, pictured in this 1938 advertisement, was the northwest corner of South University Boulevard and Hampden Avenue.

1973, when Vanderhoof moved into the statehouse after Governor John Love resigned to go to Washington. In December 1975, about a year after Vanderhoof was defeated for re-election, he initiated divorce proceedings against Merrie Lynn. By this time she lived at 966 Bonnie Brae Boulevard.

Lynn's presence in the area was apropos. The city's first radio station, KLZ, was directly south of Bonnie Brae at the home of William D. Reynolds Jr., 1124 South University Boulevard. The son of a Minneapolis railroad executive, Reynolds played the saxophone and clarinet in theaters to work his way through dental school at the University of Minnesota. From the time he was 17 in 1912, he dabbled in radio.

Shortly after he graduated from dental school in 1917, the 22-year-old Reynolds, suffering from tuberculosis, headed to Colorado Springs. Besides practicing dentistry, he continued to probe radio broadcasting and receiving. Before long, Reynolds held a federal license to send out experimental broadcasts on 9WH which subsequently became 9ZAF.

With money supplied by his father, the radio buff, now known as "Doc" Reynolds, relocated to Denver in 1920 where he opened a business manufacturing radio receivers. He simultaneously applied for a broadcast license. He was among the first 20 in the nation to receive a permit for a commercial station, leading KLZ to go on the air on March 10, 1922. (The letters were assigned by Washington; they did not have any specific meaning.)

Reynolds lived with his wife, a gifted organist and announcer, and their son near South University Boulevard and Mississippi Avenue. While KLZ's studio was officially in the Shirley-Savoy Hotel at the southeast corner of 17th Avenue and Broadway, most of the action occurred east of Washington Park. There were radio transmitters at the front and rear of the Reynolds residence. The studio was on the front porch while passersby sometimes joined the action. Before long, the dentist was blaring the messages of the Ku Klux Klan on his station, having close ties with KKK grand titan Gano Senter of 1145 South Logan Street whose Radio Cafe at 1111 15th Street always had KLZ on the air.

Early KLZ was a Reynolds family operation. The dentist played the saxophone as part of the station's programming while serving as engineer. His wife Naomi was "Mrs. Doc" who was program director, entertainer, and chief announcer. Their young son, George "Sonny" Reynolds, was "general manager." KLZ pioneered in broadcasting live performances from the Auditorium and participating in nation-wide hookups. It was the first station to broadcast a complete opera over the airwaves.

In 1925, Reynolds moved to 1385 South Marion Street, hoping to put up a more powerful broadcast tower there. Neighborhood opposition shot that down, leading KLZ to place its broadcast tower atop Ruby Hill before moving it to Dupont in 1927 when it hiked its power from 250 watts to 1,000 watts. (Dupont was a small community northeast of Denver that became part of Commerce City.)

Doc Reynolds died from tuberculosis at age 37 on November 28, 1931. Naomi Reynolds lived to age 96 in 1990. His father took over as president of KLZ. The station was subsequently part of Aladdin Broadcasting owned by movie theater mogul Harry Huffman who used the radio operation to launch Channel Seven, originally known as KLZ-TV, on November 1, 1953.

KLZ's broadcast headquarters were subsequently near the northwest corner of South University Boulevard and Hampden Avenue. Eventually, the station had most of the land between Floyd and Hampden avenues from South Downing Street to South University Boulevard. In 1951, Kent School occupied the section east of South Race Street. Nine years later, KLZ failed in efforts to convert the land west of Kent School into a shopping center. Residential development followed. After Kent School moved farther south in 1968 to the Myron Blackmer estate at South Colorado Boulevard and Quincy Avenue, the Denver Seminary, formerly known as the Conservative Baptist Theological Seminary, occupied the acreage. The real estate emerged as an exclusive residential enclave in the early 21st century when the academy moved to South Santa Fe Drive in Littleton.

For some years, Starr Yelland was KLZ's top sportscaster. He lived a mile north of the original Reynolds house at 2565 Alameda Circle. His son, Starr Yelland

Jr., was in the news when he fell from a roller coaster at Elitch's on August 14, 1965, during a KLZ picnic. The youth, who attended South High, died from his injuries on March 21, 1968.

The Bonnie Brae Tavern

$\mathcal{A}$ commercial center along South University Boulevard between Exposition and Ohio avenues is the most visible part of Bonnie Brae. The first shops opened in the mid-1920s. Among them is the oldest and most renowned business in the area, the Bonnie Brae Tavern at 740 South University Boulevard. Founder Carl Dire was a North Denver boy whose family worked at the Denver Macaroni and Noodle Company around the time of World War I when it lived at 1401 West 34th Avenue. Seeing the growing popularity of automobiles and South Denver real estate, he opened a Shell filling station at the northeast corner of South University Boulevard and Ohio Avenue in the mid-1920s, dwelling in an adjacent shack. Within a few years, he pondered expanding his operations into a Chrysler-Plymouth dealership—for a while, Dire had worked as a Chrysler mechanic. Recognizing the demand for food and drink among motorists, he returned to the food industry when he opened a bar/restaurant adjacent to his filling station upon the demise of Prohibition.

The building stood on what had been a weed-filled patch which Dire had purchased when pondering the car dealership. The tavern opened in June 1934. With

Photo by Phil Goodstein

The Little Flower Market at 709 South University Boulevard in the Bonnie Brae shopping strip occupies an old Phillips 66 filling station, a building illustrative of the fancy homes of gas stations during the 1920s and 1930s. The nearby Bonnie Brae Flowers has served the area since 1941.

Photo by Phil Goodstein

Bonnie Brae Ice Cream, at the northwest corner of Ohio Avenue and South University Boulevard, occupied the site of a popular creamery, Dolly Madison.

his wife Sue and two sons, Michael and Henry, he lived on the premises. In 1948, the family moved to a house across the alley at 745 Bonnie Brae Boulevard while the restaurant added pizza to its menu. This was right when Americans were discovering the dish. By this time, the Bonnie Brae Tavern was already a well-known neighborhood gathering spot which attracted patrons from far and near.

A 1949 expansion saw the restaurant grow from six to 26 tables. Dire worked closely with both St. Vincent de Paul Church at the northeast corner of South University Boulevard and Arizona Avenue and South High School in helping send promising neighborhood boys through college. He died at age 81 in 1982.

The owner's widow, Sue, remained a central part of the establishment. A gifted cook, her recipes for pizza and meatballs gave the restaurant a special flavor. After her husband's death, she was present daily at the restaurant, sitting in a booth near the cash register. She continued to oversee the operation until her death at age 98 on May 21, 2002. During her later years, she was something of a landmark in her own right. *Denver Post* columnist Dick Kreck celebrated her as "Grambo." Mayor Wellington Webb made June 2, 2000, "Sue Dire Day." By the time of her passing, the fourth generation of the Dire family worked at the Bonnie Brae Tavern.

(Affiliation with the bar did not equate with political success. Mike Dire, the son of Carl and Sue Dire, was active in the Republican Party in the late 1960s and early 1970s. He failed in his bids for the state House of Representatives in 1966 and for city council in 1971.)

A wide array of other businesses have come and gone from the Bonnie Brae strip. The Gobert family opened Bonnie Brae Flowers at 747 South University

Boulevard in 1941, running it into the 21st century. Back in the 1940s, the road included a meat processing plant where hunters took their game to have it chopped up and stored. One day, a young mother inadvertently got locked into a refrigerator where she froze to death. Nearby was Esquire Market, a butcher's shop at 723 South University Boulevard, which closed after 58 years in business in 2007. A former grocery store at 785 South University Boulevard emerged as a heavily patronized liquor store in the late 20th and early 21st centuries.

Before the emergence of supermarkets, three food stores were on the block including Preiser Grocery at 2331 Ohio Avenue, a shop serving the area from the 1930s to the 1980s. Around the corner was Bonnie Brae Drugs at 759–63 South University Boulevard. Between them was Dolly Madison at the northwest corner of Ohio Avenue and South University Boulevard. Opened in 1938, it was the second outlet of what was once a highly popular chain of dairy stores. Nearby were four filling stations and a hardware store. After Dolly Madison closed in 1986, Bonnie Brae Ice Cream occupied the space.

The Campus Lounge was at the other end of the block at 701 South University Boulevard. It stemmed from the Bel-Aire Cafe which dated from 1946. A liquor license followed in 1949. The establishment became the Campus Lounge in 1961. Fifteen years later, Jim Wiste, a DU hockey great, obtained it. Living up to its name, the Campus Lounge attracted many DU students, being essentially a sports bar.

Institutions and Change

*T*he Dire family's church, St. Vincent de Paul, emerged in 1926 as the Catholic congregation for Bonnie Brae and much of Washington Park. It grew out of South Denver's inaugural parish, St. Francis de Sales at the southeast corner of Alameda Avenue and South Sherman Street. After initially holding its services at the nearby St. Thomas Seminary at 1300 South Steele Street, St. Vincent de Paul occupied a joint school, parish hall, and place for worship along the north side of Arizona Avenue at South Josephine Street. It completed its sanctuary in 1953. (A couple blocks east at the southwest corner of Arizona Avenue and South Elizabeth Street is a congregation observing the rites of the Eastern Orthodox Slavic church, Holy Protection of the Mother of God Byzantine Catholic Church. Its modern building dates from 1976.)

St. Michael and All Angels' Parish, 1410 South University Boulevard, is two blocks south of St. Vincent de Paul. It stems from an Episcopal mission for those living south and east of Washington Park. The diocese organized it as a parish in 1943. The congregation grew rapidly after World War II. The faithful laid the cornerstone of their new church a decade later.

A block north of the Bonnie Brae Tavern, on the triangular lot formed by the intersection of South University Boulevard, Bonnie Brae Boulevard, and Exposition Avenue, is Bonnie Brae Baptist Church. Members incorporated it in 1946, affiliating with the American Baptists. Worshippers included men and women who had previously belonged to First Baptist at 14th Avenue and Grant Street and Broadway Baptist at Second Avenue and Lincoln Street. Their new church, they

Photo by Phil Goodstein

Huge houses, some of which are built almost up to the sidewalk, have become increasingly common in Bonnie Brae. This structure dominates the northeast corner of South Milwaukee Street and Ohio Avenue.

decreed, was a congregation for an emerging neighborhood. They broke ground for their permanent home in December 1950 and dedicated an education wing a decade later.

Under the guidance of Reverend William O. Rogers of Washington Park Congregational, locals formed the Kirk of Bonnie Brae at the southwest corner of South Steele Street and Arizona Avenue in 1946–47. Backers occupied the sanctuary in March 1950. They prepared a second section in 1954, followed by a new wing in 1958–59. Like Washington Park Congregational, the Kirk of Bonnie Brae affiliated with the United Church of Christ. Believers heralded it as "The Kirk."

While the churches and the Bonnie Brae Tavern have remained neighborhood institutions, the area was in drastic transition at the turn of the 21st century. As was the case with much of South Denver, yesterday's houses often did not satisfy the aspirations of extremely affluent buyers. The 1990s saw an increasing wave of destruction and rebuilding of neighborhood dwellings.

Settlers who liked Bonnie Brae as it had been since the 1950s decried the McMansions as monsters that were inappropriate for the area and which often came right up to the sidewalk. To preserve their enclave, they sought landmark protection. The section, they lamented, "is one big construction site. What was once a beautifully unique neighborhood featuring architectural variety, winding roads, mature trees, and gorgeous gardens is now a sea of stucco and fake rock siding." Development, they wailed, had filled their area with "a gigantic blob of mixed-up materials featuring a six-foot-wall surrounding the teeny, tiny yard." Despite such observations, advocates of preservation found as many homeowners opposed as supported their measure. Consequently, it collapsed. The wave of new buildings, seemingly ever bigger, continued apace.

Belcaro

*D*espite the McMansions, Bonnie Brae did not come close to the stature of the area directly to the east, Belcaro. The heart of that neighborhood, Belcaro Park, is between Exposition and Kentucky avenues and South Steele and South Garfield streets. Greater Belcaro extends to Mississippi Avenue on the south, South Colorado Boulevard on the east, and Cherry Creek on the north.

The evolution of Belcaro is closely linked with the man who built what has been called "Denver's grandest residence" there, Lawrence C. Phipps. Born on August 30, 1862, in Amwell Township of Washington County, Pennsylvania, Phipps was the son of a none-too-wealthy Methodist clergyman. According to the story he loved to tell, fresh out of high school at age 16, having recently lost his father, he went to work in the steel industry in Pittsburgh as a night clerk, getting $1.00 a shift. In no time, he emerged as a right-hand man of steel king Andrew Carnegie. What Phipps did not mention was that his uncle, Henry Phipps, was a close collaborator of Carnegie. When Carnegie sold his holdings to J. P. Morgan in 1901 to establish United States Steel, Lawrence Phipps retired with $15 million at age 39.

Phipps had seen his mother and first wife die young from tuberculosis. His sister Fanny had caught the disease in 1898, moving to Denver for the climate. Visiting her, he was impressed by the city's potential. Wanting to raise his children in a healthy area and fearing that he too might get TB, Phipps relocated to the Queen City in 1902.

To help others suffering from consumption, Phipps sponsored the Agnes Memorial Sanatorium at the southeast corner of Sixth Avenue and Quebec Street. He named it in memory of his mother, helping endow the operation. It opened on July 2, 1904. After he closed the hospital in 1932, Phipps persuaded Denver to buy the land from him and give it to the War Department to create a training base for the air corps which became the heart of Lowry Air Force Base.

No sooner had Phipps moved to the Mile High City than he asserted himself as a leading investor and a member of high society. Not only was he a major player in the emergence of the Denver Country Club, but Phipps owned a great deal of land adjacent to the golf course, especially to the north of First Avenue and east of High Street. By the mid-1910s, the Pennsylvania native eyed political posts, serving as the head of the Tax Payers Protective League, a business organization demanding a corporate dictatorship over city hall. Most of all, Phipps was a key stockholder in the Denver & Salt Lake Railroad, the remnants of the failed Moffat Railroad. As such, he was in the vanguard of arranging a taxpayer bailout for it via the Moffat Tunnel. Along the way, Phipps was a central figure in forming the Denver chapter of the Red Cross in 1913.

At the same time he served as a leader of the Red Cross during World War I, Phipps ran for the United States Senate in 1918, freely throwing around his money. With the help of conservative Democrats who fully endorsed his vicious attacks on incumbent John Shafroth for not being a mindless patriot, he narrowly won the election. In office, he emerged as a stalwart of the party. Phipps especially red-baited its opponents during the 1920 balloting. On the heels of this, the senator emerged as champion of the reactionary policies of President Warren G. Harding while he built his own machine in the state Republican Party.

On coming to Denver, Phipps settled in a grandiose mansion at the southwest corner of Colfax Avenue and Marion Street. As Colfax evolved from a residential boulevard into a business street, he eyed a manor in the Country Club. In the interim, he settled on Quality Hill at 738 Pearl Street. That was where he was living in 1923 when President Harding visited Denver. Phipps accompanied the president everywhere, arranging for Harding to frequent his dwelling. On the president's sudden death shortly after he left the Mile High City, Phipps was in the lead of donating for a Harding memorial.

From the beginning, Phipps stirred fierce controversy. A wing of the GOP hated him, viewing him as a boss who had used his money to buy control of the party. Labor called the senator "a gold-plated imbecile." Others, pointing to his continuing ties to the steel industry, argued Phipps was the "third senator from Pennsylvania." As he sought re-election in 1924, the politician made his peace with the Ku Klux Klan, an organization which originally opposed him because he was sometimes critical of Prohibition. Right when the robed riders were surging to political dominance that year whereby they gained control of the state Republican Party, Phipps donated at least $50,000 to them and backed their drive to capture the state government. In return, the Klan assured his return to the Senate. For a while, the Phipps wing and Klan wing of the Republicans were synonymous.

In Washington, Phipps lived in a grandiose mansion, Single Oak, on a six-acre spread. It later became the home of the Swedish embassy. By the time of his second term, his Denver home was at 360 High Street in the Country Club neighborhood, right next to his close associate Gerald Hughes at 320 High Street.

After not seeking re-election in 1930 when he knew he had no chance of remaining in office, Phipps resolved to retire to a unique Mile High estate. He decided to place his home on the open fields east of Bonnie Brae which his son had used to pasture horses for the nearby Polo Club. "Belcaro" was Phipps' name for the development. It was, he insisted, Italian for "beautiful, dear one." The official address of the chateau is 3400 Belcaro Drive.

Phipps commissioned the firm of Fisher & Fisher to design his 54-room castle. Charles Platt of New York, a recognized authority on Georgian architecture, consulted on the $310,000 effort. The 27,000-square foot house included, at Phipps' stipulation, a dining room large enough to accommodate his family which included children from three different marriages. He further requested a ground floor billiards room and a marble bath. Other than that, he left the specifics of the house to his third wife, Margaret, and her brother, Platt Rogers Jr., a leading contractor.

Platt Rogers Sr. had been a commanding figure in late 19th-century Denver, serving as mayor from 1891 to 1893. He was a powerful attorney who had numerous investments, living close to Phipps in a manor at the northeast corner of Colfax Avenue and Washington Street. John Shafroth, the man Phipps defeated for the Senate in 1918, had been Rogers' law partner.

On January 25, 1911, Phipps married Rogers' daughter. She gave birth to Allan Rogers Phipps in 1912 and Gerald Hughes Phipps in 1915. All members of the

The Belcaro Mansion of Lawrence Phipps.

family were part and parcel of the city's business, society, sporting, and culture scenes. The senator subsequently donated an organ to St. John's Episcopal in memory of Platt Rogers Sr. As a foremost builder, Platt Rogers Jr. oversaw the erection of the Belcaro palace. His nephew, Gerald Phipps, eventually inherited control of the firm that became Gerald Phipps Construction.

Completed in 1933, the manor included a built-in Kimball-Welte pipe organ, lavish wine-colored tapestries, and a 400-year old English dining room which came to Denver from a London mansion. The wood in a pine-paneled room was originally hauled to England from the New World as ballast, used as lumber in Britain, and then brought to the United States for the Phipps Villa. Carpenters made mahogany chairs in the dining room from the beams of a mansion constructed in Santo Domingo between 1509 and 1515. Craftsmen added elaborate carvings and bas-relief ceilings. Austrian oak paneling highlights the living room.

A tennis pavilion is north of the mansion. This was a pet project of Margaret Phipps. An enthusiast of the game, she pushed the Denver Country Club to have a top-notch tennis program. She insisted her sons enter tennis tournaments. Before long, with excellent coaching, Gerald Phipps was a leading competitor. So tennis would be more than a good weather pursuit, Margaret Phipps insisted that Belcaro include an indoor court.

John Gray designed the tennis house. Members of the Denver Country Club frequently used it. The facility was far more than simply a place to play the game. It included everything from a soda fountain to locker rooms and showers to a formal reception area, bedrooms, and a kitchen. A semi-glassed roof provided plenty of light. Beams and etched-glass windows decorated the dining room. Famous tennis players competing in tournaments at the Denver Country Club often stayed at the mansion and practiced at the tennis house, a hall able to host crowds of up to 300. Stretching between the pavilion and mansion were four formal gardens in addition to play yards and a bowling green.

In 1938, Gerald Phipps moved to 801 South Adams Street, a house crafted by architect Lester Varian. Allan Phipps commissioned the same man to design his home at 885 South Garfield Street. In 1965, the two brothers came to the fore as the owners of the Denver Broncos.

Football had already been on the mind of Allan Phipps in 1959 when he sold 885 South Garfield Street to Hamilton Oil as the home of former Notre Dame football coach Frank Leahy who had come to Denver as an executive with the petroleum firm. The coach did not stay long. Legal complications forced Hamilton Oil to put the manor on the market within a few months while Leahy left Denver in 1960 for a job as general manager of the Los Angeles Chargers of the new American Football League.

Before he threw himself into football, Allan Phipps had been president of the Denver Symphony. His shift was indicative of the city's transformation from a town that sought culture to a city seeing professional sports as its identity. (Janet Elway, the ex-wife of famed Bronco quarterback John Elway, purchased a modern house at 900 South Steele Street in 2008. The Symphony has its offices in the Margaret Phipps Room of Boettcher Concert Hall.)

After selling his manor to Hamilton Oil, Allan Phipps moved to a modern home directly south of his father's estate at 3481 Kentucky Avenue. Banker and oilman Thomas M. Dines of 3479 Kentucky Avenue was a next-door neighbor. Donald S. Stubbs of the powerhouse law firm of Davis, Grahams, and Stubbs lived across the

The Phipps Tennis House is a virtual mansion in itself. For years, it was the quarters of the city's high-class tennis set.

The early 21st century saw a new wave of Belcaro mansions such as 3303 Kentucky Avenue.

street at 3460 Kentucky Avenue. Trucking magnate Bill Ringsby, who owned the Denver Rockets (Nuggets) of the American Basketball Association in the 1960s, was nearby at 3500 Belcaro Drive, directly east of the Lawrence Phipps House. Members of the Burkhardt family, owners of Burkhardt Steel at 787–95 South Broadway, were neighbors at 830 South Madison Street. Office supply king William H. Kistler was at 860 South Madison Street.

The presence of these villas was indicative of how Belcaro evolved as an elite estate for the friends and business and political associates of Lawrence Phipps. His Belcaro Realty and Investment Company developed the area. His two sons-in-law by his second marriage, Van Holt Garrett and Donald Bromfield, ran it. They platted and sold off much of the land around the mansion as Belcaro Park. The section resembles the Crestmoor Park area, a product of their Garrett–Bromfield & Company.

Garrett and Bromfield worked with their brother-in-law, Gerald Phipps, a general contractor, in erecting many of the houses. In 1953, Gerald Phipps developed the eastern section of the neighborhood along Colorado Boulevard as the Belcaro Shopping Center. Until then, the land was mostly the end of the city. Typical of its isolated character was how in 1928, when Public Service began to provide homes with natural gas, the utility placed four main valves of its natural gas lines at South Colorado Boulevard and Exposition Avenue. (For many years, the field office of Interstate Gas Company, the main supplier of natural gas for the region, was at 700 South Colorado Boulevard.) The Phipps family had holdings in Public Service and other local utilities, especially Tramway and Mountain States Telephone. For years, the Belcaro Shopping Center was home of numerous neighborhood-oriented stores including Hodel's Pharmacy at 705 South Colorado Boulevard which served the area from 1958 to 1999. King Soopers opened its store in the center in 1966, designed by architect Langdon Morris who had his practice at 3950 Exposition Avenue.

Lawrence Phipps remained active in countless community ventures after the completion of the mansion. In failing health, he left the city for Los Angeles in 1949 where he died in 1958. After his death, Margaret Phipps became concerned about the future of the Belcaro Mansion, which her sons did not want. In 1960, she donated the tennis house to the University of Denver. The school has used it for conferences and retreats. She pondered the options for the chateau after her death, including turning it into apartments, a private school, or tearing it down. Not liking any of these choices, in 1964 she gave the palace to DU. She was then terminally ill in a hospital and had no intention of returning to the house. The senator's widow died in 1968. Gerald Phipps passed away in 1993. Allan Phipps followed him to the grave in 1997.

DU took over the villa as a place for receptions and special meetings in addition to renting it for private events, particularly weddings. In 1974–75, the university considered disposing of the castle as a white elephant. This led it to sell part of the land in 1979. A five-and-a-half-acre estate remained, complete with an esplanade linking the tennis pavilion with the mansion. Ornate formal gardens bordered the walkway. The college filled the Phipps Palace, officially known as the Lawrence C. Phipps Memorial Conference Center, with antiques given to the school. The former bedrooms became sitting rooms named for the members of the family who had lived in them. In response to neighborhood complaints about noise and traffic, DU limited crowds to 100 for events at the mansion and 300 at the tennis house. The school hosted an annual Christmas party at the chateau for locals, a foremost neighborhood tradition.

Naturally, rumors of ghosts pulsate in the villa. Late at night, caretakers are sure they have heard the click of pool balls near the old billiards table. Despite a no-smoking policy, there is occasionally the odor of cigar smoke. The specter of Lawrence Phipps sometimes seems omnipresent. Mysterious tennis balls sometimes show up near the grounds.

The city spruced up the Belcaro neighborhood in 1997 when the Summit of the Eight came to town. This was an international conclave of the presidents and prime ministers of the United States, Britain, France, Germany, Italy, Japan, Canada, and Russia. Mayor Wellington Webb had the police virtually close down the community so the politicians would have free sway. Included was a grand banquet at the Phipps estate. As part of the decorations, signs popped up on the borders of the neighborhood informing locals they were entering Belcaro Park.

The Specter of Spicer Breedan

*T*he heavy police presence at the Summit of the Eight was seemingly necessary so the dignitaries did not hear the snap, crackle, and pop at 3555 Belcaro Drive.

That was where Spicer Breedan killed himself on March 19, 1996. He was a scion of the Boettcher family whose parents, Victor and Charlene Breedan, had been developers of Capitol Hill apartments. Among the places Victor Breedan financed was the Summer House at 1313 Williams Street, the building replacing the mansion featured in the horror film *The Changeling*.

Ghosts seemed to haunt the Breedan family. Charlene Breedan died at a young age of cancer in 1972, right after the family had demolished the *Changeling* House. Her husband eventually had a drug and alcohol problem. So did their son. By the 1990s, Spicer Breedan repeatedly crashed fancy sports cars. This was the situation when, shortly after midnight on March 17, 1996, his specialty BMW was going more than 140 miles a hour, southbound on the Valley Highway near the South Santa Fe Drive exit, when it clipped the SUV driven by a popular *Rocky Mountain News* columnist, Greg Lopez, killing the journalist.

Breedan's vehicle did not stop, leaving behind a most distinctive bumper. After the police had identified the suspect car as belonging to the Boettcher heir, Breedan locked himself in his Belcaro house. So he could hear if anybody was coming to get him, he sprinkled the hallways with Rice Krispies. Realizing this was to no avail, he shot himself to death in the basement bathroom. To try to cloak the involvement of the Boettcher family with the hit-and-run, District Attorney Bill Ritter blamed the affair on a German immigrant artist, Peter Schmitz, who had been in the BMW with Breedan. The prosecutor used the full assets of his office to try Schmitz for vehicular homicide. The jury did not accept the district attorney's version, attributing the accident to the Belcaro resident.

To check unwanted developments, the Belcaro Park Homeowners Association has policed the area. It has covenant rights to review construction so no out-of-

Photo by Phil Goodstein

Skeletons may rattle in the Spicer Breedan House at 3555 Belcaro Drive.

A medallion at the southeast corner of South Steele Street and Virginia Avenue advertises the North Belcaro area as Stokes Place/Green Bowers.

scale edifices mar the enclave. In April 2006, after a six-day trial, Judge John McMullen (who had presided at the Spicer Breedan/Peter Schmitz case) upheld the group's power to reject a proposed gigantic house at 601 South Jackson Street as incompatible with the rest of the block on which it was planned. Architectural control committees continued to enforce covenants on the eastern edge of the area along South Jackson and South Harrison streets where most of the blocks, filled with 1950esque ranch homes, escaped the massive poptops and scrapeoffs changing the face of much of South Denver. Some McMansions went up on South Garfield Street, Belcaro Lane, and Kentucky Avenue.

Gigantic dwellings have also appeared in the North Belcaro area. This is the section stretching between roughly South Steele Street, Cherry Creek, Exposition Avenue, and South Colorado Boulevard. Hyde Park composes its northwest corner. This gated enclave dates from the early 1980s when an out-of-town developer acquired the land at 456 South Steele Street.

The real estate reflected Denver high society's fixation with horses. On July 19, 1946, El Jebel Shrine established El Palomino Patrol, a horse drill team. The group used the land to the southeast of South Steele Street and Alameda Avenue as stables and exercise grounds for its horses. The acreage was becoming too urban and valuable when the Shriners moved to 6351 South Peoria Street in 1980.

Hyde Park faced uneasy fortunes, going through bankruptcy and a building standstill in the mid-1980s. New owners bought the project in 1988, scaling down the size of the development. Generally, the walled-off enclave has provided homes for retired executives and professionals who often have summer and winter residences elsewhere.

Stokes Place is south of Hyde Park. The name recalls the Stokes Land Company, the post–World War II owner of the real estate. In January 1951, William Bennett of the firm filed the plat for the area from the alley of Dakota–Virginia avenues to Exposition Avenues between South Steele and South Garfield streets to Gill Drive.

Bennett's company designed the sloping area with twisting roads and extra large lots. Opposed to the standard 25-foot wide lots in most of Denver, those on South Monroe Way, for example, are 65 feet wide and 155 feet deep. That was where architect William Muchow built his house on two lots at 618 South Monroe Way in 1954. Neighbors included restaurateur Corbin Douglas II at 612 South Monroe Way, and John F. "Johnny" Dee Jr. at 606 South Monroe Way. The latter was a onetime Notre Dame University basketball coach and former manager of the city's department of parks and recreation who was city auditor from 1975 to 1979. By the time he held that office, Dee was at 2150 South Monroe Street. John L. J. Hart, a namesake of the law firm of Holland & Hart, was at 650 South Monroe Way. David Brofman, the head of the city's Probate Court for many years, lived at 3301 Virginia Avenue.

Muchow's house illustrated the cutting edge of modern architecture in the 1950s. Other architects designed their own houses in the area. Langdon Morris, who helped design Larimer Square, for instance, was at 520 South Garfield Street. Acclaimed attorney Walter Gerash subsequently occupied it. He was the lawyer who defended Peter Schmitz.

The Green Bowers Subdivision, filed on April 6, 1955, is east of Stokes Place. Among those living there was Harold Dill at 621 South Harrison Street. After commanding the South Denver division of the police department during the 1950s, he was chief from July 1963 to the end of 1967. He unsuccessfully ran for city

Photo by Phil Goodstein

The North Belcaro neighborhood includes show houses by the city's post–World War II architects such as the home William Muchow designed for himself at 618 South Monroe Way.

council in 1971 as a staunch Republican. In 2007, homeowners placed a medallion at South Steele Street and Virginia Avenue advertising the neighborhood as "Stokes Place/Green Bowers."

Central Christian Church has been the religious center of Stokes Place at 3690 Cherry Creek Drive South. Dating from 1871 and incorporated in 1873, it occupied an imposing temple at 1600 Lincoln Street in 1901. As was the case with many Capitol Hill sanctuaries, members started to move to the southeast after World War II. Eventually, they expected their congregation to follow them. The pioneer Mile High grouping of the Disciples of Christ, Central Christian headed to its new quarters in 1973. Besides religious programs, it has had wide-ranging educational efforts. The congregation undertook a major addition in 1998. Landscaping improvements followed in 2007. The next year saw the beginning of a gated community directly south of the church.

East of Central Christian Church is the City of Brest Park. Denver acquired this 16.7-acre stretch of greenery in 1936 when the administration planned to continue Speer Boulevard east of University Boulevard. Though nothing ever came of that, the city eventually opened Cherry Creek Drives North and South along Cherry Creek while pondering the land for a freeway. In 1962, five years after Denver made Brest, France, the Mile High community's inaugural sister city, park crews landscaped the land into open space honoring the French Atlantic seaport. On the opposite bank of Cherry Creek are parks named for other sister cities. Ironically, catercorner from Brest Park at the northeast corner of Virginia Avenue and South Colorado Boulevard is Shotgun Willie's, a stripper bar. Some confused puritans have bewailed the name of Brest Park, believing that it celebrates women's breasts.

The Polo Club

Just west of Hyde Park and north of Bonnie Brae is the Polo Club between Alameda and Exposition avenues from South University Boulevard to South Steele Street. It was a product of the days when members of the Country Club played polo.

In the 19th century, the city's elite fancied harness racing. In addition to a track for that pursuit at Overland Park, they raced at the Gentlemen's Driving and Riding Club. Initially headquartered at the northwest corner of Fourth Avenue and Downing Street, the Gentlemen's Club subsequently had the land at the southwest corner of Colorado Boulevard and 23rd Avenue in City Park.

The Denver Country Club grew out of the Overland Country Club. Its horse-riding set sought to emulate the customs of British aristocracy. Among them was fox hunting. In 1907, members of the Country Club mounted their horses, kept in stables near the equivalent of South Lafayette Street and Bayaud Avenue close to the eighth tee of the golf course, and set off on hunts to the south and east of the greenery. Included were their hunting dogs, complete with a kennel close to the stables. The sportingmen targeted coyotes more than foxes. This effort, known as the Arapahoe Hunt Club, quickly disappeared.

DMF

Dismounted polo players at the Denver Country Club in 1910.

In April 1902, the Gentlemen's Driving and Riding Club formally established a polo team. Not wishing to be upstaged, the Denver Country Club, still located on the grounds of Overland Park, created its own polo team. Even before it completed its new golf course, the Country Club installed a polo field, near the northeast corner of South Downing Street and Bayaud Avenue.

Leaders of Denver society, especially gold-mine owner Thomas F. Walsh, Lawrence Phipps Jr., and future United States District Court Judge J. Foster Symes, heavily embraced polo. By 1909, they were the Freebooters, the name of the Country Club squad. To advertise their sport, they invited one and all, including nonmembers, to come to the Country Club for matches.

Attending polo contests quickly emerged as a foremost activity. Non-polo players at the Country Club heartily objected. The outsiders, they complained, not only parked on the fairways, but invaded the clubhouse. The stables and kennels gave the elite enclave a barnyard odor. Even worse, the horses tore up the golf course and interfered with members' pursuit of knocking around little white balls.

On April 19, 1920, brothers Ira B. and Albert E. Humphreys Jr. joined Lawrence Phipps Jr. and brothers Lafayette and Gerald Hughes to incorporate the Polo Club. They obtained the William Lewis Bart Berger family farm east of South University Boulevard and south of Alameda Avenue for $62,000. (Berger, a foremost figure in Colorado National Bank, bought the land from the Kansas Pacific Railroad in 1874. Members of his family eventually lived in a mansion on the grounds of the Polo Club at 2925 Exposition Avenue.)

In 1926, the horsemen occupied a $300,000 Spanish-style clubhouse at 5 Polo Club Road, approximately the equivalent of South Clayton Street and Virginia Avenue. Architects William E. and Arthur A. Fisher designed it atop a high knoll over Cherry Creek. The resort featured pink stucco walls, a multi-colored tile roof, murals by John Thompson, and sculptures and bas-reliefs by Robert Garrison. Stables went up near the polo field at the southwest corner of Alameda Avenue and South Steele Street. Tennis courts and a swimming pool were near the rear of the clubhouse.

Throughout the 1920s and into the 1930s, the Freebooters played polo on Tuesdays, Thursdays, and Saturdays during the appropriate season, taking on teams from the United States army and Colorado Springs. Despite the wealth and devotion of the players, the club did not survive the Depression. Financial and other difficulties led to the end of polo matches after 1936.

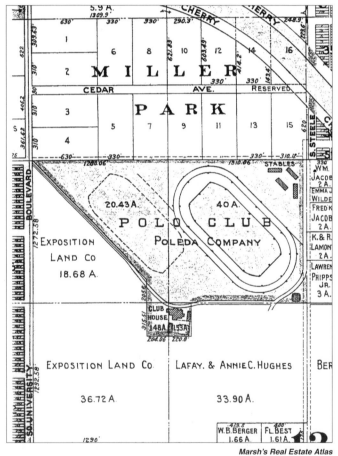

Marsh's Real Estate Atlas

This plate from Marsh's Real Estate Atlas of Denver, *c. 1937, shows the Polo Club and Miller Park.*

The ghost of Annie Hughes supposedly stalks the Lafayette Hughes Mansion at 2755 Exposition Avenue.

Lawrence Phipps Jr. would not let the game die. As residential development started to occur south and east of the Country Club, he obtained the cattle ranch of John W. Springer to the south of Littleton, the modern Highlands Ranch. There, in the late 1920s, he reincarnated the 1907 Arapahoe Hunt Club of the Country Club as a new Arapahoe Hunt Club. Under his auspices, the Denver aristocracy once more sought to imitate its British cousins with fox hunts, getting three to four coyotes a year. With the demise of the Polo Club, the Arapahoe Hunt Club became the regional center for high-class horsemen. The Polo Reserve in Littleton and a Polo Club on the Cottonwood Riding Club near Roxborough Park are other heirs of the South Denver social organization.

The Denver Polo Club proper closed in December 1941. By this time, death stalked the Hughes family. Berrien Hughes, the brother of Lafayette and Gerald Hughes, who was the foremost playboy of the family and an active figure in polo and other sporting competitions, died in May 1939 from ski injuries he suffered during a spring mountain expedition near Loveland Pass. A year later, Annie Hughes, the wife of Lafayette Hughes, killed herself at their Polo Club mansion at 2755 Exposition Avenue. The couple had occupied the residence in 1927. Its presence showed that the Polo Club was not simply a sporting center, but also an elite enclave putting the Country Club neighborhood to shame.

Annie Hughes was the daughter of John W. Springer, a leading Republican banker and rancher whose castle still stands in the center of Highlands Ranch. Her grandfather was Texas cattle king William E. Hughes. Her marriage to Lafayette Hughes in 1912 brought together the two different Hughes families. For some years, the families lived next to one another at 300 and 320 High Street.

The 48-year-old Annie Hughes was not happy by 1940. As her health declined, she was greatly depressed when doctors discovered she had a malignant growth in her ear. Fearing for the worst, she killed herself around 7:50 AM of April 19 when she fired a .32 caliber automatic into her heart. This was just before the physicians decided they had misdiagnosed her and the tumor was benign. Her husband, who was then breakfasting with their son, heard nothing. He discovered her body when he sought to say goodbye to her before leaving on a trip to Alamosa. Supposedly, her ghost stalks the place.

Explosive events also occurred at the old clubhouse. After the Polo Club ceased operations, a new owner turned it into a private residence. By January 1978, it was the home of Frederic C. Hamilton. An oilman who had come to Denver from Midland, Texas, in the early 1960s, he headed Hamilton Brothers Oil while having connections with the Murchison empire in

A terra-cotta medallion was once at the Denver Polo Club, designed by sculptor Robert Garrison. Ben Perri subsequently gained possession of it, placing it in the yard of his home at 1300 South Ogden Street.

Texas through his wife, Jane Murchison. On the side, he served on the board of International Telephone & Telegraph (ITT). That conglomerate had expanded into countless fields by the early 1970s ranging from rental cars to life insurance to mining in South America. It was closely tied to the presidency of Richard Nixon, complete with charges of unethical donations to the 1972 Nixon re-election campaign. Many hated ITT for collaborating with reactionaries in Chile in 1973 in staging a bloody coup that destroyed the country's democratically elected, self-proclaimed socialist government.

The Continental Revolutionary Army sought to do something about this. During the 1970s, it claimed credit for a number of bomb blasts in the area, including the Grinnell pipefitting plant at 15th Street near the Platte River. That company, it observed in a proclamation taking responsibility for the bombing in February 1975, was a front for ITT. It further set off explosives at the home of the local head of the CIA. This, it declared, was another act of revenge for the coup in Chile.

The group's attack failed to prevent ITT from operating as usual. Consequently, on the night of January 10–11, 1978, its operatives sneaked into the Polo Club where they targeted Hamilton in the old clubhouse. The Continental Revolutionary Army's bomb went off at 12:48 AM. The blast created a four-foot by six-foot hole in the structure, ripping through three layers of brick and the stucco. The detonation destroyed the bubble cover over the swimming pool and damaged the dining room, recreation room, and kitchen. The discharge broke numerous windows, including those in two adjacent houses. Estimates had repair costs at least $300,000 of a house valued at $500,000. The 50-year-old Hamilton was in the residence at the time of the explosion as were his wife and two of their children. None was injured.

A swimming pool was at the rear of the Polo Club headquarters at 5 Polo Club Road. The clubhouse became a private residence when the Polo Club ceased operations in 1941. The Continental Revolutionary Army bombed it in 1978. A new owner destroyed it at the beginning of the 21st century.

The police, FBI, and Bureau of Alcohol, Tobacco, and Firearms all claimed jurisdiction in investigating the attack. Residents reported smelling the odor of black power after the blast. Authorities concluded a high-explosive bomb had been placed at the west wall of the villa. The explosion was heard through central Denver and greatly frightened the others living in what was then listed as the 60-house, 32-block Polo Club.

At first, the commander of the police bomb squad, Robert Shaughnessy, denied the act was the responsibility of the Continental Revolutionary Army. This led the sect to tell the *Denver Post* in a letter that the deed had been performed by its "cell one, unit one." The police and FBI responded by insisting that they knew who was behind the cabal and were hot on the trail of the criminals. They never made any arrests for the bombings. After the attack on the Polo Club, the bombings ceased.

Hamilton remained a commanding business figure, coming to chair the board of the Denver Art Museum. He donated $20 million to its expansion program in the early 21st century. The museum honored him by naming its bizarrely de-signed, taxpayer-financed new wing the Hamilton Building which critics argued looked like the debris left by some sort of explosion. Jane Murchison Hamilton was a trustee of the University of Denver, joining its board in 1976. There she pushed women sports programs. The couple donated $3.5 million to the school in the mid-1990s whereupon the school named a gymnasium in the Ritchie Center in their honor. The Hamilton Recital Hall in the Newman Center at Iliff Avenue and South University Boulevard also recognizes their gifts to the campus.

Even before the explosion, Polo Club residents contracted with a private security firm to patrol their area. The guards stepped up their vigilance in the wake of the Continental Revolutionary Army's attack. They prominently posted no trespassing signs at entryways where surveillance cameras were in place. The Polo Club was the area's pioneer gated community.

Among those whom the Polo Club sought to keep out were Jews. Larry Mizel, a homebuilder from Oklahoma, realized this when he arrived in the city to attend the University of Denver Law School in 1964. About the time he graduated in 1967, he established himself as a developer of apartment projects. A premier effort was his 36-unit House of Rothschild in 1969 at the northwest corner of South University Boulevard and Exposition Avenue, directly west of the Polo Club. By naming it for a famous clan of Jewish financiers, he announced his presence in the city while flouting the anti-Semitism of the Polo Club—a Polo Club homeowners' association unsuccessfully sued to block the project as in violation of the zoning. The structure, which occupies nearly half of the block stretching to Center Avenue. It became condominiums in 1976.

The end of the Polo Club clubhouse came at the hands of a new occupant. Diamond dealer Tom Shane owned it by 2000 when he announced the palace was outdated and did not serve his needs. Given the secretive, exclusive character of the Polo Club, few community voices objected to this action as he sold the pipe organ and Tiffany glass which had decorated the building. A modern mansion replaced it. The Shane Company filed for bankruptcy in early 2009. Other vintage Polo Club manors have also come down. Huge open spaces remained in the enclave in the early 21st century.

In 1946, Lafayette Hughes oversaw the incorporation of the Polo Club Place Homeowners Association. High walls joined hedges along the perimeter of the Polo Club grounds. Property owners paid for private streets. Near Hughes' home were the residences of his sons Charles J., at 3100 Alameda Avenue, and Lafayette Jr., 2400 Alameda Avenue. (Polo Club addresses are often approximations. Usually the houses are isolated well away from the roads on which they are listed.)

In addition to practicing law with his brother Gerald in the lawyer-lobbyist firm of Hughes and Dorsey, Lafayette Hughes invested in cattle and oil. On January 18, 1958, he slipped on ice in a University of Denver parking lot following a basketball game. He never recovered from the injuries, remaining in the hospital till his death at age 78 on March 27, 1958.

Marjorie McIntosh Buell, the former wife of the owner of the Cherry Creek Shopping Center, Temple Buell, who was independently wealthy, acquired Hughes' Polo Club residence following his death. In August 1959, Hughes' heirs sold 34 acres between Exposition and Virginia avenues from South Clayton Street to South Steele Street to Falkenburg Construction. The new owner announced plans to divide the land into 35 building sites. Eventually, 40 elite houses arose there. Architects and landscapers designed the residences to emphasize open spaces, mountain views, and a sense of seclusion.

A quick way to escape the Polo Club was via helicopter. Or such was on the mind of industrialist Charles Gates Jr. In 1968, he convinced the association governing the Polo Club to allow him to build a heliport adjacent to his house at 444 South University Boulevard. The board of zoning adjustment rejected the proposal in the face of objections from others living in the area. By the 21st century, billionaire Philip Anschutz was among those making the Polo Club home. He decorated his house with the busts of 1920esque physicians which had once stared down at passersby from the Republic Building at the east corner of 16th Street and Tremont Place, a structure destroyed in the early 1980s by an investment firm in which Anschutz was involved.

Miller Park

*M*iller Park is the area directly north of the Polo Club between Alameda Avenue and Cherry Creek from South University Boulevard to South Steele. Once part of the John Riethmann estate, Robert Speer owned the land at the time he arranged for the Denver Country Club to purchase most of the Riethmann land. On July 22, 1918, a new owner, James H. Miller, who lived at 766 Gaylord Street, platted the spread. Having made his money in oil and mining, he designed the area for distinctive mansions.

Photo by Phil Goodstein

A windmill functioned in Miller Park near the equivalent of South Fillmore Street and Cherry Creek Drive South until development supplanted it in 2008.

Miller pulled a permit on August 7, 1918, for the area's inaugural castle at 2330 Cedar Avenue. (Though South University Boulevard is officially the 2350 east street, addresses below that number are east of it in the enclave—the road was once considered South York Street, 2300 east.) The builder received a permit for the elite house at 100 South University Boulevard on October 21, 1918. He was also responsible for the residences at 2500 and 2600 Cedar Avenue that year. The home of Edward P. Palmer at 2326 Cedar Avenue joined them in 1919. Amidst these developments, Claude W. Freed applied to erect a frame chicken house to the rear of his 2600 Cedar Avenue dwelling on November 8, 1923.

Eventually, Miller Park was a premier site where local developers and contractors lived. By the end of World War II, such prominent Denver real estate players as Van Holt Garrett, Francis J. Kirchhoff, Chuck Lower, and Herbert A. Writer dwelt in the section. Some notable financiers were in the area during the 1960s, including First National Bank chairman Eugene Adams and Walter Emery, president of the Bank of Denver. Franz A. Cramer, the president of a foremost department store, the Denver Dry, had already moved into Miller Park at 2800 Cedar Avenue in the 1920s. The James R. Arneill family, leading physicians, made 2525 Cedar Avenue their home. James R. Arneill III was the essential father of the Colorado Transportation Museum which evolved into the Forney Museum. For some years, the Alameda–Cedar Home-Owners Association claimed to speak for the neighborhood.

Controversy engulfed Miller Park in 1951 when the Conservative Baptist Association acquired an option on the house and four-acre estate at 106 South University where it hoped to build a seminary. Neighborhood opposition shot that down. Eventually, Temple Buell, the owner and developer of the Cherry Creek Shopping Center, occupied the spread.

Though the Conservative Baptist Association failed to move into Miller Park, another church did, Calvary Temple. On December 15, 1942, Reverend Verne J. Crews helped oversee the creation of Central Assembly Church at the northeast corner of Grant Street and Fourth Avenue. He did not stay long as its pastor, going on to serve as the director of the Rocky Mountain district of the Assembly of God, a Pentecostal denomination. His successor, R. Arthur McClure, left in May 1947. The church was in trouble. Membership was down to fewer than 60 and the congregation appeared to have a bleak future when it hired a charismatic 27-year-old pastor, Charles Eldon Blair, on June 22, 1947. He rapidly recruited communicants whereby the temple grew to 1,200 faithful by 1954.

By this time, the congregation had resolved to erect a new home on the block between First and Second avenues and Josephine and Columbine streets. No sooner had the recently renamed Calvary Temple acquired three acres there in June 1952 than Sears wanted the location for a store adjacent to the developing Cherry Creek Shopping Center. Blair insisted the congregation could not sell—God had told him to buy the land. Sears upped its ante. The preacher once more refused to sell. The congregation finally agreed to let Sears buy the property for $68,000 in February 1953. The deal included Sears giving Calvary Temple nine acres on the east side of South University Boulevard between Cedar and Alameda avenues.

Photo by Earle Clark Studios, Calvary Temple

The Central Assembly Church at the northeast corner of Fourth Avenue and Grant
Street grew into Calvary Temple at 200 South University Boulevard in Miller Park.

Calvary Temple broke ground for its new home in November 1953, dedicating
the sanctuary on June 26, 1955. There the congregation grew into what it claimed
was the nation's tenth largest and fourth richest Protestant church with a membership of more than 7,000. In addition to packing the church three times each Sunday morning, thousands watched its services on television. Others listened to Reverend Blair over the radio. Church buses transported worshippers to services. The
temple sponsored 100 missionaries, claiming to cater to people of all faiths in the
tradition of the circuit-riding preachers of early Colorado.

Pastor Blair emerged as a national leader of the evangelical Christian community and a pioneer of modern mega-churches. Mayor William McNichols feted
the 25th anniversary of the preacher's leadership when he declared June 25, 1972,
"Pastor Charles E. Blair Day." Clarence Decker, a former Democratic state senator who lost the 1972 nomination to Congress to Pat Schroeder, was a close Blair
associate and advisor.

The church owned houses along the 2600 and 2700 blocks of Cedar Avenue.
One was the "Castle," Pastor Blair's home. The congregation used other residences for church youth programs, activities some neighbors found extremely loud
and disturbing.

In 1964, Calvary Temple acquired 46 acres on the Polo Club to the southeast of Alameda Avenue and South University Boulevard in an exceedingly complicated real estate deal. At that time, Dorothy Lewis, the widow of Mason Avery Lewis, donated her late husband's Two Rivers Ranch in Weld County to the church. While a member of Ascension Episcopal at Sixth Avenue and Gilpin Street, she supported Blair's programs. Her husband had been a foremost corporate attorney, practicing in the firm of Lewis & Grant with the son of James Benton Grant. Mason Lewis's father was a judge on the Tenth Circuit Court of Appeals. The lawyer, who lived at 575 Circle Drive, was also a major stockholder in the Potash Company of America, a firm merged into Ideal Basic Industries, part of the Boettcher empire.

No sooner had Dorothy Lewis deeded the Weld County property to Calvary Temple, on August 13, 1964, than Blair swapped the land with construction magnate and Colorado National Bank kingpin Nicholas R. Petry for property along the northern edge of the Polo Club. Petry, a director of Public Service, sold the former Lewis ranch to the utility in 1967 at quite a good profit. The power provider placed its failed nuclear reactor, Fort St. Vrain, on the spread.

Real estate titan Lloyd C. Fulenwider had been a partner of Petry in holding the Polo Club acreage, property he estimated worth $333,000. He had pondered building on it for years, but had encountered difficulties in changing the zoning. In parting with the land, Fulenwider stated Blair would have no problems developing it for church purposes.

Photo by Phil Goodstein

A Miller Park house at 2600 Cedar Avenue is in the center of the Calvary Temple campus.

Calvary Temple announced plans for a huge 12-grade day school, a 4,000- to 5,000-seat sanctuary, a 1,700-space parking lot, and other church facilities on the western 16 acres of its Polo Club spread. It hoped to add 930 housing units on 30 acres to the east. The proposal called for four apartment buildings rising from five to fifteen stories. Polo Club residents defeated this suggestion by preventing Calvary Temple from getting the land rezoned in November 1969. Three years later, Calvary Temple presented plans for a 97,295-square-foot youth center, the sanctuary, and a possible future church college.

By the time Polo Club residents again took up their cudgels to block Calvary Temple, the church faced severe financial problems. The congregation was having trouble paying for its senior citizens nursing home, the Life Center, at Ninth Avenue and Ivy Street. In 1974, investors filed suit against Calvary Temple over the project. Disgruntled bondholders alleged Blair was borrowing funds under fraudulent premises to pay current debts, so running a Ponzi scheme. The church's enterprises filed for bankruptcy in April of that year.

In the face of the Polo Club controversy and Calvary Temple's economic difficulties, a Denver grand jury indicted Blair for securities fraud and criminal conspiracy for defrauding 3,400 investors out of upwards of $14 million. As the trial loomed, District Attorney Dale Tooley stated that the pastor's influential friends approached him, informing him that "God does not want this case prosecuted." Despite such divine intervention, in August 1976 a jury found the preacher guilty of 17 counts of fraud.

Cynics argued Tooley had filed the charges at the behest of Polo Club property owners who wanted to keep Blair's empire out of their backyard. Judge Clifton Flowers sentenced the preacher to five years of probation, ruling Blair would be best able to raise funds to pay off church debts while he remained as pastor. The controversy and unpaid bonds lingered at least into the year 2000. Dan Lynch, another Democratic Party stalwart, led aggrieved bondholders against Blair.

Despite the collapse of the church's financial empire, Calvary Temple built its school on the northwestern portion of the Polo Club. In 1993, the church sold the spread back to Fulenwider for $1.475 million. Contractors immediately destroyed the school, replacing it with elite housing.

Already in 1977, Fulenwider had reacquired the 30 acres at the southwest corner of Alameda Avenue and South Steele Street from Calvary Temple for around $1.8 million. Fulenwider developed it as Polo Club North with 126 two-unit condos and 31 custom-built houses. In 2000, a masonry wall replaced an iron fence, providing further protection for residents from the city.

The sale of the Polo Club land was indicative of Calvary Temple's waning fortunes. After Blair's conviction, the congregation failed to get new blood. By 1998, when the church board convinced Blair to retire, the temple was down to around 800 members. The church continued to operate north of Alameda Avenue into the 21st century, being home of the Colorado Christian School. By then, houses it owned by the sanctuary needed painting. Blair, through his Blair Foundation, which he established in 1967, turned his attention to Ethiopia. Heralding the country for overthrowing communism, he raised money through his charity

Cherry Creek Tower, right, is the big glass box at the southwest corner of Cherry Creek Drive South and South Steele Street. Polo Club Condominiums, left, is directly south of it.

during the first decade of the 21st century to increase a Christian missionary presence among the suffering people of Africa.

A 21-story highrise, Polo Club Condominiums, is at the southeastern edge of Miller Park at 3131 Alameda Avenue. General contractor N. Neil Wynkoop, a retired air force colonel who was born in Fruita, Colorado, on May 10, 1917, oversaw its construction in 1966–67 for his Polo Club Corporation. Far from encountering powerful and vocal opposition as a completely out-of-place skyscraper comparable to the objections that met the Calvary Temple highrise proposals, Wynkoop reaped praise for the effort. Even before the building was ready for occupancy, he had sold units to many of the people who lived in and around the Polo Club. In August 1967, the *Rocky Mountain News* touted the tower, with 158 units, as the "in" address. Roland Wilson & Associates designed it with an ornate lobby and a 5,600-square foot atrium.

No sooner had residents moved in than tensions flared between Wynkoop and the condo owners. He remained as its managing partner until his death at age 58 in May 1975. His widow, Mildred McDevitt, was long a key figure in Denver high society. The skyscraper remained home of members of the city's financial and social elite.

Firefighters rushed into the partially completed Polo Club Condominiums in the early hours of September 14, 1967, to evacuate 50 residents from a blaze caused by a carelessly discarded cigarette. A worse conflagration followed on Halloween 1991 when a three-alarm fire erupted. In no time, flames shot up to the top of the

21-story-high atrium. Members of the fire department were hampered by icy streets and slippery, narrow supports on the roof. In full packs, they climbed the stairs, breaking out the plexiglas skylights to prevent a disaster.

Cherry Creek Tower at 3100 Cherry Creek Drive South is directly north of Polo Club Condominiums. Designed by acclaimed Bauhaus architect Carl Groos, it looks like a huge glass box. Aksel Nielsen, the principal of Mortgage Investments Company and the head of Title Guaranty Company, was behind the $2.5 million effort which opened in January 1962. The building has had tenants as rich and as powerful as those in Polo Club Condominiums. Among those making it a part-time residence was Audrey Meadows after her 1961 marriage to Robert Six, the head of the Denver-based Continental Airlines.

An office building, initially known as the Citadel, stands directly east of Polo Club Condominiums at 3200 Cherry Creek Drive South. Cable television magnate Bill Daniels built it as his corporate headquarters in 1986–87. At one point, he arranged for daily gourmet-catered lunches for his staff. Cambridge Dairy had occupied the land from 1892 until it moved to 690 South Colorado Boulevard in 1933 after a flood washed away its plant.

Percival Young of 294 South Steele Street, a British immigrant, founded the dairy in 1903, naming it for Cambridge University in his homeland. (He was subsequently at 334 South Gaylord Street.) His descendants owned the property into the 1970s—their spread stretched from the west of South Steele Street to South Garfield Street. Among Young's relatives were members of the Denton family who had lived at 3035 Alameda Avenue. For a while, after Cambridge Dairy relocated, Stearns Dairy was at Cherry Creek and South Steele Street before moving to Alameda Avenue at South Birch Street. A Young Dairy was once also at Cherry Creek and South Steele Street. The Citadel subsequently became the Daniels Building.

The dairy business also impacted the modern evolution of Miller Park. H. Brown Cannon, a close friend of Mayor Benjamin Stapleton, occupied the palace at 100 South University Boulevard around 1931. The owner of Windsor Dairy and numerous other milk producers, he was the man who sold the city the heart of the land that became Stapleton Airport. For years, the *Denver Post* attacked Cannon as the monopolistic head of the dairy trust and the tycoon druggists had to see after the repeal of Prohibition. The paper asserted that a pharmacy owner had exclusively to stock milk from Cannon's companies to get a liquor license which Cannon was able to procure for them through his ties to the mayor. A member of the South Denver Civic Association, Cannon had heavy oil and bank holdings and collaborated with Stapleton in various business ventures. He died at age 84 on August 31, 1950.

At age 49 in 1915, Cannon had married the 27-year-old Margaret Reynolds, who had previously worked for Juvenile Court Judge Ben B. Lindsey. She remained in the Miller Park house until her death in September 1971. Her son Brown W. Cannon was a leading executive with Beatrice, the firm which bought the Cannon dairy holdings. Her daughter Charla married Charles Gates Jr. of the rubber dynasty. A few years after Margaret Cannon passed away, fire destroyed the house

Ornate condo complexes have grown up on the south banks of Cherry Creek in Miller Park such as this structure at 2500 Cherry Creek Drive South.

at the southeast corner of Cherry Creek Drive South and South University Boulevard. For nearly 25 years, the land remained open space, blending in with the south side of Cherry Creek. Wildlife was omnipresent, including foxes dodging through the area.

In the mid-1990s, as real estate values soared, developer Stephen Owen acquired the Cannon land and the estate of Temple Buell at 106 South University Boulevard which had been mostly empty since Buell's death in 1990. After tearing down Buell's manor, he erected One Polo Creek, a massive condominium project. Comparable complexes followed. In the early 21st century, some original Miller Park houses came down for more spacious and expensive residences. Gated communities popped up, hidden away in the middle of the section. Developers promoted part of the area as Polo Creek Court. In 2008, city crews began work on transforming Cherry Creek Drive South along Miller Park into a landscaped parkway/speedway, one on which motorists rarely stopped at a pedestrian/bicycling crossing at South Steele Street.

Knight School

By the time the new wave of building swept Miller Park, few of the people living there, in the Polo Club, or Belcaro sent their children to Denver Public Schools. This was quite a change from the post–World War II years when the neighborhood's new schoolhouse brought residents together. In September 1951, Stephen Knight Elementary opened at the northeast corner of Exposition Avenue and South Steele Street. Architect Temple Buell designed it. The academy was on what had been unplatted land, real estate which had been a dump before DPS acquired it for educational purposes. Another neighborhood dump was the land near what became Calvary Temple. The best known dump in the area was the ground that emerged as the Cherry Creek Mall.

Knight School recalled members of a family that had long been involved in the milling and baking industries while serving on the board of education. For years, Stephen J. Knight Jr., an engineer, lived nearby at 3040 Exposition Avenue. On the side, members of the Knight family were major figures in the Congregational Church. The academy pulled in the children of Bonnie Brae, Belcaro, Miller Park, and the Polo Club at a time when Denver took pride in having a foremost public school system. The academy had a capacity of 570 and was usually near that number through the 1960s. For a while, it was on double sessions.

Court-ordered school busing paired Knight with Barrett School at 29th Avenue and Jackson Street. The Belcaro academy hosted kindergarten and grades four through six; first-, second-, and third-graders went to Barrett. By 1982, amidst a wave of school closings, Knight School had seemingly seen its day. The combination of an aging neighborhood, a decreasing school-aged population, busing, and the way the wealthy increasingly sent their children to private academies led to the steep decline of its enrollment—Knight had 274 students in 1981, more than half of whom came from the Barrett district. The economically and politically powerful neighborhood was not about to let the DPS close this institution.

The school administration responded to demands that Knight remain open by transforming it into one of the city's three inaugural magnet schools, Knight Fundamental Academy. Parents of students had to sign contracts stipulating that their children would behave and do the assigned work. The school expected parents actively to participate in its programs. The goal was an old-fashioned, rigorous, drill-oriented education.

Discipline and order were the watchwords of Knight. It required students in first and second grades to walk in twin lines down hallways with their arms folded. The academy proudly emphasized "traditional American values of patriotism, good citizenship, work, honesty, pride, courtesy, and respect for self, others, and authority." The school day began with an orientation session in which the students were

Photo by Phil Goodstein

Knight School, at the northeast corner of Exposition Avenue and South Steele Street, opened in 1951 as the Belcaro/Bonnie Brae academy.

required to salute the flag and sing patriotic anthems. At times, the school seemed to have something of a quota production system as its means of assuring learning. It did not retain those who failed to meet expectations or whose parents did not cooperate. Most pupils were bused to Belcaro. Few neighborhood children attended it.

When Knight students scored near the top on standardized tests, supporters contended that the school's approach had paid off. This led more to apply to Knight School which had a enrollment of nearly 500 students with a waiting list. In response, DPS established a comparable academy at Traylor School at 2900 South Ivan Way in Bear Valley. Knight School subsequently took in only learners living east of the Platte River. It was ever less part of the Bonnie Brae–Belcaro matrix. The school board confirmed this in February 2009 when it announced the school would relocate the next year to Hallett School at 2950 Jasmine Street in Park Hill while real estate interests eyed the Knight land.

A Note on Sources:

Materials on Bonnie Brae are sparse. A 1984 interview with Mike Dire of the Bonnie Brae Tavern was helpful on the early years of the area and the Bonnie Brae Tavern. The DeBoer papers at the DPL include materials on the layout of the neighborhood. DPL has clippings on George Olinger. *DP*, May 8, 1919, p. 9, reported Olinger's land purchases and plans as a real estate developer. Tom Noel, *Rocky Mountain Gold* (Tulsa: Continental Heritage Press, 1980), 223–24, has a paid plug for Olinger's. Brief glances at the origins of Bonnie Brae are in *DP*, February 28, 1962, zone 2, p. 7, and *WPP*, February 1982, p. 7.

RMN, December 13, 1928, p. 1, December 20–24, 1928, all p. 1, December 30, 1928, p. 1, May 22, 1929, p. 9, September 11, 1929, p. 1, January 26, 1930, p. 9, February 6, 1930, p. 1, May-June 1930, esp. June 15, 1930, p. 1, and October 21, 1930, p. 1, looked at the fate of Associated Industries. James H. Baker and LeRoy Hafen, *History of Colorado* (Denver: Linderman Company, 1927), has a paid biographical portrait of Cornelius Flynn, 4:665–69.

Don Etter, *Denver Going Modern* (Denver: Graphic Impressions, 1977), heralds the art moderne homes in Bonnie Brae. Michael Paglia and Diane Wray Tomasso, *The Mid-Century Modern House in Denver* (Denver: HD, 2007), also features the houses in the area, esp. 12–15. Margaret O'Neill, *The Original Eight* ([Denver]: n.p., [c. 1986]), 81, tells the story of Laurence O'Neill and the fire department. *RMN*, March 6, 1936, p. 24, announced plans for Bonnie Brae Park.

The University of Colorado Archives hold the papers of the National Farmers Union. I mention Jim Patton in *From Soup Lines to the Front Lines*, 316–18. *Alumni Confederate*, June 2008, p. 6, highlighted the career of Merrie Lynn. She recalled her girlhood and radio career in *DP Empire*, December 2, 1973, pp. 14–20. Also see *DP*, February 21, 1973, p. 48, and December 10, 1975, p. 1, and *RMN*, February 22, 1973, p. 60. John Davoren recalled working with her at KOA in an interview on March 7, 2009.

RMN, April 22, 1934, p. 14, section 3, looked at Doc Reynolds and the origins of KLZ. Clark Secrest reviewed the rise of KLZ and the Reynolds family, "With a

Song in the Air," *CH*, Winter 1993, pp. 11–13. *RMN*, November 2, 1927, p. 14, and *DP*, November 2, 1927, p. 9, told of the station moving its broadcast tower to Dupont. *DP*, November 28, 1931, p. 2, reported Reynolds' death. Also see *RMN*, April 19, 1959, p. 42AA, *DP*, March 10, 1960, p. 30, and the ad in the unpaginated *The Story of Littleton* (Littleton: *Littleton Independent*, 1938). Tom Mulvey mentions the station's origins in "Denver Radio: 80 Years of Change," on the Web page of the Broadcast Professionals of Colorado. Allen Young, *Exotic and Irrational* (n.p.: Pilgrim Process, 2006), 10, emphasizes the KLZ opera broadcast. Dave Felice shared his extensive knowledge of Denver radio with me in various communications in February 2009. *UPN*, October 6, 1960, mentioned plans for a shopping mall on the KLZ land. *WPP*, October 2004, p. 3, and *RMN*, December 10, 2005, p. 4C, chronicled the transformation of the old Kent School/Denver Seminary property.

Retrospections about the Bonnie Brae Tavern were in *RMN*, February 28, 1988, pp. 18–19M, *WW*, December 13, 2001, p. 65, and *WPP*, June 2004, p. 3. *RMN*, May 23, 2002, p. 15B, May 27, 2002, p. 10B, and *DP*, May 23, 2002, p. 4B, reported the death of Sue Dire. *WPP* celebrated Sue Dire Day, July 2000, p. 33. Dick Kreck recalled Sue Dire as Grambo in an interview on September 1, 2008.

GCCC, August 2008, pp. 8–10, plugged Bonnie Brae businesses. *DP*, November 27, 2008, p. 11B, and *GCCC*, December 2008, p. 18, mentioned Bonnie Brae Flowers. *WPP*, December 2000, p. 7, featured Esquire Market. In May 2007, p. 4, the *Profile* told of the closing of the shop. Bob Sheets shared the story about the ghost of the woman frozen to death in the Bonnie Brae meat-processing plant in an interview on December 7, 2008. The *Washington Park Press*, October 16, 1941, and *WPP*, March 1981, p. 15, mentioned Preiser Grocery. Jim Wiste recalled his experiences at the Campus Lounge in an informal discussion in 1995.

Thomas J. Noel, *Colorado Catholicism* (Boulder: University Press of Colorado, 1989), 365–67, is a look at St. Vincent de Paul. Allen duPont Breck, *The Episcopal Church in Colorado* (Denver: Big Mountain Press, 1963), 228, 258, glances at St. Michael and All Angels. *RMN*, December 9, 1950, p. 19, *DP*, June 6, 1959, p. 4, and May 21, 1960, p. 4, dealt with the emergence of Bonnie Brae Baptist. *WPP*, June 1997, p. 27, heralded the golden anniversary of the Kirk of Bonnie Brae. Also see Virginia Greene Millikin, *The Bible and the Gold Rush* (Denver: Big Mountain Press, 1962), 113, 222, 261.

WPP, June 1999, told of efforts to gain Bonnie Brae landmark status. Diane Vertovec decried Bonnie Brae developments in a letter to the editor, *DP*, January 24, 2006, p. 6B. Comparable criticisms of the impact of rising property values were the letter by Peter Tonks, *WPP*, January 2006, p. 9, and the guest column by Teresa Keegan, *DP*, January 18, 2009, p. 2D. *DP*, November 11, 2007, p. 1R, promoted new developments in the area.

Lawrence Phipps lacks a biographer. Ingeborg Thomsen, "The Business and Political Careers of Senator Lawrence C. Phipps" (Masters Thesis, DU, 1956), is extremely superficial, mostly presenting the man's homilies about himself. Leonard Schlup, "Colorado Crusader," *Essays in Colorado History*, 9 (1989), 25–36, glances at Phipps. I mention Phipps in *Robert Speer's Denver*, 352, 400, 406, 434,

449, 482, 496, 497, *In the Shadow of the Klan*, 196–200, 234, and *From Soup Lines to the Front Lines*, 72–78, 350. CHS has a tiny Phipps collection and features the Phipps family in a wall display in the lobby of the Colorado History Museum. The DU Archives have holdings on the man and his family.

The NRHP nomination of the Phipps Mansion is also apropos. Noel and Norgren, *City Beautiful*, 40, calls the manor "Denver's grandest residence." Davis, *Denver Dwellings*, 186–205, discusses the Phipps saga and the houses of the family; also see Kohl, *Historic Mansions*, 220–30. Bonniwell, *Denver Country Club*, 126–28, emphasizes the role of the Phipps family in promoting tennis. Alice Bakemeier, *Crestmoor Park Heritage* (Denver: Heritage Press, 2005), 13–16, reviews the impact of Van Holt Garrett and Donald Bromfield. *RMN*, February 8, 1959, p. 18A, and August 14, 1959, p. 48, told of the sale of the Allan Phipps House to Hamilton Oil and the role of Frank Leahy.

CCN, January 6, 1966, p. 3, looked at developments in the Belcaro Shopping Center. Tom Swearingen, *Cooperative Century* ([Denver]: Colorado Cattlemen's Centennial Commission, 1967), 62, mentions the gas valves at South Colorado Boulevard and Exposition Avenue. *WW*, November 30, 2000, p. 18, observed the end of Hodel's.

Comments on the Summit of the Eight are based on living through it. Maxine Lankford recalled participating in protests on the edge of the Phipps Mansion banquet in conversations in 1997. I attended much of the Spicer Breedan trial in March 1997 during which testimony told about the Rice Krispies and the Breedan family's history. Walter Gerash shared his views on the case in an interview after the acquittal of Peter Schmitz. The latter informed me of his experiences and the role of Bill Ritter in pushing the prosecution.

WPP, May 2006, p. 25, glanced at the trial concerning the Belcaro Park Homeowners Association. Dan Fead educated me about the politics concerning Belcaro restrictive covenants and real estate developments in an interview on July 24, 2008.

El Jebel Temple (Denver: El Jebel Shrine, [1990]), 31, glances at El Palomino Patrol. *DP*, October 22, 1989, p. 1F, heralded Hyde Park. James M. Thoeming, who helped sell the units, discussed the project in 1990. I drew on assessor records and plats for the discussion of Stokes Place and Green Bowers. Karl Kraft shared his knowledge of the area in conversations in 1997. Paglia and Tomasso, *Mid-Century Modern Houses*, 27–28, highlights some of the post–World War II residences in the subdivision.

Central Christian Church has wall displays on the congregation's history. DPL has a clipping file on the congregation. *RMN*, May 12, 1973, p. 142, celebrated the church's first hundred years, reporting the laying of the cornerstone of its South Denver plant. *DP*, May 16, 1995, p. 10B, also profiled the congregation. My *Ghosts of Denver*, 138, tells of Central Christian's origins and Capitol Hill presence.

DPL has materials on City of Brest Park and Denver sister cities. Jim Weiss shared his knowledge of the sister city program on December 13, 2008, during which he reported that some had complained about the name of City of Brest Park, confusing it with "breasts."

Bonniwell, *Denver Country Club*, 99, 101–02, examines the rise and fall of polo at the Country Club. Lawrence Phipps Jr., *Forty Years of the Arapahoe Hunt* (n.p.: n.p., n.d.), is a superficial anthology about the origins and lore of the Arapahoe Hunt Club. CHS collection 1629 is the papers of the organization. Also see *Life*, May 30, 1949, pp. 106–07.

Noel and Norgren touch on the Polo Club in *City Beautiful*, 62. Cf. "Art in Denver," *Lookout*, 1:2 (January 1928), 32–33. DPL has an unpublished manuscript on the area in the Caroline Bancroft papers. Ann Emrich, "Denver's Polo Club was Playground for Society's Elite," *WPP*, July 1986, and Robert Johnson, "City Sports Mark o' Polo," *Denver Magazine*, September 1986, 55–56, were insightful. *DP*, December 14, 2008, p. 1R, is also apropos. Diane Paris informed me of modern polo developments during conversations in the summer of 1987.

The suicide of Annie Hughes was in *DP*, April 19, 1940, p. 1, and *RMN*, April 20, 1940, p. 7. *RMN*, March 28, 1958, p. 20, and *DP*, March 28, 1958, p. 21, reported the death of Lafayette Hughes. The *News* looked at his estate, April 4, 1958, p. 33, and chronicled the real estate transactions after his death, August 27, 1959, p. 5.

DU has a file on the Hamiltons in its collection on the Ritchie Center. The school's *The Source*, October 9, 1995, especially featured the couple. I glance at the Continental Revolutionary Army in *Big Money*, 446–47. Also see *DP*, August 8, 1975, p. 1, January 11–13, 1978, p. 1, January 16, 1978, p. 12, and March 23, 1978, p. 2, *SCJ*, July 9, 1974, p. 1, and May 8, 1975, p. 7, and *RMN*, January 12, 1978, p. 3. *WW*, April 20, 2000, p. 73, reported the doings of Tom Shane and the end of the clubhouse. *UPN*, October 3, 1968, and December 17, 1968, discussed Charles Gates' push for a heliport. Tom Manley gave me his impressions of living in the Polo Club in a conversation on December 14, 2007. Linda Lebsack shared her knowledge of the mass destruction of vintage Polo Club homes in a December 5, 2008, conversation.

Alvan Morrison called my attention to Larry Mizel's push for the House of Rothschild in a letter of November 11, 1991. *CJ*, October 9, 1968, p. 36, reported plans for it. Also see *DP*, October 22, 1969, p. 39D. *DP*, July 28, 1976, p. 57, told of its conversion into condominiums.

For the origins and evolution of Miller Park, I relied on real estate, assessor, and building records to trace early ownership and land exchanges in the area. Householder and social directories provide listings of who lived where.

DPL has an extensive file on Charles Blair and Calvary Temple. Blair told his story in *"The Man Who Could Do No Wrong"* (Lincoln, VA: Chosen Books, 1981). The church feted him on his 40th anniversary as pastor, *Commemorative Family Album* (Denver: Calvary Temple, 1987). Also see the advertisement in *DP Empire*, June 21, 1959, p. 359. Dale Tooley, *I'd Rather Be in Denver* (Denver: Colorado Legal Publishing Company, 1985), 169, mentions the pressure from the religious-business community not to prosecute Blair. *RMJ*, July 15, 1979, told about litigation surrounding the Mason Lewis estate, including the dealings of Petry and Fulenwider. Ibid., March 30, 1977, p. 1, emphasized the conflict of interest between Petry's sale of land in Weld County and his role as a director of Public

Service. Oscar Lee, a disgraced former Public Service official who landed up in a federal prison, shared his records of the land deals with me in 1996.

A sampling of articles about Calvary Temple and Blair include *WW*, January 19, 1994, p. 10, *DP*, November 3, 1960, p. 44, September 17, 1966, p. 1, May 5, 1972, p. 2, and June 8, 1974, p. 1, and *RMN*, May 5, 1972, p. 36. *DBJ*, July 7, 2000, observed that the fraud case continued into the 21st century. *WPP*, October 2002, p. 4, looked at Colorado Christian School. *DP*, March 16, 1980, p. 1G, advertised Polo Club North.

Marjorie Barrett celebrated Polo Club Condominiums as the trendiest place in town, *RMN*, August 27, 1967, p. 1F. *DP*, February 7, 1965, p. 80, and September 18, 1967, p. 42, saluted plans for the highrise as did *CCN*, December 9, 1965, p. 6. The October 27, 1971, *DP*, p. 2, and *UPN*, November 4, 1971, examined the feud between Wynkoop and the condo association. *DP*, May 12, 1975, p. 16, mentioned Wynkoop's death. *RMN*, September 15, 1967, p. 12, reported the first blaze. *Denver Fire Department,* ([Denver]: [DFD], 2003), 203, emphasized the subsequent fire.

RMN, January 7, 1962, p. 55, and *DP*, p. 2D, reported the opening of Cherry Creek Tower. Also see *CJ*, June 5, 1972, p. 1. I briefly mention Audrey Meadows in *Denver in Our Time*, 43. *DP*, October 30, 1978, p. 2, reported residents discovering shrapnel in the highrise from the explosion of a nearby pipebomb on October 28, 1978.

Jack E. and Patricia A. Fletcher, *Colorado's Cowtown* (Yuma, Arizona: Jack E. and Patricia A. Fletcher, 1981), 44, 55, focuses on Cambridge Dairy and Percival Young. It mentions H. Brown Cannon, 48, 56, 63, 72. The work further discusses the origins and evolution of the Bonnie Brae Tavern, 33. *UPN*, June 30, 1960, told the story of Cambridge Dairy and the Young family; also see *DP*, August 20, 1978, p. 1E. The DU Archives have a file on Bill Daniels and his cable empire. Also see my *Big Money*, 77–79. Jan Tyler shared the story about the catered meals at the Daniels Building in an interview on January 29, 2009.

My *From Soup Lines to the Front Lines*, 164, 166, 351, 386, 475, 514, 515, emphasizes the omnipresent role of H. Brown Cannon. The Colorado History Museum has wall displays on the Cannon and Knight families and Temple Buell in its lobby. *DP*, September 3, 1971, reported the death of Margaret Cannon. Ric Waggener recalled the fire at the Cannon Mansion and Miller Park developments in a conversation around 1995. *DP*, February 19, 1994, p. 1D, announced the Polo Creek project. Cf. *DP*, July 7, 1998, p. 2E.

DPS records and DPL clippings trace the origins of Knight School. People at the South Denver history seminar of February 17, 2008, recalled the Knight School site as a dump. The late Stephen Knight challenged my interpretation of his family in *South Denver Saga* in personal correspondence in 1991. *WPP*, March 1997, p. 4, featured the work of Knight Fundamental Academy. DP, February 6, 2009, p. 4B, told of plans to relocate Knight Fundamental Academy to Hallett School.

Chapter Eight

Cory-Merrill

Schools have been the defining institutions of Cory-Merrill, the neighborhood to the south of Belcaro and Bonnie Brae. It covers the area between South University and South Colorado boulevards from Mississippi Avenue to the Valley Highway.

S. Allen and Henrietta C. Long dubbed the area Coronado when they platted the land east of South Steele Street near Louisiana Avenue on October 26, 1883. They subsequently laid out the real estate between Mississippi and Arizona avenues from South Steele Street to South Monroe Street as Coronado Heights on March 23, 1892. For a while, South Colorado Boulevard between Louisiana and Florida avenues was Coronado Boulevard at the eastern end of the development.

Lakota Heights, platted on August 30, 1911, stretches between Kentucky and Mississippi avenues from South Steele Street to South Colorado Boulevard. The First Addition to Lakota Heights, filed on July 26, 1926, covers the real estate from South Jackson Street to South Colorado Boulevard between Mississippi and Louisiana avenues. (Lakota Heights Village was once a residential complex at 1201–45 South Colorado Boulevard.) Washington Park Heights, between Mississippi and Louisiana avenues and South Monroe and South Jackson streets, is an enclave dating from June 20, 1911.

Working with John Babcock, who had the land to the south of Coronado and played a major role in the development of the University Park neighborhood, the Long family pushed school district #35 to open an academy in their area. This was the jurisdiction dating from March 22, 1886, for the property stretching between Mississippi and Yale avenues from South Colorado Boulevard to the University of Denver campus. Babcock served as the head of the school board and was simultaneously a contractor. He erected Coronado School at the northwest corner of South Jackson Street and Florida Avenue in 1886.

225

Photo by Phil Goodstein

Here and there, frame houses dot the Cory-Merrill neighborhood, including this one shaped to resemble a log cabin at 1490 South Columbine Street. It dates from 1938.

Besides the school, Babcock and the Longs promoted a church, getting Methodists to occupy the school on Sundays in 1894 for their Coronado Mission. Before long, that outreach program was part of University Park Methodist Church. Within a few years, the Methodists moved out. Coronado School simultaneously faded. Denver Public Schools sold it somewhere between 1904 and 1907. Even so, city directories list the building as remaining in place as a school through the end of World War I. George P. and Anna Varga subsequently acquired the property. They replaced the inaugural schoolhouse with their residence at 3737 Florida Avenue in 1935.

By that time, a religious-educational establishment was nearby, St. Thomas Aquinas Theological Seminary at 1300 South Steele Street. For years, the academy deliberately isolated itself from the city. The seclusion not only kept students from concerning themselves with the mundane matters of the everyday world, but the open space, sponsors hoped, would restore the health of those aspiring to the priesthood.

The Catholic Diocese of Colorado had pondered a seminary since the 1860s. Not until 1906 did it become a reality when the Congregation of the Missions, the organization of the Vincentian Fathers in the United States, established St. Thomas. Backers hoped to redress the way tuberculosis ravished many hopeful theologians. Denver's dry, sunny climate, optimists were convinced, would assure the health of seminarians.

Upon coming to Colorado, the Vincentians examined locations from Morrison to Manitou Springs for the school which they aimed to locate in a secluded spot that would assure tubercular students plenty of sunshine and fresh air. On November 10, 1906, the order paid $15,218 for 59.9 acres. A commanding view of the mountains, the priests figured, would fill students with an awe of the wonders of their creator.

Catholics broke ground for St. Thomas in the fall of 1907. Dignitaries dedicated the school on a snowy September 29, 1908. Before moving to the Coronado land, the seminary had held its first classes in a rented house at 912 South Washington Street in 1906. St. Thomas subsequently occupied private residences at 388 South Sherman Street and 34 South Logan Street.

A priest, Nicholas M. J. Steines, working under architect John J. Huddart, designed the first building on the campus, a four-story cupola-topped structure. Known as the De Andries House for an Italian priest who had been a major figure in the Vincentians, the edifice was the home of all five faculty members and 12 students. The latter called it "Old Red Brick." Seminarians had to complete a six-year program to gain ordination.

Besides nourishing the students' souls, St. Thomas sought to feed their bodies. The Vincentians used most of the seminary land for agricultural purposes, particularly alfalfa fields. During St. Thomas' early years, students and teachers alike left class to help gather the harvest. The campus included a pig sty and a cow barn.

The seminary slowly grew, having 20 students by 1920. Five years later, it was badly overcrowded when enrollment had quintupled to 98. During the 1920s, the church rapidly expanded its outreach. In part, this was in response to the hatred directed at it by the surging Ku Klux Klan. The diocese called on the faithful to build Catholic institutions as a means of fighting the masked minions.

Photo by Phil Goodstein

"Old Red Brick" was the nickname of the first structure on the St. Thomas Seminary campus, the De Andries House.

To provide more priests for local churches, the hierarchy collaborated with the Vincentians to expand the seminary. Nearly 15,000 turned out in October 1926 to celebrate the beginning of a $600,000 St. Thomas expansion program. Jacques B. Benedict designed the new complex which included a chapel, tower, dorms, and a kitchen. Figuring the best of European church design was most appropriate for a seminary, he saw masons construct the chapel out of 900 different shapes and colors of brick to provide a mosaic effect. The building's combination of Gothic, Byzantine, and Romanesque styles is known as Lombard architecture.

The 138-foot-high Tihen Tower, honoring Bishop John Henry Tihen who led the diocese between 1917 and 1931, dominates the campus. Above the doors to the tower are carvings featuring small animals, religious symbols, and the signs of saints. Four 12–foot-high statues of angels stand on the loggia sculpted by Enrico Licari who worked closely with Benedict on the project. Worshippers consecrated the chapel in 1931 as the final part of the expansion program. In 1989, the seminary got the complex placed in the National Register of Historic Places.

The campus included a power plant, complete with tunnels linking the buildings for a steam-heating system. The school had a vegetable cellar to store its produce. Well water provided irrigation. The seminary added a recreation building with bowling alleys in 1951. In June 1956, the Vincentians dedicated a $1.5 million expansion which brought the theological institute's ideal capacity to 225 students. St. Thomas reached its peak enrollment of 274 in 1965. In addition to serving as a seminary, the school offered a bachelor of arts degree.

Enrollment was down to 175 students by the early 1970s. It continued to plummet during the next decade, stabilizing at around 50 to 55 on-campus seminarians by the late 1980s. They were joined by off-campus students seeking a master of theology or professional degrees in pastoral work. St. Thomas ended its undergraduate program in 1982.

St. Thomas had varied relations with the surrounding residential areas. At the time of the 1926 expansion, it fenced off the land and closed its roads to through traffic. By the 1970s, it mostly looked deserted. Passersby rarely saw activity on campus. The old farm fields were largely weed-filled yards. On occasion, the seminary invited people to the campus for assorted cultural affairs. Locals leased its chapel for concerts and weddings. From the 1950s to the 1990s, the school held a fall bazaar. Neighbors often referred to St. Thomas as "the priest factory."

With the declining enrollment and the need to raise an endowment, in 1979 St. Thomas sold 18 acres on its southern boundary to the Arnold Corporation. The school had never used this property. During the early 1970s it had unsuccessfully negotiated with the city about transforming the real estate into a park. Nearby residents opposed the Arnold Corporation's proposal to install a 360-unit condominium project as too dense and out of scale with the area. Eventually, a fenced-off, 134-unit effort, the Biscayne, occupied the former St. Thomas property at 3333 Florida Avenue.

The seminary did not survive the 1990s. By this time, it was usually graduating but two or three priests a year. The Vincentians were paying for up to a third of its annual $2.1 million budget. Archbishop Francis Stafford, who had taken his

Photo by Phil Goodstein

Tihen Tower dominates the complex that arose on the St. Thomas Seminary campus between 1926 and 1931.

post in 1986, was dissatisfied with the school. He visualized the land as the headquarters of the archdiocese. Both factors led to the shuttering of the college on June 30, 1995. Soon thereafter, the archdiocese purchased the land from the Congregation of the Missions for $2.59 million. Since 1906, St. Thomas had turned out around 1,100 priests.

Naming the acreage the John Paul II Center for the New Evangelization, the hierarchy sold its previous headquarters at Second Avenue and Josephine Street in the plush Cherry Creek North business district, relocating on the former seminary. By this time, Stafford had won the attention of the pope by hosting World Youth Day in 1993, an event which saw the pontiff come to the Mile High City. Stafford left Denver in 1996 for a job at the Vatican after John Paul II had named him a cardinal.

Charles Chaput succeeded Stafford as archbishop. A supporter of Opus Dei, a highly influential conservative Catholic organization, he saw great possibilities for the old St. Thomas land. In addition to arranging to have his living quarters there, the cleric believed it was an ideal site for a seminary. Building on the work of Stafford, on March 16, 1999, Chaput announced the reincarnation of St. Thomas as St. John Vianney Theological Seminary. The school honored the patron saint of parish priests. The goal was to train 50 priests a year. The archdiocese aimed at raising a $10 million endowment for the facility.

The school held its first classes on September 8, 1999. Its faculty was affiliated with the Pontifical Lateran University in Rome. Collaborating with Regis University, St. John Vianney accepted undergraduates aiming at the priesthood. It named its library for Cardinal Stafford. The main reading room recalled Archbishop Urban J. Vehr who led Colorado Catholics from 1931 to 1967—the St. Thomas library had honored Vehr.

By the time St. John Vianney was operating, a second school, the Redemptoris Mater Archdiocese Missionary Seminary, also educated priest candidates on the St. Thomas grounds. This was a Vatican effort to train missionary priests as part of a "new evangelization" known as the Neocatechumental Way. The first such facility opened in Rome in 1987–88. Before long, various dioceses established them in the United States. In part, they were a response to major inroads evangelical Protestants were making among traditional Catholic populations. The Redemptoris Mater Seminary (named for the Mother of the Redeemer, i.e., the Virgin Mary) stated its students looked to the world outside the diocese as opposed to those at St. John Vianney who focused on work within. Even so, they were under the direction of the archbishop and agreed to serve where the archdiocese assigned them, whether at home or abroad.

The Archdiocese installed works of art around the old St. Thomas campus. Among them is *Our Lady of New Life*, a statue designed by Heberto Maestas in the courtyard near the oldest church bell in Colorado. Known to the observant as "Vox Dei"—"the Voice of God"—worshippers brought the bell to Denver in 1865 for the city's first Catholic church. St. Thomas Seminary acquired it in 1942, students calling it "Old Faithful." In 2001, the seminary added stations of the cross as part of an archdiocesan park to the west of Tihen Tower.

Photo by Phil Goodstein

An old farmhouse remained standing at the southwest corner of South Jackson Street and Mexico Avenue, a remnant of the day when the Cory-Merrill neighborhood was mostly an agricultural enclave. Nearby were greenhouses. The occupant's family once owned much of the surrounding land, selling off property for commercial development to the east. Improvers targeted the residence as an eyesore in the 21st century.

Photo by Phil Goodstein

As was the case with many schools erected in the 1950s, Cory at South Steele Street and Florida Avenue is a flat, rather undistinguished structure. Supporters of international-style architecture have gotten it declared a landmark.

Cory and Merrill Schools

$\mathcal{B}$y the time St. John Vianney Theological Seminary occupied the St. Thomas land, the areas to the south and east of it were in transition. There had been little but fields and a few houses in Coronado until World War II. Residential growth swept the enclave from the late 1940s until the early 1960s. As much as had been the case in the 1880s when locals sponsored Coronado School, residents demanded educational facilities for their children.

DPS authorized a new elementary school at the southeast corner of South Steele Street and Florida Avenue in August 1949 where architect Victor Hornbein designed John J. Cory School. The academy recalled a Denver native who had worked as a mining engineer. During a slump in 1907, Cory took a temporary job teaching math at West High School. Education quickly became his career. Long living at 1175 South High Street, Cory served as principal of South High from 1919 to 1939. He thereupon became assistant superintendent of schools while overseeing Opportunity School. He died at age 62 in December 1945, ten days after asking for retirement on account of his poor health. The school board dedicated the building in his memory in 1951.

Cory School had a capacity of 492 students. It was immediately overcrowded. For a while, it was on double sessions. It went back to normal hours in early 1955 after DPS opened Bradley School near South Elm Street and Cornell Avenue. The dedication of Ellis School near South Dahlia Street and Arkansas Avenue in 1957 further eased the press of ever more students. The school system subsequently declared Cory could accommodate 540 pupils. By 1974, after the implementation of busing and the maturation of the baby boomers, the school was down to an enrollment of 142. That number slipped to 108 four years later and 81 in 1981.

By this time, Cory offered kindergarten and grades four, five, and six, paired with Hallett School at 28th Avenue and Jasmine Street as part of court-ordered school busing. The academy had a surge of enrollment in the early 1980s when it took in many of the students who had previously attended the closed Washington Park and Knight schools. DPS then stated the academy had space for 600 children.

Creative programs have come and gone from Cory. At one time, it had a veritable Indian encampment along South Steele Street, complete with a tipi. For a while, it served as the administrative offices of DPS's Barlarat Outdoor Educational Center, a 650-acre site near Jamestown, Colorado. In the modern era, Cory has adopted the Cougar as its mascot. In 1994, the city declared it a landmark as illustrative of the best of post–World War II international-style architecture. DPS counted it as having an enrollment that was 79 percent white and 21 percent minority for the 2007–08 school year. The adjacent Merrill Middle School, in contrast, was 33 percent white and 67 percent minority.

This was quite a contrast. Virtually from the time Merrill Junior High School opened to the east of Cory at the southwest corner of Florida Avenue and South Monroe Street in early 1953, it mirrored developments at the elementary school. Architect Temple Buell designed the junior high. The edifice recalled Louise Merrill, the founding principal of Byers Junior High School who kept that post until her death in January 1940.

Immediately overcrowded, Merrill Junior High expanded in 1954. Students flocked to the school in grades seven through nine through the 1960s. In addition to those living in Coronado, it pulled youngsters from University Park and much of the area east of South Colorado Boulevard. While DPS stated the academy's maximum capacity was 1,440 students, Merrill had 1,666 by the spring of 1966 with more on the way. With the opening of Hamilton Junior High School at 8600 Dartmouth Avenue in 1969, overcrowding eased before enrollment plunged with the passing of the baby boomers and the coming of court-ordered school busing.

During the late 1960s, Merrill was a quiet school under principal Roy Rebrovick who ran it with an iron hand while supporting the work of the South Denver Civic Association. By the 21st century, it attracted students from around the world. Not only have these included the children of foreign nationals teaching and studying at the University of Denver, but it has been a magnet school for those born outside the United States who need English acquisition classes. In the late 1990s, neighbors pushed the school system and the city to join with them to sod the playing fields of Cory and Merrill, linking the schools together as Cory-Merrill Park.

Near the end of the first decade of the 21st century, Cory and Merrill were on uneven paths. For the most part, Cory did quite well with classes from early childhood education through the fifth grade. It included a highly gifted program. Academic performance and community confidence, in contrast, were lacking at Merrill. Backers of the schools responded by forming the Cory-Merrill Campus Coalition in September 2007 to ponder the links between the academies and their future. Some urged merging them into a joint program, stretching from early childhood education through eighth grade. Others called for expanding the effort all the way through high school. For the most part, individuals endorsing these schemes had extremely weak ties with the parents of many of the poorly performing students. They did reach out to those who had children at University Park, Ellis, and Steele schools, academies feeding Merrill Middle School. A consensus urged a joint campus extending from early childhood education through eighth grade.

Cory and Merrill stood on what had been undeveloped land, 40 acres known as Euclid Place in the late 19th and early 20th centuries. The spread recalled a famous Greek mathematician. Off to the west was Electric Heights between Mississippi and Florida avenues from South University Boulevard to South Clayton Street. The developer filed his plat on it on October 29, 1889. Streets designated pioneers of electricity: South Josephine Street was Sprague Avenue; South Columbine Street was Edison Avenue; and South Elizabeth Street was Westinghouse Avenue. Alta Vista is the area west of South Steele Street between Mississippi and Mexico avenues. The city recorded its plat on March 19, 1890. Until well after World War II, builders designed many Alta Vista houses to emphasize a commanding view of the mountains on the steep hill sloping from South Steele Street to South University Boulevard—Alta Vista is Spanish for high view.

The House of the Good Shepherd

*I*n addition to schools, an orphanage was once a dominant Cory-Merrill landmark, the House of the Good Shepherd. Its campus stretched between Louisiana

Author's collection

The House of the Good Shepherd when it was on the west side of South Cherokee Street between West Cedar Avenue and West Byers Place.

and Florida avenues from South Jackson Street to South Colorado Boulevard. The facility dated from 1883 when Catholic Bishop Joseph Machebeuf arranged for the Sisters of the Good Shepherd of St. Louis to establish a Denver home for orphan and delinquent girls. Five nuns opened it on September 18 of that year.

After briefly occupying a couple of frame houses near West Fourth Avenue and Galapago Street, in 1885 the nuns bought five acres from the Circle Railroad on the west side of South Cherokee Street between West Cedar Avenue and West Byers Place—the railroad sold it to them at half price. The sisters liked the land precisely because it was isolated. They desired a spot where the girls would be physically separated from the temptations of the city while they learned basic job skills and how to emerge as the loving wives of deserving husbands.

The nuns insisted their facility was vitally necessary to protect girls, some of whom were no more than ten years of age, from pimps and others who sought to recruit them into criminal occupations. Before long, the House of the Good Shepherd had 300 tenants, including 50 Indians whom the federal government sent from North Dakota reservations in the course of 1885–91. The goal was to teach the young women "the ways of civilization," defined as the white middle-class ethic. To make this a reality, the institution sought to sever all connections between these wards and their tribes.

The House of the Good Shepherd experienced turbulence during the reign of a politically powerful anti-Catholic society, the American Protective Association, in 1894–97. The group, whose members included Mayor Marion Van Horn (1893–95) and Governor Albert McIntire (1895–97), vehemently objected to policies which used public funds to pay the House of the Good Shepherd to hold and discipline "incorrigible girls." Such a secular purpose, they argued, was a state function and required the establishment of a public facility. Not until 1899, after filing suit, did the orphanage receive $4,296.50 for caring for such young women from March 1894 to late 1895 as a religious and social-welfare institution.

By the early 20th century, Good Shepherd had outgrown its home on South Cherokee Street. After receiving 20 acres of Coronado land around 1911 from John Vail, it set its sights on the isolated location where neither South Harrison Street nor Arkansas Avenue cut through—Arkansas Avenue does not exist between South Steele Street and South Colorado Boulevard. In 1913, the nuns opened a four-story red-bricked building near the southwest corner of Louisiana Avenue and South Colorado Boulevard. (The official address was 1401 South Colorado Boulevard). Before long, the House of the Good Shepherd had a capacity for 650 young women. Included was a convent, chapel, and laundry.

About the time the House of the Good Shepherd moved to South Colorado Boulevard, Denver was engaged in a fervent morals crackdown. In 1912, reformers gained control of city hall. Led by the inspector of amusements, Josephine Roche, they targeted the red-light district. The women working there, Roche explained, were not criminals, but victims who needed to be set right. Toward this end, working with police commissioner George Creel, she sought to create a rehabilitation facility for arrested prostitutes on the Denver City Farm near Henderson, land which later became the Adams County fairgrounds.

The House of the Good Shepherd was well isolated from the city at the southwest corner of Louisiana Avenue, the road in the foreground, and South Colorado Boulevard on the left.

Squabbling among politicians killed that plan. In the meanwhile, Roche worked closely with the Sisters of the Good Shepherd. She arranged for the South Colorado Boulevard complex to house some of the women from the red-light district in a "Magdalene Home." There the nuns sought to cure the women of the street of venereal diseases and break their drug and alcohol habits. Before much happened, a second set of reformers ousted the incumbents in 1913 and the Roche program fell apart.

Juvenile Court Judge Ben Lindsey, a mentor of Roche, sometimes sent delinquent girls to the House of the Good Shepherd. This once more provoked the wrath of anti-Catholics. They again argued the state needed a secular facility to treat recalcitrant teenage girls. The Ku Klux Klan especially voiced this view in the mid-1920s. Despite its opposition, the House of the Good Shepherd remained an orphanage, a home for unwed pregnant women, and a place where young women in trouble with the law could regain their bearings.

In 1929, Minnie Osner of 357 Broadway, a major figure in the Good Shepherd Society—a charity backing the orphanage—donated $60,000 to the home. This led to a massive remodeling of the complex, complete with the dedication of a new chapel. For years, the orphanage functioned behind high brick walls, complete with its own school, St. Euphasia's, and an ornate garden. The institution had little connection with the people living nearby. The Sisters of the Good Shepherd were highly visible outside the grounds in their white robes.

The Coronado facility was also home to around 20 Magdalenes. They were part of an order within the Sisters of the Good Shepherd dating from 1921. Also known as the Sisters of the Cross, members shut themselves away from the world.

The women wore brown robes and had no role in the daily operations of the orphanage. Some of the Magdalenes had originally come to the facility as wards. After Vatican II, the Sisters of the Cross moved out of state.

By the 1960s, the role of orphanages was drastically changing. The House of the Good Shepherd no longer housed unwed pregnant women. Working with the Juvenile Court, the nuns focused on girls with adjustment and behavior problems. Some of the 65–70 young women staying there had been sent in from across the country. The United Way paid for many of the home's programs.

As the House of the Good Shepherd was more a social services treatment center than an orphanage, only about a third of the girls were Catholics. Increasingly, the nuns realized they created more problems than they solved if they crammed religion into those involuntarily staying there. Most of all, the facility sought to instill the young women with self discipline while teaching them basic homemaking and survival skills. Fifteen months was the average residence for those the courts ordered to the complex.

As South Colorado Boulevard property values soared in the 1960s, the nuns realized their institution was no longer the isolated abode they wished it to be. In 1966, they put the land on the market when they pondered moving to near Yale Avenue and South Syracuse Street. Before long, they selected property east of the Cherry Creek Reservoir at Quincy Avenue and South Chambers Road. They relocated there in late 1968.

Upon dedicating its new quarters in March 1969, the House of the Good Shepherd changed its name to the Neuville Center in memory of a French count who helped finance the order in the 1830s. The home did not prosper. From an enrollment of 60—its maximum capacity—the facility was soon down to 30 girls and was badly losing money. In 1973, Excelsior Youth Center took it over, operating it into the 21st century.

On December 1, 1965, F. R. Orr Construction bought an option on the South Denver Good Shepherd land excluding a filling station which was already at the northwest corner of Florida Avenue and South Colorado Boulevard. The purchase was based on getting the property rezoned from residential to business purposes. On this basis, Orr acquired the land the next year for $2.1 million. Since it opened its doors in 1948, the new owner had completed many projects, including constructing Thomas Jefferson High School.

On abandoning the South Colorado Boulevard quarters, the nuns left the House of the Good Shepherd a littered mess. A fire department inspection on January 16, 1969, found it a fire hazard. The abandoned orphanage was filled with rubbish, discarded clothing, opened fire doors, and broken windows. The firefighters ordered Orr Construction to seal the buildings pending their demolition. By this time, neighborhood youths eyed the site as a haunted house. Some of the past residents were similarly sure that ghosts were on the premises.

Before Orr could carry out the fire department's order, a conflagration consumed the orphanage the next evening. The firefighters received an alarm at 9:22 that the complex was burning. Neighbors had heard what they thought were firecrackers before the blaze erupted. In no time, flames were shooting upwards of

100 feet into the air as the main central stairway collapsed into the building. The department sounded a second alarm at 9:28. A third followed a minute later. Before long, more than 100 firefighters were on the scene who did not completely extinguish the flames until around noon the next day. A crowd of 5,000 cheered as the blaze destroyed the facility. Arson, the fire department concluded, caused the inferno. Demolition crews tore down the last ruins from the fire in late February 1969. Psychics are convinced some spirits must remain from the House of the Good Shepherd.

Since the time of the purchase, Orr Construction had pondered all sorts of plans. In 1971, it began work on a three-building Empire Park office center on the northern half of the acreage. By then other structures were in place in the block between Arkansas and Florida avenues, including a 12-story Holiday Inn dating from 1968—it later became part of the Marriott chain.

Other commercial and office developments joined Empire Park on the eastern edge of Cory-Merrill. The Denver Olympics Organizing Committee, the heir of the Denver Organizing Committee (DOC), the group charged with promoting and conducting the 1976 Winter Olympics for Colorado, had its offices at 1776 South Jackson Street in 1972. South Denver resident Carl DeTemple, who had represented the area on city council from 1963 to 1971, headed the effort. Despite the overwhelming support of the political and corporate establishments, voters said no to the games in November 1972. They partially did so because the DOC never told the truth about its plans for the competitions while it behaved most arrogantly and failed to produce realistic cost estimates about the international sporting event.

Photo by Phil Goodstein

Empire Park occupies the northern half of the real estate where the House of the Good Shepherd on the west side of the 1300 block of South Colorado Boulevard.

Office towers went up in the 1960s, 1970s, and 1980s on the southern edge of the Cory-Merrill neighborhood to the north of the Valley Highway. The building in the left-center, Centerpoint II, was the home of Silverado Savings, a notoriously corrupt financial institution.

Across the alley from the building out of which the DOC had operated was the corporate headquarters of Silverado Savings at 1777 South Harrison Street, part of a twin-towered complex, Centerpoint. The highly controversial thrift collapsed in 1988 as a result of massive fraud, shabby governmental supervision, and illegal mortgage, loan, and accounting practices. The $1 billion Silverado failure rocked the national savings and loan industry. In 2008, the city's elections division, seeking to escape the chaos and incompetence of city hall and the Denver Election Commission, moved directly south of the old Silverado abode to 3888 Mexico Avenue. There it blocked off the road during elections, causing massive inconvenience to motorists who did not have any easy detours. By 2009, it was slated to move back to a building adjacent to city hall. Prior to the erection of office towers, assorted greenhouses had been near Mexico Avenue and South Jackson Street.

Despite Silverado's failure, partly caused by the deflation of real estate values, land speculation heavily impacted the area by the seminary and Cory and Merrill schools in the early 21st century. Given the growing popularity of South Denver, many of the neighborhood's modest postwar houses would no longer do as the residential market soared. For years, a keynote of Coronado had been small houses with large lawns.

The constant erection of McMansions embittered many longtime residents who had no desire to move. The area had been their home for years. However, because of the frenzied real estate cycle, they not only found themselves annoyed by seemingly endless construction but also found themselves faced with higher tax assessments. Many found it harder to sell their properties if they were not the right sizes demanded by developers.

The Baby Boomers' Strip

$\mathcal{R}$eal estate pressures also drastically transformed South Colorado Boulevard. The throughway between Alameda Avenue and the Valley Highway was on the cutting edge of urban trends during the 1960s and 1970s. Most of all, it was a place where locals, especially baby boomers, went to play. In no place was this more so than at Celebrity Sports Center, also known as Celebrity Lanes and Celebrity Fun Center, at 888 South Colorado Boulevard.

On November 15, 1959, a Hollywood consortium that included Jack Benny, George Burns, Gracie Allen, Burl Ives, Bing Crosby, Spike Jones, and Art Linkletter announced plans for an indoor amusement park. It was linked to Celebrity Bowling Incorporated of Los Angeles, a firm looking to open a gigantic ultra-modern bowling alley. Promoters arranged for Walt Disney to invest in the Denver enterprise.

Backers vowed a $6 million effort on a seven-acre site near South Colorado Boulevard and Kentucky Avenue on which they signed a 99-year lease on what had been a dairy farm. Governor Steve McNichols led local dignitaries welcoming the Hollywood celebrities for the groundbreaking of the 122,600 square-foot hall on December 14, 1959. The firm of Powers, Daly, and DeRoss of Long Beach, California, designed the complex.

The first part of Celebrity, an 80-lane bowling alley, opened on September 17, 1960. Operating 24-hours-a-day, the facility, backers advertised, was the largest in the world and at the heart of "Colorado's fabulous recreation center." The wing could hold 2,000 people and usually was packed in the evening with members of bowling leagues. Optimists were sure that Celebrity was the first of a national chain of elite amusement centers.

Before long, poor management roiled the facility. Partners were never on the best of terms. Conflicts especially grew between Walt Disney and other investors. This led Disney to assume full ownership of the complex in October 1961. He sought to put his personal brand on the indoor amusement park.

About the time Disney took charge, Celebrity opened its swimming pool. It was 164 feet one inch by 75 feet one inch. The extra inch, the publicity department explained, was to guard against contraction and assure Celebrity's claims of having the largest and best of everything. The pool included five diving boards, three slides, a floating snack patio, and places for water games. At times, instructors taught scuba diving in it. On other occasions, kayakers practiced their skills in it. During mornings, Red Cross instructors sometimes conducted swimming classes. Now and then, the Disney Goofy character water skied on the pool, pulled by a small power boat. Enthusiasts launched model sailboats on it during what Celebrity called its Hobie Sailing Regatta. Friday nights saw Pogo Poge (Morgan White), a popular disk jockey with KIMN, the city's foremost rock-and-roll station, broadcast live from the pool. People rented the space after its 10:00 PM closing time for night owl parties.

In addition to places for bowling and swimming, Celebrity included a shooting gallery, three arcades, a pool hall, mid-sized bumper cars, a nursery, barber shop, and beauty salon. As was Celebrity's wont, it advertised having the longest slot-car track in the world, 13,500 feet. Slot-car aficionados scoffed at that assertion even as they flocked to the room that had three separate track layouts emulating famous race courses. When video games started to become popular in the 1980s, the fun center often premiered them, stating it had 300 separate game machines.

Numerous restaurants and bars came and went. Among them was Cart 'n Rib, a steakhouse. Captain's Tavern was a nightclub. The Hoffbrau was a Bavarian-style beerhouse. Walt Disney came to Celebrity on September 15, 1962, to launch a Stouffer's Restaurant. The place further had an ice cream parlor and an English-style pub serving 3.2 beer—Celebrity was the first Disney property which permitted liquor on the premises.

On occasion, Mickey Mouse and Goofy showed up at Celebrity while employees sometimes dressed in Disneyland attire. For the most part, Celebrity was a magnet for adolescents. Something, seemingly, was always going on at the complex. If nothing else, it was the place to go and be seen.

Celebrity essentially killed Glasier's Barn and the White Sands Beach Club near the northeast corner of South Dahlia Street and Mississippi Avenue. John T. Glasier ran the twin attractions. In the winter, the barn, opened in 1937, featured

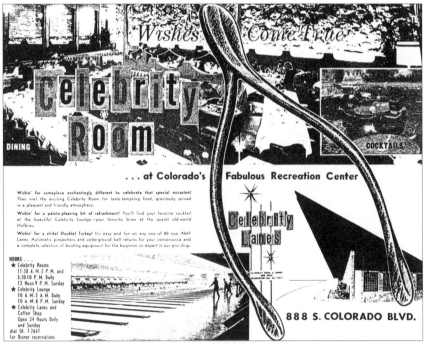

Author's collection

Walt Disney operated Celebrity Lanes in the 1960s, an indoor amusement park at 888 South Colorado Boulevard, where patrons could make their "wishes come true."

hayrides and barn dances. During the summer, locals plunged into a traditional swimming hole at White Sands Beach. The barn additionally rented horses for rides in the area. The facilities struggled after the opening of Celebrity. They closed in 1967, a couple of years before the death of Glasier at his home at 5001 Kentucky Avenue in January 1969. He had been in the area since 1914, originally operating the spread as a hay farm and feedlot. The Glasier family owned much of the nearby land, including Four Mile House near Cherry Creek and South Forest Street—the Glasiers donated that property to the city as a historic ranch house. Another popular horseback riding facility, Denver Riding Stables, closed in 1962. A devastating fire destroyed it on August 6–7, 1965. Other severe blazes consumed much of early Glendale in the late 1950s and early 1960s.

The movie theater of the future was directly south of Celebrity at 960 South Colorado Boulevard, the Cooper. It opened on March 9, 1961, as the world's most distinctive cinema. Or so promoters insisted. The Cooper Foundation of Lincoln, Nebraska, poured $1 million into a circular building designed by architect Richard Crowther. (Mel C. Glatz, a theater design consultant who collaborated on many Cooper projects, insisted he came up with the idea of a circular theater, clashing with Crowther over who deserved credit for the innovative erection.)

The money behind the effort stemmed from the fortune of the deceased Joseph H. "Joe" Cooper, the owner of a chain of theaters which had once been part of the Paramount empire. He placed his Cooper Enterprises under the protection of a foundation in 1934. Cooper had numerous cinemas elsewhere in Colorado. The sponsor concluded Denver was the ideal site for an innovative facility which showed movies in the round using Cinerama, a technique that employed three synchronized cameras to give viewers a three-dimensional sensation.

The hall, which looked like a big orange drum, featured a 105-foot-wide by 38-foot-high screen that stretched for 148 degrees, about six times the size of the screen of a traditional movie palace. More than 2,000 separate pieces of vertical ribbons made up the screen, each adjusted to reflect the image. Five stage speakers and two speakers at the back of the hall delivered the sound in an auditorium designed to accentuate the acoustic experience. Plush green seats filled the auditorium. The complex included a huge lobby dominated by a brass chandelier and space for a restaurant. It was the first theater in the world specifically designed for Cinerama, a process which backers asserted was the technology of the future. Before long, clones of the South Colorado Boulevard Cooper were in Omaha and Minneapolis, also designed by Crowther.

All 814 seats at the Cooper Theatre were reserved. In addition to one performance each evening, it had matinees on Wednesdays, Saturdays, and Sundays plus a screening for youths on Saturday mornings. Not only was the hall invariably sold out through the 1960s, but it was a foremost tourist attraction with patrons traveling for hundreds of miles to see the shows. For a while, the Cooper had arrangements with nearby motels to lodge such visitors. It had ticket outlets in 17 cities through Colorado, Wyoming, and Nebraska.

The Cooper Foundation arranged for buses to haul patrons to the South Colorado Boulevard movie palace from such towns as Cheyenne and Cripple Creek. Along

The Cooper Theatre, at 960 South Colorado Boulevard, was packed through the 1960s as the region's exclusive purveyor of Cinerama, a special way of producing and showing movies. This is the advertisement for its grand opening on March 9, 1961.

the way, it provided them with dinner at the nearby Denver Drumstick, a diner which primarily served chicken. (The theater never opened the proposed restaurant in the complex itself.) The cinema worked closely with Hollywood, having exclusive rights to such blockbusters as *How the West Was Won*, *It's a Mad, Mad, Mad, Mad World*, and *2001: A Space Odyssey*.

By the time the latter two movies came out, Cinerama had faded. Already in 1963, sponsors of the company claimed they had developed a technique to show films with only one projector. Before long, competing means of creating a three-dimensional effect brought much of the Cinerama quality to traditional movie screens while the high costs of Cinerama did not justify its continuation. Management turmoil hit the company. Actors and directors, moreover, were unable to adjust to some of the specific demands of Cinerama whereby the effort was soon put aside. The Cooper installed 70-millimeter film equipment in the fall of 1964. (Regular theaters use 35-millimeter film.) Other than for a 1967 screening of *The Best of Cinerama*, it never used the supposed technology of the future again.

Intermissions were part of the Cooper experience. At that time, rather than providing patrons with regular snack bar fare such as popcorn, the Cooper offered a few delicacies including Swiss chocolate bars and a non-carbonated orange drink that seemingly matched the orange decor of the theater. Patrons were not allowed to take food into the auditorium in the same manner that people are not permitted to snack during performances at a live theater.

By the 1970s, the cinema was increasingly losing its élan. Movie-viewers no longer had to have reservations while the Cooper ceased to bring in customers on special excursions. Even so, it remained a foremost movie house, locally premiering such exclusives as *Jaws*, *Close Encounters of the Third Kind*, and *Star Wars*.

On January 1, 1975, the Cooper Foundation sold its holdings to Highland Theatres of Cheyenne, a chain that rechristened itself Cooper-Highland. Three years later, Commonwealth Theatres of Kansas City bought the house. Already in 1975, the Cooper Cameo, a twin-screened theater, had opened as an annex. It had a standard snack bar. Eventually, United Artists ran the Cooper Theatre.

Century 21, 1370 South Colorado Boulevard, complemented the Cooper. It opened in late 1966 as a traditional ornate movie palace with a big screen able to show films with a 70-millimeter projector. Richard L. Crowther also designed it. The cinema screened foremost Hollywood pictures into the 1990s. Planned as part of the Fox Theater chain, Mann Theatres ran it.

Henritze's was among the entertainment draws on South Colorado Boulevard in the late 1950s and early 1960s. Century 21, a movie palace, displaced it in 1966.

Shotgun Willie's seems on target for a South Colorado Boulevard bank. Andy's, a smorgasbord restaurant run by Mormons out of Salt Lake City, once occupied the space at 490 South Colorado Boulevard which became Shotgun Willie's, a stripper bar.

The movie palace replaced a dinner theater, Henritze's, which featured old-fashioned western melodrama beginning in 1958. The restaurant additionally had a treasure chest into which children, who had been good during dinner, were allowed to explore for a small gift. The site had previously been the home of the Golden Lantern Restaurant.

Andy's, at 490 South Colorado Boulevard, was another diner in the area. Part of a chain run by Mormons out of Salt Lake City, it served smorgasbord in its Velkomen Room. In the mid-1950s, 490 South Colorado Boulevard had been the home of a tavern, Club Morocco. By the 1970s, a country-and-western saloon, Shotgun Willie's, had supplanted Andy's. Within a few years, Shotgun Willie's dumped its original orientation for naked women as a stripper bar.

The Denver Drumstick was a block south of Century 21 at 1490 South Colorado Boulevard. Part of a local chain which had branches in Texas, it catered to families with children. Among other attractions, the restaurant had model trains running through its dining area which passed such famous recreated Colorado scenes as Mesa Verde, the Garden of the Gods, and Cripple Creek, complete with a miniature Moffat Tunnel. The Drumstick, as locals called the place, served its meals in paper containers that looked like railroad cars, firetrucks, rockets, and boats.

The Soda Straw at 430 South Colorado Boulevard especially sought to draw in families for birthday party celebrations for young children. Next door in the 1950s was the Frontier Bar at 450 South Colorado Boulevard, a rather rowdy drinking spot. Across the street during the 1950s into the 1960s, was the Holiday Drive-In at 445 South Colorado Boulevard. Part of a local chain, it advertised it was open "25 hours a day, seven-and-a-half days a week."

Quite in contrast to Celebrity, the Cooper, and Century 21 was the Colorado Four at 360 South Colorado Boulevard. It opened in late June 1973 as the area's first movie multiplex. Essentially, the Colorado Four was nothing more than a sterile box to pack in cinema-goers. Nearby was ABC Bowling at 380 South Colorado Boulevard, a facility dating from the late 1950s. For some years, the bowling alley included the Tangerine Room, a lounge and piano bar. (The same company running ABC Lanes also operated Varsity Lanes at 2040 South University Boulevard. Colorado Bowl at 4121 Evans emphasized its banquet room as much as its 32 lanes of bowling)

The Colorado Four and ABC Bowling were close to Bob's Place, a filling station near the southeast corner of South Colorado Boulevard and Alameda Avenue. The one-armed John Robert "Bob" Gilmour ran it. He opened it in 1929, a year after he lost an arm in a railroad accident. The shop featured a big sign reading, "Howdy Folks." It promised "a bob cat for service," complete with a bobcat dressed in a tuxedo on the sign.

Oscar Garson operated another automotive facility, the White Star Garage, at 4600 Leetsdale Drive. Together, the businesses and their owners were at the heart of the formation of the independent town of Glendale which they helped incorporate on May 19, 1952, on the land east of South Colorado Boulevard between

The Galleria at 700 South Colorado Boulevard has blinded motorists with the glare from its bronze-tinted windows since it opened as a supposedly ecologically friendly office building in the mid-1970s.

approximately Alameda and Mississippi avenues to keep from being annexed by Denver. Gas-a-Mat, a self-service filling station with coin-operated pumps, was on the south side of Leetsdale near the White Star Garage.

In 1974–75, Glendale became the home of the Galleria, a 13-story office complex built to the south of Exposition Avenue on the east side of South Colorado Boulevard. Architects constructed it with bronze-tinted windows as a means of saving on utility costs at the time of the country's first modern energy crisis. Far from being an ecologically attractive edifice, the Galleria immediately stood out as a sore thumb with glaring reflections blinding those passing by on South Colorado Boulevard. Especially in the summer, heat from the building made being directly west of the complex in the late afternoon an arduous experience.

Writers' Manor was at the southern end of the South Colorado Boulevard strip to the northeast of I-25. The Writer Corporation, a local developer and house-building firm, had been in business since the mid-1920s. Right when work was underway to build the Valley Highway to what was then the edge of the metropolis at South Colorado Boulevard and Colorado Avenue, Writer announced the project in 1953. The first part opened three years later. The complex included a motel, meeting place, and a fine restaurant, the Tiffin Inn.

In 1945, Paul Shank, self-described as "the architect of appetite," opened the Tiffin Inn in a Capitol Hill mansion at 1600 Ogden Street. The restaurant was the pioneer central Denver institution joining the drift to South Colorado Boulevard when the Tiffin was the first business to occupy Writers' Manor in August 1956. Before long, the spot was packed with diners who made special trips to the eatery. The supper club featured live entertainment while it was a hangout for the University of Denver hockey crowd.

The adjacent motel, the company proclaimed, was the "country club" of highway hotels. It included an inner courtyard, complete with a swimming pool. The Writer Corporation continually expanded the lodge through the 1960s and 1970s from 104 rooms to 325 rooms. Writers' Manor was an award-winning place where affluent visitors stayed who came to town to play at Celebrity and see shows at the Cooper. The Belcaro Motel at 1025 South Colorado Boulevard and Out West Motel at 1680 South Colorado Boulevard were other lodges serving the neighborhood. The Out West Motel subsequently became Writers' Cottage Motel. (Nothing ever came of Celebrity's plans to have an Aqua Bowl Motel across the street from the fun center.)

Part of the Writer complex included space where a Safeway had once stood at 1700 South Colorado Boulevard. Safeway subsequently moved its operations to the west side of South Colorado Boulevard. Before long, the Writer Corporation expanded its presence near Mexico Avenue and South Colorado Boulevard. During the 1960s and 1970s, it erected numerous highrises stretching to the east of South Bellaire Street.

During the 1960s, the Cherry Creek Inn at 600 South Colorado Boulevard rivaled Writers' Manor as the premier South Denver motel. It opened as a $2.5 million project in August 1961 with 115 guest rooms. In many ways, its architecture was comparable to Writers' Manor, complete with an inner courtyard.

The lodge emphasized its restaurant, the Red Slipper, a place featuring an exposed charcoal broiler in the middle of the dining room. Passing motorists saw a huge revolving red slipper in front of the inn, advertising the gathering spot. The establishment included the Gay Nineties Lounge, a place featuring ragtime piano. Maxies's was the name of the restaurant by the early 1980s.

The Red Slipper sign was indicative. During the 1960s, South Colorado Boulevard featured numerous signs. Many of them had moving images to catch the eye of motorists. City planners argued this was a hideous blight. *Denver Post* columnist Joanne Ditmer joined them, leading a crusade that prohibited such displays.

In the early 20th century, a barn had been at the southeast corner of South Colorado Boulevard and Cherry Creek, a spot subsequently occupied by the Cherry Creek Inn. Cambridge Dairy moved into the space in 1933. Two years later, members of the Young family, owners of the creamery, built a house about half a block east of South Colorado Boulevard near Cherry Creek. When the Youngs sold the land for the Cherry Creek Inn, they relocated Cambridge Dairy to the Simpson Nursery at 4750 Cherry Creek Drive. On the heels of this, in 1968, they arranged for workers to move their house to 790 South Dexter Street/4700 Cherry Creek Drive where, in 1971, it became the home of a popular Glendale bar, the Bull & Bush.

During the heyday of the operations of the Cambridge Dairy, Glendale called itself "Cowtown," filled with numerous dairies. Among them was Ferndale Dairy at South Colorado Boulevard and Alameda Avenue, Country Club Dairy which had an outlet at 1625 South Colorado Boulevard, Mutual Farm Dairy at 940 South Colorado Boulevard, and the Holland

The Cherry Creek Inn at 600 South Colorado Boulevard was the home of the Red Slipper, a restaurant which had an eye-catching moving sign.

Dairy at 502 South Colorado Boulevard. The last had once been the dairy ranch of Frederick DeBoer. Eventually, a cooperative venture, the Farmers Dairy League, was at 500 South Colorado Boulevard which had been the dairy ranch of William

J. Lanting. Comparable spreads were those of William P. LeMaster at 1060 South Colorado Boulevard, Louis and Peter Nielsen at 960 South Colorado Boulevard, and Christian Noe at 1500 South Colorado Boulevard.

The Cherry Creek Inn never flourished as investors hoped. It collapsed into bankruptcy in the mid-1970s. United Air Lines purchased it in 1979, transforming the hotel into an international dormitory for pilots attending its training school near Stapleton Airport. Eventually, the hotel was part of the Sheraton chain. In 2007, Stonebridge Companies acquired it, renaming the lodge the Cherry Creek Hotel. The next year, Stonebridge wrecked the heart of the 1960s establishment. In its place, it planned a 210-room Hilton Garden Inn, building on the core of the remaining eight-story tower of the Cherry Creek Inn.

The Library, a restaurant at 800 South Colorado Boulevard, offered a distinctive dining experience in a book-encased setting. Bud Hawkins, a wide-ranging raconteur who was outspoken on his views, ran it through the 1970s, emphasizing its prime rib. It was also a premier after-work gathering spot. Back in the 1950s and 1960s, 800 South Colorado Boulevard had been home of Tommy's Fish & Chips, supposedly the first modern purveyor of that dish in the Mile High City. The community's inaugural McDonald's was nearby at the southeast corner of South Colorado Boulevard and Mississippi Avenue.

Then there was George Manley's Steak House at 1520 South Colorado Boulevard. Its namesake was born in a tiny settlement in the southern Colorado coal fields to Scottish immigrants on February 7, 1901. He came to Denver when he was five, literally fighting his way up in the world on the West Side in the 1910s and 1920s. In 1931, Manley was the leading contender for the light heavyweight championship, twice defeating crownholder Maxie Rosenbloom in non-title bouts. Rosenbloom refused to fight Manley for the belt. Shortly thereafter, the Denver boxer entered the bar business, running Manley's Grill at 224 Broadway. Tough guys frequented it, often picking fights. Manley readily intervened in the squabbles, beating those who caused trouble at his tavern. Or so he claimed. Critics argued he antagonized people, provoking them into fisticuffs that gave him an excuse for to deck them.

In 1956, Manley was among the first to relocate to the burgeoning South Colorado Boulevard strip when he opened a $100,000 dining establishment. Fights followed him. Brawls broke out on the average of twice a month at his restaurant. He insisted that he never started a fight, but ended many of them. Before long, he lost lawsuits from patrons who proved he had viciously beaten them.

Marital and legal problems led Manley to retire from the restaurant business in 1966. Two years later, on September 5, 1968, his daughter found the 67-year-old ex-pugilist dead in his home at 741 South Vine Street after he had been beaten and shot four times. There was no evidence of forcible entry or a burglary. In October, authorities got a confession from a minor criminal, Jack C. McDevitt of 85 Ogden Street. He informed them he had killed Manley at the behest of the restaurateur's estranged second wife, Sara, who was 46. After a jury rejected McDevitt's claim he was not guilty by reason of insanity, he pleaded guilty of second-degree murder in April 1970, getting a sentence of 10 to 20 years in the penitentiary.

George Manley's Steak House at 1520 South Colorado Boulevard was a center of strife in the late 1950s and early 1960s when owner, George Manley, a former professional boxer, punched out customers.

After Manley sold his restaurant, 1520 South Colorado Boulevard became home of the Playgirl Club. It predated the magazine and had no specific sexuality. In 1972, a short-lived dinner theater opened there.

Walking conditions were terrible along South Colorado Boulevard. A car was essential to get almost anyplace, including spots only a few blocks away. Sidewalks were often nonexistent while parking lots lined the road. Bus service was extremely infrequent, including when the Regional Transportation District had its headquarters at Empire Park at 1355 South Colorado Boulevard in the 1970s and early 1980s. Numerous car dealerships were on the street. Among them was Deane Buick at 1080 South Colorado Boulevard, which moved into the area in the spring of 1963. Its head, Richard L. "Dick" Deane, led the planning board under Mayor Federico Peña. He sold his business to Mike Shaw in 1994 who expanded into Chevrolets.

Off to the north in the 1960s and 1970s were Hugh Tighe Skyline Dodge at 750 South Colorado Boulevard and George Irvin Chevrolet at 390 South Colorado Boulevard. Mountain States Motors at 1260 South Colorado Boulevard was among the area's first Volkswagen dealerships. Across the street was Seifert Pontiac at

1255 South Colorado Boulevard. Farland-Buell Chrysler-Plymouth was a couple of blocks to the south at 1505 South Colorado Boulevard. Murray Motor Imports at 4300 Kentucky Avenue specialized in extremely expensive European cars which it frequently sold to those living in Belcaro and the Polo Club. The moment of fame of Jack Kent Cadillac at 1485 South Colorado Boulevard came on the evening of January 14, 1976, when Elvis Presley impulsively bought Cadillacs for friendly police officers and other associates there.

By the 1980s, the South Colorado Boulevard strip was starting to lose its élan. The evolution of Celebrity reflected changes on the road. The fun center had drifted after Walt Disney's death in 1966 and the Disney Corporation's commitment to its Florida enterprises. (Prior to the opening of Disney World, the company used Celebrity as a training spot for those staffing its Florida utopia.)

Disney put Celebrity on the market in 1978, selling it on March 29, 1979, to bankers Neil Griffin and Bob Leavitt of Texas and members of the Writer family. By this time, the amusement park had a slightly dilapidated appearance. Children complained that the pool was sometimes dirty. Some believed it had a special chemical that would change the water's color if they urinated in the pool. Adolescents did so to test the veracity of the story. A wrongful death lawsuit stemming from the drowning of a boy on June 13, 1969, showed that the pool had certain blind spots which lifeguards could not see. Henceforth, lifeguards had to get down from their stands every five minutes and stroll over to observe such locations.

During the 1980s, the Writer Corporation suffered extreme turbulence. Its projects did not pay off as it expected. The company lost immense sums, including in efforts linked to the savings and loan scandal, especially the doings of Silverado Savings. As it hemorrhaged red ink, Writer sold its interest in Celebrity to Griffin and Leavitt.

The amusement park was losing money in the early 1990s. Rather than restoring its grandeur and promoting it anew, the owners closed Celebrity on June 15, 1994. This was a month after Griffin and Leavitt had announced plans to sell the site to a real estate investment trust. In March 1995, developer Tammel Crow demolished the landmark. A big-box building supply store took its place. Sections of the Celebrity bowling alley became the dance floor of the Oxford Hotel at 16th and Wazee streets. The Lumber Baron Inn, a North Denver bed and breakfast, acquired the Celebrity star from the amusement park's sign.

About the same time they disposed of Celebrity, members of a Writer family limited partnership took control of Writers' Manor—the Writer Corporation then verged on bankruptcy. This did not save Writers' Manor. It went into foreclosure in January 1990. A new owner shuttered the lodge on August 31, 1991, citing a glut in hotel rooms. Soon thereafter, the project came down, replaced by a set of big-box stores.

In 1995, the owners of the Cooper figured the land was worth more than the theater. They sold the property at an excellent profit. Soon thereafter, demolition crews tore down the cinema. Eventually, a Barnes & Noble bookstore occupied the real estate.

⊛ VOLKSWAGEN

FACTORY AUTHORIZED SALES • SERVICE • PARTS

OUR NEW ULTRA-MODERN FACILITIES

MOUNTAIN STATES MOTORS INC.
1260 S. COLORADO BLVD.   SK 6-8317

Courtesy Dave Felice

Mountain States Motors was among the area's pioneer Volkswagen dealers. In May 1961, it moved to 1260 South Colorado Boulevard from 1300 Lincoln Street. Within a few years, numerous other car dealers joined it when South Colorado Boulevard was a foremost destination for those wanting to buy a new car.

Nor did Century 21 make it into the 21st century. The theater shut when its lease expired in early November 1993. The space subsequently became an electronics store. The Colorado Six on Alameda Avenue just east of South Colorado Boulevard replaced the Colorado Four in the early 1990s. The new cinema closed in the summer of 1999. Five years previously, a developer had demolished Bob's Place. By that time, most of the car dealerships had relocated to the suburbs. Consequently, by the turn of the 21st century, little was left of the buildings and businesses which had defined South Colorado Boulevard as the city's most dynamic drag during the 1960s and 1970s.

A Note on Sources:

Early records on Coronado are nebulous. Both the city clerk and city engineer's office have real estate records. Historic maps were also most helpful for places such as Electric Heights and Euclid Place. *RMN*, January 5, 1890, p. 19, plugged Electric Heights. Bob Sheets informed me of the history of Alta Vista in an interview on December 7, 2008. Millie Van Wyke, *The Town of South Denver* (Boulder: Pruett, 1991), 36–39, probes the origins of the area and Coronado School.

Thomas J. Noel, *Colorado Catholicism* (Boulder: University Press of Colorado, 1989), 59–60, 96–97, 123–25, 154–56, William H. Jones, *The History of Catholic Education in the State of Colorado* (Washington: Catholic University of America Press, 1955), 185–88, 278–86, and John F. Martin, "Historical Notes of St. Thomas Seminary" (unpublished manuscript which was on file at the archives of St. Thomas), focus on St. Thomas Seminary. Don DeVoria of the school discussed its operations in a phone interview c. 1985. "Art in Denver," *Lookout*, 1:2 (January 1928), 31–32, emphasized the statuary. The NRHP nomination and the seventh anniversary issue of *The Ambassador* (1962), in the DPL clipping file on St. Thomas, are also apropos. *WPP*, March 1980, p. 2, told of the zoning fight on the development south of the school.

DP, January 27, 1995, p. 1A, and *WPP*, February 1995, p. 1, announced the impending closure of St. Thomas. *National Catholic Reporter*, August 25, 1995, put it in a national setting. *DP*, March 17, 1999, p. 1A, and *RMN*, March 17, 1999, p. 5A, reported the creation of St. John Vianney Theological Seminary. *DP*, November 25, 2001, p. 29A, mentioned the installation of the Stations of the Cross. *DCR*, June 18, 2008, p. 7, highlighted the Neocatechumental Way. Its June 4, 2003, issue featured an interview with Archbishop Charles Chaput about the Redemptoris Mater Seminary. Steve Kosmicki shared his experiences as a student at St. Thomas in the late 1960s and early 1970s, and his knowledge of the workings of the Vatican and the Archdiocese in numerous conversations in the 21st century.

DPS records, clipping files at DPL, and DLPC nomination files outline the origins and architecture of Cory and Merrill schools. The South Historical Room has scattered materials on them and John Cory. *RMN*, December 6, 1935, p. 3S, celebrated Cory as principal of South. *DP*, December 20, 1945, p. 1, and *RMN*, December 21, 1945, p. 12, reported his death.

I glance at Louise Merrill in *Spirits of South Broadway*, 112. *CCN*, March 24, 1966, p. 1, and April 28, 1966, p. 1, decried the overcrowded conditions at Merrill. *WPP*, April 1998, p. 4, looked at the international dimension of the school. Ibid., May 1999, p. 9, and October 2000, p. 10, told of the push for Cory-Merrill Park. *WPP*, June 2008, p. 1, mentioned the proposals for linking Cory and Merrill schools. Also see *WPP*, July 2008, p. 16, August 2008, p. 9, and November 2008, p. 7.

The 1904 *Yearbook* of the Denver Catholic Diocese, pp. 59–63, 70–71, 75, outlines the origins and early evolution of the House of the Good Shepherd and its Ladies Aid Society. Smiley, *History of Denver*, 777, mentions the beginning of the orphanage, including the facility's role in Americanizing Indians. Noel, *Colorado Catholicism*, 32, 99, also glances at the facility. *DT*, April 5, 1899, reported the outcome of the litigation stemming from the American Protective Association's attack on the home. I treat the Protective Association in *Denver from the Bottom Up*, 230–48. My *Robert Speer's Denver*, esp. 252–56, looks at Josephine Roche and the morals crackdown of 1912–13.

Numerous newspaper articles chronicled the building and evolution of the House of the Good Shepherd on South Colorado Boulevard, e.g., *DR*, May 13, 1911, p. 1, *DCR*, April 3, 1913, and October 20, 1921, a three-part series in *RMN*, May 26–29, 1958, *RMN*, January 19, 1969, p. 5, *DP*, June 17, 1971, p. 7, *DP Contemporary*, June 28, 1964, pp. 6–7, and September 18, 1966, pp. 6–7, *CCN*, January 13, 1966, p. 1, and *CJ*, February 16, 1966, p. 4.

DP, January 18, 1969, p. 2, and January 19, 1969, p. 25, *DCR*, January 23, 1969, p. 3, and *UPN*, February 27, 1969, told of the fire. Steve Kosmicki, Randy Wren, Jim Peiker, and Bob Sheets shared their memories of watching the orphanage burn down. The fate of the Neuville Center was in *RMN*, March 2, 1969, p. 4F, *DP*, March 5, 1969, pp. 8–9, zone 1, July 11, 1970, pp. 6–7R, July 15, 1973, p. 45, and *DCR*, January 30, 1969, p. 2. *UPN*, June 17, 1971, p. 1, heralded Empire Park and the Holiday Inn.

Melissa Bradley had a letter in the March 2006 *WPP*, p. 12, about the mass negative impact McMansions had on existing small homeowners in Cory-Merrill. The June 2000 *WPP*, p. 10, mentioned the concern of residents of the area about the infestation of poptops and scrapeoffs. Cf. ibid., July 2005, p. 10, September 2005, p. 23, and January 2006, p. 12. I glance at Silverado Savings, in *DIA and Other Scams*, 310–26. The story of the Olympics is in my *Big Money*, chap. 5.

David Forsyth recalled Celebrity in "Spares and Splashes: Walt Disney's Celebrity Sports Center," *CH*, Autumn 2007, pp. 32–47. He has also put together a most informative Web page on it. Articles on the amusement center include *DP*, December 13, 1959, p. 2E, June 19, 1960, p. 2E, July 30, 1961, p. 1D, and *RMN*, December 15, 1959, p. 70, October 29, 1961, and p. 30, November 8, 1963, June 15, 1994, p. 4A, and March 17, 1995, p. 26.

Darrell Schwartzkopf recalled working as a lifeguard at Celebrity during a July 24, 2008, interview. *WPP*, January 1995, p. 3, reported the end of Celebrity. Julie Hutchinson shared her memories of Celebrity and the KIMN broadcasts in a phone conversation on November 19, 2008. Dave Felice, Ted Scott, and Sam Freeman educated me to the role of KIMN during the 1960s. MacKenzie Liman reminisced about swimming at Celebrity in the 1980s and 1990s, including how dirty the pool sometimes was, in a discussion in August 2008. Mike Huttner also talked about South Colorado Boulevard, urging me to write a book on baby boomers' Denver. He especially recalled Celebrity during a chat on January 30, 2009.

An advertisement in *UPN*, April 6, 1961, p. 3, highlighted the dedication of the Cooper Theatre. *CJ*, February 22, 1961, *RMN*, May 17, 1960, p. 50, and March 5, 1961, p. 1A, and *DP*, February 17, 1960, p. 48, November 6, 1960, p. 3E, and December 21, 1960, p. 27, reported plans for the cinema. A special supplement to *DP Empire*, March 5, 1961, featured the opening of the Cooper which advertised many nearby businesses on South Colorado Boulevard. DPL has a clipping file on the Cooper, including a booklet, *This Is Cinerama*. It also has architectural drawings by Richard Crowther. *DP*, July 29, 1964, p. 61, emphasized the theater was a tourist attraction. *DP*, June 18, 1963, p. 20, told of the changing nature of the Cinerama technique. Andrew Corsello, "Close Encounters," *5280*, November 2008, pp. 111, 142–45, was a mushy remembrance of the theater.

The former manager of the Cooper, Charles "Chuck" Kroll, talked about the house and its evolution during a phone interview on January 28, 2009. In an August 2008 conversation, Doug Gerash recalled attending the Cooper Theatre in the 1960s. He informed me of the technical evolution of Cinerama and movie production during that decade in letters of December 31, 2008, and January 19, 2009, in which he also remembered working at Writers' Manor and the slot-car tracks at Celebrity. Most of all, in a discussion on January 26, 2009, Gerash reported his research on the Cooper Foundation. He called my attention to *Behind the Silver Screen of the Cooper Theatres* (Lincoln: Cooper Foundation, [1998]), the 1996–97 report of the Cooper Foundation which includes a history of the Cooper Theatre.

Randy Wren shared his impressions of Celebrity and the Cooper in discussions on January 1 and 14, 2009. Dean Nye remembered the theater in a chat on July 24, 2008. A Google search brought up some good Web sites on the Cooper, including articles from *Motion Picture Exhibitor* of March 15, 1961, and *Boxoffice* of August 24, 1964, highlighting the national importance of the cinema.

CCN, February 17, 1966, and May 19, 1966, mentioned the plans for Century 21. Also see *DP*, November 22, 1966, p. 21, *RMN*, December 18, 1966, p. 5A, and October 28, 1993, p. 48A. *RMN*, June 29, 1973, p. 76, announced the opening of the Colorado Four. *DP Empire*, March 5, 1961, p. 4, advertised ABC Lanes. Ibid., p. 2, heralded Writers' Manor. Jerry Richmond, *Colorado: Living and Working in the Rockies* (Denver: General Communications, 1986), 216–17, has a paid portrait of the Writer Corporation.

DBJ, December 4, 1998, linked the demise of Writers' Manor to problems associated with Silverado Savings. *DP*, March 30, 1979, p. 45, and *DBJ*, February 28, 1979, p. 1, reported the purchase of Celebrity by members of the Writer family. *RMN*, March 7, 1987, p. 87, told of the Writer Corporation's severe losses; cf. *DBJ,* January 15, 1990, p. 1. Articles about the firm's various projects near South Colorado Boulevard and Mexico Avenue are: *CJ*, May 19, 1955, p. 10, and April 30, 1969, p. 9; *RMN*, June 28, 1956, p. 61, October 1, 1967, p. 51, June 6, 1969, p. 48, April 5, 1970, p. 63, and July 23, 1974, p. 66; and *DP*, August 26, 1956, p. 58, March 3, 1958, p. 29, March 28, 1966, p. 24, October 1, 1967, p. 2M, June 17, 1970, p. 73, and May 23, 1976, p. 5E. The *News* reported the end of Writers' Manor, June 15, 1991, p. 5, August 31, 1991, p. 64, and September 1, 1991, p. 6.

RMN, August 9, 1987, p. 13, had an overview of the Tiffin Inn. Also see *CJ*, July 26, 1956, p. 17, Pierre Wolfe, *Tastefully Yours* (Denver: Professional Book Center, 2001), 156–58, and *DP Empire*, June 21, 1959, p. 183. Bob Sheets recalled working as the maitre d' of the Tiffin Inn in the early 1960s during an interview on December 7, 2008. He also chatted about the wide array of signs on South Colorado Boulevard and Joanne Ditmer's war against them.

Articles on the Cherry Creek Inn include *RMN*, August 8, 1960, p. 33, August 6, 1961, p. 52, August 30, 1961, p. 63, and March 29, 1977, *DP*, August 6, 1961, p. 3D, and March 13, 1979, p. 1, *GCCC*, November 2008, p. 23, and *WPP*, December 2008, p. 5. Jim Peiker, Patsy Vail and Bob Sheets discussed it during a session on the history of South Denver on December 7, 2008. Sunny Maynard shared her memories of the Red Slipper sign in a conversation on September 24, 2008. So did Fred Zitkowski and Jim and Barb Weiss in a chat about South Colorado Boulevard on December 13, 2008.

Jack E. and Patricia A. Fletcher, *Colorado's Cowtown* (Yuma, AZ: Jack E. and Patricia A. Fletcher, 1981), 45–47, 55, focuses on dairies along South Colorado Boulevard. The work highlights the history of Glendale, especially Bob's Place, 34, and mentions Glasier's Barn, 73. *CJ*, August 20, 1955, p. 1, reported Cambridge Dairy's expansion in the area. *UPN*, May 18, 1961, p. 3, January 23, 1969, and *CCN*, February 10, 1966, looked at White Sands. *DP*, January 9, 1969, p. 46, and *RMN*, January 17, 1969, p. 112, recalled the life of John T. Glasier. Jim Peiker, Patsy Vail, and Bob Sheets remembered White Sands and Glasier's Barn in a discussion on December 7, 2008. Stuart H. Frankel reminisced about South Colorado Boulevard businesses and the Glasier family on December 29, 2008. Doug Gerash gave me his memories of Glasier's and Glendale in the 1960s in a January 19, 2009, letter.

DP, April 7, 1964, p. 38, reviewed the Denver Drumstick. Bud Hawkins recalled the Library with me in informal discussions in 1992. Lou Mozer shared his immense knowledge of the city's restaurant scene in a conversation on October 23, 2008, especially the operations of Henritze's, the Library, and the Tiffin. Advertisements for Henritze's and Andy's are in *DP Empire*, June 21, 1959, pp. 303, 330.

Jim Peiker reflected on the wild events associated with George Manley in a chat on September 16, 2008. Patsy Vail echoed him in an interview on December 7, 2008. Walt Young also remembered Manley and talked about the history of boxing in Denver on November 26, 2008. Looks at Manley were in *DP Empire*, September 6, 1959, pp. 4 5, and June 21, 1959, p. 351. Reports of lawsuits against the boxer were in *RMN*, November 17, 1959, p. 6, and *DP*, December 28, 1959, p. 19. Stories on his death, the police investigation, and the guilty plea of Jack McDevitt include *DP*, September 5, 1968, p. 3, September 7, 1968, p. 3, October 22, 1968, p. 1, April 22, 1970, p. 38, and May 28, 1970, p. 40, *RMN*, September 6, 1968, p. 5, October 26, 1968, p. 8, June 18, 1969, p. 33, April 23, 1970, p. 13, April 29, 1970, p. 65, and May 29, 1970, p. 39.

Glances at the Galleria were in *DP*, March 17, 1974, p. 75, and November 5, 1975, and *SCJ*, September 15, 1977, p. 1. Bud Wells, *The Colorado Car Book* (Boulder: Johnson Printing, 1996), glances at Deane Buick and other dealerships. Dave Felice shared his immense knowledge of Denver car dealerships with me in conversations on January 3 and February 3, 2009, and a letter on February 16, 2009. The December 2008–January 2009 *Mile Higher*, pp. 1, 3, glances at the evolution of Deane Buick. I mention Elvis Presley's Cadillac caper in *The Seamy Side of Denver*, 220–22.

Chapter Nine

Papers and Politicians

*N*ewspapers have been part and parcel of the South Side. On occasion, local publications have taken politicians to task. At other times, they have been tools of elected officials. Some sheets have had a strict political neutrality. Now and then, politicians have owned the papers.

Both the publications and public officials have come face to face with neighborhood improvement associations. Such groups popped up close to Washington Park at an early date. They have come and gone into the 21st century, having extremely diverse characteristics. Some have exclusively focused on the interests of homeowners with the avowed goal of increasing property values. Others have claimed to represent everyone, including renters and merchants. Now and then, the societies have primarily been social clubs. In places, they have been nothing more than personal organizations. In more than one instance, rival groups have emerged that more fight each other than stand for the populace of South Denver.

Nobody more personified the links between newspapers, politicians, and neighborhood activists than Harry Risley. Born in Utica, Missouri, in October 1876, he apprenticed as a printer. Eventually, he turned to journalism. He arrived in Denver around the turn of the century. After serving as a police reporter for the *Rocky Mountain News,* Risley acquired a pioneer South Denver newspaper, the *South Denver Eye*, in 1905. It had appeared since 1886. Risley insisted it was the heir of the neighborhood's first paper, the *South Denver Advocate*, launched in 1882. As such, he asserted, it was the South Side's oldest functioning community institution and business.

Merging with the *South Denver Bulletin*, Risley ran the weekly as the *South Denver Eye and Bulletin* out of his print shop at 203 Broadway. For the most part, it was an advertising sheet, notices for businesses filling three-fourths of the front

Advertisements dominated the front page of the South Denver Eye and Bulletin.

page. Nestled between them were choice tidbits about developments in the area. Sometimes, the inside of the paper consisted of national and international feature stories with no South Denver focus. The sheet ranged from four to eight broadsheet pages.

Come election time, the *South Denver Eye* championed the Democratic ticket. Above all else, Risley was a party loyalist. In reward, Governor Elias Ammons (1913–15) appointed him state printer in 1913. As such, Risley's shop printed state documents. Shortly after taking office in January 1915, Republican Governor George Carlson ousted Risley, claiming the South Denver printer was a crook who had inflated state printing contracts.

On the side, Risley was secretary of the South Denver Improvement Association while he was a staunch backer of Mayor Robert W. Speer (1904–12, 1916–18). During World War I, he used the *Eye* to cast doubts about the loyalty of the University of Denver because the school taught the German language. After the return of peace, Risley called for outlawing the display of the red flag while insisting the city must prohibit "unpatriotic gatherings" and "suppress seditious utterances." The editor simultaneously urged subscribers to read the scriptures and go to church.

A strong racist streak was obvious in the *Eye*. This came out in May 1921 when African-Americans held a dance at a rental hall near Second Avenue and Broadway. Locals complained that blacks had no business being in their part of town. Risley echoed them in his paper, insisting African-Americans must stay in their own section of the city. In plugging woman suffrage, the paper observed it would not threaten white supremacy.

After living at 393 South Pennsylvania Street and 64 South Lincoln Street, in 1922 Risley moved to a commanding $7,000 house at 1274 South Gilpin Street. He shared it with his wife Bijou. On occasion, she was president of the South Side Woman's Club and the Washington Park Garden Club.

By the time he was living directly east of Washington Park, Risley was more politically involved than ever. After losing a race for the school board in 1917, he won a place on city council two years later. Holding the seat during the 1921, 1923, and 1925 elections, he emerged as the Ku Klux Klan president of the city legislature when four outright kluxers won places on the nine-member council in 1925.

Risley was the fifth Klansman on council. Realizing that many greatly hated and feared the cabal, some prominent hoodwearers did not publicly disclose their affiliation. Klan membership books at the Colorado Historical Society show the printer applying for membership on July 24, 1924, and gaining admission to it four days later. He was a longtime associate of Klan leaders Gano and Laurenta Senter of 1145 South Logan Street.

Photo by Phil Goodstein

Newspapers have consumed massive amounts of trees. Locals have simultaneously sought to save street trees. Here and there, artists have transformed the trunks of dead trees into sculptures such as is the case at 1545 South Franklin Street.

As council president, Risley worked closely with a fellow kluxer at city hall, Mayor Benjamin Stapleton. After Klan grand dragon John Galen Locke broke with Stapleton and the KKK in the summer of 1925 when he formed the Minute Men as a rival organization, Risley and Stapleton stuck with the knights of the fiery cross. The South Denver city councilman retained his place as council president in 1926 with the help of anti-Locke, anti–Minute Men members when the other one-time Klansmen on council sought to oust him.

In the spring of 1927, differences between Risley and Stapleton led the South Side councilman to run for mayor against the incumbent. After he lost that race, coming in third in a crowded field, the printer returned to the city legislature in 1931, serving until he failed re-election in 1943 to Henry M. Duff. In the interim, he had been president of the Colorado State Taxpayers League, a conservative group of 9,000 members lobbying the city and state governments. He sold the *Eye* in the mid-1920s. The paper collapsed in 1929.

(The 41-year-old victor in the 1943 council contest, Henry Duff, was the manager of Brake & Duff, a lumber company at 1475 South Broadway. Duff, who lived at 1501 South Elizabeth Street, subsequently operated Duff's Cafe and Lounge with his wife at 1930 South Broadway. He did not seek re-election in 1947.)

In 1944, Risley lost a bid for a place in the state Senate. He likewise failed in other efforts to return to elected office. For a while, he was publicity agent for National City Bank at South Broadway and West Bayaud Avenue. In addition, during the 1930s, he worked as the business manager for the *South Denver Monitor*. The paper, not disclosing the connection, heavily praised his activities on council.

Eventually, Risley was the *Monitor*'s political columnist. Already in the 1930s, his political presence was heavily felt at the *Monitor* with its endorsement of Franklin Roosevelt and the New Deal. The weekly also eagerly backed Ben Stapleton— Risley had made his amends with the mayor by then. The printer-politician spent his last years living in the First Avenue Hotel at West First Avenue and Broadway where he died at age 82 on February 24, 1959.

Neighborhood Newspapers

*T*he *Eye* had never been alone. Newspapers continually popped up. Virtually from the time Arthur Pierce announced his intention of issuing the *South Denver Advocate* in 1882, papers came and went. The *South Denver Tribune*, located at 17 First Avenue, for example, competed with the *Eye*. William A. Payne of 47 West Cedar Avenue and later 146 West Irvington Place published it with George H. Beyer of 58 Corona Street between 1908 and 1929.

The *South Denver Standard*, a weekly, came out between 1913 and 1947. Originally located at the rear of 1571 South Broadway, it soon relocated to 1403 South Broadway where Jason I. Ellsworth of 1579 South Washington Street had his print shop. He ran the operation with his son Alonzo. The latter, who lived at 1318 South Corona Street, eventually was publicity director for the Chamber of Commerce.

Commercial gazettes highlighting the area's businesses included the *South Denver Budget, a* weekly, in 1912–13. The *South Denver Independent* appeared in 1928–29, a weekly, followed by the short-lived *South Denver Daily* in 1932–33. The *South Denver Neighborhood News* was a weekly in the course of 1938–39. The *South Side Observer* appeared in 1944–45. Few or no copies of any of them have survived.

The foremost sheet from the 1920s to the 1950s was the weekly *South Denver Monitor.* It hit the stands on December 4, 1925. Initially, the broadsheet highlighted business developments, focusing on the area from Bannock Street to Colorado Boulevard between Cherry Creek and Yale Avenue. Before long, the *Monitor* had sister papers reporting on East Denver and North Denver. By the 1930s, the South Side weekly claimed a circulation of 15,500.

Frank J. Wolf of 792 South Emerson Street was the moving force behind the *Monitor.* After apprenticing as a printer and salesman at local firms, he teamed up with Victor Neuhaus to acquire the Colorado Herald Publishing Company in the mid-1920s. It issued the *Colorado Herold*, a daily German-language newspaper that included a Sunday edition. Wolf used the *Herold*'s presses to build the *Monitor* empire, printing various weeklies at its plant at 1950 Curtis Street. For a while, the *South Denver Monitor* had its editorial office at 81 South Broadway, later moving to 17 First Avenue. Before long, it shared office space with the South Denver Civic Association (SDCA), a business promotion group, at 9 First Avenue. Virtually from the time of its first issue, the *Monitor* was something of the unofficial voice of the SDCA.

Now and then, the *Monitor* peeked at the politics and power of the area. During its early years, the sheet was highly partisan in its endorsements, never mentioning opposition candidates. The paper frequently blasted the *Denver Post* for undermining the city through the daily's critical coverage of city hall. Against this, the *Monitor* was an echo of the Chamber of Commerce, insisting the public should receive only positive news. Additionally, the *Monitor* included local gossip and the doings of the Boy Scouts and various PTAs. A church page told of South Side worship services. Its movie page highlighted neighborhood cinemas.

From the beginning, the *Monitor* used its front page to tout favored business ventures such as Gray Goose Airways of 4150 Josephine Street. In 1930–31, that company announced it was building an airship comparable to a luxury ocean liner. The *Monitor* eagerly urged readers to invest in the venture, arguing that Albert Einstein's theory of relativity assured the company's success. The weekly also plugged a miraculous air motor and suggested readers invest in gold mine stocks. Such stories gave it a huckster tone.

Generally, the publication was from 10 to 16 pages, often including a four-page advertising supplement from Montgomery Ward. On occasion, the newspaper printed obituaries. For a while, the weekly referred to itself as the *South Side Monitor.* By the early 1940s, it was simply the *Monitor* when it averaged from 20 to 28 pages. The sheet did not then have a local address. It filled much of its space with radio and movie listings and grocery advertising.

The First Avenue Hotel was close to the offices of the South Denver Monitor *in the 1930s. In 2007, graffiti artists besmirched the abandoned landmark at the northwest corner of West First Avenue and Broadway. The next year saw its purchase and promise of renovation.*

Already in the 1930s, the *Monitor* had ever less focus on South Denver. In some ways, it was the city's alternative weekly. Its front page frequently had far more news about the New Deal and Colorado state politics than it did about neighborhood developments. This, in part, reflected the political guidance provided by Risley. At times, the *Monitor* mentioned meetings of the Socialist Party when that organization advertised in its pages. By the 1950s, the weekly readily commented on international events, fervidly denouncing communism and endorsing the Cold War. Like the *Eye*, it heavily plugged religion, especially revival meetings.

The *Monitor* arranged for high school boys and girls to deliver the paper for free. In exchange, it urged those getting it to pay carriers 15 cents a month for the effort—the young men and women who put it on people's porches at dawn on Friday morning depended on such contributions for their income. The newspaper disappeared in the mid-1950s, shortly after the death of Frank Wolf in January 1954. By the time of his passing, he had been retired from the *Monitor* for 12 years.

The *University Park News* followed the *Monitor* as the neighborhood booster paper. It stemmed from the *Pioneer–Buchtel News*. This was a four-page tabloid that appeared in 1947 to report on happenings of Pioneer Village and Buchtel Village, two DU housing projects for veterans to the north of Evans Avenue and east of South Garfield Street. In 1949, the paper caught the attention of the newly established University Park Community Council (UPCC), changing its name to *University Park News.*

Genevieve Wyant purchased the *University Park News* in 1955. After having previously taken charge as its editor, she quickly realized that the sponsoring groups, the UPCC and the University Hills–Southridge Civic Association, did not know how to run the four-page weekly. Editorial and business disputes led her to buy it from them.

Besides news of University Park, the publication focused on developments east of South Colorado Boulevard and in Arapahoe County. The paper also was full of gossip, reporting the doings of locals. It additionally emphasized sports, especially competitions of organized little leagues. Advertisements from University Hills department stores filled its constantly expanding pages.

In December 1965, *University Park News* launched a sister sheet, *Cherry Creek News.* That weekly focused on the area from Downing Street to Quebec Street between Eighth and Mississippi avenues. In no time, *Cherry Creek News* was an eight-to-sixteen page tabloid with a weekly circulation of 15,000. *University Park News* printed 20,000 copies, often having 32 pages. Many picked up the publications for their listings of television shows.

Wyant sold her holdings in April 1966 to George I. Sanford of Kansas City, Missouri. Before long, the new owner had a chain of comparable papers in the suburbs and northern Colorado. In the course of 1967, *University Park News* and *Cherry Creek News* frequently published the same articles and had joint sections.

South Denver's newspaper of the 1950s and 1960s, University Park News, *started as a publication for the University of Denver's Pioneer Village. This was a settlement for married students in former World War II barracks-type buildings. Evans Avenue is in the right foreground. South Garfield Street is at the bottom left. South Colorado Boulevard is on the top. What became the Valley Highway is on the upper left.*

The publisher combined them into the *University Park and Cherry Creek News* in early 1968. Carriers delivered it free to residents.

Besides its television page, the paper included an astrology column and listing of area churches. It printed numerous bridal photos, heavily reporting weddings. During the school busing war of the late 1960s and early 1970s, *University Park News* focused on the way South Denver improvement associations were in the vanguard of opposing the scheme. The area, it proudly observed, was predominantly a Republican bailiwick. While it remained mostly a giveaway publication, the tabloid listed 15 cents as the cost of a copy on the cover. On the side, *University Park News* allowed *Chinook*, a local hippie newspaper, to use its presses in the late 1960s.

The *Minneapolis Star & Tribune* bought the *University Park and Cherry Creek News* in November 1971. The Minnesota daily was attempting to emerge as a national newspaper chain. It announced the South Denver paper would henceforth be part of Community Publications Company that would issue a weekly with a circulation of 150,000 copies, complete with special sections for different parts of the metropolis. Former owner George Sanford, it promised, would stay in charge of the publication for southeast Denver and Arapahoe County. Soon thereafter, *University Park News* vanished from sight.

Clarence Stafford

*B*y the time *University Park News* was going strong in the 1960s, Clarence M. Stafford was a virtually forgotten part of South Denver's past. For a while, he served on city council with Harry Risley. Like Risley, Stafford represented part of the South Side and was a Klansman and a printer.

A native of Fort Wayne, Indiana, born on September 30, 1893, Stafford came to Denver in 1905. Eventually, he operated his own shop, Stafford Printing Company at 1668 Pennsylvania Street, a commercial press which had no specific South Denver orientation. He held KKK card 2291, showing he was an early devotee of the hooded haranguers.

A major figure in the Masons who headed the city's prestigious lodge #5 in 1935, Stafford served as a Republican in the General Assembly from 1929 to 1933 before winning election in May 1933 to represent council district four. He retained the post in balloting in 1935, 1939, 1943, and 1947. Before moving to his longtime home at 103 South Pearl Street, he had dwelt at 664 South Sherman Street. Stafford was subsequently at 22 South Pearl Street. After failing in his bid to win election as a Republican as secretary of state in 1940, the printer gave up his seat on council in 1951 when he took on Mayor Quigg Newton for city hall. He lost that race and the contest for auditor four years later. Now and then, he put out special magazines touting his views and political campaigns.

In 1956, Stafford printed the "pink sheet." This was an election flyer anti-Catholics had been issuing since the late 19th century. Printed on glaring pink paper, it listed the religion of candidates. Voters, sponsors insisted, must support only Protestants and keep the United States out of the hands of the Vatican. During the 1920s, the Ku Klux Klan had made the pink sheet its own.

A longtime associate of Stafford, E. Page Wingate, a used-car salesman who was once clerk of the Denver County Court, was behind the 1956 pink sheet. It especially targeted the Democratic candidate for governor, Steve McNichols, and Democratic United States Senate hopeful John Carroll. The electorate, the document stated, had to reject them because of their Catholicism.

The flyer failed to list the printer or sponsor. By not doing so and attacking a candidate for federal office, it violated a new regulation which required those behind political literature to identify themselves in races for the presidency and Congress. After McNichols and Carroll both won their races, the United States attorney's office accused Stafford and Wingate of breaking the law via the pink sheet.

Stafford initially insisted on his innocence. Not only did the First Amendment protect the pink sheet, but he claimed he was simply printing a commercial job. Nonetheless, he pleaded guilty in May 1957. Federal District Court Judge William Lee Knous fined him $500, giving him a four-month suspended prison sentence and a year's probation. By the time of the case, Stafford had left South Denver for a residence at 75 Harrison Street. The former Klan councilman declared bankruptcy in February 1960. He was an also-ran when he sought a place on council as a member at large in 1971. The onetime South Side representative was living in Castle Rock at the time of his death in September 1982.

The Washington Park Profile

Opposed to the political impetus of publications flowing from the presses of Stafford and Risley, the *Washington Park Press* was a neighborhood advertising sheet. Mabel Hamilton established it in late 1929 at 2210 Mississippi Avenue. For the most part, it was an eight-page tabloid touting the businesses on South Gaylord Street and Bonnie Brae. It contained some light neighborhood gossip but lacked any substantive reporting.

In 1943, Julian and Mildred Jordan of 750 South Gilpin Street obtained the *Washington Park Press*. They also ran the *West Side Hustler* at 670 Santa Fe Drive. That paper dated from 1897. While it primarily focused on developments in the heart of West Denver, especially along the Santa Fe Drive business corridor, its reportage sometimes looked at the Miracle Mile and South Denver.

In addition to putting out the *Hustler*, the Jordans had a commercial press which printed the *Washington Park Press*. After they bought the Myrtle Hill publication, Mildred Jordan took hold as editor, locating her office at 1085 South Gaylord Street. She emphasized the positive in the *Press*, asking readers to contribute juicy tidbits about the people of the neighborhood. At its peak, the paper had a circulation of about 7,500.

The Jordans retired in 1963, moving to 9 South Downing Street. A new owner sold the *Press* in early 1964. The subsequent publisher was dissatisfied with the paper as it was. He renamed it the *Southeast Bulletin*, a publication which soon vanished.

A short-lived *South Denver News* in the 1970s spurred the creation of the neighborhood's modern newspaper, the *Washington Park Profile*. South Denver

The entry into Washington Park near South Marion Street Parkway around 1910. The park has been the defining spot of the neighborhood's modern newspaper, the Washington Park Profile.

Realty of 1040 South Gaylord Street sponsored the *News*. An amateur publication with a typewritten text, the *News* was as much an advertising sheet as it was an objective source of news on the area.

Individuals displeased with the *South Denver News* established the *Profile* as a monthly in October 1978. Originally a 12-page half tabloid, it emanated a good deal of 1960s idealism. A loosely organized cooperative issued the sheet in the name of the Washington Park Profile Association. Members held informal editorial meetings during which they pasted together the gazette.

The early *Profile*, which was photo offset, included listings of Southeast Denver Free University, a children's page, and articles on the history of South Denver by staff writer Joan McCarthy. For the most part, hard-hitting neighborhood news was absent from it. The monthly emphasized the doings of improvement associations right when they were re-emerging as defining neighborhood institutions. After operating out of a home at 1115 South Emerson Street, the paper established its office at 617 Jewell Avenue where it offered its space to readers as a community resource.

Paul Kashmann emerged the central figure at the *Profile*. A native of New Jersey, he relocated to Breckenridge in 1971, pulled to Colorado by the mystique of the Rocky Mountain High. Before long, he worked as a bookkeeper in Denver and for a computer firm. He stepped aboard the *Profile* as an advertising salesman three months after its establishment. Within a year or so, he was co-publisher/

editor with Deborah "Debi" Brown. She had been the powerhouse in forming the monthly. Marriage and motherhood led her to leave the paper after four years.

Under Kashmann, the *Profile* was well designed with an emphasis on the people and businesses of the area. While usually in sync with the corporate agenda, its letters to the editor sometimes contained critical comments about what others called "progress." Over the years, the gazette's focus expanded to include the area east of South Colorado Boulevard. At one time, it sought to embrace Capitol Hill to Colfax Avenue. By the early 21st century, it had an excellent distribution system through Colorado Free University, showing up on newsstands throughout central Denver.

Besides heavy restaurant advertising, politicians' columns filled the *Profile*'s pages. As such, it was frequently a forum for elected officials to address readers rather than serving as a watchdog reviewing their actions. Reading its pages, one would have no doubt that neighborhood groups were the essence of those living in South Denver, saying nothing about the intense disputes between members of rival improvement associations. In the process, the *Profile* illustrated the close working relationship between leaders of some of the neighborhood societies and city hall.

Sometimes neighborhood news was missing from the *Profile*. While it heavily focused on business developments, it often ignored the history of the neighborhood and literature about it. Frequently, it had a moralistic environmentalist agenda, repeating the clichés about the need for conservation while never questioning the economic system or why sprawl and waste had become central parts of the economy. Ballooning from about 16 tabloid pages, the *Profile* was sometimes more than 50 pages in two sections.

Redistricting City Council

*I*n 1916, Robert Speer returned as mayor. He had not sought re-election in 1912 in the face of a strong reform movement. Voters completely reshaped the municipal government in 1913, replacing city council and the mayor's office with a five-member city commission. Not only did Speer reinstate a strong mayor's office, but he oversaw the creation of a unicameral nine-member nonpartisan city council. Until council expanded to 13 seats in 1971, districts three and four included most of the South Side. District three stretched from West Sixth Avenue and the Platte River to the area south of Mississippi Avenue on the east side of Washington Park to the city's southern, western, and eastern boundaries. A good chunk of district four not only included southern Capitol Hill, but ranged all the way to 24th Avenue and Yosemite Street.

A December 1950 redistricting saw a massive modification of South Denver's council lines. District four was increasingly Capitol Hill/Montclair, going from approximately Eighth Avenue to Hudson Street to Alameda Avenue to South Colorado Boulevard to Kentucky Avenue to Broadway. The next year, voters elected Robert S. McCollum to represent the area when Clarence Stafford gave up the seat to run for mayor.

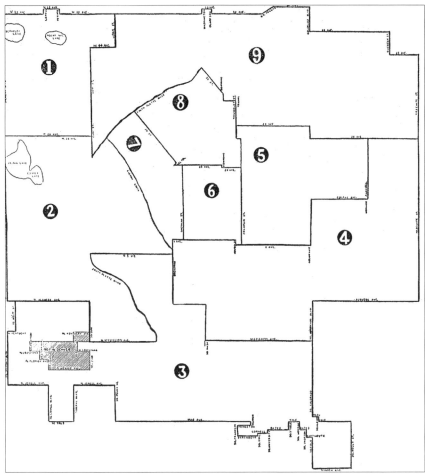

City council borders in 1947 showed how districts three and four encompassed most of South Denver and a lot more areas.

A Denver native, born in 1916, McCollum was a graduate of Deerfield, an elite New England prep school. After service in World War II, he took over his parents' auto distributorship, adding an appliance distributorship to it. Active in the Junior Chamber of Commerce, McCollum gained election to council in 1951 at the behest of his good friend, Mayor Quigg Newton. An eager young Republican, McCollum did not seek re-election in 1955 when he joined the administration of Mayor Will F. Nicholson. The next year he lost a bid for Congress against incumbent Byron Rogers.

Soon thereafter, McCollum left Denver for a job with the State Department. He returned to Denver in the summer of 1960 as vice chancellor for public affairs at DU. Besides promoting the school, he was also a direct conduit to the State Department, attending its conferences and attempting to explain its policy to the public. In the process, he brought many prominent figures of the foreign policy establishment to the South Denver university. Among other posts, McCollum was state chairman of the Crusade for Freedom, a CIA front raising money for Radio Free Europe while he was a prime promoter of the fallout shelter program of the early 1960s.

In 1964–65, McCollum served on the Denver school board, being the conservative choice against liberals who wanted an African-American, Rachael Noel, to receive the appointment to fill a vacancy. By the time he left his post at DU in 1968 to form a consulting firm, McCollum was the vice chairman of the drive for the 1976 Winter Olympics. The former councilman was president of Lutheran Hospital from 1977 to 1982, dying in early 1987. During his years on council McCollum lived at 5345 Sixth Avenue. For a while, especially when he was DU vice chancellor, he was at 3241 South Monroe Street.

At the same time McCollum represented district four, Robert H. McWilliams Sr. of 2025 South Fillmore Street held the seat for district three. Between 1927 and 1946, he was a professor at DU, essentially creating the school's sociology department. On his retirement, he threw himself into politics. In 1947, he gained election to the open council seat, defeating Harry Risley, 5,205–3,591, who sought to retake the post.

A non-driver, McWilliams commuted to city hall via public transportation while he continually walked the neighborhood, discovering if anything was amiss. On his re-election in 1951, McWilliams emerged as president of council. He did not seek another term in 1955. The professor died at age 78 on January 2, 1959. His son, who grew up in University Park and graduated from South High and DU, was subsequently on the Colorado Supreme Court and the Tenth Circuit Court of Appeals. McWilliams Park, along Harvard Gulch near South Fillmore Street and Yale Avenue, recalls the city council member.

After the 1950 redistricting, district three stretched from near West Sixth Avenue and the Platte River on the north to the western edge of Washington Park. To the south of Kentucky Avenue, it extended to the city's southeast borders. South Federal Boulevard was generally its western limit. The 57-year-old William Flor gained the seat in 1955. A retired police captain, he lived at 1666 South Ogden Street. He lost his re-election bid four years later to a young attorney and accountant, Irving Hook of 1470 South Navajo Street. The new member immediately emerged as a most dynamic councilman.

Hook easily breezed to re-election in 1963 and 1967 as a backer of development and the urban renewal policies of Mayor Tom Currigan. Political insiders praised Hook for his acute understanding of the city. Rather than seeking a post in the new district seven for the area west of Washington Park in 1971, Hook remained on council that year as a member at large. In 1973, he led the charge for the city to drop statutes that targeted the conduct of homosexuals in their private lives. After leaving council in 1975, he associated with Bobby Rifkin, a man who ran strip clubs. Hook was among those endorsing Rifkin's efforts to open such an establishment near Hampden Avenue and South Tamarac Street in 1988. The former councilman remained active as an accountant into the 21st century.

A dinosaur is in the playground of McWilliams Park near Yale Avenue and South Fillmore Street. The greenery recalls South Denver councilman Robert H. McWilliams.

The 1971 expansion of council to 13 members gave the city legislature a completely new alignment, including two members at large. Districts six and seven emerged as the South Denver seats. The neighborhood also had a say in districts four and nine.

District nine was a product of ethnic gerrymandering. The politically correct created it so a Hispano would be on council. It stretched from Globeville through the heart of North Denver to much of downtown to old West Denver to West Mississippi Avenue and the Platte River, encompassing the land west of South Broadway. Latinos were outraged when a conservative North Denver Italian, Eugene "Geno" DiManna, won the race in 1971. Sal Carpio, a North Denver resident who had run for Congress in 1970 as the candidate of La Raza Unida, a radical Chicano party, gained the council post in 1975. Other North Denver residents, Debbie Ortega and Judy Montero, subsequently held the seat. The South Broadway section was always an afterthought in the vortex of district nine politics.

For years, district seven was primarily a Capitol Hill area. The 1960 redistricting saw it move south when it covered the area from Colfax Avenue to approximately Downing Street on the east, Ohio and Kentucky avenues on the south, to Broadway to West Bayaud Avenue to the Platte River. A West Washington Park resident, L. Paul Weadick, gained the seat in the 1963 balloting. A graduate of St. Francis de Sales High School who lived at 735 Cedar Avenue with his wife and seven children, he had served as clerk of the County Court. After joining the bar in 1954, Weadick assisted Charles S. Vigil, former United States attorney for Colorado, in various high-profile cases. Among them was the defense of John Gilbert Gra-

ham who was executed for the November 1, 1955, bombing of the airplane on
which his mother and 43 other people flew. Weadick's law office was at 271 South
Downing Street.

After unsuccessfully seeking a place on council in 1955 and 1959, Weadick
gained the open post four years later. No sooner was he on council than the West
Washington Park resident wanted to join the bench. After he failed in his bid for
the Denver District Court in 1964, he quit council in January 1965 when Mayor
Tom Currigan appointed him to a vacancy on the Denver County Court. Weadick
kept the post until his retirement 20 years later, dying in 1986.

Currigan named Leo Gemma to fill Weadick's seat. The chief probation officer of the Denver Juvenile Court, the 37-year-old Gemma lived at 1149 Downing
Street. The new representative had lost his race for the state senate in the fall of
1964. He did not seek re-election to council in 1967 when the 31-year-old Edward
F. Burke gained the spot.

Until 1983, Burke was the area's highly controversial representative. By that
time, especially after the 1971 modification, district seven was essentially the West

District seven of council mostly encompassed Capitol Hill when Ed Burke
gained election to the seat in 1967. Among others, he defeated Bernard
Duffy, the namesake of Duffy's, a well-known downtown tavern.

Washington Park district even while it reached to South Federal Boulevard to the southern city limits. In one place district seven did not quite extend to Washington Park. Burke saw that the boundary was gerrymandered in 1971 to keep Gary Tessler of 637 South Corona Street out of his constituency. Active in the Washington Park Action Council, Tessler had made it known he was interested in winning the seat.

A Denver native who graduated from St. Francis de Sales High School and Regis College, Burke grew up in a politically charged household. His home at 315 South Sherman Street had once been the rectory of St. Francis de Sales Church. In the early 1930s, it was the home of Patrick J. Devlin, the district captain of the Democratic Party who used his political connections to become police telephone operator. Burke's uncle, Edward C. Day Jr., who lived next door at 311 South Sherman Street (a house Devlin once also occupied), was on the Colorado Supreme Court from 1957 to 1976. Burke subsequently moved to 1202 South Clarkson Street.

In 1967, Burke triumphed by defeating bar owner Bernard Duffy and Albert Moore. The latter ran an independent store affiliated with Associated Grocers. At the time of his election, Burke managed Adams' Thriftway at 1211 Alameda Avenue which was also part of Associated Grocers. Before long, he was personnel director of Sky Chef, the company overseeing food concessions at Stapleton Airport. As a member of council, Burke oversaw airport contracts.

Even while the Washington Park councilman was a close political ally of Mayor William McNichols (1969–83) and the conservative majority that ran council under the mayor, Burke opposed the administration's plans to constantly add traffic capacity to South Denver streets. Constituents revolted against him in 1981 over the development of the Harvard Gulch Golf Course. After the election commission rejected a petition to recall him in 1982, voters overwhelmingly said no to the incumbent in 1983 when Burke came in fourth in a field of six, with 15 percent of the vote. The former officeholder died at age 72 on February 12, 2008.

Nieves McIntire succeeded Burke as the representative for district seven. The wife of a leading South Denver Realtor, she lived at 875 South Corona Street. She and her husband poured their personal wealth into the race. Over the years, McIntire had worked as a speech pathologist and in Head Start. Locals knew her from her involvement with the South Central Improvement Association (the forerunner of the West Washington Park Neighborhood Association) and the Washington Park Community Center. McIntire had also served as secretary of the Denver Democratic Party. Most of all, during the campaign, she emphasized she had been a commissioned officer in the Marines who had a "top secret security clearance."

By 1987, many constituents were unhappy with McIntire. They saw her as a do-nothing councilwoman. Some further attacked her husband, seeing him as the area's worst slumlord. On this basis, Dave Doering, an attorney who had had ties to the administration of Governor Richard Lamm and members of improvement associations, ousted the incumbent. He lived at 281 Sherman Street. In 1995, Doering failed in a bid for auditor. The former councilman subsequently suffered severe personal problems, losing and regaining his law license.

Photo by Phil Goodstein

In 1909, the Brethren laid the cornerstone for their church at the southwest corner of Mississippi Avenue and South Washington Street. Numerous other congregations have come and gone from the sanctuary during the past century. None have had any direct political involvement with the neighborhood.

Bill Himmelmann of 571 South Emerson Street, the head of the Denver Area Labor Federation from 1977 to 1992, gained the open council seat. Not happy in the city legislature, he retired after one term. Kathleen MacKenzie of 997 South Pearl Street, a veteran council aide and neighborhood activist who had good ties with city hall and the labor movement, succeeded him, serving to 2007. After she left office, she traveled extensively, settling in Belgium.

The ties between Himmelmann and MacKenzie and the labor movement were indicative. Unions had previously backed the election drives of Nieves McIntire and Dave Doering. Since the time the United Rubber Workers gained recognition as the union representing workers at Gates Rubber and Samsonite in the early 1940s, organized labor had a strong South Side presence. Numerous Gates and Samsonite employees lived west of Washington Park. While the labor movement was generally a minor player in defining the area's destiny at the turn of the 21st century, it retained a strong political clout, being able to turn out the vote. The nonpartisan character of city elections gave organized labor extra influence in selecting candidates and putting them in office.

Despite nonpartisanship, most of those elected to council had intimate connections with the Democrats or Republicans. The parties frequently had their informal slates in city contests. Strong links existed between members of improvement associations and the Democrats. The affluent, educated residents of West Washington Park, moreover, tended to be much more involved in politics than those living in poorer areas to the southwest. Generally, candidates from sections of district seven outside of West Washington Park were also-rans where turnouts were much less than in precincts close to the greenery.

Chris Nevitt of 994 South Ogden Street won the race to succeed the term-limited MacKenzie in 2007. He gave voters a mixed message. Before the election, he had been extremely critical of the giveaways associated with tax-increment financing, a means by which developers essentially did not have to pay taxes on their projects while receiving subsidies from city hall. Nevitt had led such groups as the Front Range Economic Strategy Center and the Campaign for Responsible Development which forced the developer of the former Gates Rubber site to make gestures to organized labor. The Denver Area Labor Federation was among the sponsors of these assemblages. Even while he campaigned on this, the victor also identified himself closely with Mayor John Hickenlooper, a politician who embraced tax-increment financing.

District Six

*F*or years, district six included the South Country Club area and parts of Washington Park East. For the most part, it was a Capitol Hill seat, stretching from 17th Avenue and Colorado Boulevard at the northeast to about Kentucky Avenue and South Downing Street at the southwest.

C. Paul Harrington, a major figure in the Chamber of Commerce, gained the post in 1933. A resident who lived in various apartments west of Cheesman Park, he was the owner of Merchandise Warehousing. That company provided storage space for the city's newspapers which backed him in his efforts to remain in office. Generally, he was the council voice of the Country Club while he frequently socialized with members of high society. On the side, as a talented singer, Harrington performed with and backed various choral groups. George V. Kelly upset the incumbent in 1959 after the United States attorney's office announced a grand jury had indicted the 66-year-old Harrington for income tax evasion the day before the runoff balloting.

The new councilman lived at 641 Columbine Street. A native of Leadville, born in 1914, Kelly had been in Denver since 1919. For a while, the councilman aspired to the priesthood, attending St. Thomas Seminary before gaining his degree from the University of Denver. During the 1940s, he was a reporter for the *Denver Catholic Register*, *Denver Post*, and *Rocky Mountain News*. More than anything, Kelly was a political insider who had worked for mayors Quigg Newton and Will F. Nicholson. The councilman, who did not seek re-election in 1963, was subsequently an assistant to mayors Thomas Currigan and William McNichols. He ran unsuccessfully for auditor in 1971, vowing to abolish the post as an elective office. In 1974, he published a history of mid-20th-century Denver politics, *The Old Gray Mayors of Denver*. Kelly died in 1986.

The 1960 modification of council borders extended district six to Mexico Avenue at South Emerson Street to near Colfax Avenue and Colorado Boulevard. Carl DeTemple (1920–1995) of 648 South York Street represented the area from 1963 to 1971. A staunch Republican and Denver native who graduated from North

High and the University of Denver, he was an FBI agent in Washington between 1947 and 1953. He subsequently worked as community representative for Climax Molybdenum. Under Mayor Richard Batterton, he was manager of welfare from 1960 to 1962. DeTemple won the race in a field of six. (Harrington, who had been cleared of the tax charges, came in third in a come-back bid. The former Capitol Hill/South Denver councilman died in 1973.)

At the same time he served on council, DeTemple was a corporate booster. In addition to his elected post, he was a foremost functionary for the Colorado Association of Commerce and Industry, a group functioning as something of the union-busting Colorado state chamber of commerce. Most of all, DeTemple was president and general secretary of the Denver Organizing Committee for the 1976 Winter Olympics right when the group managed to alienate much of the city with its arrogant plans, leading the populace to reject the games.

To promote the Olympics, DeTemple did not seek re-election in 1971. That year's reorganization of council saw district six defined as the area from the west side of Washington Park to South Quebec Street. Extending to Sixth Avenue on the north, it included Cherry Creek North. Sections were south of the Valley Highway east of South University Boulevard. For the most part, it was the seat of Washington Park East.

Don Wyman, a dynamic 35-year-old Republican attorney, succeeded DeTemple as the area's councilman in 1971, winning a four-way race with the endorsement of DeTemple and former district attorney Mike McKevitt who was then in Washington representing Denver in Congress. Wyman, who had started out as a teller at First National Bank, had served as a deputy prosecutor under McKevitt. He lived at 1305 South Hudson Street at the time of his election, soon moving to 1580 South University Boulevard. Besides serving on council and having an independent law practice, he was a vice president of First National Bank.

The father of five, Wyman was part of a Republican surge in Denver in the early 1970s. Southeast Denver repeatedly elected Republicans while a GOP council bloc collaborated with Mayor McNichols in assuring a conservative business leadership of the city. After Wyman breezed to re-election in 1975, pundits touted him as the Republicans' hope for regaining the mayor's seat in 1979.

Bob Carr, the son of Governor Ralph Carr (1939–43) and an assistant attorney general, interfered with that. On October 4, 1977, he stabbed Wyman two times with a steak knife outside of Wyman's bachelor's pad near Ninth Avenue and Sherman Street: Wyman, who projected himself as a devout family man, had been conducting an affair with Carr's wife. When Wyman sought to retain his seat as a martyr in 1979, voters rejected him as a philanderer who had not been worthy of their trust. By that time, he was separated from his wife and living in the Park Lane apartment complex—she kicked him out of their South Denver house and divorced him in the wake of the Carr affair. Ten years later, the Colorado Supreme Court disbarred Wyman for "an extreme indifference to the welfare of his clients and the status of their cases." The former councilman died at age 65 in February 2001 from injuries suffered in an automobile accident.

A sculpture by Jonathan Stiles, Aegis, *which includes a bench and a mobile, is in front of the district #3 police station at the southwest corner of Iowa Avenue and South University Boulevard. Don Wyman, the area's city councilman in the 1970s, lived catercorner from it at 1580 South University Boulevard.*

John Silchia, a 43-year-old restaurateur living at 550 Milwaukee Street, replaced Wyman on council after walking the district and outcampaigning the incumbent. A libertarian, Silchia believed that the less the government did, the less it did wrong. He was frequently most skeptical of the claims of the planning office. Often extremely blunt, Silchia sometimes offended the sensitivities of voters when he dismissed their pleas for token city resolutions as meaningless irrelevancies. By the time he sought re-election in 1987, many were dissatisfied with Silchia as a do-nothing councilman. The incumbent agreed this was an issue: Silchia told constituents to reject him if they wanted a high-spending, full-time council representative. They booted him from office. He subsequently moved to California.

Mary DeGroot of 2660 Tennessee Avenue defeated Silchia. Not only was she a voice of change, but she was also politically well connected through her husband, a ranking figure in the Denver Democratic Party who headed the Urban Drainage and Flood Control District. Before going to city hall, she had been a cost analyst for the phone company. During her first term, DeGroot more or less went along with administration projects. By 1995, she was extremely dissatisfied with Mayor Wellington Webb. That year, the councilwoman took on the incumbent. Though she received a narrow plurality in the May contest, she failed to receive a majority. The African-American Webb, implying that only racists would oppose him, defeated her by a margin of 54 percent to 46 percent in the runoff.

Republican South Denver

 $\mathcal{D}$ eGroot's 1987 triumph was indicative of a major political shift. For decades, parts of South Denver, especially such areas as Belcaro, Bonnie Brae, the South Country Club, and Polo Club, had been solid Republican districts. During the 1960s and 1970s, leading GOP representatives and senators in the General Assembly, such as Ted Bryant of 1590 South Birch Street, Don Friedman of 3206 South St. Paul Street, Paul W. Powers of 480 South Marion Street, and Cliff Dodge of 1851 South High Street, were from the area. Members of the interlinked Shoemaker and Wham families long held at least one legislative post for Washington Park/University Park.

Attorney William Joseph "Joe" Shoemaker of 3260 South Monroe Street first won election to the state Senate in 1962 when he was living at 963 South Ivy Street. A graduate of the United States Naval Academy who worked for the powerhouse law firm of Holland and Hart before serving as administrative assistant for Mayor Richard Batterton (1959–60) and manager of public works (1960–62), he built his house on the edge of the Wellshire Country Club in 1965. It came to include a tennis court and swimming pool.

Unsuccessful in a 1966 bid for lieutenant governor, Shoemaker returned to the Senate in 1968, emerging as a dominant figure in the legislature through his membership on the Joint Budget Committee. After he failed in his run for mayor in 1971, Shoemaker took charge of efforts to rehabilitate the Platte River, leading to the establishment of the Platte Greenway. Additionally, he helped create the Urban Drainage and Flood Control District, serving as its legal counsel. Despite his commitment to the GOP, the party faithful rejected him in 1978 when he lost the primary for governor.

Robert "Bob" Wham of 2790 South High Street was Shoemaker's partner in the firm of Shoemaker & Wham. He was city attorney from 1961 to 1963 under Batterton after serving as acting United States attorney for Colorado in 1958–59. Wham succeeded Shoemaker in the state Senate in 1977, holding the post to 1981. His wife, Dorothy S. "Dottie" Wham, subsequently served in both the state House (1985–87) and Senate (1987–2001). Jeff Shoemaker, the son of Joe Shoemaker, succeeded Dottie Wham in the state House of Representatives, holding the seat from 1987 to 1993.

A close personal and political associate of Shoemaker was Robert E. "Bob" Lee, the man who oversaw the success of the Denver Republican Party in the 1950s, 1960s, and 1970s. He came to the Mile High City in the early 1940s at the behest of his wife, working at 280 South Downing Street in the real estate business of his father-in-law, Earl Johnston. The latter lived at 452 South Ogden and 35 South Ogden Street before relocating to 765 South Vine Street. A member of the Johnston family ran a hardware store on South Gaylord Street.

Lee, who built his own house at 1040 South Gilpin Street, coached the Redskins team in the Young American League. After serving as Denver clerk and recorder under Republican Mayor Will F. Nicholson (1955–59), Lee was eventually a functionary for oil magnate John M. King whose empire spectacularly collapsed in the

The Daniels Building at the northeast corner of South Steele Street and Alameda Avenue was the headquarters of cable television magnate Bill Daniels. South Denver Republican political operative Bob Lee had his office there for some years, assisting Daniels' effort to dominate the state Republican Party.

early 1970s. Always an extreme opponent of trade unions who worshipped Richard Nixon as his political idol, Lee was subsequently a political operative for cable television king Bill Daniels. Most of all, he was an exponent of hardball politics, constantly painting Democrats as nothing less than Bolsheviks. He assisted Republicans in key races nationally. Lee was among those using the hysteria over school busing in the late 1960s and early 1970s to help the Republicans temporarily assert themselves in Denver politics.

Carl Gustafson of 901 South Williams Street was among those standing out as a Denver Republican in the legislature. A native of Eaton, Colorado, who was an investment banker, he won a place in the Colorado House of Representatives in 1966. Two years later, he kept his seat when he ousted Democrat Barbara Frank of 983 South Gilpin Street who was also in the legislature for a new district #12. (Until the 1968 balloting, Denver elected members of the General Assembly at large.) By this time of his second victory, Gustafson was at 974 South Franklin Street.

Gustafson quickly asserted himself in the statehouse. He defeated Gary Tessler in 1970 to keep the seat—Tessler was subsequently a leading talk radio personality before becoming a mortician. The Washington Park representative was House majority leader in 1971–74 and 1977–78. (The Democrats controlled the House in 1975–76.) Simultaneously, Gustafson emerged as city bond adviser, arranging for his municipal bond firm of Quinn & Company to profit greatly from a 1975 refi-

The area west of Washington Park, especially west of South Broadway, has tradi-
tionally been a Democratic enclave. Numerous low-income residences remain
such as these Victorian survivors at 1324–28–32 South Acoma Street.

nancing of city bonds on Mile High Stadium. The legislator did not seek re-election in 1980. Two years later, Gustafson signed on as Democratic Mayor William
H. McNichols' manager of revenue. The next year, he announced he would run for
mayor if McNichols did not. The incumbent ran and was defeated, leading
Gustafson to leave the political stage.

   On returning to his home, then at 710 South Harrison Street, at around 4:45 PM
on July 31, 1974, Gustafson found his wife of one year, the 45-year-old Elizabeth
"Beth" Roser, dead with a plastic bag over her head and a man's sock wrapped
around her neck. The bedroom was in disorder with the deceased suffering from
facial contusions. There were no signs of a forced entry into the house. The
coroner could find no evidence of foul play or drugs in her system, ruling the death
an asphyxiation. The politician refused to believe she had killed herself, claiming
she had been murdered. The exact cause of death was never determined. Gustafson
subsequently relocated to 499 South Garfield Street. He died at age 59 in January
1989.

   On September 12, 1980, Gustafson had quit the legislature. He did so to assist
the election campaign of Ruth Prendergast of 580 South Harrison Lane who had
recently won the Republican primary for his seat. She had resigned as the vice
chairwoman of the Denver GOP in 1975, claiming the party lacked leadership.
Four years later, she was part of a Republican sweep of the election commission.
Despite asking voters for a four-year term, she abandoned the post in June of the
next year to run for the legislature. The district GOP committee named her to
succeed Gustafson in the House in late September, leading to her victory in November. Her district stretched along Cherry Creek, including the Country Club
neighborhood. She gained re-election to the seat in 1982.

Linden Blue was another Republican star in the early 1970s. A resident of Cherry Creek Tower at 3100 Cherry Creek Drive South, he overwhelmingly won a post as councilman at large at age 34 in 1971. In part, his triumph reflected on his mother, Virginia Neal Blue, a highly active real estate investor who had triumphed in the race for state treasurer in 1966. She died while running for re-election in September 1970.

The new councilman had been raised in a culture of wealth, flying airplanes and running a banana plantation in Nicaragua. Cuba forced down Blue's plane in March 1961 when he was flying over the island. It accused him of being a CIA spy/provocateur. Blue gained his freedom after 11 days in captivity, just before the Bay of Pigs invasion. He later criticized the White House for not adding air cover to the attack. The politician did not seek re-election in 1975, soon leaving town to serve as a top executive with Gates Learjet.

In contrast to Washington Park East, the area west of the greenery generally leaned Democratic, especially in Rosedale and Overland. Richard Lamm, for example, was at 2500 South Logan Street, when he gained re-election to the House of Representatives in 1968 after living at 531 Emerson Street at the time of his first legislative triumph two years earlier. He remained the representative of this part of the South Side until his election as governor in 1974.

Lamm's brother, Tom, lost a bid for the state Senate from the neighborhood in 1970 when he ran a do-nothing campaign. Democrat Wayne Knox, who graduated from South High in 1945, represented sections of West Washington Park and parts of southwest Denver in the state House of Representatives from the 1960s to the 1990s, living at 1373 West Gill Place before moving to 761 South Tejon Street.

Not only was Mary DeGroot's 1987 council victory indicative of the shift to Democratic dominance east of Washington Park, but, before long, the Democrats swept all of South Denver in legislative voting. Ken Gordon, a onetime resident of 2323 South Jackson Street, went from being in the Colorado House to state Senate leader when his party regained that chamber in the early 21st century. His legislative assistant, Andrew Romanoff of 887 South Gilpin Street, succeeded Gordon in the House in 2000, serving as speaker from 2005 to 2009 when term limits forced Romanoff from office.

South Denver was once also the headquarters of post office politicians. Frank L. Dodge of 1434 South Pennsylvania Street won election to the state Senate in 1914 and 1918 as a staunch Republican while working for Joslin's, a local department store. In 1922, he gained appointment as the area's postmaster. Previously a member of school board #7, he was part of a reform slate in 1912 when he gained a place on the board of aldermen (the lower house of city council). Dodge retired as postmaster at the end of his third term in 1934, dying eleven years later.

James Orren "Jim" Stevic of 1051 South York Street succeeded Dodge as postmaster. A native of Michigan, he dropped out of school after sixth grade to become a printer. After arriving in Colorado for his wife's health in 1922, Stevic emerged as a leading figure in the labor movement. For a while, he was editor of the *Colorado Labor Advocate*. Most of all, he was extremely close to leading Democratic politicians, helping them gain election.

The South Denver Post Office at the southwest corner of West Cedar Avenue and South Broadway dates from 1940 when James Stevic, a resident of Washington Park East, was the city's postmaster.

The Democrats rewarded Stevic by making him postmaster. Over the years, Stevic threw himself into numerous community causes. He remained postmaster until 1949. The Washington Park resident died at age 87 in 1965. His wife had preceded him to the grave. She had been president of the Washington Park Garden Club in 1942–43.

Modern Politics

Sue Casey succeeded DeGroot in 1995 as the Washington Park East council member. A native of New Hampshire, she married an investment banker. In 1983, she made connections with United States Senator Gary Hart of Colorado, helping him win the 1984 New Hampshire Democratic presidential primary. During that campaign, the term "yuppie" first appeared, describing individuals such as Casey who found Hart their ideal political inspiration.

The woman was part of the Hart team as the senator eyed the White House in 1988. On this basis, she relocated to Denver in 1986 to assist Hart's presidential bid. Though it collapsed the next year, she settled at 792 South Gilpin Street as an avid outdoorswoman. On council, she always projected immense energy, including leading bicycle rides around the area.

The councilwoman resigned her seat in February 2001. By doing so, she explained, she was saving the city. Because of term limitations and the lack of any real political opposition, the bulk of council was slated to leave office in 2003. A new Washington Park member, the incumbent believed, would provide continuity in the city legislature. Besides, being out of office shielded Casey from the responsibilities of power as she sought election as mayor. Her 2003 campaign never took off. She received 7.2 percent of the vote, coming in fifth in a field of seven.

In a sexually charged contest where most of the candidates were women in a nine-person field, Charlie Brown of 2181 South Cook Street won the race to succeed Casey. He had previously served one term in the Colorado House of Representatives for district 11 in 1983–84 when he lived at 782 South Vine Street. The candidate won the legislative seat in an upset on the coattails of Governor Richard Lamm's re-election. Many constituents immediately found him most arrogant. He lost his place in the House to Republican Dottie Wham in 1984. Brown won the council race by a plurality of 21 votes over his closest challenger, Peggy Lehmann. In office, he was most outspoken, being something of a conservative voice mocking the political correctness and trendiness of the day. More than a few Democrats were convinced he was really a Republican.

Some locals hated Brown. They were sure that if Lucy Van Pelt ran for office, she would win in a landslide against him. Despite this, Brown had no trouble retaining his post in 2003 and 2007. In many ways, he was a quintessential Democratic yuppie, personifying this group which was increasingly omnipresent in University Park and Washington Park East.

After her narrow loss to Brown, Peggy Lehmann of 2496 South Leyden Street still wanted to serve on council. A past president of the League of Women Voters, she got her chance when, shortly after Brown's victory, council rearranged its borders in the light of the 2000 census. The new alignment put Lehmann in district four. Following the revision of council borders in 1970, this was the constituency for southeast Denver stretching south from Mexico Avenue at South Downing Street to the southeast limits of the city. Modifications of the boundaries have included parts of the greater University Park neighborhood, mostly to the south of Iliff Avenue. Lehmann gained a place on council from district four in 2003.

In 1955, attorney Paul A. Hentzell of 2265 South Adams Street won election to council from the old district four. Born in Littleton on September 8, 1918, he earned his law degree from Westminster Law School. From 1944 to 1946, he was an assistant city attorney under Mayor Ben Stapleton. The father of two boys, Hentzell served as president of the University Park School PTA while playing a visible role in the Boy Scouts, Highlander Boys, and the South Denver Civic Association. As Denver annexed land to the east of South Colorado Boulevard, he relocated to 3820 South Dahlia Street.

A staunch conservative who called himself a "maverick Republican," Hentzell crusaded for quiet streets, especially checking noisy ice cream trucks and barking dogs. At times, he got along better on council with the Democratic majority than he did with Republicans in his district. In 1963, the GOP machine tried to unseat him. In response, Democrats and organized labor rallied to Hentzell's successful re-election bid.

At times, Hentzell engaged in redbaiting. Typical was his 1971 attack on the Denver Public Library for stocking supposedly "revolutionary" books. Despite being an outspoken advocate of law and order, Hentzell was never on the best of terms with the police. Right when he was urging a reform of the department in

The clubhouse of the Wellshire Country Club, 3333 South Colorado Boulevard, has been a meeting and dining spot. It is in district four, the council seat encompassing the southernmost sections of historic South Denver.

January 1974, he parked his car at police headquarters at 13th and Champa streets. When he returned, he found his vehicle vandalized with three flat tires. The councilman stormed into the police building to complain. The next thing he knew, two officers slammed him against the wall and beat him. Explaining they did not know he was a member of council, they treated him like an everyday citizen. The police subsequently arrested Hentzell for drunk driving when he was on medication for a heart problem.

By the early 1980s, despite his Republican registration, Hentzell increasingly sided with liberal opponents of Mayor William McNichols on a closely divided city council. He fought against the city's strong mayor system of government, demanding that council assert itself against the executive. After suffering a severe heart attack in October 1982, he announced he would not seek an eighth term. The longtime southeast Denver councilman died on August 14, 1983, six weeks after he left office.

After his 1963 triumph, Hentzell rarely faced any meaningful political opposition during his bids for re-election. This was indicative of the city's nonpartisan municipal races. Seeing how politicians like Hentzell seemingly stayed on council forever, voters adopted term limitations in the 1990s. Some of the incumbents, who were virtually professional jobholders, bitterly decried this. Many who won council seats had previously been council aides. They sometimes described themselves as full-time candidates in election questionnaires. Eventually, they got the populace to allow them three terms. All the while, council salaries soared.

Stephanie Foote of 3275 South Steele Street, another Republican, succeeded Hentzell in 1983. She stepped down in 1993 to become chief of staff for Mayor Wellington Webb. Joyce Foster of 3344 South Niagara Way won the vacancy election. Besides her own civic activism, she was known for her husband, Rabbi

Stephen Foster of Temple Emanuel. Prior to winning the seat, she had been the director of Jewish Family Services of Colorado. With her on council, the politically correct started to view district four as something of the Jewish seat on council. Foster was a Democrat, the first person of her party to represent the district since the 1971 reorganization of council. This was another sign of the political shift in the area as Denver became virtually a one-party Democratic city. After leaving council in 2003, forced out by term limitations, Foster won a place in the state Senate in 2008 from district #35 as something of the handpicked choice of the term-limited Ken Gordon.

Political and newspaper developments were part and parcel of the South Denver saga. By the 1990s, the areas south of the Valley Highway sought to emulate if not surpass the Washington Park neighborhoods. Their evolution, the central presence of the University of Denver, the wars over Harvard Gulch, the development of the Platt Park district, and how traffic patterns have defined the area are the subjects of *The Ghosts of University Park, Platt Park, and Beyond.*

A Note on Sources:

Volume three will have a greater look at South Denver neighborhood groups, including those close to Washington Park. *Baker Bark,* May 2002, p. 2, recalled the *South Denver Eye.* My judgment of the papers mentioned is primarily based on reading the available copies. I glance at the origins of the *South Denver Advocate* and *Eye* in *Spirits of South Broadway,* 46–48.

SDE, May 25, 1918, is Risley's attack on DU for teaching German. His view of the red flag and "unpatriotic gatherings" is November 23, 1919; cf. *SDE,* November 29, 1919. His religiosity is in April 24, 1920. He attacked allowing blacks on the South Side in the May 20, 1921, issue. The article on suffrage is February 24, 1917—all are on p. 1. FF 20 of the SDCA papers at CHS includes some Risley columns from the 1950s.

CHS holds Klan membership books. My *In the Shadow of the Klan,* 306–07, 338–42, dissects Risley's links to the robed riders. It and *From Soup Lines to the Front Lines,* 132–34, 136, 137, look at Risley's role in city politics. *SDM,* April 17, 1931, p. 1, heralded the Colorado State Taxpayers League and pushed Risley for council. The sheet told of his joining the paper as business manager, June 5, 1931, p. 1. *DP,* February 26, 1959, p. 63, reported the former councilman's death.

Members of the Ellsworth family recalled the *South Denver Standard* on September 16, 2008, during the reunion of the South High class of 1953. *SDM* explained its subscription policies, May 11, 1951, p. 1. I glance at the *Monitor*'s place in the local media scene in *From Soup Lines to the Front Lines,* 110. The weekly reported the death of Frank J. Wolf, January 14, 1954, p. 1.

George V. Kelly, *The Old Gray Mayors of Denver* (Boulder: Pruett, 1974), 29, 48, 158, makes brief reference to Clarence Stafford. *RMN,* September 18, 1982, p. 61, was the obituary of the longtime South Denver councilman. The paper told of his guilty plea to issuing the smear sheet on May 25, 1957, p. 5. *DP,* June 7, 1957, p. 3, noted the court's sentence. Stafford's bankruptcy was in the *News,* February 13, 1960, p. 30.

CCN, April 7, 1966, p. 1, discussed the history of *University Park News* and *Cherry Creek News* and their sale to George Sanford. Edward Humes, *Over Here* (New York: Harcourt, 2006), 129–30, glances at Pioneer Village and Buchtel Village. The April 21, 1966, *UPN* emphasized morning home delivery. The late Kevin Tannenbaum recalled *Chinook* and how he arranged for *UPN* to print it during conversations in 1995–96.

DPL has a few scattered issues of the *Washington Park Press*. *WPP* recalled the Jordans, May 1981, p. 6. *WPP*, April 1982, p. 10, and October 1982, p. 2, looked at Deborah Brown and Paul Kashmann. The latter reflected on the *Profile* in personal conversations. He discussed the paper on its 25th anniversary, *WPP*, October 2003, p. 2, and its 30th anniversary, September 2008, p. 2. He had an autobiographical statement in December 2007, p. 2.

The DU Archives have a file on Robert McCollum. Newspaper features on him include *RMN*, January 20, 1951, p. 17, November 3, 1968, p. 18, September 19, 1976, p, 41, and January 3, 1987, p. 42, and *DP*, April 18, 1962, p. 3, and February 27, 1964, p. 2. *DP*, January 4, 1959, p. 2A, reported the death of Robert McWilliams and recalled his career. There is also information about McWilliams at the DU Archives. *RMN*, August 8, 1953, p. 62, profiled his work on council. Also see *WPP*, April 2009, p. 11. Volume three looks at the origins of McWilliams Park.

Denver County Court Judge Larry Bohning informed me of the career of Paul Weadick in a conversation on August 15, 2008. Andrew J. Field, *Mainline Denver: The Bombing of Flight 629* (Boulder: Johnson Books, 2005), is about the John Gilbert Graham case. It has a brief look at Weadick, 98, 228. *RMN*, January 24, 1965, p. 13, told of his appointment to the County Court. *RMN*, May 18, 1992, p. 12, profiled Irving Hook. It reported his advocacy of topless dancing, September 24, 1988, p. 24. Gerald Gerash highlighted Hook's fight in behalf of homosexuals in a 2009 video, *The Gay Revolt and the Troublemakers Who Made It Happen.*

Volume three will examine the fate of Ed Burke and the controversies over the Harvard Gulch golf course. Gary Tessler shared the tale of Burke's gerrymandering district seven in a phone interview on July 17, 2008, during which he discussed South Denver politics during the 1960s and 1970s, including the roles of Carl Gustafson and Tom and Dick Lamm. Dick MacRavey, a longtime resident of South Ogden Street, recalled state and local politics in a chat on July 20, 2008.

WPP reported the 1983 district seven city council race, March 1983, p. 3, April 1983, p. 7, May 1983, pp. 1, 10, 15, June 1983, p. 1, July 1983, pp. 1, 4, and August 1983, pp. 4, 18. Bill Himmelmann shared his views about serving on council in discussions in the late 1990s. Chris Nevitt critiqued tax-increment financing in *WPP*, November 2005, p. 18. Charlotte Winzenburg shared the gossip about neighborhood politics and city council members in an interview on February 13, 2009. Among other points, she mentioned labor support for McIntire, the woman's do-nothing role on council, her husband's real estate investments, and Dave Doering's unhappy fate after he left council.

Kelly, *Old Gray Mayors*, 112–15, looks at the politics of council district six and the 1959 election. *DP*, May 15, 1959, p. 63, sketched the candidates in that year's council contest, including Kelly. *DP*, March 13, 1973, p. 20, reported the death of Paul Harrington. It told of George V. Kelly's passing, September 26, 1986, p. 7E, and October 2, 1986, p. 6B.

CCN, April 6, 1967, p. 1, examined the political career of Carl DeTemple and that year's city council race. *DP*, May 18, 1963, p. 3, reviewed the district six race which DeTemple won. I tell of the fight over the 1976 Winter Olympics in *Big Money*, chap. 5. My *Seamy Side of Denver*, 232–33, dissects the fate of Don Wyman. *UPN*, May 13, 1971, p. 2, profiled the campaign in which Wyman was elected; compare, May 20, 1971, p. 1, June 3, 1971, p. 1, and June 10, 1971, p. 1. The weekly reported his victory and biography, June 17, 1971, p. 1. Mike Davenport shared his observations about Wyman, John Silchia, and other neighborhood politicians in ongoing discussions since the mid-1980s. I covered city council during the mid-1980s when Silchia was on council, listening to his remarks about the planning office and the problems with government intervention in the lives of everyday citizens. My *DIA and Other Scams*, 423–26, glances at Mary DeGroot and her run for mayor in 1995. I have a file on the 2003 mayoral election that has literature outlining the background of Sue Casey.

Penny Dykstra Shoemaker, *A Grandmother's Collections for her Grandchildren* ([Denver]: n.p., 1993), tells the epic of the Shoemaker family, including the political careers of Joe and Jeff Shoemaker. Joe Shoemaker celebrated his work on the Joint Budget Committee in *Budgeting Is the Answer* (n.p: World Press, 1977). The Colorado political establishment heralded him in Morgan Smith, ed., *Joe Shoemaker: A Straight Shooter for Colorado* (Santa Fe: Cowdin Press, 2007). I glance at Shoemaker's role in redeveloping the Platte in *Big Money*, chap. 14.

UPN, November 5, 1970, p. 1, stressed South Denver as a Republican bailiwick. John Suthers and Melba Deuprey, *That Justice Shall Be Done* (Denver: United States Attorney's Office, 2004), 73–75, mentioned Robert Wham's role as acting United States Attorney. Articles on the Whams' political involvement include, *DP*, April 24, 1960, p. 15A, July 17, 1961, p. 3, January 9, 1963, p. 3, June 24, 1963, p. 3, and *RMN*, March 11, 1980, p. 8, September 10, 1984, p. 7, July 14, 1991, p. 32, and January 15, 1992, p. 7.

Joe Shoemaker with Bill Miller, *Robert E. Lee of Colorado: One Man Who Did Make a Difference* ([Denver]: A. B. Hirschfeld Press, 1999), celebrates the Republican boss. Jan Tyler remembered Lee and Ruth Prendergast in interviews on November 11, 2008, and January 29, 2009.

DP, September 17, 1970, p. 1, and *RMN*, p. 5, told of the death of Virginia Blue. The *Post* profiled her November 23, 1952, p. 6. The *News* reported her being honored with a stained glass window in the state Senate chambers, February 20, 1975, p. 8. *DP*, April 5, 1961, p. 3, mentioned Linden Blue's release from Cuba. He spoke of it in *RMN*, November 5, 1961, p. 59. Also see *DP*, February 21, 1975, p. 2, and *RMN*, February 22, 1975, p. 5, and August 20, 1975, p. 8.

Portraits of Carl Gustafson include *DP*, January 16, 1977, p. 1, and July 5, 1978, p. 3, and *RMN*, November 13, 1978, p. 13, April 24, 1980, p. 10, September 13, 1980, p. 8, March 4, 1982, p. 21, and June 5, 1983, p. 6. Stories about the death of his wife are *RMN*, August 1, 1974, p. 5, August 2, 1974, p. 5, August 14, 1974,

p. 5, and *DP*, August 1, 1974, p. 3, August 2, 1974, pp. 3, 55, and October 19, 1974, p. 3. *DP*, January 5, 1989, p. 4, and *RMN*, p. 111, reported his death. Miller Hudson and John Davoren recalled service in the General Assembly with Gustafson and the state's politics in the late 1970s and early 1980s in a conversation on October 4, 2008. Glances at Ruth Prendergast include *RMN*, October 24, 1975, p. 13, June 7, 1980, p. 5, and September 27, 1980, p. 73.

RMN, October 28, 1945, reviewed the career of Frank L. Dodge. The 1928 *Year Book of Organized Labor*, p. 21, feted James Stevic. His obituary was in *RMN*, December 25, 1965, p. 5, and *Colorado Postmaster*, January 1966, p. 1.

WPP, August 2002, p. 1, celebrated Sue Casey. Come election time, the paper gave the views of candidates and briefly sketched their backgrounds. The monthly looked at Charlie Brown's election to the Colorado House, December 1982, p. 3. The June 2001, p. 1, issue reported his triumph in the city council race. In a series of conversations in 2003 and 2007, Julie Wells discussed the politics of South Denver, especially the 2003 city council race won by Peggy Lehmann—Wells reviewed a draft of this chapter. Steve and Katie Fisher likewise gave me their views of South Denver council politics in numerous chats. They especially focused on developments around the University of Denver and the way Lucy Van Pelt would have defeated Charlie Brown if she ran against him for council.

DP, May 13, 1963, p. 1, told of the controversies provoked by Paul Hentzell and how the Republicans were out to get him. *RMN*, August 15, 1983, p. 1, and August 16, 1983, p. 18, and *DP*, August 15, 1983, p. 1, had retrospections on the councilman. Also see *UPN*, April 1, 1971, p. 9, *DP*, January 28, 1974, p. 3, January 31, 1974, p. 1, and October 24, 1979, p. 19, and *RMN*, January 28, 1974, p. 8, March 15, 1974, p. 5, December 14, 1979, p. 8, October 9, 1982, p. 6, and April 19, 1983, p. 8.

Index

(V1 refers to South Denver topics in volume 1; V3 to volume 3. A street is always listed before an avenue in identifying intersections, e.g., First Avenue and Broadway is under Broadway. Discussions of specific streets are in the general index. Addresses are limited to locations in South Denver.)

Addresses

9 1st Av., 260
17 1st Av., 259, 260

Acoma St. and W. 3rd Av., 104
1324–28–32 S. Acoma St., 270
801 S. Adams St., 198
538 Alameda Av., 66
616 Alameda Av., 64
1101–05–09–13 Alameda Av., 54
1121 Alameda Av., 105
1211 Alameda Av., 180, 271
1919 Alameda Av., 141
1929 Alameda Av., 143
2001 Alameda Av., 139
2201 Alameda Av., 142
2303 Alameda Av., 146
2400 Alameda Av., 210
3035 Alameda Av., 217
3100 Alameda Av., 210
3131 Alameda Av., 216
110 W. Alameda Av., 64
123 W. Alameda Av., 164
W. Alameda Av. and Platte
    River, 140
2565 Alameda Cir., 190
120 W. Archer Pl., 64
1717 Arizona Av., 93
1800 Arizona Av., 84, 85

1157 S. Bannock St., 99
1805 S. Bannock St., 95
S. Bannock St. and W. Evans
    Av., 60
7 Bayaud Av., 64
1112 Bayaud Av., 162
1134 Bayaud Av., 162
1322 Bayaud Av., 157, 158
30 W. Bayaud Av., 62, 64
3400 Belcaro Dr., 196
3500 Belcaro Dr., 199
3555 Belcaro Dr., 200–01
Bonnie Brae Blvd. and
    Kentucky Av., 186
745 Bonnie Brae Blvd., 192
930 Bonnie Brae Blvd., 187
954 Bonnie Brae Blvd., 188
966 Bonnie Brae Blvd., 189
2 Broadway, 64

Broadway and 1st Av., 259, 261
121 Broadway, 78
Broadway and 2nd Av., 179, 257
203 Broadway, 256
220 Broadway, 34
224 Broadway, 248
357 Broadway, 235
400 Broadway, 64
500 block of Broadway, 64
Broadway and 6th Av., 132
81 S. Broadway, 260
S. Broadway and Bayaud Av., 259
281 S. Broadway, 180
S. Broadway and Alameda Av., 28
316 S. Broadway, 180
S. Broadway and Dakota Av., 90
S. Broadway and Virginia Av.,
    55, 188
S. Broadway and Center Av., 45
S. Broadway and Exposition
    Av., 132
787–95 S. Broadway, 95, 199
S. Broadway and Kentucky Av., 94
S. Broadway and Mississippi
    Av., 39, 53, 98
1403 S. Broadway, 259
1419 S. Broadway, 98
1451–53 S. Broadway, 98
1475 S. Broadway, 259
1571 S. Broadway, 259
S. Broadway and Jewell Av., 12
1930 S. Broadway, 259
S. Broadway and Evans Av., 20

326 Cedar Av., 56
735 Cedar Av., 269
939 Cedar Av., 179
1681 Cedar Av., 151
1701 Cedar Av., 147
1805 Cedar Av., 146
1900 Cedar Av., 141, 142
2326 Cedar Av., 212
2330 Cedar Av., 212
2500 Cedar Av., 212
2525 Cedar Av., 212
2600 Cedar Av., 212, 213
2700 Cedar Av., 213
2800 Cedar Av., 212

2975 Cedar Av., 153
47 W. Cedar Av., 259
20 Center Av., 135
Cherokee St. and W. 5th Av., 104
S. Cherokee St. and W. Cedar
    Av., 233, 234
2500 Cherry Creek Dr. S., 218
3100 Cherry Creek Dr. S., 217, 279
3200 Cherry Creek Dr. S., 217
3690 Cherry Creek Dr. S., 204
1202 S. Clarkson St., 271
S. Clarkson St. and Florida Av., 87
S. Clarkson St. and Iliff Av., 3, 9, 20
S. Clayton St. and Virginia Av., 206
S. Clayton St. and Louisiana
    Av., 103
S. Clayton St. and Florida Av., 233
3000 S. Clayton St., 60
S. Colorado Blvd. and Alameda
    Av., 245, 247, 251
360 S. Colorado Blvd., 245
380 S. Colorado Blvd., 245
390 S. Colorado Blvd., 249
430 S. Colorado Blvd., 244
445 S. Colorado Blvd., 245
450 S. Colorado Blvd., 244
490 S. Colorado Blvd., 244
S. Colorado Blvd. and Virginia
    Av., 204
500 S. Colorado Blvd., 247
502 S. Colorado Blvd., 247
S. Colorado Blvd. and Cherry
    Creek, 247
600 S. Colorado Blvd., 18, 246
690 S. Colorado Blvd., 217
S. Colorado Blvd. and Exposi-
    tion Av., 199, 200, 246
700 S. Colorado Blvd., 199, 245
705 S. Colorado Blvd., 200
750 S. Colorado Blvd., 249
800 S. Colorado Blvd., 248
888 S. Colorado Blvd., 239, 240
S. Colorado Blvd. and
    Kentucky Av., 225, 239
940 S. Colorado Blvd., 247
960 S. Colorado Blvd., 241,
    242, 248
1025 S. Colorado Blvd., 246

1060 S. Colorado Blvd., 248
1080 S. Colorado Blvd., 249
S. Colorado Blvd. and
  Mississippi Av., 225, 248
1201–45 S. Colorado Blvd., 225
1255 S. Colorado Blvd., 250
1260 S. Colorado Blvd., 249, 251
S. Colorado Blvd. and
  Louisiana Av., 225, 234, 235
1300 S. Colorado Blvd., 237
1355 S. Colorado Blvd., 249
1370 S. Colorado Blvd., 243
S. Colorado Blvd. and
  Arkansas Av., 237
1401 S. Colorado Blvd., 234
1485 S. Colorado Blvd., 250
1490 S. Colorado Blvd., 244
S. Colorado Blvd. and Florida
  Av., 236, 237
1500 S. Colorado Blvd., 248
1505 S. Colorado Blvd., 250
1520 S. Colorado Blvd., 248, 249
1625 S. Colorado Blvd., 247
1680 S. Colorado Blvd., 246
S. Colorado Blvd. and Mexico
  Av., 18, 246
1700 S. Colorado Blvd., 246
3333 S. Colorado Blvd., 282
S. Colorado Blvd. and Quincy
  Av., 148, 190
S. Columbine St. and
  Tennessee Av., 186
1490 S. Columbine, 226
2266 S. Columbine St., 106
2181 S. Cook St., 281
58 Corona St., 259
112 S. Corona St., 162
186 S. Corona St., 164
S. Corona St. and Cedar Av., 71
S. Corona St. and Virginia Av.,
  55
555 S. Corona St., 178
618 S. Corona St., 56
637 S. Corona St., 271
875 S. Corona St., 271
950 S. Corona St., 56
1107 S. Corona St., 56
1111 S. Corona St., 56
1301 S. Corona St., 56
1318 S. Corona St., 259
S. Corona St. and Harvard Av., 20

1312 Dakota Av., 170
25 Downing St., 168
S. Downing St. and Ellsworth
  Av., 166
9 S. Downing St., 264

99 S. Downing St., 154
S. Downing St. and Bayaud
  Av., 162–65, 205
101 S. Downing St., 162
152 S. Downing St., 164
155 S. Downing St., 164
211 S. Downing St., 176
234 S. Downing St., 180
266 S. Downing St., 179
271 S. Downing St., 270
280 S. Downing St., 179, 276
284 S. Downing St., 179
290 S. Downing St., 178
291 S. Downing St., 178
295 S. Downing St., 178
S. Downing St. and Alameda
  Av., 162, 178–81
309 S. Downing St., 180
S. Downing St. and Virginia Av., 45
555 S. Downing St., 57
811 S. Downing St., 57
S. Downing St. and Kentucky
  Av., 42
1025 S. Downing St., 57
1051 S. Downing St., 56
1059 S. Downing St., 57
S. Downing St. and Arizona Av., 42
S. Downing St. and Louisiana
  Av., 17, 42
1636 S. Downing St., 188
2010 S. Downing St., 130

Elati St. and W. 3rd Av., 61
S. Elizabeth St. and Arizona
  Av., 193
1501 S. Elizabeth St., 259
32 W. Ellsworth Av., 77
119 W. Ellsworth Av., 78
420 S. Emerson St., 60
571 S. Emerson St., 272
792 S. Emerson St., 260
1115 S. Emerson St., 265
S. Emerson St. and Evans Av., 80
2292 S. Emerson St., 81
2324 S. Emerson St., 80
2332 S. Emerson St., 90
1725 Evans Av., 64
1744 Evans Av., 22
620 Exposition Av., 62
2755 Exposition Av., 207
2925 Exposition Av., 205
3040 Exposition Av., 219
3950 Exposition Av., 200

S. Fillmore St. and Cherry
  Creek Dr. S., 211
2025 S. Fillmore St., 268

S. Fillmore St. and Yale Av.,
  268, 269
3333 Florida Av., 228
3737 Florida Av., 226
Fox St. and W. 6th Av., 121
100 S. Franklin St., 153, 155
140 S. Franklin St., 156
175 S. Franklin St., 152
271–73 S. Franklin St., 139
364 S. Franklin St., 178
381–83 S. Franklin St., 112
S. Franklin St. and Virginia Av.,
  45, 46
S. Franklin St. and Exposition
  Av., 36, 37, 38, 39
700 S. Franklin St., 104
800 S. Franklin St., 90
840 S. Franklin St., 94
842 S. Franklin St., 94
850 S. Franklin St., 94
876 S. Franklin St., 94
880 S. Franklin St., 94
S. Franklin St. and Kentucky
  Av., 13, 76
900 S. Franklin St., 77, 79
918 S. Franklin St., 89
932 S. Franklin St., 89
942 S. Franklin St., 94
966 S. Franklin St., 94
974 S. Franklin St., 89, 277
1048 S. Franklin St., 94
1074 S. Franklin St., 90
1080 S. Franklin St., 94, 95
1100 S. Franklin St., 90
1130 S. Franklin St., 92, 93
1140 S. Franklin St., 94
1150 S. Franklin St., 90
1190 S. Franklin St., 83, 90–92
S. Franklin St. and Arizona Av., 24
S. Franklin St. and Louisiana
  Av., 11
1545 S. Franklin St., 258

W. 4th Av. and Galapago St., 234
499 S. Garfield St., 278
520 S. Garfield St., 203
885 S. Garfield St., 198
S. Garfield St. and Evans Av., 261
S. Gaylord St. and Alameda
  Av., 35, 140, 142
300 block of S. Gaylord St., 144
334 S. Gaylord St., 217
665 S. Gaylord St., 178
925 S. Gaylord St., 89
S. Gaylord St. and Tennessee Av., 3
1004 S. Gaylord St., 101
1004–06 S. Gaylord St., 98

1010–12 S. Gaylord St., 98
1028 S. Gaylord St., 64, 101, 102
1040 S. Gaylord St., 265
1052 S. Gaylord St., 103
1065 S. Gaylord St., 98
1075–83 S. Gaylord St., 98
1076 S. Gaylord St., 100, 101
1085 S. Gaylord St., 103, 264
1088 S. Gaylord St., 100
1092 S. Gaylord St., 98
1093–95 S. Gaylord St., 98
1096 S. Gaylord St., 100
S. Gaylord St. and Mississippi
    Av., 98
1192 S. Gaylord St., 18
1283 S. Gaylord St., 99
1312 S. Gaylord St., 83
1370 S. Gaylord St., 101
1381 S. Gaylord St., 98
S. Gaylord St. and Iowa Av., 134
208 S. Gilpin St., 151
445–47 S. Gilpin St., 108
568 S. Gilpin St., 110
S. Gilpin St. and Center Av., 103
692 S. Gilpin St., 84
750 S. Gilpin St., 264
792 S. Gilpin St., 280
811 S. Gilpin St., 90
887 S. Gilpin St., 279
983 S. Gilpin St., 277
1040 S. Gilpin St., 276
1101 S. Gilpin St., 95
1111 S. Gilpin St., 95
1112 S. Gilpin St., 28
1120 S. Gilpin St., 95
1125 S. Gilpin St., 95
1136 S. Gilpin St., 95
1137 S. Gilpin St., 95
1164 S. Gilpin St., 93
1168 S. Gilpin St., 96
1171 S. Gilpin St., 92
1187 S. Gilpin St., 92
1195 S. Gilpin St., 92
S. Gilpin St. and Arizona Av.,
    19, 93
1200 S. Gilpin St., 95
1220 S. Gilpin St., 95
1234 S. Gilpin St., 90
1248 S. Gilpin St., 94
1260 S. Gilpin St., 95
1274 S. Gilpin St., 94, 258
1284 S. Gilpin St., 93
1286 S. Gilpin St., 94
S. Gilpin St. and Louisiana Av., 42
S. Gilpin St. and Evans Av., 159
Grant St. and 3rd Av., 35
Grant St. and 4th Av., 212, 213

S. Grant St. and Cedar Av., 63
S. Grant St. and Florida Av., 3
S. Grant St. and Colorado Av.,
    121

580 S. Harrison Ln., 278
621 S. Harrison St., 203
710 S. Harrison St., 278
1777 S. Harrison St., 238
205 S. High St., 146
250 S. High St., 146
401 S. High St., 105
416 S. High St., 78
725 S. High St., 78, 79
S. High St. and Tennessee Av., 79
1045 S. High St., 101
1175 S. High St., 231
1194 S. High St., 83
1284 S. High St., 99
1851 S. High St., 94, 276
2790 S. High St., 276
101 S. Humboldt St., 153, 154
369 S. Humboldt St., 178
S. Humboldt St. and Virginia
    Av., 178

501 Iliff Av., 14
146 W. Irvington Pl., 259

601 S. Jackson St., 202
S. Jackson St. and Mississippi
    Av., 225
S. Jackson St. and Louisiana
    Av., 225
S. Jackson St. and Florida Av.,
    225
S. Jackson St. and Mexico Av.,
    81, 230, 238
1776 S. Jackson St., 237
2323 S. Jackson St., 279
617 Jewell Av., 265
848 S. Josephine St., 186
S. Josephine St. and Arizona
    Av., 193

549 Kalamath St., 159
S. Kalamath St. and W.
    Alameda Av., 19
614 Kentucky Av., 67
1923 Kentucky Av., 64
3303 Kentucky Av., 199
3460 Kentucky Av., 199
3479 Kentucky Av., 199
3481 Kentucky Av., 198

S. Lafayette St. and Bayaud
    Av., 157, 204

140 S. Lafayette St., 156
175 S. Lafayette St., 158
S. Lafayette St. and Dakota
    Av., 105, 169, 174
401 S. Lafayette St., 169, 170
Lincoln St. and 2nd Av., 193
Lincoln St. and 5th Av., 34
64 S. Lincoln St., 258
260 S. Lincoln St., 180
Logan St. and 3rd Av., 20
Logan St. and 4th Av., 184
34 S. Logan St., 227
S. Logan St. and Virginia Av., 63
620 S. Logan St., 103
1145 S. Logan St., 190, 258
1275 S. Logan St., 63, 175
S. Logan St. and Florida Av., 4
S. Logan St. and Iliff Av., 14
2500 S. Logan St., 279
2797 S. Logan St., 86

830 S. Madison St., 199
860 S. Madison St., 199
S. Marion St. and Bayaud Av., 14
100 S. Marion St., 159
S. Marion St. and Cedar Av., 111
480 S. Marion St., 276
490 S. Marion St., 169
S. Marion St. and Virginia Av.,
    18, 171, 172, 188
1385 S. Marion St., 190
3888 Mexico Av., 238
S. Milwaukee St. and Ohio Av.,
    186, 194
S. Milwaukee St. and Asbury
    Av., 98
S. Milwaukee St. and Evans
    Av., 102
2210 Mississippi Av., 264
2375 Mississippi Av., 78
W. Mississippi Av. and the
    Platte River, 269
730 W. Mississippi Av., 159
S. Monroe St. and Mississippi
    Av., 225
S. Monroe St. and Arizona Av.,
    225
S. Monroe St. and Florida Av., 232
2150 S. Monroe St., 203
3260 S. Monroe St., 276
606 S. Monroe Way, 203
612 S. Monroe Way, 203
618 S. Monroe Way, 203
650 S. Monroe Way, 203

85 Ogden St., 248
35 S. Ogden St., 276

S. Ogden St. and Bayaud Av., 167
103 S. Ogden St., 167
S. Ogden St. and Cedar Av., 168
452 S. Ogden, 276
500 S. Ogden St., 54, 55
S. Ogden St. and Ellsworth Av.,
    166
700 block of S. Ogden St., 55
994 S. Ogden St., 273
1195 S. Ogden St., 55
1300 S. Ogden St., 208
1666 S. Ogden St., 268
622 Ohio Av., 67, 68, 105
2331 Ohio Av., 193

128 Pearl St., 66
22 S. Pearl St., 263
S. Pearl St. and Bayaud Av., 4
103 S. Pearl St., 263
259 S. Pearl St., 66
264 S. Pearl St., 67
295 S. Pearl St., 67
S. Pearl St. and Alameda Av.,
    65, 66, 67
300 S. Pearl St., 67
312 S. Pearl St., 64, 65
324 S. Pearl St., 65
350 S. Pearl St., 65, 66
383 S. Pearl St., 64
386 S. Pearl St., 63
387 S. Pearl St., 63
508 S. Pearl St., 60
675 S. Pearl St., 63
695 S. Pearl St., 62
700 S. Pearl St., 62
714 S. Pearl St., 62, 63
715 S. Pearl St., 59
716 S. Pearl St., 62
890 S. Pearl St., 66
S. Pearl St. and Kentucky Av., 66
997 S. Pearl St., 272
S. Pearl St. and Louisiana Av., 178
1590 S. Pearl St., 81
S. Pearl St. and Colorado Av.,
    120, 121
S. Pennsylvania St. and Cedar
    Av., 35
393 S. Pennsylvania St., 258
429 S. Pennsylvania St., 60
S. Pennsylvania St. and
    Exposition Av., 62
900 block of S. Pennsylvania
    St., 57, 58
931 S. Pennsylvania St., 70
959 S. Pennsylvania St., 58
1434 S. Pennsylvania St., 279
1831 S. Pennsylvania St., 98

38 Polo Club Cir., 145
5 Polo Club Rd., 206, 209

S. Race St. and Cedar Av., 139, 140
S. Race St. and Alameda Av., 140
300 block of S. Race St., 144
S. Race St. and Exposition Av., 80
801 S. Race St., 111
S. Race St. and Kentucky Av.,
    64, 103
S. Race St. and Tennessee Av.,
    77, 84, 85
1017 S. Race St., 79
1025 S. Race St., 89
1067 S. Race St., 113
S. Race St. and Mississippi Av.,
    20, 61, 84, 85
1178 S. Race St., 95
S. Race St. and Arizona Av., 18, 82
1846 S. Race St., 134
S. Race St. and Asbury Av., 132

281 Sherman St., 271
235 S. Sherman St., 86
S. Sherman St. and Alameda
    Av., 193
311 S. Sherman St., 271
315 S. Sherman St., 271
388 S. Sherman St., 227
664 S. Sherman St., 263
S. Steele St., and Cherry Creek
    Dr. S., 216, 217
294 S. Steele St., 217
S. Steele St. and Alameda Av.,
    202, 206, 215, 277
456 S. Steele St., 202
S. Steele St. and Virginia Av.,
    202, 204
S. Steele St. and Exposition
    Av., 61, 218–19
S. Steele St. and Kentucky Av.,
    225
900 S. Steele St., 199
S. Steele St. and Arizona Av.,
    194, 225
S. Steele St. and Mississippi
    Av., 225
S. Steele St. and Louisiana Av.,
    78, 225
1300 S. Steele St., 193, 226
S. Steele St. and Florida Av., 231
3275 S. Steele St., 283

2660 Tennessee Av., 275

S. University Blvd. and Cherry
    Creek Dr. S., 218

100 S. University Blvd., 212, 217
106 S. University Blvd., 212, 218
S. University Blvd. and Cedar
    Av., 213
200 S. University Blvd., 213
229 S. University Blvd., 143
S. University Blvd. and
    Alameda Av., 3, 205, 214
444 S. University Blvd., 211
S. University Blvd. and
    Exposition Av., 3, 186, 191,
    193, 210
701 S. University Blvd., 193
709 S. University Blvd., 191
723 S. University Blvd., 193
740 S. University Blvd., 191
747 S. University Blvd., 192–93
759–63 S. University Blvd., 193
785 S. University Blvd., 101, 193
S. University Blvd. and Ohio
    Av., 38, 191, 192, 193
864 S. University Blvd., 106
993 S. University Blvd., 78
1001 S. University Blvd., 103
1044 S. University Blvd., 186
S. University Blvd. and
    Mississippi Av., 190, 233
1124 S. University Blvd., 189
S. University Blvd. and
    Arizona Av., 192
1317 S. University Blvd., 80
1325 S. University Blvd., 40
1410 S. University Blvd., 193
1485 S. University Blvd., 96–98
1495 S. University Blvd., 98
S. University Blvd. and Florida
    Av., 96, 97
1580 S. University Blvd., 274, 275
S. University Blvd. and Iowa
    Av., 9, 36, 44, 135, 275
S. University Blvd. and I-25, 23
S. University Blvd. and Jewell
    Av., 78
2040 S. University Blvd., 245
S. University Blvd. and Iliff
    Av., 209
S. University Blvd. and
    Hampden Av., 91, 189, 190

300 block of S. Vine St., 144
S. Vine St. and Virginia Av., 103
667 S. Vine St., 100
741 S. Vine St., 248
765 S. Vine St., 276
782 S. Vine St., 281
S. Vine St. and Mississippi Av., 109
3301 Virginia Av., 203

300 block of S. Washington St., 66
700 block of S. Washington St., 63
S. Washington St. and Ohio
 Av., 20, 68
809 S. Washington St., 70
912 S. Washington, 227
S. Washington St. and
 Mississippi Av., 272
1579 S. Washington St., 259
200 block of S. Williams St.,
 138–39
219 S. Williams St., 139
225 S. Williams St., 139
298 S. Williams St., 106–08

S. Williams St. and Dakota Av.,
 35, 68, 105, 106
400 S. Williams St., 104
600 S. Williams St., 84
644 S. Williams St., 1
648 S. Williams St., 80
777 S. Williams St., 80–81
S. Williams St. and Ohio Av., 80
901 S. Williams St., 77, 277
995 S. Williams St., 92
1089 S. Williams St., 111
S. Williams St. and Mississippi
 Av., 111
1150 S. Williams St., 83

1157 S. Williams St., 83
1165 S. Williams St., 78
1225 S. Williams St., 99
1243 S. Williams St., 96

300 block of S. York St., 144
300 S. York St., 144
648 S. York St., 273
S. York St. and Ohio Av., 78
1051 S. York St., 279
1090 S. York St., 84
S. York St. and Mississippi Av., 77
1190 S. York St., 84, 85
1800 S. York St., 134

General Index

ABC Bowling, 245
Adams County, 59; fairgrounds, 234
Adams, Eugene, 212
Adams Street School, 85
Adams' Thriftway, 271
Adler, Carl E., 101
Aegis, 135, 275
Afton, Emory, 94
Agape Coffee House, 106
Ager-Tabell Drugs, 179
Agnes Memorial Sanatorium, 195
Aladdin Broadcasting, 190
Aladown, 178
Alameda Grocery, 180
Alameda Tavern, 64
Alameda Theater, 64, 65
Alameda–Cedar Home-Owners
 Association, 212
Albright, Madeleine K., 91, V3
All City Stadium, 126, 131–35
Alsop, Marin, 78
Alta Vista, 233
American:
—Basketball Association, 151, 199
—Bible Society, 83
—Civil Liberties Union, 106, 157
—Football League, 198
—House, 8
—Legion, 25, 134, 135
—Penwomen, 37
—Protective Association, 234, V1
Ameter, Frederick W., 26
Ammons, Elias, 257, V1, V3
Amuzu Theater, 64
Andersen Ballet, 64
Andersen's Market, 99
Anderson, Al, 66–67
Anderson, Arthur J., 94, 95
Andy's, 244
Anema, Charles, Jr., 173
Anschutz, Philip, 211

Aqua Bowl Motel, 246
Arapahoe County, 59, 262,
 263, V1, V3
Arapahoe Hunt Club, 204, 207
Arizona Avenue Parkway, 19
Armstrong, Hamilton, 81
Arneill, James R., family, 212
Arnold, Cora, 157
Arnold Corporation, 228
Arnold, Henry J., 169
Arsenault, Marcel, 87
Arthur Young & Associates, 154
Arts for All, 63
Asbury School, 188, V3
Ascension Episcopal, 214
Aspen, Charles B., 178
Assembly of God, 212
Associated Grocers, 271
Associated Industries, 184–87, V3
Ault, Charles, 102

Babcock, John, 225–26, V3
baby boomers, 61, 85, 108,
 133, 231, 232, 239
Bailey, Frank and Carrie,
 family, 77–79, 82, 88, 89
Baker neighborhood, 2, 4, V1
Bancroft, Caroline, 150
banks and banking, 8, 146, 212,
 238, 244, 250, V1, V3
Baptists, 80, 193, V1, V3
Barbara, Frank, 277
Barber, Max, 103
Barlarat Center, 232
Barnard, Harry F., 84
Barnes & Noble, 250
Barnes, Richard, 33, 70
Barnum neighborhood, 165
Barrett School, 219
Bartels, Carrie, 77, 78
Bartels, Louis F., Jr., 78

Basanow, Sugar, 33–34
baseball, 42, 135
Batterton, Richard, 274, 276
Bayes, Ginny, 112
Bear Valley, 220
Beatles, 173
Beatrice, 217, V1
Beattie, Albert B., 78
Becker, Carryl M., 103
Bel-Aire Cafe, 193
Belcaro, 4, 195–04, 218, 219,
 225, 250, 276; Mansion, 197–
 200; Motel, 246; North, 202–
 04; Park, 195; Park Homeown-
 ers Association, 201; Realty
 and Investment, 199; Shopping
 Center, 199–200
Bell, Doug, 173, 174
Belmont Plumbing, 100, 101
Benedict, Jacques, 32, 93, 96,
 147–48, 228
Bennett, William, 203
Berger, Bart, family, 205
Bethesda Sanatorium, 87, V3
Beyer, George H., 259
bicycles, bicyclists, 30, 31, 42,
 99, 100, 104, 181, 218, 280
Big D Diner, 103
Billings, David, 102
Biscayne, the, 228
Bishop, Tina, 169
Blackmer, Myron, 147–48, 190
blacks, African-Americans,
 civil rights, 28, 42, 61, 87,
 128, 129, 130, 131, 186,
 257, 268, V1, V3
Blair, Charles E., 212–15
Blamey family, 178
Blee, Joseph, 96
Blossom Drive, 14
Blue, Virginia and Linden, 279

Bob's Grocery, 101
Bob's Place, 245, 251
Boettcher, Charles and Claude,
    family, dynasty, 77, 81–82,
    152, 167, 201, 214, V1, V3;
    Concert Hall, 198; Founda-
    tion, 142; Boettcher, Newton
    & Company, 153, 154–55
Bohm, George, family, Addition,
    76–80, 88, 90
Bohn, Eddie, 172–73
Boland, Kate, 31
bombs, 208, 209
Bonfils, Frederick, family, 150,
    170, V1, V3
Bonnie Brae, 4, 184–88, 189,
    194, 195, 196, 204, 219, 220,
    225, 276; Baptist, 186, 193–
    94; business strip, 101, 191–
    93, 264; Drugs, 193;
    Flowers, 191, 192–93; Ice
    Cream, 192, 193; map, 185;
    McMansions in, 194; Park,
    186, 188; Plumbing, 101;
    stone pillars, 186; Tavern,
    191–94; transformation, 194
Boorman, William J., 187
Botanic Gardens, 15, 19, 141
Bowen, Gwen, 63
bowling, 228, 239, 240, 245,
    250, V1, V3
Bowman, William Norman, 63,
    164–66, V1
boxers and boxing, 172, 249
Boy Scouts, 106, 163, 260,
    281, V1, V3
Braconier, Ben, Plumbing, 100, 101
Bradley, John, 81
Bradley School, 231
Brake & Duff, 259
Breedan, Spicer, family, 200–02
Brethren, 272
Brick, John, 130
brickyards, 134, 184, V1, V3
Brico, Antonia, 58–59
Brinkerhoff, Zachary K., 153
Broadway:
—Baptist, 193, V1
—Department Store, 169, V1
—Heights, 76, 77
—Park, 12, V1
—Stadium (Park), 132, V1
—Terrace, 2, V1
Broe, Pat, 167–69
Brofman, David, 203
Bromfield, Donald, 199
Brooks, Stan, 144

Brown, Charlie, 281
Brown, Debi, 266
Brown, Joseph G., 37, 38
Brown, Molly, 37, 38
Brown, Sherman T., family, 169
Brunetti, Wayne, 146
Bryant, Ted, 276
Bryn Mawr, 53, 54
Buchtel, Henry, 82, V3
Buchtel Village, 261
Buell, Temple, 91, 210, 212,
    218, 219, 232
Bull & Bush, 247
Burke, Edward F., 270–71, V3
Burkhardt family, Steel, 95,
    199, V1, V3
Burnett, William H., 90
Burr, Raymond, 151
Bush, George, family, 146, V3
busing, see school busing
Busy Corner, 179, 180
Butler, Brad, 146
Byers Junior High School,
    4, 165, 232, V1, V3
Byers School, 88, V1
Byers, William Newton, 7–8, V1

cable television, 217, 277, V3
Cahill, Willie, 60, 61
Calvary Temple, 212–16, 219
Cambridge Dairy, 217, 247
Camp Fire Girls, 17–18, 33, 83
Camp Rosalie, 83
Campaign for Responsible
    Development, 273
Campus Lounge, 193
Candle Light, 64
Cannon, H. Brown and
    Margaret, family, 217
Capitol Hill, 2, 5, 9, 10, 76, 78,
    109, 147, 154, 201, 204,
    245, 266, 269, 270, 273, 274
Capitol Hydraulic Company, 7
Captain's House, 56, 57
Captain's Tavern, 240
Carlson, George (governor),
    257; (sculptor), 16
Carnegie, Andrew, 195, V3
Carpio, Sal, 269
Carr, Bob and Ralph, 274
Carroll, John, 264
cars, car dealers, 172, 249, 251,
    264, V1, V3; also see by name
Cart 'n Rib, 240
Casey, Sue, 43, 280–81
Castle Rock, 264
Caston, Saul, 59

Catholics, Archdiocese, 55,
    147, 148, 193, 226–30, 234,
    236; anti-Catholicism, 60,
    234, 235, 263
Causey, James, 83, 90–92
Cecil's Supermarket, 101
Celebrity Sports Center, 4,
    239–41, 245, 246, 250
Centerpoint, 238
Central Assembly Church,
    212, 213
Central Christian Church, 204, V1
Central City Opera, 148, 150
Central One, 67
Century 21, 243, 244, 245, 251
Cervi, Gene, 156
Chamber of Commerce, 8, 24,
    93, 122, 259, 260, 273;
    Junior, 267
Changeling, The, 201
Channel: Four, 188; Seven,
    190; Six, 92; Two, 170
Chappell, Dos, 31
Chaput, Charles, 229
Charney, Leo, 100
Chatfield Reservoir, 8
Chavarria, Albino, 157
Cheesman, Walter, 11, 139, 141,
    V1; Park, 12, 13, 40, 42, 59, 90,
    273, V3; Realty, 142, 145
Cheltenham School, 175
Cherrelyn, 188
Cherry Creek, 2, 3, 4, 9, 13, 14,
    31, 59, 66, 67, 120, 138, 140,
    152, 162, 206, 218, 241, 278,
    V1, V3; Dam, 81, 236; Hotel,
    248; Inn, 18, 246–48; News,
    262–63; North, 102, 229, 274;
    Shopping Center, 91, 210, 212,
    219; Tower, 216, 217, 278
Cherry Hills, 91, 133
children, 12, 15, 25, 33, 37, 42,
    104, 146, 150, 175, 177, 265;
    Children's Fountain, 36;
    Children's Hospital, 145,
    158, 166; Children's Museum,
    20; Children's Theater, 173
Chinook, 263, V1
Chipotle, 159, V3
Christmas blizzard, 36
Chrysler, Jeremiah, family,
    Chrysler & Sons, Chrysler
    & Brunner, 98–99
Chuck's Donuts, 67
churches, see by name,
    denomination
CIA, 208, 268

Cinerama, 241–42
Citadel, The, 217
city council, 43, 45, 57, 77, 78, 85, 94, 99, 111–14, 168, 237, 258, 259, 263, 266–73, 279, 280–83; district 3, 266–73, 279, 280–83; district 4, 263, 266–69, 281, 283; district 6, 269, 273–75; district 7, 268–71, 273; district 9, 269; expansion, 266, 269; members, 264, 278—also see by name
City Ditch, 7–10, 14, 15, 20–27, 29, 34, 37, 39, 41, 125, 126, 135, 174, V1, V3; as a landmark, 23; flooding, 20
City of Brest Park, 204
City Park, 9, 10, 12, 13, 17, 22, 24, 36, 40, 42, 204
Civic Center, 34, 40, 90
Clark, Elizabeth, 68
Clayton, George W. and William M., 53
Club Morocco, 244
coal, 96, 248
Cody, Buffalo Bill, 60
coffee business, 180
Colburn Hotel, 165
Cole Junior High, 130, 165
Collins, John, 79, V1, V3
Collins, Judy, 58
Colonial Dames, 154
Colonial Room, 169
Colorado, state government: Athletic Commission, 172; attorney general's office, 90, 157, 274; Bureau of Child and Animal Protection, 11; Capitol, 9, 12, 93, 164; Division of Wildlife, 25; General Assembly, legislature, House, Senate, 90, 99, 159, 172, 263, 276, 277, 278, 281, 283; Historical Society, 89, 112, 127, 145, 158, 258; School of Mines, 96; State Detention Home for Women, 159, V1; State Home for Dependent and Neglected Children, 3, 9, 20–21, V3; State Penitentiary, 81, 187; State University Extension Service, 20, 29; Tax Commission, 99
Colorado:
—Academy, 31
—& Southern Railway, 122, V3
—Association of Commerce and Industry, 274

—Blueprint Company, 90
—Bowl, 245
—Christian School, 216
—Federation of Garden Clubs, 19
—Forestry and Horticulture Association, 141
—Four, 245, 251
—Free University, 266
—Fuel & Iron, 92
—Herald Publishing, 260
—Humane Society, 11
—*Labor Advocate*, 279, V1
—Land & Home, 88
—*Miner*, 15, 16
—Mountain Club, 157
—National Bank, 155, 156, 206, 214
—Retail Merchants Association, 99
—Rockies, 135
—Royals, 64
—Six, 251
—Springs, 13, 142, 171, 189, 206
—State Taxpayers League, 259
—Transportation Museum, 212
Commerce City, 190
community centers, 33, 82, 86
Community Publications, 263
condominiums, 173, 174, 218
Cones, Joseph M., 169, V1
Congregation of the Missions, 226, 229
Congregational Church, 105, 106, 194, 219
Conservative Baptists, 190, 212
Continental Construction, 153
Continental Revolutionary Army, 208–10
Contos, Pete, 84
Cooper Theatre, 4, 241–43, 245, 246, 250
Coronado, 225–27, 231, 232, 234, 235, 238; Heights, 225; Mission, 226; School, 225, 226, 231
Cory, John J., 122, 231, V3; School, 231–33, 238–39
Cory-Merrill, 4, 225–39, V1; as agricultural enclave, 230; Campus Coalition, 232; defined, 225; evolution, 231, 238; office buildings, 230, 237–38; Park, 232
Cosmopolitan Hotel, 165
Cottonwood Riding Club, 207
Council on Foreign Relations, 158
Country Club: Dairy, 247; Gardens, 164, 166–69;

neighborhood, 9, 138, 195, 196, 207, 278; Towers, 167–68; also see Denver Country Club, South Country Club, West Country Club
courts: Colorado Supreme, 55, 60, 82, 90, 174, 268, 271, 274; Denver County, 90, 264, 269, 270; Denver District, 90, 270; Denver Juvenile, 12, 86, 217, 235, 236; Denver Probate, 203; US District, 205; US Circuit, 214, 268; US Supreme, 84
Covillo–Park School of Ballet, 64
crabapple trees, 14
Craft, Jane, Neighborhood Award, 70, 156
Craig Subdivision, 54
Cramer, Franz A., 212
Crane, Richard M., 187
Cranmer, George, 42, V3
Creel, George, 234
Crestmoor Park, 199
Crews, Verne J., 212
Cripple Creek, 241, 244
Crocker & Ryan, 92
Croft, Frank B., 94
Crofton School, 176, 177
Crowther, Richard, 241, 243
Crusade for Freedom, 268
Crystal Ballroom, 34, V1
Cub Scouts, 83
Currigan, Thomas G., 84, 90, 104, 268, 270, 273, V1, V3
Curtis Park, 10, 109, 177

Dad's Cookie Company, 65
Dailey, John L., 76, V1
dairies, milk, 65, 162, 180, 217, 239, 247
dancing, 33, 64, 87, 170, 171, V1
Daniels, Bill, Building, 217, 277, V3
Daughters of the American Revolution, 17, 154
Davoren, John, 155
Dawson, Thomas F., 89
Day, Edward C., family, 90, 271
De Andries House, 227
De Jong, John, 126
Deane Buick, 249
DeBoer, Frederick, 247
DeBoer, Saco R., 13, 14–15, 19, 91, 184, 186, 188, V3
Decker, Clarence, 213
Decker, Jesse and Velma, 179

Dee, Johnny, 203
DeGroot, Mary, 275, 276, 279, 280
Democrats, 90, 91, 99, 154,
    155, 156, 188, 215, 271,
    272, 275, 277–81, 283
Dempsey, Jack, 172
Denton family, 217
Denver: administration, mayor's
    office, 1, 29, 68, 131, 266,
    272, 273; as a city of lights,
    32; auditor's office, 263, 271,
    273; Auditorium, 135, 190;
    City and County of, 59, 120,
    133; city attorney's office, 82,
    281; city commission, 266;
    City Farm, 234; city forester,
    29; Commission on Commu-
    nity Relations, 84, 155; Com-
    munity Development Agency,
    45, 70, V3; district attorney's
    office, 55, 56, 187, 201, 215,
    274; election commission, 85,
    238, 271, 278; Fire and Police
    Board, 81; General Hospital,
    16; Landmark Commission,
    168, 169; parks and park-
    ways, 10, 12, 14, 15, 29, 33,
    35, 35, 38, 42, 45, 93—also
    see by name; plans and plan-
    ners, 4, 24, 67, 111, 113; Pub-
    lic Library (DPL), 38,
    83, 281; Water Department
    (DWD), 21, 22–23, 78, 93,
    142; also see city council,
    courts, fire department, police
Denver:
—Academy, 86–87
—& Rio Grande, 90, 96, 139, 143
—& Salt Lake, 195
—& Santa Fe, 59, V1
—Area Labor Federation, 272,
    273, V1
—Art Museum, 57, 209
—Boulder Turnpike, 92
—Broncos, 198, 199
—*Catholic Register*, 273
—Christian School, 87, V3
—Circle Railroad, 59, 234, V1, V3
—Civic Ballet, 64, 150
—Civic Theatre, 150
—Country Club, 3, 4, 9, 12, 14,
    24, 53, 135, 138, 143, 144,
    145, 150, 151, 158, 162,
    164, 167, 195, 197, 204,
    205, 207, 212, 273; also see
    Country Club neighborhood
—Croquet Club, 24

—Digs Trees, 155
—Drumstick, 242, 244
—Dry, 212
—International School, 87, 88
—Macaroni Company, 191
—Medical Society, 94
—Municipal Band, 40
—Museum of: Natural History,
    Nature and Science, 123, 142
—National Bank, 56
—Naval Officers Club, 171
—Northwestern, & Pacific, 141
—Organizing Committee
    (DOC), see Olympics
—Philharmonic, 59
—Players Guild, 102, 150, 151
—*Post*, 90, 112, 150, 155, 156,
    170, 192, 209, 217, 247,
    260, 273, V1, V3; fishing
    tournament, 25; Opera, 59
—Pressed Brick, 57
—Public Schools, see schools
—Real Estate Investment, 167
—Retail Grocers Association, 99
—Riding Stables, 241
—Rockets (Nuggets), 151, 199
—Seminary, 190
—South Park, & Pacific, 8
—Tramway, 11, 46, 82, 139,
    143, 199, V1, V3
—*Tribune*, 36, 37
—Union Water Company
    (DUWC), 11, 139, 140
—Urban Gardens, 177
—Waldorf School, 87, V3
Depression, New Deal Programs,
    38, 42, 127, 132, 142, 158, 170,
    187, 207, 259, 261
DeTemple, Carl, 237, 273–74
Devlin, Patrick J., 271
Dickson, Dick, 101
Dill, Errett B., 187
Dill, Harold, 203
DiManna, Geno, 269
Dines, Courtland, 169
Dines, Thomas M., 198
Dire, Carl, family, 191–93
Disciples of Christ, 204
Disney, Walt, 239, 240, 250
Diss, William and Minnie, 154
Ditmer, Joanne, 247
Dodds, John H., 60
Dodge, Cliff, 276
Dodge, Frank L., 279
Doering, Dave, 271, 272
Dolly Madison, 192, 193
Dolly Varden, 25

Dominick, Peter, Jr., 94
Dorsey, Clayton, 141
Douglas, Corbin, II, 203
Downing Street Parkway, 14
drugstores, 62, 100, 178,
    179, 217; also see by name
Druif, Meredith and Clara, 179
Dryden, David W., 174
Duff, Henry M., 259
Duffy, Bernard, 270, 271
dumps, 132, 219
Dunklee, George, 89
Dutch community, 87, V3

Early, James A., 178
East High, 120, 132, 157, V1
Edwards, Ellwood, 172
El Jebel Shrine, 165, 202
Electric Heights, 233
Elitch's, 148, 191, V1
Elkins, Bradbury, family, 164
Ellett, Virginius, 80
Ellipse Park, 188
Ellis School, 231, 232
Ells, M. Stephen, 159, V3
Ellsworth, Jason I., family, 259
Elway, Janet and John, 198
Emery, Walter, 212
Empire Park, 237, 249
Endres, George, 138
Endsley, Abner, 90
Englewood, 3, 9, 170, 188, V1, V3
Epiphany Lutheran, 69, V1
Episcopalians, 155, 193, V1, V3
Esquire Market, 193
Euclid Place, 233
Evans, John, II, family, Hill,
    Mansion, 82, 139–41, 142,
    143, 145, 147, V1, V3
Evans, Josephine, Chapel, 145, V3
Evans Store, 102, V3
Evans, William G., 11, 82, 139, V3
Excelsior Brick, 134
Excelsior Youth Center, 236

Fairmont School, 61, V1
Fairmount Cemetery, 12, V3
Falcone's, 103
Falkenburg Construction, 210
Fallis, Edwina, 60
fallout shelters, 181, 268
Farland-Buell Chrysler-
    Plymouth, 250
Farm Crest, 66
Farmer, Joseph P., and
    Elizabeth F., 54
Farmers Dairy League, 247

farms, farming, farmhouses, 2, 10, 14, 53, 88, 96, 230, V1, V3; also see dairies
Federally Assisted Code Enforcement, 68, V1
Feldhauser, Mable, 143
Fellowship House, 33, 70
Ferguson, John A., Jr., 144
Ferndale Dairy, 247
Field, Eugene, Cottage, Library, 36–39
filling stations, 99, 178, 191, 193, V1, V3
fire department, fires, 25, 28, 45, 66, 126, 174, 187, 216–17, 236, 237, 241, V1, V3; station #13, 45, V1; station #21, 45–46
First Avenue Hotel, 259, 261, V1
First Baptist, 194
First National Bank, 139, 141, 143, 212, 274, V1
First Plymouth, 69, V3
Fisher, William E. and Arthur A., Fisher & Fisher, 91, 122, 123, 140, 141, 142, 166, 196, 206, V1, V3
fishing, see Smith Lake, Washington Park
Fitzgerald, Edward, Jr., 112
Fitzsimmons, Thomas, 95
Fix-It Shop, the, 100
Flag Day, 135
Flood, Joe, family, 170
floods, flood control, 20, 132, 134, 135, 138, V1, V3
Flor, William, 268
Flowers, Clifton, 215
Flynn, Cornelius, 184, 186, 187
Foote, Stephanie, 282
Force, Anna Laura, 60
Ford assembly plant, 2, 94, V1
Forney Museum, 212
Foster, Alexis, 91
Foster, Joyce, 282–83
Four Mile House, 241
Freebooters, the, 205, 206
Freed, Claude W., 212
French-Americans, 87
Friedman, Don, 276
Friends and Neighbors of Washington Park, 20
Friends of the Downing Street Waiting Station, 163
Friends of Washington Park School, 88
Frontier Bar, 244

Frothingham, Will, 103
Fulenwider, Lloyd, 173, 214, 215

Gallagher, Jimmie, 64
Galleria, 245, 246
Gallup, Avery and Charolette, 54
garages, 71, V1
gardens, gardeners, 18, 19, 126; *Gardener's Forum*, 29
Garland, David T., 66
Garret, John, 65
Garrett, Van Holt, 199, 212
Garrison, Robert, 123–24, 206, 208
Garson, Oscar, 245
Garver, Arlene, 64
Garwood, Omar, 56
Gas-a-Mat, 246
Gates, Charles C., family, Rubber, 2, 24, 39, 53, 54, 144, 210, 217, 272, 273, V1, V3; Learjet, 279
Gates, Charles M., 64
Gemma, Leo, 270
Genesis Investments, 150
Gentlemen's Driving and Riding Club, 204, 205
George Washington High School, 133
Georgetown, 158
Gerash, Walter, 203
German-Americans, 77, 104, 143
ghosts, 4–5, V1, V3; at 186 S. Corona St., 164; at 298 S. Williams St., 106; at S. Williams St. and Dakota Av., 106; at Washington Park Methodist, 83; in the House of the Good Shepherd, 236, 237; in the Mary Grant House, 154; in the Phipps Mansion, 200; in South High, 126–27; in Washington Park, 1, 2, 3, 41; of a gold miner, 98; of Annie Hughes, 207, 208; of Beatrice Haven, 41; of Spicer Breedan, 201
Gilmour, Bob, 245
Glasier, John T., 240
Glatz, Mel C., 241
Glendale, 241, 245–47
Glick, Jerold and Sandra, 154
Gobert family, 192
Golden Lantern Restaurant, 244
Gonner, John, 77
Good Shepherd Lutheran, 45
Goodell, Roswell, family, 153

Goodheart, Harry, 90, V1
Gordon, Ken, 279, 283
Governor's Mansion, 90
Grace, Walter A., 152
Graham, John Gilbert, 269–70
Grant Avenue Methodist, Community Center, 63, 79, V1
Grant, Bill, 155, 156–57
Grant, Gertie, 24, 155
Grant, James Benton, family, 153–54, 214
Grant, Mary, House, 153–56
Grant School, Junior High, 84, 120, 121–22, 123, 188, V1, V3
Grant Smelter, 153
Grant Subdivision, 59, 120
Grant, Ulysses S., 120, 127
Grant, William W., family, 153, 154–56
Grasmere Lake, 15, 17, 19–25, 31, 37, 40, 56, 125—also see Washington Park; algae, 22; caiman scare, 21–22; drained, 21, 22; Parkway, 21, V3
Gray Goose Airways, 260
Gray, John, 197
Great Western Sugar, 142, 167
Greek-Americans, 67, 84, 100
Greek Theater, 33, 90
Green Bowers, 202–04
Green Gables, 163, 164
greenhouses, 230, 238
Griffin, Neil, 250
Griffin Wheel Company, 95, V1
Griffith, Emily, Opportunity School, 92, 231, V1
grocery stores, 8, 62, 64, 65, 66, 98, 100, 103, 180, 193, V1, V3; also see by name
Groos, Carl, 217
Guild Theatre, 102
Gunter, Julius, 82
Gustafson, Carl, 277–78

Hallett School, 220, 231
Hamilton, Frederic C. and Jane, Oil, 198, 208–09, V3
Hamilton, James H., 85
Hamilton Junior High, 232
Hamilton, Mabel, 264
Handle Bar & Grill, 181
Harding, Warren G., 196
hardware stores, 63, 193, V1, V3
Harper, Heber, 91
Harrington, C. Paul, 273, 274
Harrington, Orville, 96–98

Harrison, William Ray, 56
Hart, Gary, 280
Hart, John L. J., 203
Hart, Stephen, 158
Harvard Gulch, 268, 283, V3;
    Golf Course and Park, 9, V3
Hatton, John, 95
haunted houses, see ghosts
Havekost, Daniel J., 92
Haven, Beatrice, ghost of, 41
Hawkins, Bud, 248
Hemingway's, 103
Henritze's, 243, 244
Hentzell, Paul A., 281–82
Herman's Hermits, 174
Hewitt, George W., 105
Hewson, Bill, 173, 174
Hickenlooper, John, 273, V1, V3
Highlander Boys, 40, 184, 281,
    V1, V3
Highlands Ranch, 207
Hilltop Reservoir, 140
Hilltop Stadium, 132, V3
Himmelmann, Bill, 272
hippies, 4, 40, 106, 109,
    131, 263, V1
Hispanos, Latinos, Chicanos,
    42, 61, 87, 131, 176, 269, V1, V3
Historic Denver, 32, 112
Hi-Y, 129
Hobie Sailing Regatta, 239
Hock, Del, 146
Hodel's Pharmacy, 200
Hodge, Robert V., 153
Hoffbrau, the, 240
Holiday Drive-In, 245
Holland & Hart, 158, 203, 276
Holland Dairy, 247
Holland, Erik, 131
Holland, Ruth, 33
Holy Protection Church, 193
homeowners' association, see
    neighborhood groups
Hook, Irving, 268
Hoover, Herbert, 158
Hornbein, Victor, 156, 231
House of Rothschild, 210
House of the Good Shepherd,
    233–37
houses, housing stock, styles,
    7, 53, 54, 56, 94, 176, 187,
    188, 194, 203, 226, 231, 232
Hovey–Billings, 102, V3
Howell's, 62
Howze, Isham P., 57
Hoyt, Merrill and Burnham,
    143, 144, 154, 175

Huddart, John J., 227
Huffman, Harry, 190
Hughes, Gerald and Mabel,
    family, House, 141–42, 143,
    145–47, 196, 205, 207, 210
Hughes, Lafayette and Annie,
    family, 205, 207–08, 210
Humphreys, Albert E., family,
    154, 205
Hunt, Alexander C., 7
Hunter, James H., 99
Hunter, Nathaniel, 80
Huntington, Glen, 106
Hutchinson, Julie, 163
Hutchison's Pharmacy, 62
Hyde Park, 202, 203, 204
Hyder, James B., 26, 57

I-25, see Valley Highway
ice-skating, 26, 35; also see
    Smith Lake, Washington
    Park
Iliff School, 106, 145, V3
improvement associations, see
    neighborhood groups
Indian Hills, 184
Indian House, 157–59
Indians, 157, 234, V1
Innes, Frederick, 40
International Telephone &
    Telegraph (ITT), 208
International Trust, 143
Inter-Neighborhood Coopera-
    tion, 155
Interstate Gas Company, 199
Irvin, George, Chevrolet, 249

Jackson, Arthur C., Robert,
    Drugs, Pharmacy, 178–80
Jackson, Josie J., 159
Jaeger, J. Rudolph, 96
Japanese-Americans, 27, 83, 84
Jefferson County, 84
Jefferson Territory, 174
Jews, 94, 186, 210, 283, V3
Jewish: Consumptives Relief
    Society, 94; Family Services,
    283; Relief Society, 170
John Paul II, 229
Johnson, Axel P., 57
Johnson, Ed, 99
Johnson, Gary, 57
Johnson, Howard L., 92, 93
Johnson, Opal, 68
Johnston, Earl, family, 179, 276
Jolly Rancher, 101
Jones, Ben B., 60

Jones, F. W. "Billy," 103
Jordan, Julian and Mildred, 264
Joslin's, 279
JR's Malt Shop, 103
Junior League, 173
juvenile delinquents, see courts

Kansas Pacific Railroad, 184, 205
Karstedt, George, 163
Kashmann, Paul, 265–66
Kelly, George V., 273
Kenney, Frank W., 94
Kent, Jack, Cadillac, 250
Kent School, 148, 190
Kentucky Inn, 66
Kessler, George, 14
KGMC, 188
KHOW, 188
KIMN, 239
kindergartens, 60, 78, 85, 87,
    88, 175
King, John M., 276
King Soopers, 200
Kinzie, Phillip, 95
Kirchhoff, Francis J., 212
Kirk of Bonnie Brae, 69, 194
Kirkland, Vance, 141
Kistler, William H., 199
KLZ, 189–91
Kniffin, Alice May, 165
Knight, Stephen J., family, 219;
    School, 61, 219–20, 232
Knott, Mary Frances, 188
Knous, William Lee, 264
Knox, Wayne, 279
KOA, 106, 155, 156, 188
Koby, Paul, 57
Kohankie, Adam, 15, 19, 20,
    28, 80
Korbel, Josef, 91, V3
Korean Christian Church, 97, V3
Kreck, Dick, 192
Kreiling, Charles and Cora, 64
KRMA, 92
Krott, Paul, 86
KTLN, 170
Ku Klux Klan, 28, 56, 83, 90,
    99, 112, 159, 196, 227, 235,
    258, 263, 264, V1, V3
KVOD, 188

La Raza Unida, 269
labor, unions, union-busting,
    101, 180, 196, 272, 273,
    277, 279, 281, V1
Lacey, John B., 22
Lacker, Hersh, 145

Lake Junior High, 60
Lake View, School, 54, 174
Lakeside, 54
Lakota Heights, 225; Village, 225
Lamm, Richard, 172, 271, 279, 281
landmarks, 23, 62, 79, 112, 154, 167, 168, 177, 194, 228, 231, 232; also see by name
Lang, John B., 12–13
Lanting, William J., 248
Larimer Square, 101, 203
Leadville, 16, 153, 154, 273
League of Women Voters, 94, 281
Leahy, Frank, 198
Leavitt, Bob, 250
Leavitt, Ralph, Shirley, and Virginia, 106–08
Lee, Bob, 276
Lehmann, Peggy, 281
Leick, John S., 40
LeMaster, William P., 248
Lenicheck, Ed, 40
Levin, J. Clifton, 178
Lewis, George, 95
Lewis, Mason and Dorothy, 214
Liberal Church, 63
Library, the, 248
Licari, Enrico, 228, V3
Life, 129
Life Center, the, 215
Lincoln, Abraham, 37, 59; High School, 133
Lincoln:
—Creamery, 63
—Drugs, 62
—Hardware, 63
—Hotel, 62, 63
—School, 59–62, 63, 68, 70, 84, V1
—Subdivision, 59
Lindsey, Ben, 12, 217, 235, V1, V3
Listen Up, 63
Little Flower Market, 191
Little, Rosaman L., 56
Littleton, 9, 92, 190, 207, 281, V1, V3
Loan, Jim, 87
Locke, John Galen, 259, V1
Lomonaco, Charles, 90
Long, S. Allen, family, 225–26
Longmont, 64, 66, 163
Lopez, Greg, 201
Lort, Frank J., family, sisters, Ella, Hattie, Joseph, Lydia, Martha, 78–80, 83, 85
Love, John, 188, V3
Love, Minnie, 158–59
Lower, Chuck, 212

Lowry: Air Force Base, 88, 177, 195; Landfill, 23
Loyalty Group Insurance, 170
Lumber Baron Inn, 250
Lutherans, 45, 69, 104, V1, V3; Hospital, 268
Lynch, Dan, 215
Lynch, Philip A., 84
Lynn, Merrie, 188–89

MacFarland, Finley, 93
Machebeuf, Joseph, 234; High School, 88
MacKenzie, Kathleen, 272, 273
Maestas, Heberto, 230
Magdalenes, 235–36
Majestic Theater, 64, 65
Manitou Springs, 78, 226
Manley, George, 248–49
Manning, Harry, 85, V1, V3
Manual High, 132
Mapelli Brothers, 101
Marean, Willis, Marean and Norton, 57, 62, 82, 90, 91, 96
Marine Bar & Grill, 103
Marine Deck, 171
Marion Limited, 173
Marion Park, 174
Marion Street Parkway, 14, 21, 31, 42, 163
Mason, Perry, 151
Masons, 99, 104, 263, V1
Massaglia, Joseph, Jr., 173
Matteson, Joel, 153
Matz, Nicholas, 147
Max Gill & Grill, 103
Maxies's, 247
Mayan Theatre, 179, V1
McCarthy, Joan, 265
McClure, R. Arthur, 212
McCollum, Robert S., 266–68
McConnell, Francis, 83, V3
McCrary, Culley, & Carhart, 90, 140
McDevitt, Jack C., 248
McDevitt, Mildred, 216
McDonald's, 181, 248
McDowell, William F., 79, V3
McInroy, James, 99
McIntire, Albert, 234
McIntire, Nieves, 43, 271, 272
McKevitt, Mike, 274
McKinley School, 63, 175, V3
McMansions, 108, 110, 111, 112, 113, 194, 195, 202, 238, V3
McMeen, George, 84–85
McMullen, John, 202

McNichols, Steve, 239, 264
McNichols, William H., 84, 213, 271, 273, 274, 278, 282, V1, V3
McWilliams, Robert H., Sr., Park, 268, 269, V3
Meadows, Audrey, 217
Melton, Lydia, 97
Menheh, William, 64
Merchandise Warehousing, 273
Merchants Park, 132, V1
Merrill, Louise, 232, V1, V3; Junior High, 232–33, 238, V3
Mesa Verde, 153
Methodists, 69, 79, 80, 82, 83, 145, V1, V3
Metropolitan State College, 151
Metropolitan Television, 156
Mile High Stadium, 278
Miles, Alfred, 11
milk, see dairies
Miller, Alexander, 134, V1
Miller, James H., 211–12
Miller, Jonathan, 88
Miller Park, 211–18, 219; map, 206; windmill, 211
Miller, Paul R., 65
Miller's, 98, V1, V3
Milligan, Charles, 106
Milliken, Charles R. and Hazel, 180
Millikin, Eugene, 169
Milton School, 60, V3
Minneapolis Star & Tribune, 263
Mint, 96–97
Minute Men, 259
Miracle Mile, 3, 4, 264, V1
Missouri Synod, 104, V1
Mitchell, Maurice, 145, V3
Mizel, Larry, 210
Moffat, David, 141; Railroad, 141, 195; Tunnel, 95, 195, 244
Monkey Island, 40, 41
Montclair, 266; Academy, 88
Montero, Judy, 269
Montgomery Ward, 35, 55, 188, 260, V1
Moore, Albert, 271
Moore, Hudson, Jr., 142–43, 145
Moore, Orville, 57
Moorman, Edwin H., 94
Morey, Chester and John, family, Hill, House, Mercantile, 100, 107, 142–44, 146
Morgan, Harry L., 56
Mormons, 244
Morris, Langdon, 154, 200, 203
Morris, Mike, 181

Morrison, Singleton M., 57
Morse, Jared B., 92
Moulton, Jennifer, 32
Mount Olivet Cemetery, 149
Mountain States Motors, 249, 251
Mountain States Telephone,
    62, 94, 142, 165, 199
movies, theaters, 64, 101, 241,
    243, 245, V1, V3; also see
    by name
Muchow, William G., 106, 203
Muck, Karl, 58
Mullen John, family, 8, 147–
    53, V3; High School, 152;
    Home for the Aged, 152
Munz, Charles J., 18
Murray, Charles A., 90
Murray Motors, 250
music, musicians, concerts, 40,
    57, 58–59, 80, 102, 104, 170
Mutual Farm Dairy, 247
Myers, Elijah E., 164
Myrtle Hill, 2, 76–80, 86–88,
    98, 108, 109, 112, 113; at
    Washington Park Place, 88;
    Community Church, 79, 82,
    84; name fades, 82, 85;
    origins of, 77; School, 77,
    84, 85

National:
—City Bank, 259, V1
—Farmers Union, 188
—Jewish Hospital, 170
—Mining and Industrial
    Exposition, 59, V1
—Register of Historic Places,
    23, 131, 167, 228
—Western Stock Show, 156
natural gas, 178, 199
neighborhood activists, groups, 3,
    18, 56, 68, 70, 210, 212, 256,
    266, 272; also see by name
Neilsen, Oluf N., 38
Nell's Service Club, 17
Neocatechumental Way, 230
Neuhaus, Victor, 260
Neuville Center, 236
Nevitt, Chris, 114, 273
New Deal, see Depression
NewHeight Group, 167
Newman Center, 209, V3
newspapers, 256, 259–63, 283
Newton, Quigg, 92, 155, 156,
    263, 267, 273
Nicholson, Samuel D., family,
    16–17

Nicholson, Will F., 267, 273, 276
Nielsen, Aksel, 217
Nielsen, Louis and Peter, 248
Nine/Eleven, 87, 168
Nixon, Richard, 208, 277
Noe, Christian, 248
Norman, the, 154, 164–66, 167, 169
North Denver, 109, 186, 191,
    250, 269
North High, 120, 132, 177,
    186, 274
Norton, Albert, 57, 62, 82, 90,
    96, V1, V3
Notre Dame, 198, 203
Nuckolls, George L., 80, 83
Nyiri, Louis, 164

Ochs, Arthur R., 112
O'Connor, Katherine Mullen,
    family, House, 151–53
Ogden Street South, 167
Ohio Avenue Congregational,
    67–70, 105
oil, boom, oilmen, 109,
    153, 198, 208, 210, 211
Old One Eye, 25–26
Old South Gaylord Street, 3,
    98–103, 264, 276
Olinger, George, 184–86, V1, V3
Olmstead, Frederick Law, Jr., 15
Olympics, 132, 237, 238, 268, 274
One Polo Creek, 218
O'Neill, Laurence, 187
organs, 83, 153, 169, 197
orphans, orphanages, 3, 98,
    234–36, V3
Orr Construction, 236, 237
Ortega, Debbie, 269
Orthodox Christians, 193
Osner, Minnie, 235, V1
Ott, George and Margaret,
    family, 178
Out West Motel, 246
Overland Park, neighborhood,
    2, 4, 28, 204, 205, 279, V1, V3
Owen, Stephen, 168, 218
Owens Dairy, 65
Oxford Hotel, 250

Palmer, Edward P., 212
Papooses, the, 79
Paragon Builders, 30
Park Hill, 220; Methodist
    Church, 165; School, 175
Park Lane, 18, 93, 169–
    74, 188, 274; Cafe, 181;
    Delphian Society, 170

Park Mayfair, 174
Park People, 32, 38, 39, 155
Park Theater, 102
Patton, Jim, 188
Payne, William A., 259
Peabody, James H. and Cora, 157
Pearl Street Meats, 62
pedestrians, sidewalks, walk-
    ing, 30–31, 66, 89, 164, 218,
    249, V1, V3
Peet, Jane and Creighton, 93
Peña, Federico, 34, 36, 249, V1, V3
Peonio, Joseph, 130
Perich, John, 135
Perri, Ben, 208
Pesman, Walter, 126
Pete's, 84
Petry, Nicholas R., 214
pharmacies, see drugstores
Phillips, David, 170
Phillips 66, 191
Phipps, Lawrence C. and
    Margaret, family, Mansion,
    195–200, 205, V3; Allan,
    196–98, 200; Gerald, 196–
    200; Lawrence Jr., 205, 207;
    Tennis House, 197–98, 200
Pierce, Arthur E., 76, 259, V1
Pig 'n Whistle, 172
Piggly Wiggly, 62, 98, 180
pink sheet, the, 263–64
Pioneer–Buchtel News, 261
Pioneer Village, 261, 262
Pisko, Seraphine, 170
Plaisted, Daniel H., 80
plans and planners, planning
    board, 22, 31, 33, 67, 113, 247,
    249; also see Denver plans
Platt, Charles, 196
Platt, James H., 4, V1, V3
Platt Park, 3, 4, 64, 283, V1, V3
Platte River, 2, 8, 28, 53, 59,
    90, 120, 140, 208, 266, 276,
    V1, V3; Greenway, 276, V1
Platte Water Company, 7, 8, 10
Playgirl: Club, 249; Lounge, 173
playgrounds, 33, 71
Pogo Poge, 239
police, 22, 40, 42, 44, 80, 84,
    107, 108, 126, 131, 146,
    150, 200, 201, 203, 209,
    250, 271, 281, V1, V3;
    ambulance, 1; station #3, 44,
    135, 275, V1
Polo Club, 3, 145, 196, 204–
    11, 214, 215, 218, 219, 250, 276;
    clubhouse, 206, 208–09,

210; Condominiums, 216, 217; map, 206; North, 215; Place Homeowners Association, 210

Polo Creek Court, 218

poptops, 81, 94, 107, 108, 110–13

Porter, Henry Miller, Hospital, 10, 41, V3

Portis, H. Baxter, 81

Portland Mine, 95

post office, 62, 178, 179, 189, 279–80, V1, V3

Potash Company, 214

Potter, J. Stewart, 95, V1

Powell's, 178, V3

Powers, Daly, and DeRoss, 239

Powers, Paul W., 276

Pozner, Larry, 94

Preiser Grocery, 193

Prendergast, Ruth, 278

Prentice, Charles, 56

Presbyterian Hospital, 16

Presley, Elvis, 250

Prindle, Helen, 155

Proctor & Gamble, 146

Progress and Preservation Together, 112

Prohibition, 55, 56, 93, 152, 191, 196, 217, V1, V3

PTAs, 177, 260, 281

Public Lands Council, 30

Public Service, 142, 146, 199, 214

Puls, Louis, 95

Quality Hill, 196

Quinn & Company, 277

Rabb's, 25

Radetsky, Ralph and Martha, 156–57

radio, 105, 106, 170, 188–91, 239, 277; also see station call letters

Ragatz, Arthur and Ruth, 83

railroads, 8, 90, 157; workers, 64

Rainbow Ballroom, 34, V1

Rainbow Row, 57–59, 70

Raine, William MacLeod, 165

real estate, developers, speculation, 2, 7, 54, 59, 62, 63, 80, 84, 87, 88, 89, 93, 99, 101, 111, 112, 184, 191, 212, 214, 218, 220, 238, 239, 273; Real Estate Exchange, 93

Red and White, 100, 180

Red Cross, 20, 60, 195

Red Slipper, the, 247

Reddy, Paul R., 92

Redemptoris Mater, 230

Redskins, the, 79, 276

Reed, William, 98

Rees, Joseph, 85

reform and reformers, 234, 266

Regional Transportation District, 163, 249, V3

Regis, 229, 271

Reid, Frederick H., 94

Reid, Roderick and Grace, 94

Reivers, 103

Republic Building, 211

Republicans, 56, 57, 89, 90, 99, 139, 192, 196, 207, 263, 272, 274, 278, 281, 283; South Denver as Republican enclave, 263, 274, 276–78

Reum, Earl, 129

Reynolds, Doc and Naomi, 189–90

Reynolds, Margaret, 217

Rhodes, Bill, 151

Rhodes, Burt, 54

Rice, Condoleezza, 91, V3

Rice, Frank Hamilton, 63, 64

Rich, Sherman, 179

Richards, Daniel F., 80–81

Richthofen Castle, 154

Rickert, Lori, 63

Ricketson, Frank, Jr., 101, V1, V3

Ries, Jane Silverstein, 39

Riethmann, John J., 9, 138, 210, V1

Rifkin, Bobby, 268

Ringsby, Bill, family, 151, 199

Risley, Harry and Bijou, 94, 256–59, 261, 263, 264, 268, V1

Ritchie Center, 36, 209, V3

Ritter, Bill, 201, V3

Riverboat House, 56, 57

Roberts, Doc, 103

Robinson Brick, 134, V1

Robinson Dairy, 151

Robinson, L. Kent, 93

Robinson, Thomas D., 59

Roche, Josephine, 234, 235

Rocky Mountain News, 25, 111, 150, 155, 201, 216, 256, 273, V1, V3

Roe, John F., 90, 96

Roems, Dorothy, 85

Rogers, Byron, 267

Rogers, James Grafton, 157–58

Rogers, Platt, family, 196–97

Rogers, William O., 105, 194

Romanoff, Andrew, 279

Romer, Roy, 146

Roosevelt, Franklin, 158, 188, 259

Root, Robert, & Associates, 30

Rosedale, 279, V1, V3; Sanitarium, 12, V1

Rosen, Herbert, 95

Rosenbloom, Julius, 1

Rosenbloom, Maxie, 248

Roser, Beth, 278

ROTC, 128, 130, 131

Roxborough Park, 12, 207

Royal Crest Dairy, 65–66

Royal Publications, 151

Ruby Hill, 190, V1

Russell, John L., 17, 28, 45, V1

Russell, Thomas P., 81

Ryan, Alfred J., 92

Safeway, 178, 246

Saint Joseph Hospital, 149

Salem Church, 69

Samsonite, Shwayder Brothers, 2, 53, 272, V1, V3

Sanford, George I., 262, 263

Sankey, Verne, 81–82

Santa Fe Drive corridor, 264

Satire Lounge, 84

savings and loans, see banks

Schlachter, Dennis, 111

Schlesinger, Melvin, 166

Schmitz, Peter, 201, 203

schools, Denver Public Schools, 2, 4, 57, 59–62, 70, 78, 79, 83, 85–87, 92, 120–34, 142, 174, 175, 218, 219, 220, 226, 231, 232, V1, V3—also see by name; board, 60, 93, 128, 130, 159, 210, 219, 220, 258, 268; busing, 61, 85, 92, 128, 133, 157, 175, 176, 177, 219, 231–32, 263, 277; church, private, and Sunday, 62, 79, 82, 83, 86, 87, 104, 105, 176; district #1, 59; district #2, 59, 84, 120, V1; district #7, 120, 279, V3; district #35, 225, V3

Schreimer Brick, 134

Schroeder, Pat, 213

Schuetze, Reinhard, 12–14, 31

Schultz, Otto W., 67

Scottish Village, 186

Scotty's, 181

scrapeoffs, 110, 112, 113

Sears, 212

Secret Service, 96, 97

Seifert Pontiac, 249

senior citizens centers, 45, V3

Senter family, 190, 258, V3

Sertoma, 17
Seventeenth Street, 91, 141, 158
Shackleton Place, 138, 139
Shafroth, John, 195, 197, V3
Shane, Tom, 210
Shank, Paul, 246
Shattuck Chemical, 95, V1
Shaughnessy, Robert, 209
Shaw, Mike, 249
Shell Oil, 191
Shepperd, Orian, 92
Sheraton Hotels, 248
Sherman School, 35, V1
Sherman Subdivision, 59, V1
Shirley–Savoy Hotel, 190
Shoemaker, Joe, family, 276
Shotgun Willie's, 204, 244
Shotwell, Lauddale, 95
Shwayder, see Samsonite
sidewalks, see pedestrians
Siebers, Edmund, 80
Siebers, Hugo R., 1
Silchia, John, 111, 275
Silverado Savings, 238, 250
Simpson Nursery, 247
Sirkle, Chester, 1
sister city program, 204
Sisters of the Cross, 235
Six, Robert, 217
skiing, 36, 207, V3
Sky Chef, 271, V3
Sky Room, 173
Skyline Urban Renewal
    Project, 167, V1
Slavens, Leon, School, 60, V3
sledding, 35, 36, V1, V3
Sloans Lake, 13, 42
slot-cars, 240
Smith, John W., family, 8–
    10, 11, 25, 54, V3
Smith Lake, Smith's Ditch, 1–3,
    9–13, 15, 16, 20, 21, 25, 26,
    31, 32, 37, 42–44, 60, 127,
    169, V1, V3; boating, 1, 25;
    city buys, 10; fishing, 25–26;
    ice-skating, 35–36; swim-
    ming in, 26–29; also see
    Washington Park
Smith, Robert, 56
Snow, Frank, 95
socialism, communism, red-
    baiting, 28, 94, 158, 196,
    216, 208, 261, 281, V3
Soda Straw, 244
Sodano, Ralph, 177
Sons of Colorado, 89
Sopris, Richard, 7

South Broadway Christian, 69, V1
South Broadway industrial
    district, 2, 4, V1
South Broadway Theatre, 180, V1
South Capitol Hill, 11
South Central Improvement As-
    sociation (SCIA), 24, 68, 69,
    271
South Colorado Boulevard,
    4, 239–51; decline, 250;
    poor walking conditions,
    249; signage, 247
South Country Club, 3, 67, 138–
    59, 273, 276; aging of neigh-
    borhood, 145; housing, 139,
    151, 156; rolling terrain, 144
South Denver, as middle class
    neighborhood, 2; defined, 2,
    V1; divisions, 2–3; historical
    preservation, 111; popular-
    ity, 7, 238; schools, 120—
    also see by name
South Denver:
—Advocate, 256, 259
—Budget, 260
—Bulletin, 256
—Civic Association (SDCA),
    134, 170, 217, 232, 260, 281, V1
—Daily, 260
—Drugs, 62
—Eye, 256–57, 259, V1
—Improvement Association,
    18, 257, V3
—Independent, 260
—Monitor, 259, 260–61
—Neighborhood News, 260
—News, 264–65
—Park District, 13
—Realty, 264–65
—Standard, 259
—Tribune, 259
—Women's Association, 170
South Gaylord, see Old South
    Gaylord
South High School, 3, 4, 5, 9,
    20, 28, 40, 53, 62, 79, 92,
    100, 114, 120–33, 151, 179,
    188, 191, 192, 231, 268,
    279, V1, V3; academic
    excellence, 132; Activist,
    130; Aeronaut, 127; Alumni,
    130, 131; as a landmark,
    131; athletic fields, 131–32;
    Booster Club, 131; building
    by Washington Park, 122;
    building symbols, 123–25;
    Confederate, 127, 128, 129,

130, 188; cornerstone, 123;
    dedicated, 123; gargoyles,
    Gertie Gargoyle, 5, 124,
    125, 126, 129; ghost in,
    126–27; graduates, 133,
    134; griffin as symbol, 129;
    historical room, 130, 131;
    library, 121, 124, 125, 127;
    murals, 127, 131; over-
    crowded, 132–33; parking
    lot, 42, 126; racial tensions,
    131; radio club, 129; Rebels,
    127–29; Senior Hall, 125;
    tower, 124, 127, 129, 131;
    weather vane, 124, 131
South Pearl Street, 3, 62–67, V1, V3
South Platte River, see Platte
    River
South Side Observer, 260
South Side Woman's Club, 258
Southeast Bulletin, 264
Southeast Denver Free
    University, 265, V1
Speer, Robert W., 16, 36, 41,
    93, 138, 139, 211, 257, 266,
    V1, V3
Spelman, Mary Lou, 175
Spivak, Charles D., 94
Springer, John W., 207
St. Euphasia's, 235
St. Francis de Sales, 69, 193,
    271, V1; High School,
    86, 269, 271, V1
St. John Vianney Seminary,
    229–30, 231
St. John's Episcopal, 197
St. John's Lutheran, 104, V1
St. Luke's Hospital, 97
St. Michael and All Angels, 193
St. Philip's Hospital, 65
St. Thomas Seminary, 78, 193,
    226–28, 229, 230, 231, 273;
    artwork at, 230; closed, 229
St. Vincent de Paul Church,
    192, 193
Stafford, Clarence M., 263–64,
    266
Stafford, Francis, 228–29
Stapleton, Benjamin, 14, 217,
    259, 281, V1, V3
Stapleton Airport,
    61, 217, 248, 271
Star Dance Center, 87
Starbucks, 180
Starkweather, James C., 187
Stearns Dairy, 217
Steck, Amos, 7

Stedman School, 85
Steele Community Center, 34
Steele, Everitt, 57
Steele, Mary Clark, 57
Steele, Robert W., School, 45, 105, 174–78, 232; Greening of Steele, 177; Improvement Association, 89; kindergarten, 175; planetarium, 177–78; Steele–Crofton Organization of Parents and Educators, 176
Stein, Paul, 169, 170
Steines, Nicholas M. J., 227
Steinhauser, Frederick C., 184
Stephens, William P., 80–81
Sterling, Joseph, 90; Park Front Home Addition, 90
Sterne, William C., 92
Stevic, Jim, 279–80
Stiles, Jonathan, 135, 275
Stokes Place, 202–04
Stonebridge Companies, 248
Stouffer's, 240
Straight Johnson's, 63, V1
streetcars, 62, 76, 80, 101, 162, 163, V1, V3; shelters, 163–64; shopping strips, 62, 63, 98
Strickler, Gertrude, 33
stripper bars, 204, 244, 268
Stroessner, Robert, 57
Stuart, Theodore M., 90
Stubbs, Donald S., 198
Stude, Charles E., 104
Students for a Democratic Society (SDS), 130
Sudler, Carol K., 153
Summer House, the, 201
Summit of the Eight, 200
Sunderland, Jim, 180
Sutherland, Jerry, family, 92
Swansea School, 60, 84
Sweet, William, 91, V3
swimming, swimming pools, 19, 29, 43, 44, 150, 169, 174, 206, 209, 210, 239, 240, 241, 246; also see Celebrity, Smith Lake, Washington Park
Swiss Haven, 170
Symes, J. Foster, 205
Symphony, Denver and Colorado, 40, 59, 78, 145, 149, 198

Tabor Center, 167
Tammel Crow, 250
Tangerine Room, 245

Tank Hill, 139, 140, 141, 145
Tax Payers Protective League, 195
tax-increment financing, 273
Teapot Dome, 147
television, 21, 151, 156, 170, 188, 190
Teller, Henry M., 89
Temple Emanuel, 283
Temple of Youth, 20, V1
tennis, 25, 31, 169, 197–98, 200, 206
term limitations, 280, 282, 283
Tessler, Gary, 271, 277
Thatcher School, 84, 88, 121, V3
Thomas Jefferson High School, 133, 236
Thomas, Sam and Dorothy, 65
Thompson, John, 206
Tiffin Inn, 246
Tighe, Hugh, Skyline Dodge, 249
Tihen, John Henry, Tower, 228, 229, 230
Title Guaranty Company, 217
Tommy's Fish & Chips, 248
Tooley, Dale, 66, 215
Tooley, W. L., 173
Top of the Park, 170–73
Torrey, Mabel Landrum, 37
Town of South Denver, 2, 3, 7, 11, 12, 17, 28, 45, 54, 76, 120, 134, V1, V3
traffic, 271, 283, V1, V3
Traylor School, 220
trees, 12, 14, 17, 19, 23, 27, 39, 67, 109, 111, 155, 258
T-REX, 23, V3
Trident Theater, 102
Trinity Methodist Church, 59, 79
True, Allen, 127, 175
tuberculosis, 14, 91, 92, 175, 189, 190, 195, 227, V1, V3
Tuesday Community Club, 83
tunnels, 55, 104, 164, 228, V3
Twist & Shout, 63
Twist, W. N., 100

Ulley and Jackson Drugs, 178
unions, union-busting, see labor
United Air Lines, 248
United Artists, 243
United Church of Christ, 68, 69, 106, 194
United Rubber Workers, 272, V1
United States: attorney's office, 264, 269, 273, 276; Bureau of Reclamation, 95; Forestry

Service, 95; Housing Administration, 167
United States Olympic Festival, 132
United States Steel, 195
United Way, 70, 236
University Boulevard: as a parkway, 18; widening of, 143; Church of Christ, 97, 98, V3
University Hills, 78, 262, V3; Civic Association, 262
University of Colorado, 142, 144, 158
University of Denver, 2, 8, 9, 21, 31, 36, 70, 79, 80, 91, 132, 139, 144, 151, 188, 200, 209, 225, 232, 257, 261, 267, 268, 273, 274, 283, V1, V3; hockey, 193, 246, V3; Law School, 157, 158, 210, V3
University Park, 2, 80, 225, 232, 262, 268, 276, 281, V1, V3; Community Council (UPCC), 262, V3; Methodist, 226, V3; *News*, 261–63; School, 281, V3
Urban Drainage and Flood Control, 275, 276
urban renewal, 268, V1

Vail, John, 234
Vaile, William, 93
Valley Highway, I-25, 4, 19, 23, 66, 68, 92, 131, 134, 135, 225, 238, 246, 262, 274, 283, V1, V3
Van Horn, Marion, 234, V1
Van Stone, Frederick A., 90
Vanderhoof, John, 188–89
Varga, George P. and Anna, 226
Varian, Lester, 198
Varsity Lanes, 245, V3
Vehr, Urban J., 229
Veterans of Foreign Wars, 25
Veterans Park, 9, 23, 134–35
Victor-American Fuel, 96
Vigil, Charles S., 269
Vincentians, 226–28
Vine and Iowa Ballfield, 135
Volunteers for Outdoor Colorado (VOC), 29–31
Vox Dei, 230

Wagner, Florence M., 58
Walgreen's, 179, V1, V3
Wall Street, 158
Walsh, Thomas F., 205

Washington Park, 1–2, 3, 4, 5, 7–
    46, 54, 59, 68, 80, 82, 89, 104,
    105, 120, 126, 133, 162, 169,
    256, 258, 265, 266, 268, 271,
    276, V1, V3—also see Gras-
    mere Lake, Smith Lake; alco-
    hol problems, 20, 40, 41; as a
    middle-class park, 27; as a
    state of mind, 45; bandstand,
    40; barn, 13; bathhouse, beach,
    26–31, 36, 42, 43, 174; bicy-
    clists, 30, 42; boathouse, see
    pavilion; Bowling Club, 24;
    concerts and music, 31, 40;
    croquet, 24; dancing in, 33–34;
    discrimination, 27, 28; drugs
    in, 20, 40, 41; Ecology Pavil-
    ion, 17, 18; Evergreen Hill, 15;
    fishing, 25–26, 43; flower gar-
    dens, 14, 19, 20; gazebo, 40;
    George Washington tree, 17–
    18; hippies in, 40; Huck Finn
    Day, 25, 26; ice-skating, 35–
    36, 45; jogging, 30, 31; land-
    scaped, 12, 14; lily pond,
    13, 15, 20, 25; litter, 18, 22, 41,
    42; Lovers Lane, 13; Lullaby
    Fountain, 37; meadow, 12, 40,
    42, 43; Mount Vernon Garden,
    15, 19; mountain view, 23,
    155; named, 12; New Year's
    Eve, 28; noise, 40–42; pavil-
    ion, 19, 31–34, 36, 40, 104;
    playground, 33; poor city
    maintenance, 15, 32, 36, 39;
    pump house, 13; riots, 28, 40;
    rock garden, 13, 15, 20; size
    of, 13; soccer, 43; swimming,
    26–29, 43; tennis, 35, 42; toi-
    lets, 31–32; traffic, 20, 40, 41–
    42; trails, 30; vandals, 15, 39;
    volleyball, 42, 43; winter
    sports, 35
Washington Park neighbor-
    hoods, 4, 45, chaps. 2–3,
    138, 175, 177, 178,
    193, 283; as white areas,
    109; East versus West, 53,
    59, 76; housing, 88–96,
    108–12; transformation of,
    2, 108–10
—East, 2, 20, 43, 64, 72, 76–112,
    151, 273, 274, 279, 280, 281;
    as yuppie neighborhood, 2,
    110; historic preservation ef-
    forts, 112; Neighborhood As-
    sociation, 68, 86, 106, 112

—North, 135, 159—also see
    South Country Club, West
    Country Club
—West, 2, 4, 20, 43, 53–72, 112–
    14, 162, 268, 269, 270, 272,
    279; changing character, 59,
    67, 72; downzoning of, 113–
    14; Neighborhood Associa-
    tion, 24, 68, 69, 113, 155, 271
Washington Park:
—Action Council, 42, 68, 271
—Addition, 88
—Community Center, 20, 33,
    34, 67, 68–72, 155, 271
—Community (Methodist)
    Church, 18, 69, 82–84, 99,
    101, 104
—Congregational Church (UCC),
    68, 69, 83, 104–06, 194
—D&R Theater, 64, 101–03
—Garden Club, 18–20, 258, 280
—Grille, 103
—Heights, 225
—Pharmacy, 100, 103
—Place, 88
—Press, 264
—Profile, 163, 264–66
—Recreation Center, 23, 29,
    43–45, 71, 82
—School, 20, 61, 84–88, 176, 232
—Theater, 102
—View, 88
—Woman's Club, 83
Washington Street Community
    Center, see Washington Park
    Community Center
water, waterworks, 21, 22, 23,
    76, 140, 157, 178, 188
Weadick, L. Paul, 269–70
Webb, Wellington, 33, 44, 192,
    200, 275, 282, V1
Weckbaugh, Ella, Ellie, family,
    Mansion, 147–51
Weinberg, Benjamin F., 170, 173
Weinberger, Morris, 67
Weld County, 214
Wellshire, 184, 276, 282, V1, V3
West Country Club, 162–81
West Denver, West Side,
    8, 248, 264, 269, V1
West High School, 60, 92, 120,
    132, 231, V1
West Side Hustler, 264
West Washington Park, see Wash-
    ington Park neighborhoods
Western Cine, 64, 65
Western Enterprises, 101

Westminster Law School, 281
Wettengel, Earl, 55–56
Wham, Robert and Dottie, 276, 281
Wheelhouse, the, 56–57
When Denver and I Were
    Young, 60
White House of Denver, the, 154
White Sands Beach Club, 240
White Star Garage, 245
Whitehead, Andrew and Edwin,
    Brothers, House, 11–13, 28
Whitmore, James and Annie, 153
Wilcox, Henry, Manor, 162–64
Willbanks, Roger and Beverly, 151
Williams, Harold and Carol,
    68, 70
Wilson, Roland, & Associates, 216
Windsor Dairy, 217
Wingate, E. Page, 264
Wiste, Jim, 193
Witwer, Anne, 177
Wolcott, Edward, 89, V1
Wolcott's, Miss, School, 57
Wolf, Frank J., 260, 261
women, women's clubs, suf-
    frage, feminism, 18, 83, 154,
    159, 170, 258, 281, V1, V3
Woodruff, Hazel Gates, 39
Woodward, Frank, 37
Woolridge, Ross, 64
Works Progress Administra-
    tion, 14, 28, 42
World Youth Day, 149, 229
Writer family, Corporation,
    Manor, 4, 18, 212, 246–50
Wyant, Genevieve, 262
Wyman, Don, 274, 275
Wynken, Blynken and Nod, 36–
    37, 39
Wynkoop, N. Neil, 216

Yamecila, 165
Yasui, Minoru, 83–84
Yelland, Starr, 190–91
YMCA, 30, 40, 91, V1, V3
Youmans, Vincent, 171
Young American League
    (YAL), 42, 79, 276
Young, Percival, family, 217, 247
Younger, Corine, 106
yuppies, 2, 109, 110, 280, 281
YWCA, 154

Zang family, 169
zoning, downzoning, 88, 103,
    111–14, 174, 210, 214
zoo, 22, 99